The Sikhs

The Sikhs

PATWANT SINGH

DOUBLEDAY

New York   London   Toronto   Sydney   Auckland

PUBLISHED BY DOUBLEDAY
a division of Random House, Inc.
1540 Broadway, New York, New York 10036

DOUBLEDAY and the portrayal of an anchor with a dolphin
are registered trademarks of Doubleday,
a division of Random House, Inc.

Originally published in Great Britain by
John Murray (Publishers) Ltd., London, in 1999

The Sikhs was originally published in the U.S. in hardcover by Knopf,
a division of Random House, Inc.

The Library of Congress has cataloged the 1999 hardcover edition as follows:

Singh, Patwant.
The Sikhs / Patwant Singh.
p.   cm.
Includes bibliographical references and index.
1. Sikhs—History.   I. Title.
DS432.S5S48   2000
954'.00882946—dc21
99-31807
CIP

ISBN 0-385-50206-0

1   3   5   7   9   10   8   6   4   3   2

To those noble exemplars
whose inner strength,
deep convictions and
heroic deeds continue to
inspire Sikhs the world over

Contents

Illustrations

Daljit Singh and the war artist Serbjeet Singh in the foreground

The author and publisher are grateful to the following for the illustrations reproduced in this book: Plates 1, 3, 4, Deidi von Schaewen; 2, V&A Picture Library; 5, 7, 8, Lahore Fort; 6, 9, Hotel Imperial, New Delhi; 10, 5th Battalion, Sikh Regiment; 11, Pushpindar Singh; 12, Serbjeet Singh.

Maps

Acknowledgements

It is difficult to express my gratitude to all those whose illuminating insights, and endurance in the face of my unending demands on their time, made this book possible. I could not have tracked down so many different records—to the extent I was able to—without their help. I am also deeply indebted to friends who offered to read various chapters in manuscript form. Their observations and suggestions helped bring coherence and consistency to the more elusive segments of the book. I owe to them whatever exactitude I have succeeded in bringing to a vast canvas.

My special thanks go to H.L. Agnihotri, Iradj Amini, Jagjit Singh Anand, Gurcharan Singh Attariwala, Rasil Basu, Ajit Battacharjea, Ominder Singh Chowdhary, Lt.-General J.S. Dhillon, Kartar Singh Duggal, Kirsty Dunseath, David Fisher, S.S. Gill, N.S. Kapany, Rajni Kothari, Ashwini Kumar, Fali Nariman, H.S. Phoolka, Lt.-General K.S. Randhawa, Padam Rosha, Jasdev Singh, Pushpindar Singh, Rear-Admiral Satyindra Singh, Lt.-Colonel Thawar Singh, Jivat Thadani, Romila Thapar, and Philippa Vaughan. And even more so to Lt.-General J.S. Dhillon, Rajni Kothari and Ashwini Kumar for so frequently and unstintingly setting aside time to enrich me with their inspiring inputs.

I am no less indebted to the generosity of Jasdev Singh who opened up the splendid picture archives of the Hotel Imperial in New Delhi for me. Nor to Serbjeet Singh, a gifted painter, cartographer, and film-maker who helped with the maps, which were drawn by the versatile Denys Baker. Susan Stronge was equally magnificent in locating old illustrations.

I found some of the finest translations of passages from the Guru Granth Sahib—rendered with sensitivity and rare clarity—in the following three books: *Selections from the Sacred Writings of the Sikhs*, edited by Trilochan Singh et al. (George Allen & Unwin, London, 1960; UNESCO Collection of Representative Works—Indian Series); *The Heritage of the Sikhs* by the late Professor Harbans Singh (Asia Publishing House, Bombay, 1964); and *Guru Nanak and Origins of the Sikh Faith* by Harbans Singh (Panjabi University, Patiala, 1969).

I am particularly grateful to three exceptional women: Sara Stewart and Christine Sutherland for introducing me to John Murray, and Caroline Knox for commissioning the book.

I am also very grateful to Antony Wood for his invaluable editorial advice.

The tenacity of Ram Narayan Singh Rawat, my research assistant, deserves praise not only for brilliantly unearthing material buried long back, but for persuading librarians to let him borrow twice the number of books he was entitled to.

My secretary, Anita Mauji, coped with the pressures of looming deadlines and seemingly endless revisions with confidence and aplomb.

The co-operation and guidance of the staff of Bhai Vir Singh Sahitya Sadan, the Nehru Memorial Museum and Library, the India International Centre Library and the National Archives of India are also gratefully acknowledged.

It goes without saying that the book could never have been written without the unfailing encouragement, help and support of my dear Meher.

Preface

"Do you have any particular reason for writing this book?" a friend asked me when I started work on it. I told him I had a compelling desire to tell the stirring story of a people and a faith to which I belong myself, and which has been the source of lifelong inspiration to me. The full story of the Sikhs, I felt, needed telling, from the emergence of Sikhism just over 500 years ago up to the present time. It was necessary, I felt, for people to know something of the conditions in which Sikhism originated and everything Sikhs have experienced since then: the invasions and inquisitions, triumphs and tragedies, piety and sense of divine purpose, devotion and depravities, loyalties and betrayals, courage and convictions. I saw a clear need to chronicle all these. But why at this particular time?

Because the systematic disinformation campaign about current events crafted by successive Indian administrations from the 1970s onwards really ought to be placed in perspective. Although the mandarins of modern India precipitated the most dangerous crisis the Republic has faced in the first fifty years of its existence, which was largely due to their short-sighted and unstatesmanlike moves with regard to Sikh sensibilities, the Sikhs were held responsible. This distortion needs to be corrected. Since Sikhs now live in the farthest corners of the world, a need also exists for people of those countries to know something of the history, traditions and beliefs of the new arrivals in their midst.

Prone as it is to religious chauvinism, Indian society has to realize that it is an incomparably rich though fragile mosaic of cultures, creeds and customs. An appreciation of its own fragility is essential if this society is not to fragment. I am sad to see little such realization at the present time. A country of huge size and wealth of human talent and natural resources is still bedevilled by religious and caste rivalries which continue to impede its progress and stability. For this reason alone, India's future will remain uncertain so long as its political leaderships keep fuelling religious hate and using caste divisions to dominate each other.

It has been suggested—all too frequently—that the caste system's "integrative" and ideological dimensions have enabled Hindu society to survive and respond to many challenges. Possibly. On the other hand, caste distinctions have also created debilitating divisions which work against a collective sense of national purpose. To illustrate this point I have provided, in the Prologue to this book, a backdrop against which the evolution of Sikh thought should be viewed. Nothing happens in isolation from preceding events, and there is a recognizable historical pattern in the drama unfolding in India today, especially in relation to the "ethos of separateness" that is reflected in segments of Indian society.

I have always admired the range, depth and quality of Brahminical scholarship, and its contribution to philosophical and metaphysical understanding. If I sound critical of Brahmins at times, it is with regard to their role in keeping large segments of India's population out of their own exclusive domain of privilege and power. I have at no time experienced such exclusion myself, but I have never aspired to political power or public position. As an observer of India's social and political scene, however, who has also read a great deal about his country and its people, I am convinced that it is not the quality of our people but the lack of vision and political wisdom of their leaders that has been responsible for humiliations past and present.

By refusing to learn from the past—or the present—we Indians continue to injure ourselves grievously. This is especially regrettable at a time when large new power blocs, driven by an acute awareness of their own self-interest, are emerging around the globe. It will be a monumental tragedy if a myopic India continues to follow its divisive policies and practices, and falls behind in the international contest for prestige, power and influence.

If an energetic and vital community like that of the Sikhs is irretrievably estranged, modern India as a whole—and not merely a handful of politicians in power who are causing the damage—will suffer. India will be pushed back into the medieval times from which it is still trying to extricate itself.

This book is written in the hope that those who lead India will be able to avoid past follies, and adopt less self-destructive and more pragmatic policies in the future. Only then will they be able to honour the social contract with Indians of every background and persuasion. There is, in fact, no other option open.

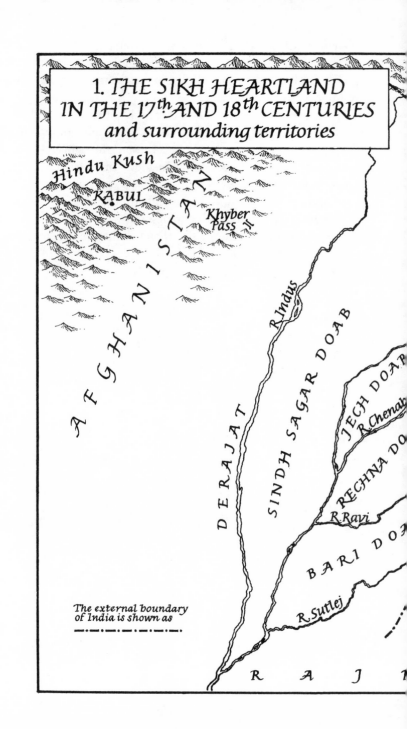

1. THE SIKH HEARTLAND IN THE 17th AND 18th CENTURIES
and surrounding territories

Hindu Kush

KABUL

Khyber Pass

AFGHANISTAN

R.Indus

DERAJAT

SINDH SAGAR DOAB

JECH DOAB

R.Chenab

RECHNA DO

R.Ravi

BARI DO

R.Sutlej

The external boundary of India is shown as
—··—··—··—··—··—

R   A   J

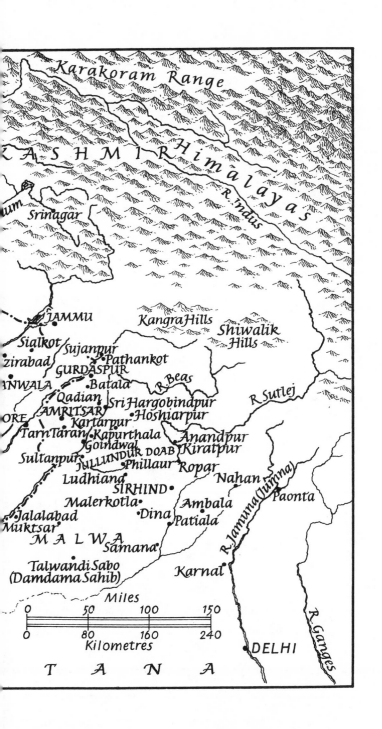

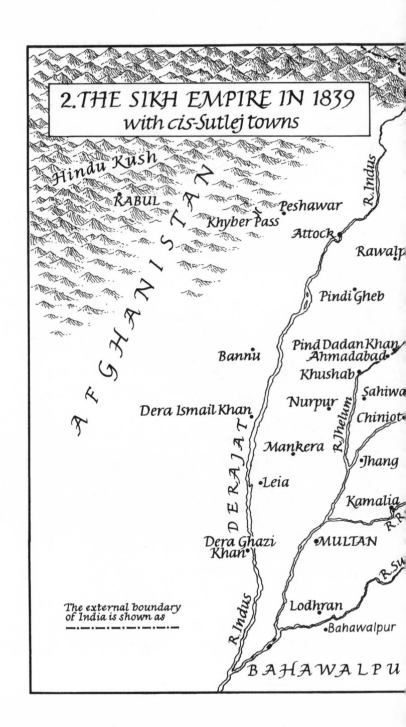

2. THE SIKH EMPIRE IN 1839
with cis-Sutlej towns

Hindu Kush

AFGHANISTAN

KABUL

Khyber Pass

Peshawar

Attock

R. Indus

Rawalp

Pindi Gheb

Pind Dadan Khan
Ahmadabad

Bannu

Khushab

Nurpur

Sahiwa

R. Jhelum

Chiniot

Dera Ismail Khan

DERAJAT

Mankera

Jhang

•Leia

Kamalia

R.R.

Dera Ghazi
Khan•

•MULTAN

R.Su

The external boundary
of India is shown as
▬•▬•▬•▬•▬•▬

R. Indus

Lodhran

•Bahawalpur

BAHAWALPU

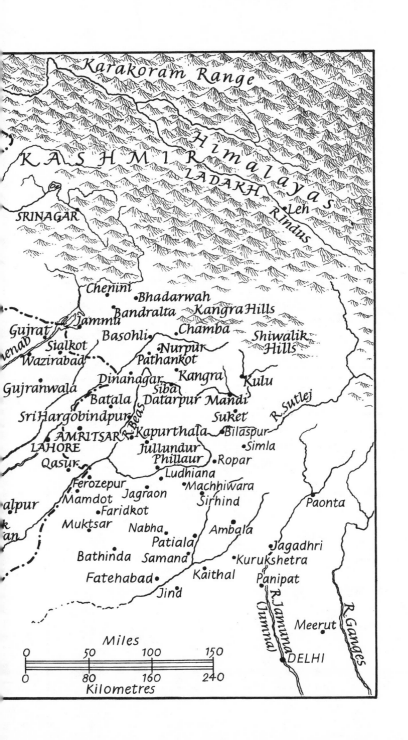

Karakoram Range

KASHMIR

Himalayas

LADAKH

•Leh
R. Indus

SRINAGAR

Chenini

•Bhadarwah

•Bandralta Kangra Hills

•Jammu

Gujrat

Basohli• •Chamba

Shiwalik Hills

Sialkot

•Nurpur

Wazirabad

Pathankot

Gujranwala

Dinanagar •Kangra •Kulu

R. Sutlej

Batala •Siba

SriHargobindpur Datarpur •Mandi

Suket

AMRITSAR •Kapurthala •Bilaspur

LAHORE Jullundur •Simla

Qasur Phillaur •Ropar

•Ludhiana

Ferozepur •Machhiwara

alpur Mamdot Jagraon Sirhind Paonta

•Faridkot

Muktsar Nabha• Ambala

Patiala

Bathinda Samana •Jagadhri

•Kurukshetra

Fatehabad• Kaithal Panipat

Jind

Meerut

DELHI

R. Jamuna (Jumna)

R. Ganges

Miles
0   50   100   150

0   80   160   240
Kilometres

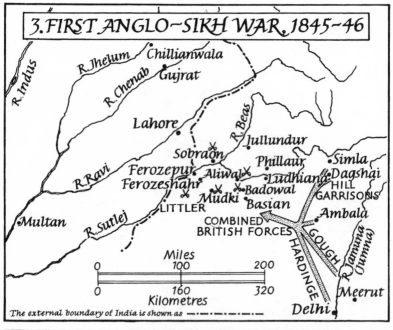

3. FIRST ANGLO-SIKH WAR, 1845-46

R.Indus
R.Jhelum
Chillianwala
R.Chenab
Gujrat
Lahore
R.Beas
Jullundur
Sobraon
R.Ravi
Ferozepur
Phillaur
Simla
Ferozeshahr
Aliwal
Ludhiana
Dagshai
HILL
Mudki
Badowal
GARRISONS
LITTLER
Basian
Multan
R.Sutlej
Ambala
COMBINED
BRITISH FORCES
GOUGH
R.Jamuna (Jumna)
HARDINGE

Miles
0   100   200
Kilometres
0   160   320

Delhi
Meerut

The external boundary of India is shown as —··—··—··—··—

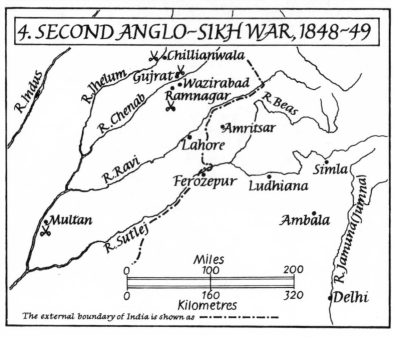

4. SECOND ANGLO-SIKH WAR, 1848-49

R.Indus
R.Jhelum
Chillianwala
Gujrat
R.Chenab
Wazirabad
Ramnagar
R.Beas
Amritsar
R.Ravi
Lahore
Simla
Ferozepur
Ludhiana
Multan
R.Sutlej
Ambala
R.Jamuna (Jumna)

Miles
0   100   200
Kilometres
0   160   320

Delhi

The external boundary of India is shown as —··—··—··—··—

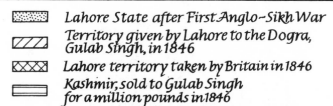

5. THE DISMANTLING OF THE SIKH EMPIRE, 1839~49

Lahore State after First Anglo~Sikh War

Territory given by Lahore to the Dogra, Gulab Singh, in 1846

Lahore territory taken by Britain in 1846

Kashmir, sold to Gulab Singh for a million pounds in 1846

N.W.F.P. (North~West Frontier Province), carved out of Punjab after British annexation in 1849

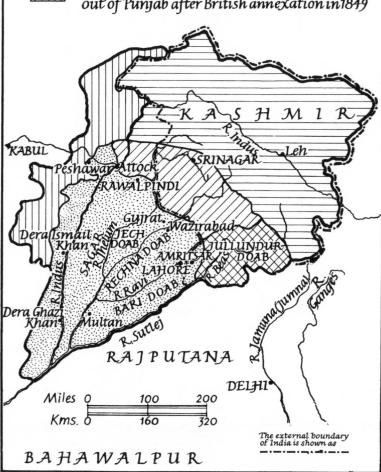

KASHMIR

KABUL

Peshawar Attock

RAWALPINDI

SRINAGAR

R. Indus

Leh

Gujrat

Wazirabad

Dera Ismail Khan

JECH DOAB

R. Jhelum

SAGAR

RECHNA DOAB

R. Chenab

JULLUNDUR DOAB

AMRITSAR

LAHORE

R. Ravi

R. Beas

BARI DOAB

Dera Ghazi Khan

Multan

R. Indus

R. Sutlej

RAJPUTANA

R. Jamuna (Jumna)

R. Ganges

DELHI

Miles 0   100   200

Kms. 0   160   320

The external boundary of India is shown as
—·—·—·—·—·—

BAHAWALPUR

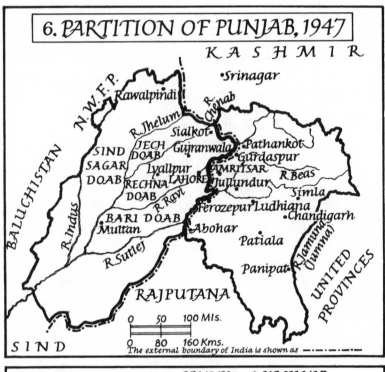

6. PARTITION OF PUNJAB, 1947

KASHMIR

•Srinagar

N.W.F.P.

Rawalpindi

R.Jhelum

R.Chenab

Sialkot•

BALUCHISTAN

SIND SAGAR DOAB

JECH DOAB

Gujranwala

•Pathankot
•Gurdaspur

Lyallpur

RECHNA DOAB

LAHORE

AMRITSAR

Jullundur

R.Beas

Simla

R.Indus

R.Ravi

BARI DOAB

Multan•

•Abohar

Ferozepur•Ludhiana

•Chandigarh

Patiala

R.Jamuna (Jumna)

R.Sutlej

Panipat•

UNITED PROVINCES

RAJPUTANA

0   50   100 MIs.

0   80   160 Kms.

The external boundary of India is shown as ·—··—··—

SIND

7. PUNJAB AFTER REORGANIZATION IN 1966

JAMMU & KASHMIR

HIMACHAL PRADESH

TIBET

•Gurdaspur
Hoshiarpur

AMRITSAR•

Simla

Jullundur

Chandigarh

PAKISTAN

•Ferozepur
PUNJAB

Patiala•

The external boundary of India is shown as ——

HARYANA

•DELHI

RAJASTHAN

UTTAR PRADESH

0   50   100   150 Miles

0   80   160   240 Kilometres

The Sikhs

Prologue

India's internal divisions and conflicts make sense only if you know something of her caste system. A unique *tour de force* with deep philosophical and spiritual underpinnings, it took its present form at about the beginning of the Christian era, even though the groundwork was established with the Aryan migrations into northern India around 1500 BC. On the physical side, the Aryans included a taller, larger-boned type distinguished by strong hair growth, especially beard, who settled mainly in the north, principally in the area that became known as Punjab. This type became the core of the military castes of the region, as also of the people who are the subject of this book.

"The coming of the Aryans," it has been said, "was a backward step, since the Harappan culture had been far more advanced than that of the Aryans who were as yet pre-urban." Robust and virile, with heroic appetites—which included beef eating and great intakes of an amazingly potent liquor called Soma—the light-skinned Aryans brought three distinct social groupings with them: Kshatriyas, the warrior rulers; Brahmins, the priestly class; and Vaishyas, who eventually evolved into traders and entrepreneurs.

After destroying the sophisticated urban North Indian civilization of the Dasyus, who peopled the Indus Valley where the Harappan culture flourished, the Aryans set about making India their home. And as with all those who have invaded India over the millennia, the Aryans

3

too experienced a slow but steady assimilation with the existing beliefs and customs of India. Neither side, in fact, was left untouched by the assimilative experience, the attitudes and outlook of both being affected by the merging of distinctly different cultural streams. As the metamorphosis progressed over the centuries, the open society of the Aryans was gradually reshaped in the closed and distinctive mould of the subcontinent's rituals and beliefs. What emerged was unrecognizable from its Aryan origins.

From hard-drinking, beef-eating beginnings, the Aryans came to consider alcohol internally polluting and taboo, whilst the cow, seen as more sacred than all other animals, was to be venerated not eaten. Based on concepts of purity and pollution, an elaborate system was established in which forms of behaviour, rituals and much else were clearly set down. For instance, death was considered polluting, so the widow's remarriage was banned since she had dealt with death.

The most significant change for the assimilated Aryan social order had to do with institutionalizing a hierarchy of upper and lower classes in the almost inviolate system of social engineering known as "the caste system," which is still active today. The Brahmins emerged at the top of the caste hierarchy whilst the Kshatriyas—who had led the Aryans into India—found themselves in second place. The Vaishyas continued to occupy the third position, with a new category, the Shudras, added to bring the total to four. The Shudras, or cultivators and the like, were denied the initiation rite which gave the other three castes the privilege of being called the "twice-born." The Shudra also had to forego the opportunity of becoming rich, "for a Shudra who makes money is distressing to the Brahmins." Yet another classification, even lower than the Shudras, was also added: the Chandalas or untouchables. They were outside the caste system and considered the lowliest of the low, whose vocations had to do with "polluting elements," like cobblers, sweepers and cleaners, washermen, barbers, butchers and those who cremated dead bodies.

A hymn in the Rig Veda, the oldest of the Vedas, or Hindu scriptures laid down by the Brahmins, describes the origin of the four Varnas, or caste groups, through the symbolic sacrifice of Purusha, the Primeval Man, from whose head rose the Brahmins, from his arms the Kshatriyas, from his thighs the Vaishyas and from his feet the Shudras.

The operation of the caste system is an "ordering mechanism" which enables the exercise of power through social control and spiritual notions of the sacred and profane, as spelt out by an exclusive class of spiritual interpreters. These are the Brahmins, the great interpreters of tradition, who are to be found in all locations, literally every village, certainly at every point of dispensation of power and patronage. Hence their dominance over both the ruler (Kshatriya) and the merchant (Vaishya), and their "legitimate" control and exploitation of the Shudras (the toiling masses, the landless, the cultivators, bonded labour, women, the lot). Dominance is exercised through rules, rituals and rigmarole.

It is argued in favour of this system that despite the multiplicity of cultures and communities, and the many ideological challenges it has faced, India has "produced a high degree of ideological tolerance and flexibility." Not really. Because institutionally "Indian society has been traditionally very rigid, working out a precise and clearly identifiable hierarchy, formalized rules, and conventions, conformity with which was mandatory and defined by birth, and a system of substantive and symbolic distances which articulated the hierarchy in a definitive and predictable manner." In the end, India was landed with "a kind of tolerance" which is "only another name for intolerance, namely tolerance of injustice and disparities and of humiliation and deprivation by superior individuals and groups." This is what the caste system has been about over the centuries. Only in recent years—with the upsurge of consciousness among the lower castes and the democratic political process—has the slowly emerging challenge to the hegemony of the Brahmins and other "twice-born" upper castes led to some loosening of their total grip over society.

From Alexander's invasion of India in 326 BC till the closing years of the twentieth century, Brahmin influence has helped shape the destiny of courts, kingdoms, nations and religious movements in India's long history. Behind the rise and fall of many, if not most, was the hand of Brahmin courtiers, counsellors and priests. Their supremacy was as much due to scholarship, erudition and intellect as to their matchless skills in statecraft and intrigue.

When Alexander turned back from the banks of Punjab's River Beas to return to Macedonia, Vishnugupta Chanakya, or Kautiliya, the astute Brahmin, urged the commander-in-chief of the powerful Magadha Kingdom's army, Chandragupta Maurya, to organize a revolt against the Greek forces left behind. After defeating them, Chandragupta—again on Kautiliya's advice—headed back to Pataliputra (present-day Patna, capital of the state of Bihar) from where he had fled after a failed attempt to take over the Magadha Kingdom. More successful this time, Chandragupta slew the ruler and founded the Maurya Dynasty (322–185 BC). To Kautiliya* is also attributed the astonishingly comprehensive *Artha Sastra* or manual of politics.

The increasing inclination of Chandragupta's illustrious grandson Ashoka towards Buddhist teachings, philosophy and practices culminated in his eventual conversion, and led to the ascendance of Buddhism. Buddhism, a philosophical-cum-political movement founded by Gautama Buddha (563–483 BC), represented fundamental dissent against Brahminic political and priestly dominance and promoted alternative theologies, value systems and lifestyles, as did Jainism, founded by Vardhamana (599–527 BC). Ashoka's passionate commitment to Buddhism, and its expanding hold on the state, eventually precipitated a Brahmin revolt, spearheaded by the Shunga family working under the Buddhists. Pushyamitra Shunga, after assassinating the last Mauryan ruler, usurped his throne and founded the Shunga Dynasty (185–73 BC). He persecuted Buddhists and razed their monasteries. During the first millennium AD, however, Buddhism steadily reestablished itself in India.

Both Buddhism and Jainism opposed the caste system. "Not by birth does one become an outcast," said Buddha, "not by birth does one become a Brahmin. By deeds one becomes an outcast, by deeds one becomes a Brahmin." Both movements, appealing to the socially downtrodden, in course of time made inroads on the Brahmins' power and privileges. Once more a Brahminical reaction built up, and in the ninth century a South Indian Brahmin religious leader, Aadi Shankara or Shankaracharya, decisively ejected Buddhism from India. He endorsed the law of Manu (framed between 200 BC and 200 AD):

* Historians are divided on Kautiliya's identity. Many believe Chanakya and Kautiliya were one and the same person. Others disagree. In a tribute to both, the diplomatic enclave in New Delhi has been named Chanakyapuri.

"According to Manu, the Brahmins are appointed by the Supreme Being and they should be venerated as god-like creatures. A ten-year-old Brahmin must be respected as if he were the father of a hundred-year-old Kshatriya . . . If a Brahmin finds buried treasure, it belongs to him; if the King finds such, he must share it with the Brahmins. By his deferential behaviour to a Brahmin, a man of a lower caste can attain rebirth in a higher." The Shankaracharya is reputed to have remarked: "whatever Manu says is medicine." The Shankaracharya and others directed their deep learning to conceiving a brilliant combination of ideas, ideology and state power with which to turn the tables on the Buddhist and Jain revolts.

Buddhism virtually vanished from the land of its birth, although it flourished in almost all other countries in South and East Asia. Jainism survived with a small following, a far cry from the days of its apogee.

Even during Islamic rule, there was no serious threat to Brahminical privileges. From the time of Muhammad bin Qasim (711) till Feroz Shah Tuglak (1350), Brahmins, unlike other castes, did not pay taxes. Abbé J.A. Dubois, the French scholar who lived in India from 1792 to 1823, observed that "the rule of all the Hindu princes, and often that of the Muhammadans, was, properly speaking, Brahminical rule, since all posts of confidence were held by Brahmins." Even if this is a slight exaggeration, Brahmins certainly held powerful positions of patronage in the courts of successive rulers. "Large sections of the Mughal," according to one modern historian, "and even earlier Muslim, financial administrations south of the Narmada had been staffed by Brahmins . . . Kolhapur Brahmins formed the fiscal administration in the Carnatic, especially in the Bangalore area; Brahmins from Ahmednagar and northern Maharashtra were earlier recruited by the invading Mughals to administer areas further south." The Brahmin Rai Ranjan Patr Das was made governor of Gujarat under the great Mughal emperor Akbar in 1613–14. During Akbar's son Jahangir's rule, Keshav Dass Braj exercised great influence with the emperor, writing a collection of paens praising him. Another Brahmin, Chander Bhan, was Mir Munshi, or Chief Secretary, in Shah Jahan's court. Raja Daya Bahadur and Raja Chuhela Ram Nagar were both governors during the reign of the Mughal emperor Farrukh Siyar.

The Mughals were not unappreciative of Brahminical help in consolidating their rule. If the Rajputs—the warlike clans who traced descent from the ancient Kshatriyas and settled the area known today as the state of Rajasthan—were the bedrock of their empire until the end of the seventeenth century, and helped lead numerous Mughal campaigns, this was only possible with Brahminical approval of their alliance with the latter, including intermarriage.

Brahminical hold was consolidated still further in Mughal times through *madad-i-mash*, tax-free grants and subsidies to Hindu temples. Mughal rulers gave grants to temples in Benares, Mathura and Vrindavan. In the South "even the famous *math* of Sringeri and its venerated Jagadgurus were well protected and even patronised by Muslim rulers of the South . . . the Jagannath temple of Puri and the Sringeri *math* are thus excellent examples to show to what extent Muslim rulers were willing to cooperate with Hindu institutions in order to rule the country." And since these institutions were controlled by the Brahmins, such help led to a proportionate increase in their power.

Not all grants to royal temples came from Muslim rulers. They received far more from regional Hindu kingdoms—reflecting the ruler's piety and status—and each new structure vied with the next in grandeur and scale. The diversion of state resources to these temples obviously meant more wealth and power for the Brahmins, their traditional keepers, and less for the common people: "The settlement of Brahmins and the establishment of royal temples served the purpose of creating a new network of ritual, political and economic relations." Such networking obviously helped to get the grants in the first place.

With land grants given personally to the Brahmins as well, they too emerged as a powerful landed gentry. In Eastern UP and Bihar, Mughals gave generous support to Brahmin landlords and Rajas and helped create princely kingdoms such as Benares and Mathura. The Brahmin hand in the creation of some of these, as in the case of Darbhanga, is interesting. After defeating the Rajput Rajas of Tirhut in Bihar, Akbar appointed Mahesh Thakur, a Maithili Brahmin, to collect land revenue since the emperor was impressed by "his great erudition." But he had more than that in mind: "By relying on and supporting Mahesh Thakur and his successors, Akbar and his descendants helped entrench the Maithili Brahmins as a local ruling élite, displacing the Rajput Rajas of Tirhut." Under Emperor Aurangzeb in the seventeenth century, Mahinath Thakur, of the same family, helped "the Mughal forces in the conquest of Palamau in South Bihar and in the suppression of the zamindars [big landowners] of Morang." As reward he was given what came to be known as the state of Darbhanga.

When the Marathas from the South took the field against the Muslims in the seventeenth and eighteenth centuries, Shivaji, founder of the Maratha Empire and chief source of inspiration to his people, was a devoted follower of Swami Ram Das, a Brahmin, whom he held in great reverence. Ram Das's exhortation to Shivaji was: "Places of pilgrimage have been destroyed; homes of the Brahmins have been desecrated; the whole earth is agitated; *Dharma* [the Brahmins' right to preside over the Hindu religious and moral order] is gone."

Brahminical control is best illustrated by the problems Shivaji faced in getting himself crowned. According to ancient Hindu scriptures (written by Brahmins) only the Kshatriyas were entitled to kingship, and thus to the homage of their Hindu subjects. So how could a Bhonsle, a clan to which Shivaji belonged, aspire, as a mere tiller of the soil, "to the rights and honours due to a Kshatriya"? Brahmins from all over India let it be known they would attend Shivaji's coronation only if he was declared a Kshatriya. An obliging Brahmin was found who agreed—for a suitable fee—to arrange for Shivaji's elevation to the Kshatriya caste. Shivaji had to bow before Brahminical power, despite his contribution to the consolidation of Maratha power. During Shivaji's reign prominent subcastes of the Deccan Brahmins occupied six of the eight positions in his council of ministers.

After Shivaji's death in 1680, and with the investiture of his grandson Shahu in 1708, a far-sighted Brahmin, Balaji Visvanath, emerged as his principal adviser. Impressed by his qualities of statesmanship, Shahu conferred the title of Peshwa or Prime Minister on him. Balaji not only restored the rule of law which had been in disarray since Shivaji's death but succeeded in getting the Mughal ruler in Delhi to recognize his master as the independent ruler of his grandfather Shivaji's territories. Some regard Balaji as the second founder of the Maratha Empire.

After Balaji's death in 1720, a grateful Shahu—despite the resentment of Maratha nobles against growing Brahmin ascendancy—

invested Balaji's son, Baji Rao, as the Peshwa. Even more ambitious and far-sighted than his father, Baji Rao decided to point the Marathas north, to the very seat of the Mughals. Their victories and territorial acquisitions shook the Mughal Empire to its foundations and when Baji Rao died in 1740, his son Balaji Baji Rao was also made Peshwa by Shahu. After Shahu's death nine years later, Balaji Baji Rao staged the ultimate *coup d'état* by seizing all powers himself.

This was a departure from the Brahminical élite's preference for the number two position in the power hierarchy, not only because of the influence, status and wealth it brought, but, more importantly, because it enabled a versatile man, well-versed in statecraft, to exercise power without the danger or ridicule the top position attracts. Moreover, the top man is accountable for all his actions, which the man behind the throne is not. Interestingly, it was a Brahmin named Sissa who invented the game of chess (*chatur-angam* as it was called then) in the fifth century, to convince his monarch that even though the king was the most important piece of all, he could neither attack nor defend himself without the alert and constant support of his subjects. Naturally, the second most important piece in Indian chess is *mantri*, or minister of state (most often a Brahmin), whilst in the West it is called the queen. Abbé Dubois, in his *Hindu Manners, Customs and Ceremonies*, rightly mocks the form chess took in the West: "What can be more ridiculous than the castles which move about from place to place, the queen who rushes about fighting with the king's people, or the bishops who occupy such an exalted position?" (In the Indian version of chess the castles are elephants and the bishops chariots.)

Astute and calculating, the British, with a keen sense for the wealth to be made out of India, had been quietly expanding their presence from the year 1585, when William Leeds, Ralph Fitch and John Newbury first arrived in India, sent by enterprising London merchants with instructions to find a sea route to India and bring back a first-hand account of the trading possibilities. Fitch's report on returning to England eight years later led to the founding of the East India Company on 24 September 1599. By the nineteenth century it ruled over large tracts of India, which were taken over by the Crown in 1858. It was not so much English courage and qualities of leadership as the chronic infighting and self-destructive urges of the Indian ruling classes that led to India's colonization. The eminent political thinker Rajni Kothari is of the view that one of the major weaknesses of the Brahmin and upper-caste-dominated social structure in India was the absence of a political state with a clear centre, supported by effective military technology. He makes the point that the British, who came as merchants, understood and exploited these weaknesses, which enabled them to establish their own political and military ruling apparatus.

The British made great use of the Brahmins' long experience in court intrigue and ability to enforce caste discipline. As British contacts with India in the seventeenth and eighteenth centuries grew, so did the need to know more about its peoples' customs, languages, traditions, social structures, land systems, demographic distinctions and seemingly endless religious beliefs and practices. The erudite Brahmins were the obvious source of knowledge to which the British and other Western travellers turned.

The reports of Jean-Baptiste Tavernier, a Frenchman who visited India several times between 1631 and 1667, were largely based on conversations with Brahmins. In the same period, Abraham Roger, a chaplain at the Dutch factory near Madras, developed his understanding of Hinduism from a Dutch-speaking Brahmin, Padmanubha; Roger's treatise was published in 1670 with extensive quotes from Padmanubha. Alexander Dow, an army officer in the East India Company, who published *The History of Hindustan* in 1768–71 (an English translation from the Persian), derived the basis for his introductory essays largely from Brahmins and their view of the sacredness and centrality of the Brahmin in Indian life.

As Britain's grip on India tightened towards the end of the eighteenth century and orientalists and administrators alike made concerted efforts to learn Sanskrit and other languages of India, Brahmin scholarship again proved useful—this time to the Brahmins directly. The Indian Public Service Commission reported in 1887 that of 1,866 Hindu members of the judicial and executive services, nearly half were Brahmins, the figure for Madras being 202 of a total of 297, and in Bombay 211 out of 328. Of sixteen successful Indian candidates for the Indian Civil Service in Madras between 1892 and 1904, fifteen were Brahmins. Even though Brahmins—like others—were at the receiving end of colour discrimination and such, the coarse racial prejudices of the British gradually gave way to more pragmatic views of India's human talents. From the nineteenth century onwards, institutions for Western education were established in India, and then Indians—especially Brahmins—entered schools and universities in Britain and ultimately the top grade of the Indian Civil Service. At the time of India's Independence in 1947, Brahmins constituted 226 out of 349 Indian ICS officers, or roughly 65 per cent.

The quality of Brahmin intellect and learning is not in doubt. What is open to question is the manner in which powerful Brahminical cliques perpetuated their hold and in the process excluded non-Brahmins from the real centres of power. Thirty-five years after Independence: "In the senior echelons of the civil service from the rank of deputy secretaries upwards, out of 500 there are 310 Brahmins; of the 26 state chief secretaries, 19 are Brahmins; . . . of the 16 Supreme Court judges, 9 are Brahmins; of the 330 judges of the High Courts, 166 are Brahmins; . . . of 438 district magistrates, 250 are Brahmins; of the total of 3,300 IAS* officers, 2,376 are Brahmins." A caste which accounted for 3 per cent of the population controlled from 50 to 70 per cent of the country's key positions. In the half-century since Independence, Brahmins have fielded five out of eleven Indian presidents, six out of ten vice-presidents, and six out of twelve prime ministers.

After 2,000 years of ceaseless turbulence, wars, conquests, defeats, bloodshed, destruction and conversions during which great civilizations, religions, languages and customs have flourished and vanished, the Brahminical order has not only survived but spread with unerring purpose. Although there have been setbacks—for example, the anti-Brahmin agitation in South India in the early twentieth century—they have been overcome.

In time, to be a Brahmin meant you belonged to an exclusive club, and not just in jobs or positions of privilege. Exclusivity became an end in itself and was taken to extremes even in the twentieth century. For instance, the low-born had to keep their specified distance from the high-born: from a few paces to 50 or 96 paces or more depending on

---

* Indian Administrative Service—the equivalent of the ICS after Independence.

how low the low-born was, the idea being to prevent the lowly from accidentally touching their betters and polluting them or their immediate environment. The Purada-Vannan, a low-caste category in South India, were not even allowed outside their homes during the day: they were considered unfit to be seen by the upper castes and the high-born would not risk the shadow of the lowly-born falling on them, so that the members of this caste had to live nocturnal lives. In the southern state of Travancore lower-caste women were forbidden to cover their breasts in the presence of the higher castes. "In the elaborate hierarchy of caste ranking, the Nairs, for example, bared their breasts before the Nambudiri Brahmins, and the Brahmins did so only before the deity. The Nadars, like all of the lower castes, were categorically forbidden to cover their breasts at any time." This practice was finally given up after a prolonged struggle, largely owing to the efforts of Christian missionaries.

Despite the political pressure from contemporary Dalits (the former low castes), the abolition of untouchability on 29 April 1947, and many other social reforms, attitudes and customs of two millennia have not changed much. A caste system which has withstood the challenge of Buddhism and the onslaughts and fervour of Islamic and Christian rulers and reformers does not easily disintegrate.

As an exquisite piece of social engineering, the caste structure has no parallel. Monopoly of privileged status and sharp social divisions are of course seen in other societies. But "the real triumph of the caste system," as an Indian government report has pointed out, "lies not in upholding the supremacy of the Brahmin, but in conditioning the consciousness of the lower castes into accepting their inferior status in the ritual hierarchy as a part of the natural order of things."

In other countries a worker or the offspring of a worker can cross class boundaries through education, industry and financial success, but lower-caste Indians cannot cross the line that divides them from others at birth. Even after acquiring wealth and high positions they cannot cut through the encrusted privileges of upper-caste Brahmins. As the thinker Swami Vivekanand has noted: "In modern India one born of Shudra parents, be he a millionaire or a great pundit, has [n]ever the right to leave his own society, with the result that the power of his wealth, intellect or wisdom, remains confined within his own caste limits . . ." And the Brahminical doctrine, impregnable to all challenges to its authority, makes a virtue of the "condescending benevolence of the upper castes and grovelling submission of the lower castes and gives them religious sanctity."

But the Hindu social order rests on other institutions as well which have ensured its continuity over time. As Nirad Chaudhuri suggests in his *Autobiography of an Unknown Indian:* "Hinduism has an uncanny sense of what threatens it. No plausible assurances, no euphemism, no disguise can put its ever-alert instinct of self-preservation off its guard." So, aside from the vertical structure provided by *varna* (caste), there is the horizontal structure of *jati:* "While *varna* has all the appearance of a neat and logical structure, *jati* on the other hand is characteristically ambiguous. It has several meanings, refers to *varna* at one level and to other meanings of segmentation at other levels." Through this kind of horizontal movement and ambiguity, *jati* can cover doctrinal, economic, political, occupational and ritual territories, providing an "all-India frame into which myriad *jatis* in any single linguistic area can be fitted." Into the *jati* structure is provided room—through marriages and other associations—for other communities and groups, which not only gives them confidence, contentment and status, but also creates space for the newly emerging merchant-industrial class—all this tending to support and strengthen the vertical caste structure, *varna.*

Any faith that believes in equality among human beings, and sees God in each of them, is an intrusion—an assault—on those who constitute the caste hierarchy. Such intruders have to be removed, as was Buddhism. The Sikhs and their beliefs, which threatened Brahmin supremacy by rejecting the idea of caste, also fell into this category, and resentments against them began with Nanak's enunciation of his principles of equality. When on 30 March 1699 the tenth Guru, Gobind Singh, baptized five Sikhs from different social backgrounds to form the brotherhood of the Khalsa, the "pure ones," the first five of the Sikh Faith—and in turn asked them to baptize him—he reiterated the same principle. And one far removed from "a way of thought that survived seventeen conquests and two millennia . . ."

This difference in their approach to life and religious obligations accounts for the uneasy relationship between the Sikhs and India's caste élite. Their differences have led to frequent clashes. And no matter what attempt is made to explain these away, the root cause of the unsettled relationship belongs to the continuum of history; a tangled web of religion and caste. The Sikhs and their evolution cannot be understood unless the manner in which power is wielded in India's social fabric is also understood.

In his *Antimemoirs,* André Malraux quotes Jawaharlal Nehru as saying: "André Malraux asked me a strange question: what was it that enabled Hinduism to expel a well-organized Buddhism from India without any serious conflict, more than a thousand years ago? How had Hinduism managed, so to speak, to absorb a great and widespread popular religion without the usual wars of religion? . . . But I could not give a satisfactory answer either to him or to myself. For there are many answers and explanations, but they never seem to get to the heart of the problem."

This is a disingenuous anecdote because Malraux could not have been unaware that far from being expelled from India "without any serious conflict," Buddhism was cast out after its followers were put to the sword and their monasteries destroyed. Nehru was too knowledgeable to have been ignorant either of where the "heart of the problem" lay.

The "problem" lay, and still lies, with the dominant caste's proven ability to overthrow other faiths with or without the usual wars of religion, depending on what appears appropriate. Today, in step with the changing times, the Brahmins have penetrated the rural areas through new alignments with the landed gentry belonging to the intermediate castes, or the "dominant castes" as they have recently been called. This further consolidates their hold even in the present democratic age—in a way because of it, since numbers are manipulated in elections to benefit politicians and political parties, and eventually the Brahmins.

The Sikhs have no illusions about this whole edifice of domination, and the despotic hold of the upper castes. But having opposed repression, and the tyranny of caste, a number of times in their history, they know how to stand their ground. And that is what this book is about.

I

The Gurus of the Faith
1469–1708

It was a time of turmoil and terror, and of conquests, cruelties and despair, with the constant spectre of more calamities ahead. If fifteenth-century Hindustan had already seen centuries of invasions and indignities, it had also been moved—even if peripherally—by the mystical outpourings of Sufi scholars who presented the humane side of Islam's unpredictable and capricious rulers. The Afghans Mahmud of Ghazni and Muhammed of Ghor, Tamerlane of Samarkand, and other invaders from the north-west had destroyed cities, towns and temples and plundered their immense wealth. But the five hundred years from the tenth to the fifteenth century were witness to surprising self-certainties as well, which found expression in two appealing movements of spiritual quest and humanitarian concerns.

Each was rooted in the great religions of Hinduism and Islam which were on a collision course in Hindustan. Whilst the Bhakti movement evolved from its Hindu origins, the Sufis were Muslim. The doctrine of Bhakti, or devotion to a personal deity, originated in southern India in the thirteenth century and was further propagated in the next by a new sect in Benares, which made no distinction of caste or creed. A more extreme version of it was evolved by a Muslim weaver named Kabir, who ridiculed all institutional religion, ceremony, asceticism and learning, addressing his teaching to the most humble people. Sufism, a school of Islamic mysticism which reached the climax of its development in the eleventh century AD, included among its adherents many of the finest Persian poets. Enthused by the mystical and philosophic content of Hinduism and Islam respectively, and preferring a liberal, humane and broad-minded interpretation of them, Bhaktism and Sufism drew inspiration from each other without sacrificing their identities or loyalty to their parent faith. Each was in thrall to the divine being, not to the rituals and symbols of religious power. The two movements were enthusiastically received in Punjab—gateway to India and the land of five legendary rivers*—whose people had paid such a punishing price in the continuing clash of arms on their soil. The region's key city—the seat of power—was Lahore, for whoever ruled Punjab did so from here.

The founder of the Sikh religion, Nanak, was born in the village of Talwandi near Lahore, on 15 April 1469. The fifteenth century was a time of comparative peace in northern India, of respite between the barbarous invasion of Tamerlane at the end of the fourteenth century and the conquest by Babur, founder of the Mughal Empire,† in the next. Rare stability at the time of Nanak's birth was provided by the rule of the Afghan nobleman Bahlol Khan, founder of the Lodhi dynasty (1450–1526).

Nanak's destiny was shaped as much by his own extraordinary qualities of head and heart as by those eventful times. The very location of Talwandi, on the direct route of invading armies which kept pouring in through the majestic mountains of the Hindu Kush, toughened its inhabitants and made them remarkably resilient; just as often as their village was razed to the ground, they rebuilt it. To move away was unacceptable. Another inescapable fact of life was the mutually destructive struggle for supremacy between warring Hindu kingdoms, clans and castes, which was largely responsible for Hindustan's dominance by outsiders. Their internecine warfare had also led to the country's increasing colonization by Muhammadans, not that that prevented other Muslim adventurers, lured by the subcontinent's

---

* The Jhelum, Chenab, Ravi, Sutlej and Beas.
† The word "Mughal" or "Mogul," a corruption of "Mongol," was loosely applied to Muslims of Central Asian origin in India, and designates the Emperors of Delhi descended from Tamerlane, beginning with Babur (1526–30).

riches, from invading India. Nanak's awareness of the prevailing religious, political and social forces was shaped by this welter of violence. And by the conciliatory promise of the Sufi and Bhakti movements, although in his own spiritual quest, and its final achievement, he would go far beyond their confines.

Nanak's father, Kalyan Chand, of a Hindu family of the Bedi branch of the Kshatriyas, kept revenue records for a prosperous landlord and Rajput convert to Islam named Rai Buler. In Talwandi, where Hindus and Muslims lived side by side, a Muslim midwife brought Nanak into the world. Since the birth of a son called for much rejoicing, Kalyan Chand's friends gathered to celebrate the joyful event at which both Pandit Hardyal, the family's Brahmin priest, and the midwife agreed that the child had an exceptional aura. The horoscope prepared by Hardyal predicted that Hindus and Muslims alike would acknowledge Nanak as a philosopher-teacher and that he in turn would make no distinction between them. So not very surprisingly one of Nanak's earliest observations:

There is no Hindu
There is no Mussalman

GURU GRANTH SAHIB
RAG BHAIRON, P. 1136

whilst acknowledging the distinctive beliefs and nature of each, stressed the fact that in the eyes of the divine being all are equal, and that appreciation of this central truth was important if humanity was to surmount the barriers that divide people.

These insights, extraordinary for one so young, were greatly helped by the happy household in which Nanak grew up. His mother Tripta and sister Nanaki doted on him, whilst his father quietly nursed high hopes for a prosperous future in business for him. But when he took his son to the village school at the age of seven, the teacher soon realized he had a very unusual pupil on his hands. Within days of starting school Nanak would write verse on his slate tablet, and not only was the structure of his poems impressive, but their content possessed a sensitive feel for nature and its many moods. And Nanak had a mind also given to probing the metaphysical.

But his father worried. He couldn't understand his son's lack of interest in business. A change of teachers didn't help either, although Nanak did learn Sanskrit from his second instructor and Arabic and Persian from the third. In the chronicles of his life, the *Meharban Janamsakhi,* his second instructor is quoted as saying: "He is a blessed one . . . he grasps instantly what he hears once." Both instructors saw in his contemplative nature and inquiring mind, which included a facility with languages, a potential for scholarship and spiritual quest. Even more astonishing was his tendency to question the logic of traditional practices.

This he did at eleven, an age when boys of the twice-born castes have to don the *janeu,* or sacred thread of the Hindus, consisting of strands of cotton woven into a thin cord which is looped from the left shoulder around the right hip. Nanak stunned the family's friends and relations gathered for his initiation by refusing to wear the thread, and asking the presiding Brahmin priest to explain the difference a thread could make. Shouldn't deeds, merits and actions, he asked, differentiate one man from another? Since he was unconvinced that the *janeu* created any true distinction, he preferred not to wear it.

As if this weren't enough, Nanak recited his own composition to a thoroughly baffled Pandit Hardyal and his father's guests:

> *Out of the cotton of compassion*
> *Spin the thread of contentment,*
> *Tie the knot of continence,*
> *   and the twist of virtue;*
> *Make such a sacred thread,*
> *O Pundit, for your inner self.*
> GURU GRANTH SAHIB
> ASA, P. 471

His spirited stand against an unacceptable practice set Nanak apart, and marked him for an unusual journey through life; what preoccupied him was far removed from the pranks of his boyhood friends. When grazing his father's cattle he was given to spending hours on end listening to the mystics, saints and spiritualists who have always been a part of India's human mosaic, leading lives of self-denial and introspection, and expounding the virtues of their own faith. Nanak heard them with rapt attention, but drew entirely different conclusions—in verse—on tenets long accepted without question. He questioned most of them:

> *Pilgrimages, penances, compassion and alms-giving*
> *Bring a little merit, the size of a sesame seed.*
> *But he who hears and believes and loves the Name*
> *Shall bathe and be made clean*
> *In a place of pilgrimage within him.*

GURU GRANTH SAHIB

JAPJI, P. 4

He assessed Islamic practices too with the same analytical mind and the same sharp eye for empty rituals and customs, neither challenging nor deriding prevalent beliefs, but posing questions and presenting his own convictions:

> *Let compassion be your mosque,*
> *Let faith be your prayer mat,*
> *Let honest living be your Koran,*
> *Let modesty be the rules of observance,*
> *Let piety be the fasts you keep;*
> *In such wisdom try to become a Muslim:*
> *Right conduct the Ka'ba; Truth the Prophet;*
> *Good deeds your prayer;*
> *Submission to the Lord's Will your rosary;*
> *Nanak, if this you do, the Lord will be your Protector.*

GURU GRANTH SAHIB

ASA, P. 141

Around the age of sixteen Nanak set out for the town of Sultanpur—a hundred miles or so away to the east of the Ravi and the Beas—at the invitation of Nanaki and her husband Jairam. After her marriage his sister had moved there with her husband who worked for Nawab Daulat Khan Lodhi, a relation of Delhi's ruler, Bahlol, and governor of the region. Daulat Khan was an exceptional man, a powerful official of the Lodhis, builder of fine buildings and superb gardens, and patron of scholars and theologians who were increasingly drawn to him by his interest in their work. He made Sultanpur a great centre of learning.

Jairam was held in high esteem by the nawab, who received him graciously when he took Nanak to meet him. As others had done who had met Nanak, Daulat Khan too took a liking to him, and offered him a job. Notwithstanding his indifference to occupations without a goal, Nanak gratefully accepted, as he was reluctant to impose himself on his sister and brother-in-law for too long. His diligence impressed the nawab, as it did the never-ending stream of people who came to pay their taxes in kind, or draw part of their salaries in kind. Even in the *modikhana* (the granary and stores), despite the earnestness he brought to his work, his thoughts were never far from the Divine Being. Professor Harbans Singh tells this story: "While weighing out rations one day, [Nanak] was so entranced with the utterance of the figure *tera*, or thirteen, which is also the Punjabi equivalent of the word 'thine,' that he kept repeating it—*tera, tera* (Thine, Thine, all is Thine, O Lord!)— and dealing out the provisions."

In the midst of his mundane responsibilities, his mind remained focused on the Creator:

> *God has His seat everywhere,*
> *His treasure houses are in all places.*
>
> GURU GRANTH SAHIB
> JAPJI, P. 5

And:

> *If I remember Him I live,*
> *If I forget Him I die . . .*
>
> GURU GRANTH SAHIB
> REHRAS, P. 9

Slowly and intuitively, as he looked for the elusive truth, his unceasing inner search was helping him to develop his unusual mind, on which he preferred to depend more than on tomes written by others:

One may read for years and for years,
And spend every month of the year in reading only;
And thus read all one's life,
Right up to one's last breath.
Of all things, a contemplative life
Is really what matters;
All else is the fret and fever of egoistic minds.

GURU GRANTH SAHIB
ASA, P. 467

An increasing number of men and women were beginning to gravitate towards him. In a rented house near his place of work, where he lived with two boyhood companions, people congregated for recitations, prayers and contemplation. To Nanaki, an ardent admirer of her gifted brother, this was, however, only one side of his life. The other side, she felt, was incomplete without a wife and children. And since Nanak too believed that "the secret of religion lay in living in the world without being overcome by it," he was persuaded. Through Jairam's initiative a match was arranged with Sulakhni, the daughter of a Kshatriya named Mulchand, from the village of Pakhoke near Batala, and Nanak was married at the age of nineteen.

During the next eight years he spent in Sultanpur, his two sons, Srichand and Lakhmidas, were born. Alongside the nawab's growing respect and confidence, his circle of loving disciples also grew, coming from distant places as news of him spread far and wide. But a restlessness was building up in Nanak, an urge to discover the nature of the world he lived in, to meet and understand different people and their beliefs, to find out what they looked for in their faith. He knew he had to travel far to get the answers. Hard as it was to leave those whose love had sustained him, he had to go if his mission in life was to succeed. He had already established the parameters of his faith.

There is but one God. He is all that is.
He is the Creator of all things and He is all-pervasive.
He is without fear and without enmity.
He is timeless, unborn and self-existent.
He is the Enlightener
And can be realized by his grace alone.
He was in the beginning; He was in all ages.
The True One is, was, O Nanak, and shall forever be.

GURU GRANTH SAHIB

JAPJI, P. I

If he could apply his integrating genius to making the concept of "one god" a reality, he could harness it to serve a strife-torn society, erase divisions and despair, and help people overcome their prejudices and mindless preoccupations. This concept would become central to the Sikh faith.

And so in the summer of 1496 Nanak's travels began. The first phase took him eastward to Hardwar, Benares, Kamrup (Assam) and Jagannath (Orissa), and to southern India and Ceylon, and the second to Tibet, Kabul, Mecca and Baghdad, no small feat considering the times and distances involved. But the saintly Nanak had an iron will, and he knew what he wanted from his exchanges with the scholars, thinkers and mystics he met at each of these great centres of religious learning. The encounters helped crystallize his own ideas and give sharper definition to the contours of the faith he was developing. Faith in one God. Not a God with a physical form but an amalgam of truth, integrity, courage and enlightened thinking. An inner God present in every person. Not the property of a few purveyors of priestly wisdom but of all living beings. "While [he was] at Hardwar, the Brahmins . . . pointed out the advantages of sacrifices and burnt-offerings, and of the worship of cremation-grounds, gods and goddesses. The Guru replied that the sacrifices and burnt-offerings of this age consisted in giving food to those who repeated God's name and practised humility."

In the course of his travels Nanak not only studied the religious beliefs and practices of others but preached his own developing faith, in any venue he could find, Hindu temple, mosque or in the open. In many of the traditional anecdotes about his life, the *janam-sakhis*, it is related how he would call at people's houses and join with them in the singing of hymns he had composed. An anecdote from one such source illustrates Nanak's fearless criticism of high-caste power and privilege. In Sayyadpur (now Eminabad in the district of Gujranwala) he stayed in the house of a carpenter named Lalo. Hearing of Nanak's reputation, a high-caste official of the region invited him to a banquet he was giving for holy men. Nanak at first refused to go, saying he cared for the company only of the low-born. But at last he did accept, declining, however, to eat. Asked why he did so when, a holy man of Kshatriya descent, he had not declined to eat a carpenter's food, he replied to the official: "Your food reeks of blood, while that of Lalo, the carpenter, tastes like honey and milk." And further, when asked for explanation: "Lalo earns with the sweat of his brow and out of it offers whatever little he can to the wayfarer, the poor and the holy, and so it tastes sweet and wholesome, but you being without work, squeeze blood out of the people through bribery, tyranny and show of authority."

Nanak's travels lasted twenty-eight years, until he finally settled down at a peaceful spot on the Ravi above Lahore for the remaining fifteen years of his life. Here he built a village called Kartarpur, which soon exercised a magnetic pull on persons of the new faith as it developed into a community of learning and shared beliefs. It was a perfect setting for the distillation of Nanak's experiences and, most of all, his inner search for a new direction for mankind. The pastoral environs provided a serene backdrop to his endeavour to translate his ideas and ideals into the new faith of Sikhism.

Most of Nanak's converts came from the Hindu farming population of Punjab among whom Nanak naturally moved, with occasional Muslims, among whom was Nanak's close confidant, Mardana, who accompanied him on his travels. The high-placed urban mercantile Khatri caste was the origin of many of Nanak's and later Gurus' disciples and closest associates, while the ranks of the widespread Jat caste of village cultivators came to make up a sizeable proportion of the Sikh community.

.   .   .

The word "Sikh" evolved from the Sanskrit term *shishya*, a disciple or devoted follower, and the name was appropriate since Nanak's followers gravitated in increasing numbers to idyllic Kartarpur. His daily involvement in the activities of the community made a profound impression on the participants as did his prolific writings in verse. In order better to communicate both with his congregations and his more distant followers he used Gurmukhi, since it could best enunciate Punjab's spoken language. The script that came to be called Gurmukhi— "from the Guru's mouth"—belongs to the Brahmi family, the script used by the Aryans. Whilst Nanak used Gurmukhi letters for his writings, his successor, Angad, developed the script by giving it new form and precision.

Nanak's 974 hymns are a significant part of the Sikh scriptures, the Granth Sahib, which the fifth Guru, Arjan Dev, would compile at Amritsar sixty-five years later. The word *Guru*, incidentally, is a term of respect which really means "teacher," and Nanak and his nine successors were reverentially addressed by all Sikhs as Gurus.

Guru Nanak's writings repeatedly revert to the need to wean people from idolatry and the pernicious caste system on the one hand, and from fanatical attitudes which make people destroy temples and idols on the other. The striking symbolism of his verses portrays this continuing concern:

> *If you believe in pollution at birth,*
> > *there is pollution everywhere.*
> *There are creatures in cow-dung [considered sacred by Hindus]*
> > *and in wood.*
> *There is life in each grain of corn.*
> *Water is the source of life,*
> > *sap for all things.*
> *Then how can one escape pollution?*
> > *Pollution pollutes only the ignorant.*
> *The pollution of the mind is greed,*
> > *the pollution of the tongue lying.*
> *The pollution of the eyes is to look with covetousness*
> > *upon another's wealth, upon another's wife*

and upon the beauty of another's woman.
The pollution of the ears is to listen to slander.

The pollution in which people commonly believe
is all superstition.
Birth and death are by divine will,
by divine will men come and go.
What is given to us to eat and drink is pure.
They who have arrived at the truth
remain untouched by pollution.

GURU GRANTH SAHIB

ASA, P. 472

On different occasions Nanak had incurred the wrath of both Hindus and Muslims who resented his philosophic equation: *there is no Hindu, there is no Mussalman.* When Muslims complained to Nawab Daulat Khan Lodhi of his effrontery in equating the ruling race with the subject people of Hindustan, Nanak's response—with which the nawab wholly agreed—was characteristically forthright:

It is not easy to be called a Mussalman:
If there were one let him be so known.
He should first take to his heart the tenets of his faith
and purge himself of all pride.
He will be a Mussalman who pursues the path
shown by the founder of the creed;
who extinguishes anxiety about life and death;
who accepts the will of God as supreme;
who has faith in the Creator and surrenders
himself to the Almighty.
When he has established his goodwill for all, O Nanak,
then will he be called a Mussalman.

GURU GRANTH SAHIB

VAR MAG, P. 141

Impressed by the basic compassion of Hinduism and the essential brotherhood of Islam which looked upon the faithful as equals in the sight of God, Nanak emphasized the inconsistencies that detracted from these inspired origins and set the two religions on a course of hatred and intolerance. It has been suggested that the rule of the Lodhi Sultanate and the early Mughals was not characterized by religious violence, and that wherever violence was resorted to, for example, the destruction of temples, it was for political rather than religious reasons. This is a moot point. Destruction of its places of worship cannot denote respect for another religion, it can only signify the ruling race's arrogance towards the faith of a subject people. The degree of intolerance certainly varied, but not the antipathy.

Alongside his efforts at helping people to reach beyond their prejudices, Nanak brought his clarity of thinking to highlighting the jarring social inequalities then prevailing, especially discrimination against women:

> *Of woman are we born, of woman conceived,*
> > *to woman engaged, to woman married.*
> *Woman we befriend, by woman is the civilization continued.*
> *When woman dies, woman is sought for.*
> *It is by woman that order is maintained.*
> *Then why call her evil from whom great men are born?*
> *From woman is woman born,*
> > *And without woman none would exist.*
> *The eternal Lord is the only one, O Nanak,*
> > *Who depends not on woman.*

> GURU GRANTH SAHIB
> ASA, P. 473

It goes without saying that amongst his own followers Guru Nanak insisted on complete equality between men and women. In this he was far ahead of his time.

Amongst the other reforms initiated by him—formalized by the third Guru, Amar Das—was the institution of *langar*: the community kitchen in which Sikhs would cook, serve and eat together wherever they congregated. Its deeper purpose was not only to instil a sense of equality in Sikhs, but to help them overcome caste prejudices, which prohibit the higher and lower castes from eating together. The social significance of this had a revitalizing effect on those drawn to Sikhism.

This man of courage, compassion, intellect and tireless pursuit of his goals, who believed that "death was the privilege of the brave," died in Kartarpur on 7 September 1539. That he died in peace was indeed a privilege for someone as courageous as he, because the times did not encourage dissent, nor favour those who questioned despotism:

> *The times are like drawn knives, kings like butchers,*
> *Righteousness has fled on wings.*
> *The dark night of falsehood prevails,*
> *The moon of truth is nowhere visible.*

GURU GRANTH SAHIB

MAJH, P. 145

Nanak's life coincided with a period of religious renaissance in Europe, Martin Luther (1483–1546) and John Calvin (1509–64) being among his contemporaries. Their emphasis on the sovereignty of God, the supreme authority of the scriptures, and condemnation of idolatry and false rituals paralleled Nanak's approach. But whilst opposing discriminatory doctrines and practices, he also addressed the question of self-indulgent and corrupt religious and political hierarchies. He wanted to bring those who had been pushed to the fringes of human concerns back into the mainstream. "Religion lies not in empty words. He who regards all men as equal is religious."

Sikhism went beyond the older established religions of India in its liberal and sensitive concern for the individual. In exalting the concept of caring for every human being irrespective of caste or creed, it replaced dogma and doctrine by a basic belief in truth. It elevated truth to the level of a Divine Being. Sikhism emerged not as a synthesis of established religions but as an alternative to them.

Joseph Davey Cunningham, an official of the East India Company, in his classic *History of the Sikhs* (1849), provides another perspective on Nanak: "It was reserved for Nanak to perceive the true principles of reform, and to lay those broad foundations which enabled his successor Gobind to fire the minds of his countrymen with a new nationality, and give practical effect to the doctrine that the lowest is equal with the highest, in race as in creed, in political rights as in religious hopes."

Guru Nanak, instead of appointing one of his two sons to succeed him, chose Lehna, his devout follower and former worshipper of the Hindu goddess Durga who had converted to Sikhism. Born on 31 March 1504 in Sarai Naga, a village ten miles from Muktsar in the present-day Faridkot district of Punjab, he was of the Khatri caste. To emphasize his confidence in him Guru Nanak renamed him Angad, or an "inseparable part" of himself. He lived at Khadur in the present district of Amritsar. A man of extreme religious sensitivity, he was so affected by Nanak's death that he tried to go into seclusion. It has been suggested by some historians that he was seeking to avoid the hostility of Nanak's two sons, and alternatively that he was testing the strength of the Sikhs' faith. The latter would appear the most likely explanation, since withdrawal from the world was not in the spirit of Nanak. Angad was soon persuaded to return to the world, and took up his stewardship with a will.

Angad amply justified Nanak's confidence. During the thirteen years of his stewardship, the fledgling faith grew with discipline, and norms of personal conduct were diligently upheld. He also made the Gurmukhi script pre-eminent and collected Guru Nanak's hymns into a book which included 62 composed by himself. His own ethical concerns were in line with his predecessor's:

> *Whom should I despise,*
> *Since the one Lord made us all?*
>
> GURU GRANTH SAHIB
> VAR SARANG, P. 1237

One of Angad's last acts was to ask a wealthy disciple, Gobind, to build a new village on the Beas not far from Khadur, naming it Gobindwal after its builder; eventually the new settlement came to be known as Goindwal. One of Guru Angad's most devoted disciples, Amar Das, helped to make it a centre of Sikh devotion. When Guru Angad died on 29 March 1552, he had chosen Amar Das as his successor.

This man, also a Khatri, although already in his seventies, was filled with eagerness to consolidate the new faith. The *sangats*, or assemblies of the Sikhs, now existed in far-flung places as more and more people joined the fold. In order to develop cohesiveness and continuity, Guru Amar Das organized the *sangats* into twenty-two *manjis*—the equivalents of ecclesiastical districts. He also institutionalized the *langar* and all visitors were expected to eat—just as he did—with others. When the Mughal emperor visited him at Goindwal in 1567, he too willingly ate in the community kitchen.

Among his other far-ranging social reforms was the prohibition from practising *sati*, the self-immolation of widows on their husbands' funeral pyres. He also stopped women wearing veils, allowed widows to remarry, and broke with tradition by appointing women preachers. Women headed many of the *manjis* established by Amar Das. The cultural distinctiveness of the Sikhs was underscored by equality between their men and women.

Guru Amar Das also took the first step towards the construction of one of the world's holiest shrines. Although it took several decades for the symbol of the Sikh faith—the Golden Temple—to be built in the centre of a serene stretch of clear water, the site was chosen by him because of the tranquillity of the forested terrain around it. Hitherto the Gurus had lived in places of their choice: the first in Kartarpur, the second in Khadur, and the third at Goindwal. This place by a pool was destined to become the emblematic core of Sikhism. In the third Guru's time all it had was a mud hut he had built on the water's edge for meditation and prayer.

Guru Amar Das's 907 hymns in the Granth Sahib, in the main deeply devotional, continuously and emphatically reiterate Sikhism's opposition to the prejudices of caste:

> *Let no man be proud because of his caste.*
> *For the man who has God in his heart,*
> *He, no other, is the true Brahmin.*

So, O fool, do not be vainglorious about your caste.
For vainglory leads to most of mind's evils.
Though they say there are four castes,
One God created all men,
All men are moulded of the same clay.
The Great Potter has merely varied their shapes.
All men are made of the same five elements,
None can reduce an element in one, increase it in another.

GURU GRANTH SAHIB
RAG BHAIRON, P. 1128

With Guru Amar Das's death on 1 September 1574 when he was over ninety, the mantle of leadership fell on Ram Das (1534–81). This devoted disciple of the third Guru had been selected by him as his successor. His name had previously been Jetha; Amar Das renamed him Ram Das, or Servant of the Lord. He had greatly impressed Amar Das both by his commitment to the principles and purposes of the faith and by his extraordinary industriousness; and he had married the third Guru's younger daughter. The development of the new site by the pool was taking place under his direction; and Guru Amar Das had seen him dig and built the *baoli*—a wide well with steps leading down to the water—in Goindwal, which in time would become another place of pilgrimage. The Sikh Gurus, unlike religious heads of some faiths, worked in the kitchens, washed dishes, tilled the fields, cut firewood and lent a hand in all community activities. They did not use their positions to lead privileged lives.

In a move which would prove of great spiritual and political relevance, Guru Ram Das—even before assuming the responsibilities of leadership—chose to live by the same beautiful expanse of water that had appealed to his predecessor. It lay between the rivers Ravi and Beas some fifty miles north-west of Goindwal and a hundred miles east of Lahore. Convinced of its appropriateness as a future centre of the Sikh faith, Ram Das bought the pool and much of the land around it. This is where the Harmandir Sahib (which means "the house of God"), also known as the Golden Temple, fountainhead of Sikh inspiration, would be built, and around it the holy city to which Sikhs would come for the sheer joy of seeing their beloved shrine in the middle of the immortal pool.

In its early years this place of pilgrimage was known by various names, such as Guru-ka-Chak, Chak Guru Ram Das and Ramdaspur, but by the beginning of the eighteenth century the name Amritsar—derived from *amrit sarowar*—had come to stay. *Amrit*, in Sanskrit, means the elixir of life or water sanctified by the touch of the sacred, whilst *sarowar* is a lake or pool.

A colourful human mosaic soon converged on the small settlement by the *sarowar*. Along with the masons, joiners and other artisans and inspired people, came the bards, balladeers, scholars, savants and mystics; all of them drawn by the excitement in the air, by a sense of purpose. In time they and the many enterprising craftsmen and traders converted the makeshift houses, bazaars and meeting-places into a new city. But in the construction of the spiritual centre the faith's enduring principle remained constant: the Sikh tradition of voluntary labour and self-reliance. This pride in their ability to sustain their beliefs had in fact made Guru Ram Das decline the benevolent Akbar's offer to give land to the Sikhs.

Guru Ram Das's compositions, like his predecessors', also reflect his unswerving resolve to strengthen the bonds between the faith and its followers:

> *Even in a gale and torrential rain,*
> *I would go to meet my Guru.*
> *Even if an ocean separates them,*
> *A Sikh would go to meet his Guru,*
> *As a man dies of thirst without water,*
> *A Sikh would die without his Guru.*
> *As parched earth exults after a shower,*
> *A Sikh rejoices on meeting his Guru.*

> GURU GRANTH SAHIB
> RAG SUHI, PP. 767–8

These prophetic words foretold the magnetic hold the Gurus—Nanak and his successors and then the Granth Sahib—would exercise on the Sikhs in the coming years, and of their inner urge to be in constant communion with their faith's founders.

Guru Arjan Dev, who succeeded Guru Ram Das after his death in 1581, was born on 15 April 1563 at Goindwal. The first three Gurus had looked beyond their own line to appoint their successors (although in Ram Das the third Guru, Amar Das, had appointed a son-in-law), choosing one of their followers for their qualities of spiritual authority. The succession of the Sikh Gurus now followed a new principle—that of heredity, though not of primogeniture; for Arjan Das was the third son of Ram Das. Through a hereditary system of succession the Sikhs may have hoped to avoid a disputed succession.

Amritsar's pre-eminence grew in the fifth Guru's lifetime, helped greatly by his initiatives in the twenty-five decisive years of his stewardship. The first was to make Amritsar more than a place of pilgrimage. It became the rallying-point for Sikhs, a powerful and indestructible symbol of their pride. The soul of the city would be the Harmandir, the house of God (the complex of buildings around the Harmandir and including it would in later years be known as Darbar Sahib). By the time of his tragic death Guru Arjan Dev had made Amritsar the seat of Sikh religion.

The natural pool had been widened by Guru Ram Das in 1577. Guru Arjan Dev now lined it with bricks, with steps going down to the water on all sides, because bathing in the *sarowar* had become customary even before 1559—the year work on the Harmandir began. Its foundation-stone was probably laid in 1588, though historians cannot agree on who actually laid it. Some say it was Guru Arjan Dev, whilst others assert that Mian Mir, a Qadirite Sufi saint of Lahore, laid it on the Guru's invitation. With the destruction of valuable written records in the unending battles fought over the Darbar Sahib, oral tradition is the source of most information of this period.

Guru Arjan Dev's role in constructing the first phase of the Darbar Sahib was crucial, even though the complex is not the work of a single designer or master builder. Nor was it all built at a given point in time. It evolved over the centuries, as successive generations lavished their wealth, time and devotion on it. Guru Arjan Dev's continuing emphasis on the spiritual rather than the material led him to build a modest structure—in brick and lime, in the centre of the "pool of nectar"—so that its design and construction mirrored the logic and coherence of Sikh beliefs. The symbolic significance of the design is striking. The Harmandir's location in the water is a synthesis of *nirgun* and *sargun*—the spiritual and temporal realms of human existence. And with its base situated lower than the surrounding land, the building emphasises the faith's inner strength and confidence, which does not depend on lofty, awe-inspiring structures. In further contrast to the traditional design of temples, with only one entrance, the Harmandir has four—one on each side. Its doors are thus open to all four castes, since Guru Arjan Dev was convinced that "the four castes of Kshatriyas, Brahmins, Shudras and Vaishyas are equal partners in divine instruction."

Quite a few buildings of that age, it must be remembered, were monuments to monarchies, celebrations of the power and riches of the church, or extravagant statements by wealthy merchant princes, like the ornate structures built by India's Islamic and Hindu rulers, or Europe's Renaissance architecture with its overstated ornamentation and scale. The attitude of many religious orders towards extravagant buildings was outlined on his deathbed in 1455 by Nicholas V, the first Renaissance Pope: "A faith sustained only by doctrine will never be anything but feeble and vacillating . . . If the authority of the Holy See were visibly displayed in majestic buildings all the world would accept and revere it. Noble edifices combining taste and beauty with imposing proportions would immensely exalt the chair of St. Peter." But the philosophy of the Sikh faith was diametrically opposite to this. People had to be drawn to it by the nobility of the idea that all human beings are equal in the eyes of God, not by the majesty of the buildings built in His name.

So the place of worship built in ordinary bricks and mortar by the side of a small pool in a place called Amritsar was not obsessed with scale. Nor was it built with plundered wealth, despotic levies, or riches appropriated from other countries. What it had was simple materials and the élan of its worshippers.

By 1601 the core of the complex had taken shape with the completion of the Harmandir and the causeway, and the levelling of the ground around the pool for *parkarma* or circumambulation. Either through fortunate chance or a highly sensitive feel for scale, the visual relationship between the Harmandir and the pool as seen from the *parkarma*, creating a mood of serenity, certitude and unruffled calm, is remarkable.

Guru Arjan Dev now took his momentous decision. Based on his conviction that the dynamic in the relationship between the Sikhs and the centre of their faith could not be sustained by an empty structure, he set about making the Harmandir synonymous with wisdom and learning; a repository of rational thought and sound judgement; a place which elevated and inspired in an age of uncertainty and despair. Those who came to the Harmandir, he felt, must return whence they came more resolute and enriched. With this in mind his work on compiling the Sikh scriptures, which he had already begun, now took on a new dimension. If, on their completion, he were to instal these scriptures, with their magnetic pull, in the Harmandir, they would accord it the sanctity and status impossible without them. It was, moreover, irrational for a religion that stressed rationality to sustain its momentum in a vacuum, or try to impress its followers with empty buildings. So Guru Arjan Dev's compilation of the inspired thoughts and insights of that age was as logical a move as his decision to make them the focal point of the Harmandir.

He had worked ceaselessly on this anthology, which not only included the writings of the first four Gurus and his own, but also those of Hindu and Muslim scholars and saints like Farid (twelfth century), Namdeva (thirteenth century), Sain (fourteenth century), Kabir (fourteenth and fifteenth centuries), Ravi Das (fifteenth century), and many others. They represented a cross-section of the culture and talent of India: men who spoke out against religious and social injustice. As Kabir, a Muslim weaver, put it:

> *The images are all lifeless, they cannot speak:*
> *I know, for I have cried aloud to them.*
> *The Purana and the Quran are mere words:*
> *Lifting up the curtain, I have seen.*

And again:

> *What makes you a Brahmin*
> *And I merely a Sudra?*
> *If blood runs in my veins*
> *Does milk flow in yours?*

GURU GRANTH SAHIB
RAG GAURI, P. 324

By his inclusion of the writings of others besides the Sikh Gurus, Guru Arjan Dev gave a clear message: anyone who showed compassion and concern for his fellow humans would be honoured by the Sikhs. Once completed, the scriptures were set to the *ragas* (the classical system of Indian music) so that the rationality of thought was rendered lyrically. What emerged at the end of Arjan Dev's prodigious efforts was a Granth Sahib (Granth means compilation of sacred scriptures, Sahib is a term of respect), of 1,948 pages containing more than 7,000 hymns. Of these, 2,218 were his own. The writings of the Gurus were compiled in chronological order followed by the works of saints and sufis. In setting the entire volume in 31 *ragas*, an exacting method was followed, making the compositions correspond to the time of day and different moods and occasions. For a balanced outlook, the joyous and the sad were subtly interwoven with moods of yearning and rejoicing. These scriptures compiled by Arjan Dev are known as the Adi Granth (or the "original edition").

The final shape to the Adi Granth was given by Guru Gobind Singh, the tenth and last Guru, who added hymns of his father Tegh Bahadur to it. Just before his death in 1708, he enjoined his followers to look to the Granth Sahib as their supreme guru, to worship wisdom and knowledge and not an individual. And with that ended the tradition of living Gurus.

The elevation of the Granth Sahib to the status of a guru was to introduce a unique concept of leadership which has worked admirably over the centuries, since the scriptures have provided spiritual direction to the Sikhs ever since. They have turned to them in tragedy or triumph, rejoicing or grief, for guidance or calm and intelligent insights, and found philosophical answers to many questions. With print technology overtaking the art of calligraphy, the size of the

Granth Sahib has been fixed at 1,430 pages for every single copy, anywhere in the world. The original Gurmukhi script is kept, even where the original hymns were in medieval Punjabi, Hindi and other languages of the time.

Guru Arjan Dev crowned his achievements by installing the Granth Sahib in the Harmandir on 16 August 1604, three years after its completion. From that date till now the Granth Sahib has been ceremoniously carried from the place where it is kept each night to this sanctum sanctorum before the break of dawn each day. Passages from it are then read throughout the day, interspersed with the singing of excerpts, so that those who come to listen leave enriched by the words of their spiritual forefathers.

In less than two years after the Granth was placed in the Harmandir, the dedicated existence of this peaceable community ended in the turbulence that marked the beginning of the reign of Jahangir, son of Akbar and fourth in the line of Mughal Emperors. Ironically, Jahangir's father had not only visited Guru Amar Das at Goindwal, he had also offered Guru Ram Das a gift of land for their shrine. But Jahangir was made of inferior stuff. Lacking Akbar's vision, one of the first promises he made on ascending the throne was to protect the Muhammadan religion; the powerful lobby of the Ulema in fact demanded it in exchange for their support in the succession crisis Jahangir was then facing.

Sheikh Ahmed, the revivalist head of the Naqshbandi Sufis of Sirhind in eastern Punjab, was one of the fanatics who had Jahangir's ear. He was of the view that "the glory of Islam consists in the humiliation of infidelity and the infidels." Another one of his kind was Chandu Shah, a Brahmin Dewan in the service of Lahore's Mughal Viceroy, the extent of whose contribution remains controversial. His personal role aside, he is certainly seen as representing the opposition of orthodox Hindus to the Guru. Whilst Sheikh Ahmed bitterly resented Akbar's insistence on religious tolerance, he—along with several others—was also resentful of the independent ways of the Sikhs. Sheikh Ahmed "had no sympathy for those who believed that Ram and Rehman were the same." Nor was the upper-caste Hindu view any different, since Sikhism was anti-Brahminical in character. So both the Ulema and the

Brahmins around Jahangir were opposed to the Sikhs. These two elements seized the opportunity—when the Guru was produced in Court—"to institute new proceedings against him on the old charge of having compiled a book which blasphemed the worship and rules of the Hindus and the prayers and fastings of the Muhammadans." Jahangir came round to their view. "So many simple-minded Hindus, nay, even foolish Muslims too had been fascinated by the Guru's ways and teachings . . . many times the thought had been presenting itself to my mind that either I should put an end to this false traffic, or that he be brought into the fold of Islam," he wrote in his memoir, *Tuzuk-i-Jahangiri*.

Matters came to a head over the emperor's eldest son Khusru. Sir Thomas Roe, the English ambassador, described Khusru as a man who favoured "learning, valour and the discipline of war, abhorring all covetousness and . . . [other] base customs . . . [of] his ancestors and the nobility." Although the people rose against Jahangir in favour of Khusru, he was defeated and captured in Punjab, and Jahangir stamped out the rising with utmost cruelty. He had two of his son's principal supporters sewn up in raw hides which contracted in the sun, and three hundred of the rebels impaled in front of Khusru, who was later near-blinded with a hot iron. Another of those on whom the vengeful emperor visited his anger was Guru Arjan Dev, since he had met Khusru, just as Nanak had met his grandfather Babur, and Amar Das had received his father, Akbar. Primed with hate by those around him, Jahangir had the Guru arrested, and as he recorded in his memoir: "I ordered them to produce him and handed over his houses, dwelling places and children to Murtaza Khan, and having confiscated his property commanded that he should be put to death with torture."

The torture was savage. The Guru was seated on a hot iron plate whilst burning sand was poured over him. He was immersed in near-boiling water as well and eventually drowned in the River Ravi. Amongst his last words, to his Sufi friend Mian Mir, were: "I bear all this torture to set an example to the teachers of the True Name, that they may not lose patience or rail at God in affliction." Sheikh Ahmed Sirhindi, who had influenced the emperor's actions, recorded his satisfaction at "the execution of the accursed *kafir* . . ."

In the words of Professor Harbans Singh, "The event marked the fulfilment of Guru Nanak's religious and ethical injunctions. Personal piety must have a core of moral strength. A virtuous soul must be a courageous soul. Willingness to suffer trial for one's convictions was a religious imperative."

The event also turned a peaceful movement of reconciliation and reform into the most militant ever witnessed in India. Because of this senseless murder the towering rage of the Sikhs carried them into bitter battles with Mughal and other Islamic forces for over 150 years. It also left an indelible impression on Sikh minds, bringing them face to face with the concept of martyrdom, and imbuing them with a resolve to take an implacable stand against tyranny. A new orientation was now added to the Sikh sense of mission and purpose.

The parting message Guru Arjan Dev wanted delivered to his son Hargobind was: "Not to mourn or indulge in unmanly lamentations, but to sing God's praises." He also advised him to "sit fully armed on his throne and maintain an army to the best of his ability." Born on 19 June 1595, Hargobind was only eleven when he succeeded his father in September 1606. The task before him—of canalizing the burning rage of the Sikhs into a formidable military community—was daunting. But he rose to it. He sent far and wide for the finest horses and weapons, and started intensive training camps for swordsmanship, archery and physical endurance. These were now seen as an integral part of Sikh ideals, since skills and valour in combat were necessary if the religion was to be saved from those wanting to destroy it.

Out of this awareness emerged Hargobind's concept of *meeri* and *peeri*, meaning equal time for temporal (*meeri*) and spiritual (*peeri*) matters. After the crime against their beloved Guru, this distinction—and equation—was to become a cornerstone of Sikh faith. But even as the importance of worldly concerns was brought home to the community, the search for spiritual grace continued to be paramount. Whilst the expanding Sikh communities' spiritual needs were served with unflagging dedication, the looming conflict with the Mughals—more temporal than spiritual—was also faced with exemplary determination. While the Harmandir reigned supreme in all matters, purely material concerns were dealt with by the Akal Takht, seat of temporal authority. Representatives of the Sikhs, assembled before the Akal Takht, which literally means "the Almighty's throne," took all major decisions. This emphasis on consensual decision-making was a rare assertion of democratic rights in feudal times.

In order of importance, the Akal Takht ranks, in fact, a fraction below the Harmandir. Located across a wide open space opposite the causeway to the Harmandir, it was only an earthen embankment in Guru Hargobind's time, with a raised platform of bricks for him to sit on and receive those who came with their aspirations, hopes, fears and feuds. It also became an open-air forum for discussions and decisions taken by the community in its epic struggles. In time the square onto which the Akal Takht looked was paved with inlaid marble and the Takht itself raised to five storeys with a gold-leafed dome on top. But in 1609 this was a distant dream.

Jahangir was increasingly disturbed by Guru Hargobind's raising and equipping of a body of troops. Since this was a radical change of course for what till then had been a purely religious movement, he sent a force to arrest and detain the Guru at Gwalior fort. He was released after a few months, but not before he succeeded in freeing some of the many Hindu feudal chiefs detained there: "The Guru's imprisonment does not seem to have dampened his military ardour in any way, and there is evidence to show that he continued the same old policy which he had adopted at the beginning of his pontificate." According to the Mughal chronicler of that period, Mohsin Fani, "the Guru had 800 horses in his stables, 300 troops on horseback and 60 men with firearms were always in his service." Jahangir's son Shah Jahan proved even more implacable than his father. Within a year of his ascending the throne in 1627, contingents of the imperial army clashed with the Sikhs—the first of many, increasingly bloody encounters.

The first showdown took place in 1628 over the ownership of a hawk. Shah Jahan and the Guru had been hunting in the vicinity of each other near Amritsar, and a dispute between their followers—each of whom claimed the rare white hawk—led to the encounter. An annoyed emperor dispatched a detachment of troops under Mukhlis Khan to arrest the Guru. In the clash of arms which lasted two days the imperialist force was beaten and Mukhlis Khan killed in action. The die was cast. "Though successful in his first struggle, [Hargobind] had the sagacity to perceive that the anger of the king would only be appeased by his own overthrow and death." Being aware of the consequences of this challenge to Mughal authority, Hargobind decided to leave Amritsar rather than endanger the sacred Harmandir in the next round of hostilities. He would never see Amritsar again.

In the next two clashes between Mughals and Sikhs, at Lahira in 1631 and Kartarpur in 1634, the Mughals were defeated and their commander Painde Khan killed at Kartarpur. The historical importance of these battles did not lie in their scale, but in the fact that the aggressor's writ was rejected and his power scorned. A mood of defiance was generated against the Mughals and an example set for others.

Hargobind's life away from Amritsar was nomadic, marked by military actions between small bodies of Sikh troops on the one hand and the Mughal army on the other. But he also undertook extensive tours to communicate Sikh beliefs in different centres of pilgrimage and learning in the country. As he moved from place to place attending to the affairs of his religious ministry and inspiring an increasing number of new entrants to join the faith, the fighting qualities of his men were also honed. He instilled a valorous spirit into those who fought by his side and helped establish a tradition which changed the ideology of the Sikhs and Sikhism forever. Towards the end of his life Guru Hargobind lived in the distant foothills of the Himalayas in eastern Punjab. Here he built the settlement of Kiratpur, which in later times became famous as Anandpur Sahib, home of another major Sikh shrine. His death on 3 March 1644 marked the end of a life during which, aside from ceaselessly contributing to the spiritual goals set by his forebears, he also highlighted the ongoing importance of striking back at those who dared raise their hand against Sikh beliefs. He transformed the passive Indian mood of servility into one of confident defiance of autocratic rulers, and a fierce pride in Sikh prowess.

The *gurdwara*, the Sikh house of piety and prayer, is yet another abiding legacy of Guru Hargobind. It was for the Sikhs what the *mandirs*, *masjids*, churches and synagogues were to followers of other faiths. The Sikhs' places of congregation before Hargobind's time were known by many names, *dharamsala*, *dharam-mandir* and such, which meant places where those with shared beliefs, or similar spiritual and social concerns, would meet. But after the Guru Granth Sahib's consecration in the Harmandir, the gurdwara took form as the Sikh place of worship. It literally means "the door to the Guru," or "the Guru's house," or "the abode of the divine being." It was Guru Hargobind who made it not only inseparable from Sikh religion, but the enduring symbol of Sikh faith.

The gurdwara has provided the Sikhs, from the seventeenth century onwards, with the most intense and elevating moments of their lives. A large high-ceilinged hall with lime-washed white walls—bare, since idols and depictions are antithetical to Sikhism—the gurdwara is the magnetic core of the Sikh faith. On a wide raised platform at one end of it is a pedestal draped with many pieces of fine silk on which rests the Guru Granth, the large volume which contains the sacred writings of the Sikhs. Seated cross-legged on the ground before it, a priest reverently reads passages from the Granth Sahib. Singers also sing excerpts from it so those who visit the gurdwara are elevated by the totality of their experience in its sacred environs.

The congregation sits on the floor at a level lower than the pedestal on which the Guru Granth rests—on carpets covered with freshly laundered white cotton sheets to add to the mood of serenity. The atmosphere in the gurdwara is further enhanced by the respectful silence which attends all readings from the scriptures. At the end of the day the Guru Granth is closed with deep reverence and wrapped in rich layers of silk and muslin before being opened again with ceremony and enthusiasm early the next morning.

Guru Har Rai succeeded his grandfather as the seventh Guru. Born at Kiratpur on 16 January 1630, he was a saintly man immersed in the scriptures who, whilst he did not compose any hymns himself (there are none by him in the Guru Granth), travelled extensively to spread the word of Nanak and bring people into the Sikh fold. His emissaries travelled across eastern India to Rajasthan, to Kashmir and Kabul, as well as to all corners of Punjab. His kindly interest in a poor young lad, Phul, led the boy eventually to found the families that later ruled the princely states of Patiala, Nabha and Jind. Although there were no major military engagements between Sikh and Mughal troops in his time, Har Rai did incur the displeasure of Aurangzeb, son of the reigning Mughal emperor, Shah Jahan, because he had received his elder brother, Dara Shikoh, heir apparent to the throne that Aurangzeb coveted. When in 1659 this ruthless and bigoted man ascended the Mughal throne, he instructed Amber's Raja Jai Singh to bring Guru Har Rai to Delhi, his ire having been fanned by courtiers resentful of the Sikh faith in the same way as his grandfather Jahangir had been led to persecute Guru Arjan Dev.

Har Rai refused to go. As he put it: "I am not a king who payeth thee tribute, nor do I desire to receive anything from thee, nor do we stand in the relation of priest and disciple to each other, so wherefore hast thou summoned me?" He sent his son Ram Rai instead, enjoining him "to fix his thoughts on God, and everything would prove successful. He also impressed on him the propriety of not countenancing any objections the Emperor might make to the Granth Sahib . . ." But Ram Rai faltered in the Mughal's presence and whilst reciting a passage from the Granth Sahib deliberately misread it, possibly because it could be construed as derogatory to Islam. When this was reported to Guru Har Rai he refused to receive his son ever again for daring to alter Guru Nanak's hymns. He then anointed his youngest son Har Krishan as the eighth Guru before his death at Kiratpur on 6 October 1661. Some tried to exploit Ram Rai's resentment, but their efforts proved of little consequence.

Born at Kiratpur on 7 July 1656, Har Krishan was five when his father died. Sadly he himself died of smallpox three years later, on 30 March 1664. The comparative calm of the last few years was now nearing its end. A cataclysmic turbulence in Sikh-Mughal relations was already building up, and it would burst forth with full fury eleven years later, driving the avenging Sikhs to change forever the political configuration of India.

Tegh Bahadur, the youngest of Guru Hargobind's five sons, was born on 1 April 1621 in Amritsar. Legend has it that just before Guru Har Krishan's death he had uttered the words *"Baba Bakale,"* "the venerable man of the village of Bakala." What it meant, his followers felt, was that they should look for the next Guru in the village of Bakala. It was soon evident when they arrived there that the person Guru Har Krishan had in mind was Tegh Bahadur, because after Hargobind's death his wife Mata Nanaki had taken their son to Bakala where her parents lived. Whilst still in his teens and despite the mystic in him, Tegh

Bahadur had earned his spurs in the battle of Kartarpur, greatly impressing his father with his superb horsemanship and bold conduct in battle. Guru Hargobind had predicted that his son, and his son after him, would do the Sikhs proud. For his part Tegh Bahadur, although he had to stay away from his beloved father for many years, was deeply aware of his spiritual and martial heritage. So when the Guru's mantle was placed on him, he was ready for what would prove to be a momentous period in Sikh history.

Like his predecessors, Tegh Bahadur travelled the length and breadth of India to visit Sikhs settled in remote places. On one of his journeys, after stopping at Delhi, Mathura, Agra, Allahabad, Benares, Sasaram, birthplace of Sher Shah Suri who had defeated the Mughal emperor Humayun at Panipat, and Gaya, he reached Patna which would become one of the five great centres of Sikhism with a gurdwara called the Takht Sri Harmandir Sahib, built on the site of the house in which his only son Gobind—the tenth and last Guru—was born on 22 December 1666.

Leaving his family in Patna, Guru Tegh Bahadur travelled on to Bengal and Assam. Struck by the number of Sikhs in Dacca, capital of present-day Bangladesh, he called it "the citadel of Sikhism," and it was here that news of Gobind's birth in Patna—where his wife had stayed on—reached him. Towards the end of 1668, whilst in Dhubri in Assam—which Guru Nanak too had visited 163 years earlier—he started work on the historic gurdwara Damdama Sahib.

His journeys through the easternmost parts of India had many purposes. Aside from visiting Sikh *manjis* and *sangats* established across India, he was satisfying his deep philosophical interest in other faiths. To better inform himself of their beliefs he had extensive exchanges with the Mughal emperor Aurangzeb in Delhi, with Brahmin priests in Prayag (Allahabad), Buddhist pilgrims in Gaya (even though the Brahmins had long since taken it over), Sufis in Malda, and with Assam's Ahom tribesmen regarding their tantric practices.

Guru Tegh Bahadur was reunited with his family at Chakk Nanaki on his return to Punjab in early 1672. Chakk Nanaki, famous today as the redoubtable settlement of Anandpur, had interesting beginnings. Lying in the foothills of Bilaspur State, the land was offered to Guru

Tegh Bahadur by its owner, Dowager Rani Champa, in 1665 and he had bought the site—which included the villages of Lodhipur, Mianpur and Sahota—for 500 rupees. On the high promontory of Makhowal, in the middle of this rugged and muscular landscape, ground for the new village was broken on 19 June 1665, and over the following years it grew into a formidable stronghold.

By 1672 the countdown to a tragedy had begun. It was a time of religious intolerance aggravated by the bigotry of Aurangzeb. He found the "infidels" insufferable and made this clear to his provincial governors. According to the chronicler Mustaq Khan (*Maasir-i-Alamgir,* 8 April 1669): "His Majesty, eager to establish Islam, issued orders to the governors of all the provinces to demolish the schools and temples of the infidels and with utmost urgency put down the teachings and public practice of the religion of these misbelievers." His injunction did not end with the destruction of institutions, it was also used to exterminate those who refused to embrace Islam. The Mughal governor of Kashmir, Iftikhar Khan, more rabid than most, carried out his emperor's policy with particular viciousness.

How Guru Tegh Bahadur took up cudgels on behalf of the pandits of Kashmir is best explained by a contemporary Kashmiri historian, P.N.K. Bamzai, in his *History of Kashmir:* "Iftikhar Khan . . . was using force to convert the Pandits in Kashmir to Islam. Some pious men among the Pandits then met and decided to go to Amarnath and invoke the mercy of Siva there for deliverance from the tyrannies of the bigot. At the Amarnath cave, one of the Pandits saw Lord Siva in a dream who told him to go to Tegh Bahadur, the ninth Sikh Guru, in the Punjab, and ask for his help to save the Hindu religion. He spoke to his companions about the revelation [and] about 500 [then] proceeded to Anandpur where Tegh Bahadur lived."

The Guru listened long to the pandits' moving account of the forcible conversions and of the atrocities Aurangzeb's sadistic satrap was inflicting on the Hindus. After deep deliberation, Tegh Bahadur declared that if the emperor could make him convert to Islam, the pandits too would accept conversion. By throwing down the gauntlet he had decided to demonstrate that a man convinced of the moral purpose of his religious beliefs had the strength to stand up to a despot determined to subjugate people to his will; that the inalienable right of a people to practise their own faith could not be denied to them by bigoted rulers.

Aurangzeb, already enraged by reports of Guru Tegh Bahadur's sympathetic response to the Kashmiris, ordered him to be brought to Delhi. According to his instructions to the governor of Lahore, he was to be "fettered and detained . . ."

Tegh Bahadur, who had left for Delhi on his own volition, was arrested en route on 12 July 1675 in the village of Malikpur Rangharan near Ropar and taken to Sirhind, then sent to Delhi in an iron cage. He arrived in the capital on 5 November 1675. For the next five days the daily routine of his captors alternated between persuasion to bring him around to Islam and torture on his refusal to do so. His message to Aurangzeb was simple: "The Prophet of Mecca who founded your Religion could not impose one religion on the world, so how can you? It is not God's will." On 11 November 1675 the Guru's three close companions, Bhai Mati Das, Dayal Das and Sati Das, were killed in his presence: the first was sawn into two, the second boiled to death in a cauldron, the third burnt alive. When even this was of no avail, Guru Tegh Bahadur was publicly beheaded on the same day on the spot where the Sikhs—after they captured Delhi years later—built Gurdwara Sis Ganj in Delhi's Chandni Chowk. Reflecting his own preparation for the ultimate test of his beliefs, these lines composed by him are included in the Guru Granth:

> *The truly enlightened ones*
> *Are those who neither incite fear in others*
> *Nor fear anyone themselves.*

GURU GRANTH SAHIB
SLOK, 16, P. 1427

Guru Tegh Bahadur's head was recovered by his follower Bhai Jaita during a raging storm on the night of his execution, and after a perilous journey brought to Anandpur where his nine-year-old son Gobind received it. It was cremated on 16 November 1675 by the Sikhs, outraged by this murderous act of the Mughal but immensely inspired by their Guru's resolute character. As the sandalwood pyre was lit by Gobind, the chanting of verses from the Granth Sahib filled the air.

In faraway Delhi too, a man called Lakhi Shah Lubana and his companions had taken his body out of the walled city in the dead of night—during the same storm—to a place called Rakabganj, on the city's outskirts. Since a formal cremation was fraught with danger, Lakhi Shah reverently placed the Guru's body in his house, then set the house on fire to avoid detection: a fitting farewell by his devotees to a man who had stirred their imagination by his unique sacrifice.

The full measure of his father's unrivalled act was not lost on his young son Gobind. As he later acknowledged in his autobiography in verse, "a deed like Tegh Bahadur's none had dared before." He was equally clear about why his father had taken the risk:

> *To protect their* tilak *and* janeu
> *He performed a heroic deed in the age of Kali.*
> *He gave his head for men of faith without flinching*
> *And chose martyrdom in the cause of righteousness.*

> BACHITTAR NATAK

Gobind's early grasp of the concept of martyrdom in defence of man's essential freedoms—the right to life, to religious beliefs, and to ideals and principles—served him well through the dangerous years ahead. He was clear that the mark on the forehead, the *tilak*, and the sacred thread, the *janeu*, which represented upper-caste Hindu customs, had no place in the Sikh faith, but had nevertheless to be respected since countless Hindus venerated them. No less clear was the uniqueness of his father's deed—a bold defiance of the imperium which demanded that its subjects compromise their beliefs by giving in to its arrogant diktats. In voluntarily setting out for Delhi—while most had to be dragged to their persecutors—Tegh Bahadur had challenged the arrogant assumptions of imperial power, accustomed to having its own way with a shackled people. None of this was lost on Gobind.

The experience of his father's martyrdom shaped his outlook and actions during the next thirty-three years—between the age of nine, when his father died, and his own death at the age of forty-two. According to J.D. Cunningham, a political official in the East India Company and author of a classic history of the Sikhs: "he resolved upon awakening his followers to a new life and upon giving precision and aim to the broad and general institutions of Nanak. In the heart of a powerful empire he set himself to the task of subverting it, and from the midst of social degradation and religious corruption he called up simplicity of manners, singleness of purpose, and enthusiasm of desire."

Gobind Singh, it seems clear, was convinced, even at the young age when he had held his father's severed head in his hands, that the flames lit by Guru Hargobind had to be stoked still further, that the enemy must be made to take notice. Fully convinced that the tyrant's injustice and cruelty had to be met by armed warriors with an iron will, he set about building up his troops and concentrating on their intensive military training.

He would see to it that whilst there was no deviation from religious or moral goals, the Sikhs would not allow their self-esteem to be compromised. Their foes, who inflicted pain on innocents, would be made to pay for their inhumanity, thereby adding a new dimension to Guru Nanak's dictum "truth is pure steel." Steel would now seal the fate of those who mocked the rights of others. His own acceptance of the sword, in effect of steel, as a symbol of the divine being and his will, was neither accidental nor whimsical, as is evident from the *Bachittar Natak:*

> *You are the subduer of kingdoms,*
> *The destroyer of evil armies.*
> *You adorn the brave on the battlefield.*
> *Your arm is unbreakable, your brightness dazzling,*
> *Your radiance is like the sun's.*
> *You bestow happiness on the good,*
> *You terrify the evil, you scatter sinners.*
> *I seek your protection.*
> *Hail! hail to the world's creator,*
> *I cherish you, the saviour of creation,*
> *Hail to you, O Sword!*

In his study *The Mantle of the East*, Edmund Candler writes perceptively of the sword's profound significance for the Sikhs: "When Guru Gobind Singh inaugurated the sacrament of steel he proved himself a wise and far-sighted leader. For of all material things which genius has inspired with spiritual significance, steel is the truest and most uncompromising . . . [it] welded the [Sikhs] into a nation; and in the dark days of Muhammadan rule in the middle of the eighteenth century, when the Sikh was slain at sight and no quarter was given, it drove them on to those gallant crusades in which they rode to Amritsar in the dead of night, leapt into the sacred tank and out again, and galloped back through the enemy's lines purified. Hundreds were slain, but no one abjured his faith or perjured his soul to preserve 'his muddy vesture of decay.'"

Gobind Singh has been described as a "sharp-featured, tall and wiry man," superbly dressed, wearing a tall plume-topped turban, always armed with a variety of weapons and, when seated on the throne or out hunting, with a white hawk perched on his left hand. Emphasis on military preparedness was only a part of his agenda. At the same time, with intense concentration, he learnt Sanskrit, Braj, Persian, Arabic and Avadhi, and studied the classics in these languages, which helped nurture his own poetic genius and broadened the range of his enquiring mind. Years later, these scholarly foundations would result in literary work which included a book of psalms, a narrative of his times, an autobiography, inclusion of his father's hymns into the Granth Sahib, and poetic compositions of penetrating insight into the gamut of human existence. The diversity of his interests ranged from astronomy, geography, metaphysics, yoga and botany to Ayurvedic healing and warfare.

Alongside these concerns was his ongoing commitment to Sikhism's secular principles, laid down by Guru Nanak and reiterated by his successors, most dramatically by Guru Tegh Bahadur. As Gobind Singh observes in his poetic composition *Akal Ustat*:

> *Recognize all mankind as one,*
> *whether Hindus or Muslims,*
> *The same Lord is the creator*
> *and nourisher of all:*

Recognize no distinctions between them.
The monastery and the mosque are the same,
So is Hindu worship and Muslim prayer.
Men are all one!

The years from 1675–76—from the death of Guru Tegh Bahadur and his own succession as the tenth Guru—to 1685 were a time of preparation for what lay ahead. He knew that following Guru Tegh Bahadur's martyrdom, the Sikhs had to be inspired by his own exemplary conduct and confidence. And it was not long before his qualities of leadership were put to the test.

The first trouble came from the neighbouring hill states. It was precipitated by Raja Bhim Chand of Bilaspur (also known as Kahlur), who was irked by the increasing number of the Guru's followers. Resentful of an earlier rebuff when the Guru had refused to give him his elephant and personal canopy, the raja attacked him at Anandpur. His defeat fuelled the resentments of other hill rajas in the neighbouring Kangra Hills who now formed a united front against the Sikhs. To them, as well as to the imperial court, the emergence of a new centre of Sikh power in the remote fastnesses of Anandpur was a disquieting development. And since Sikhism embraced all castes, irrespective of their place in the Hindu hierarchy, the resentments of the upper castes were an added factor to reckon with, alongside the hostility of the chieftains who viewed democratic Sikh doctrines as a threat to their own feudal privileges. The belligerence of these feudatory interests was the immediate concern of the Sikh community at Anandpur, although Mughal anger—frequently fanned by these rajas—would in time pose far greater challenges.

In 1685 Guru Gobind Singh decided to accept a friendly invitation from Raja Medini Prakash of Sirmur State who, disagreeing with the aggressive temper of his contemporaries, was keen to cultivate the Guru. His overture was not entirely disinterested, for he had seen the Sikhs defeat Raja Bhim Chand, and with the hostility of his rival, Raja Fateh Shah of Srinagar, very much on his mind, he saw Guru Gobind Singh as a future ally whose presence in Sirmur could deter Fateh Shah's forays into Sirmur territory. Whatever the reasons for Medini

Prakash's hospitality, the three years or so that Guru Gobind Singh spent there proved highly rewarding both from the scholar's point of view and from the soldier's.

Reluctant to stay for too long as the raja's guest in his palace at Nahan the Guru chose—at his host's invitation—a site on a bend of the River Yamuna which he named Paonta, derived from *pav*, or foot, since his favourite horse had left an imprint on the banks of the river. The setting at Paonta, where an imposing gurdwara now stands, was inspiring with its clear fast-flowing river, the hilly terrain against the backdrop of mountain ranges, and thick forests full of game. Here the Guru's eldest son Ajit Singh was born to his wife Mata Sundari.

This sylvan existence ended with yet another battle, this time with the combined forces of some of the hill rajas assembled by Bhim Chand and Fateh Shah. The two sides clashed at Bhangani, six miles from Paonta. The bitter and bloody battle had its highs and lows, which saw 500 Pathan mercenaries who had joined the Sikhs cross over to the enemy with another segment of the Sikh force, the Udasis, although their leader Kirpal Das valorously made up for his men's defection, as did Pir Budhu Shah, a follower of Guru Gobind Singh who joined him with his four sons and several hundred men. At battle's end the victorious Sikhs and their comrades had accounted for two Pathan leaders and the hill chieftain Hari Chand. The enemy's casualties in the Battle of Bhangani decisively demonstrated that the Sikhs could not be trifled with.

Returning to Anandpur soon after this, Gobind Singh set about fortifying Anandpur in anticipation of attacks from the humiliated hill rajas. The Mughal forces too, he was sure, would not be long in coming. The forts built at Anandgarh, Lohgarh, Keshgarh and Fatehgarh, on craggy promontories around Anandpur, were a part of his defence plan. A wise plan, as it turned out. Emboldened by Aurangzeb's prolonged absence from Delhi on military campaigns in South India, the hill chieftains, who had stopped paying their dues to the imperial court, formed a confederacy to challenge Mughal suzerainty. When in 1690 Mian Khan, the Mughal overlord of the region, sent his commander, Alif Khan, to discipline them, two rajas crossed over to him to help bring down their colleague Raja Bhim Chand. The frightened raja, who had twice fought the Guru, now beseeched him for help. Not

THE SIKHS

only did Guru Gobind Singh agree, he personally led his men against
Alif Khan. In a decisive action at Nadaun on the Beas river, the routed
Khan fled. Within days of this, the devious Bhim Chand once again
accepted Mughal suzerainty!

Aurangzeb was becoming increasingly incensed by Guru Gobind
Singh's ascendance. In an imperial edict of 20 November 1693 he
announced: "All military commanders concerned [in Punjab] are
ordered to prevent him [Guru Gobind Singh] from assembling his followers." The Guru responded by summoning distant Sikh *sangats* to
Anandpur for Baisakhi (New Year's Day in the Punjab) at the end of
March 1694. They were to come bearing arms, with their beards
uncut, so as to leave no doubt in Mughal minds about their identity.
After pitched battles with imperial pickets along the way, the huge
gathering which assembled before the Guru provided proof of the triumphant Sikh spirit; of its refusal to be daunted by the Mughals.

When told of this defiance of the Emperor's *firman*, Dilawar Khan,
the Mughal chief for the Kangra Hills, sent a force to chasten the Guru
in his fastness at Anandpur. But when the attack at dead of night—
designed to catch the Sikhs unawares—was greeted with their war cries
and the booming beat of Guru Gobind Singh's war drum, Ranjit
Nagara, the attacking force under Dilawar's son retreated without
joining battle. His livid father next ordered his commander Husain
Khan to tame the Guru. As the Khan's columns headed for Anandpur
early in 1695, the same duplicitous Bhim Chand of Bilaspur joined the
Mughal force, along with several other hill chiefs, in yet another conspiracy to bring down the Guru. When on his way Husain Khan
attacked Raja Gopal of Guler—who could not pay the tribute demanded of him—the latter sought Gobind Singh's help. The Guru
promptly dispatched a troop of horsemen to his aid. In the ensuing
battle Husain Khan and Raja Kirpal Chand of Katoch were killed and
their forces defeated, but a key Sikh commander, Bhai Sangatia, was
also killed.

Now followed a period of respite, although an imperial force under
Prince Muazzam, Aurangzeb's son and successor, was sent to Punjab to
teach the recalcitrant hill chieftains a lesson, and to deal with Guru
Gobind Singh as well. Whilst Muazzam's commander, Mirza Beg,
took a heavy toll of the rajas, the prince and his commanders felt it

prudent to leave the Sikhs alone in their fortified region of Anandpur. As the Sikhs were openly advocating revolt against Mughal misrule, Muazzam's apparent strategy was to subdue the rajas before taking on the Sikhs. His hesitation, however, could also have been due to a genuine respect for men of religion.

These peaceful years, from 1697 to 1700, were put to good use. Guru Gobind Singh completed the *Bachittar Natak* and oversaw the translations of many classics including the Upanishads. He also tightened control of the organizational structure of Sikh communities scattered around the country by abolishing the institution of *masands*. The appointment of these officials had been conceived during the time of Guru Amar Das in order to administrate and take care of Sikh congregations, but they had become corrupted, prone to pocketing offerings at places of worship and acting in ways contrary to the community's religious principles. They had also tried to create schisms in the fledgling Sikh community which could have weakened it from within. With their abolition each Sikh occupied his rightful place in the scheme of things, needing no intermediaries between him and the founders of his faith.

Gobind Singh's most dramatic step was to set the Sikh community apart once and for all. He baptized the Sikhs into a brotherhood which he called the Khalsa, or "pure ones." This innovation aimed at providing every Sikh with cultural distinctiveness, imbuing him with a strong sense of self-esteem and purpose, committed to opposing tyranny and despotism, and the appearance, too, of every Sikh would be emblematic of the Khalsa.

Attitudes to caste, idols, rituals, orthodoxy, priesthood, fanaticism and bigotry had already set the Sikhs apart from Hindus and Muslims, but the time had now come to develop even more assertive Sikh characteristics and to establish a visible and separate Sikh identity. The creation of the Khalsa reflected Guru Gobind Singh's conviction that Sikhism was a *tisar panth*, a third religion, distinct from Hinduism and Islam.

The decree that the Khalsa's unshorn hair would be a proud symbol of this new fraternity was a move of deep psychological significance. The distinctive appearance of each Sikh, a celebration of his individualism, would instil in him the confidence to stand out in a crowd—unself-consciously and confidently. It would set him apart from what Professor Puran Singh would later call "barber-made civilizations." Each member of the Khalsa would wear five distinctive items, the names of all of which began with a K, which would be the bedrock of Khalsa beliefs. These were *kesh* (long hair), *kanga* (comb), *kara* (steel wristband), *kachh* (short breeches) and *kirpan* (short sword). Each had a definite meaning and purpose. The comb—while keeping the hair tidy—symbolized cleanliness; the short breeches were a reminder of the need for continence and moral restraint. The circular steel band protected the wrist that wielded the sword; it also symbolized the circle in Indian thought—the wheel of *dharma*. The sword was a constant reminder of the Khalsa's readiness to repel aggression. As Bhai Gurdas, a contemporary and chronicler of several Gurus including Arjan and Hargobind, put it: "The orchard of the Sikh faith needed the thorny hedge of armed men for its protection."

As a final stamp of distinction and dedication, Guru Gobind Singh gave each Sikh the surname Singh, or Lion—a fitting tribute to a people who had been fighting for their identity for almost 230 years. And because of the distinctive turban which Sikh men tie around their hair each day, they stand out in a crowd and are easy to identify. The turban, of fine muslin, evolved as a means of managing long hair which is left unshorn as a sign of respect for the God-given form; the turban's colour and its shape when tied are matters of personal preference.

The act of transforming the Sikhs into the Khalsa was a highly dramatic event. It coincided with the Baisakhi festival, a time of celebration in Punjab, heralding a good harvest. In 1699 this date corresponded to 30 March in the Western calendar. (Owing to the divergence between the Christian and Bikrami years, Baisakhi now falls on 13 April.) The gathering of over 80,000 Sikhs at Anandpur that year was especially large.

There was an air of expectancy, because none knew why everyone had been summoned from all over India. Having long meditated on the step he was about to take against the grand backdrop of Fort Keshgarh and the mountains beyond, Guru Gobind Singh, aware of the need to restructure the faith for the exacting times ahead, had very carefully selected Baisakhi for injecting a new vitality into the community. It was the day on which Gautama Buddha too had received Enlightenment, had pledged himself for "the good and benefit of all living things, mortal and immortal."

What startled the Sikhs that day was the sight of their Guru drawing his sword and demanding that one of those assembled should come forward and sacrifice his head in the honoured tradition of laying down his life for his faith, *dharma*. For a while the bewildered audience sat transfixed, too shocked to respond. Then a few left, while others, although fearful of this astounding demand, stayed on. Finally Daya Ram from Lahore came forward to offer his head. The Guru took him into an adjacent tent and when he emerged his sword was dripping with blood. The next man, Dharam Das, was from Hastinapur. When the Guru reappeared with his sword even more bloodied than before, and demanded yet another head, Mohkam Chand from Dwarka was the third to volunteer, followed by the fourth, Himmat of Jagannath, and the fifth, Sahib Chand of Bidar.

In an entirely unexpected dénouement, the Guru emerged from the tent with the five reattired Sikhs—dressed in saffron-coloured robes and turbans—and the audience realized that what had been on trial was its mettle. And in those who had fled on seeing the sword with dripping blood, it had been found wanting. It was a singular lesson in overcoming that most debilitating of all emotions—fear. It was also a significant ceremony for the birth of a new and martial race—the Khalsa.

Guru Gobind Singh's message to the assembled Sikhs was clear. "You are the sons of Nanak, the Creator's own, the chosen ones . . . You will love man as man, making no distinction of caste or creed . . . You will only bow your heads to your Master. You will never worship stock, stone, idol or tomb. Remember always, in times of danger or difficulty, the holy names of the Masters: Nanak, Angad, Amar Das, Ram Das, Arjun Dev, Hargobind Sahib, Har Rai Sahib, Har Krishan, Tegh Bahadur. I make you a rosary of these names and you shall not pray each for himself, but for the entire Khalsa. In each of you the whole brotherhood shall be incarnated. You are my sons, both in flesh and spirit."

The emphasis on *flesh and spirit* was a reiteration of the idea of the *fellowship* of the Khalsa—not a hierarchical order of the high above and the dispossessed below, but a casteless community of inspired people; a family knit together by its ideals and beliefs. Gobind Singh was to prove the strength of his own belief in this ideal time and again, especially in the face of personal tragedy: he was soon to lose his four sons. When news of the younger two was brought to him, he would tell the assembled Khalsa that even though he had lost four sons, thousands of his beloved ones were still alive.

In a practical demonstration of the fellowship idea he first baptized, in the presence of the entire gathering, the first five members of the Khalsa, the *panjpiyare*, or "beloved five," then knelt before them to be baptized in turn—a reaffirmation of the principle of absolute equality. The ceremony of baptism was simple. Into an iron bowl full of clear water he added sugar, then stirred it with a double-edged sword accompanied by recitations from the Granth Sahib. This magical mix of sweetness and steel, which he called *amrit*, or life-giving ambrosia, was administered to the *panjpiyare*, as it has continued to be given to all baptized Sikhs ever since. He then recited in a resonant voice a line he had composed for the occasion and which has been a rallying-cry for the Khalsa since then: *"Sri Wahe Guruji Ka Khalsa, Sri Wahe Guruji Ki Fateh"*—"The Khalsa belong to God, and God's truth will always prevail."

The distinguished Sikh scholar Kapur Singh was convinced that Guru Gobind Singh believed in "an aristocracy dedicated and consciously trained—but not by right of birth—[and] which is grounded in virtue, in talent and in the self-imposed code of sacrifice to humanity, [and that] such men should group themselves into the order of the Khalsa . . ." He further suggests that "Guru Gobind Singh clearly seemed to believe that aristocracy is one of the goals of democracy. For what is more basic to democracy than careers open to talent, a doctrine that so clearly presumes that talent is of supreme value? The Guru believed that democracy can justify itself only by including aristocracy as its goal, and because democracy alone cannot guarantee freest scope to talent was, it would seem, the Guru's reason for having faith in it."

Proof, if any is needed, of the democratic foundations of the faith is provided by the composition of the first five members of the Khalsa, or *panjpiyare*, initiated and baptized with a double-edged sword. Of these five one was a Kshatriya, the second a Jat (tiller), the third a washerman, the fourth a cook and the fifth a Shudra. This reflected an emphasis on equality a century and more before the rest of the world awoke to the idea, and to the need for legislative safeguards to ensure equal opportunities for all.

Although estimates vary, at least 50,000 Sikhs appear to have been baptized during those first few days. The excitement at achieving greater self-definition was palpable. But the exhilaration at Anandpur was in marked contrast to the jealousy of the hill rajas—even more resentful now of Sikh élan. In a petition to the imperial power in Delhi, they wrote: "The Guru [has] established a new sect distinct from the Hindus and Muhammadans, to which he has given the name of Khalsa. He has united the four castes into one, and made many followers . . . he suggested to us that if we rose in rebellion against the Emperor, he would assist us with all his forces . . . we cannot restrain him and have accordingly come to crave the protection of this just government against him. If the government considers us its subjects we pray for its assistance to expel the Guru from Anandpur. Should you delay his punishment, his next expedition will be against the capital of your Empire."

This craven representation reached Aurangzeb in the South, and on his orders two Mughal commanders, Painda Khan and Din Beg, were sent to settle the Sikh problem, and that of their Guru, Gobind Singh. Not surprisingly the hill rajas joined the Mughals. In the ensuing battle Painda Khan was killed in single combat with Guru Gobind Singh, Din Beg was wounded, the hill rajas fled the field of battle, and the end came with the rout of the Mughal expedition. Soon afterwards, the embittered rajas of Mandi, Srinagar, Kulu, Keonthal and Jammu again joined forces to lay siege to Anandpur, but when Sikh reinforcements arrived from the Majha they were defeated and driven off. Between 1701 and 1704 there was no end to the skirmishes and pitched battles between the Sikhs and the hill rajas, until Ajmer Chand, son and successor to the treacherous Bhim Chand of Bilaspur, travelled to the Deccan to urge Emperor Aurangzeb to put down Guru Gobind Singh and his defiant Sikhs once and for all.

Aurangzeb ordered the Mughal satrap of Lahore to march on Anandpur under the overall command of Nawab Wazir Khan of

Sirhind. But the Mughal and Hindu rajas' forces—the largest ever assembled—were still unable to break Sikh resistance after several bloody battles, and so settled down to a prolonged and meticulously planned siege. The besieged were gradually cut off from their food supplies and despite lightning forays for victuals outside their fortifications the situation worsened, especially when a hill stream which provided water to Anandpur was diverted. At this point Aurangzeb sent a message to Gobind Singh assuring him and his entourage safe passage if he agreed to leave Anandpur. It was a difficult decision. The very thought of walking away from a challenge was alien to the Guru's nature; but the cost of staying on and seeing his loyal ones die of starvation was equally unacceptable. In the end, with conditions worsening each day, he opted to leave. And so, at the close of 1704, he evacuated the place he had grown up in and which had helped shape his personality, intellect and character. It was the last time he would see it.

The Mughals and the hill rajas, perfidious to the end, did not honour their word. The Sikh contingent, including women and children and the Guru's mother, two wives and four sons, was attacked soon after reaching the plains on the banks of a small river, the Sarsa. One of Guru Gobind Singh's ablest commanders, Ude Singh, and several of his men died in a heroic rearguard action aimed at enabling others to get away. As the main body of men and women forded the chilly waters of the river swollen by winter rains, many lost their lives while others were separated from the rest on reaching the opposite bank. Amongst the latter were Mata Gujri, the Guru's mother, and his two younger sons, Zorawar Singh and Fateh Singh. Guru Gobind Singh's own group, reduced from 500 to scarcely 40 fighting men including his two elder sons, Ajit Singh and Jujhar Singh, managed to reach the village of Chamkaur several miles away, with a considerably augmented Mughal force in hot pursuit.

The battle of Chamkaur, on 22 December 1704, is seared in every Sikh heart. Here a small band of just over 40 Sikhs took on an enemy vastly superior in numbers. Both Ajit Singh and Jujhar Singh, along with Mohkam Singh and Himmat Singh, two of the original five *panjpiyare*, were killed in hand-to-hand combat. The Sikhs, by then reduced to the Guru and three others, Daya Singh, Dharam Singh and

Man Singh, managed to evade the enemy and head for territory favourable to the regrouping of a resurgent Khalsa.

But this tragic phase was still to reach its nadir. With the break of dawn—after leaving Chamkaur at the dead of night—the Guru found himself separated from his companions and alone in the heart of the Machhiwara forest. He was without food, shelter or his trusted mount, his mind filled with thoughts of Mughal betrayal and the loss of his men and sons; only his iron will sustained him in that bleak hour. As luck would have it his three companions, following the route they had agreed upon, were eventually reunited with him. The four, with the help of loyal Sikhs and at least three friendly Muslims, made their way through the enemy patrols who were searching for them.

They finally reached the village of Jatpura where the Guru was warmly received by the Muslim chief of the area, Rai Kalha. The help of Muslims, who admired Sikhs for their unflinching stand against the tyranny of Islamic rulers, is significant, reflecting the decencies that were observed, even in those troubled times, by people of different faiths. A modern historian of the period comments on Aurangzeb's mindlessly repressive policy of crushing religious minorities: "Many Muslims, who considered Guru Gobind Singh to be fighting for the cause of truth and justice, supported him . . . the Caliph of Mecca had shown disagreement with the religious policy of Aurangzeb. The Khalifa of Baghdad had even refused to see the envoy of Aurangzeb."

While Guru Gobind Singh's two wives, Mata Sundari and Mata Sahib Kaur, had gone to Delhi with a distinguished scholar and contemporary of the Guru, Bhai Mani Singh, the tragic news of his mother and two younger sons, Zorawar Singh and Fateh Singh—separated during the retreat from Anandpur—was brought to him at Jatpura. They had been betrayed by a servant who had offered them shelter and then alerted the agents of the governor of Sirhind, Nawab Wazir Khan, who had them arrested and imprisoned in Sirhind fort. He offered the brothers inducements to convert to Islam, but to his astonishment the two—aged eight and six—refused. He then ordered them to be bricked up alive. When only their heads and shoulders remained above the masonry they were again asked to convert, but they refused. Extricated from the tomb-like structure they were produced before Wazir Khan, who, enraged by their unrelenting stand, ordered them put to the sword. On hearing the news, their grand-mother died of shock.

Chroniclers of the period are agreed on the astonishing fearlessness of the two boys on that fateful morning of 27 December 1704. They also agree on the principled—though unsuccessful—intervention by the nawab of Malerkotla, Sher Muhammad Khan, who had tried to prevent the debased act. In Punjab the Sikhs, remembering the Malerkotla chief's noble stand, have honoured his role to this day and ensured his descendants' protection.

Guru Gobind Singh's next significant stay after leaving Jatpura was in Dina, in what would later become Nabha State. Here he wrote the first of his two forceful letters to Aurangzeb around 26 December 1704. Some refer to this as the *Fatehnamah*, while the second is widely known as the *Zafarnamah*. In the first he told the emperor: "Your name does not become you, Aurangzeb, since your ways are deceitful." (Broadly translated, Aurangzeb means "pride of the throne.") And fur-ther: "You are accustomed to conduct your statecraft through decep-tion and diplomacy. I do not approve of what does not accord with ethical principles and the dictates of conscience."

Written in Persian, the *Zafarnamah* was a public indictment of Aurangzeb for his breach of faith in allowing his troops to attack the Sikhs after they had vacated Anandpur on a guarantee of safe conduct. The letter stressed the centrality of truth in statecraft, and under-scored the importance of rulers abiding by the same moral principles they expected of the ruled. Guru Gobind Singh's communication to the emperor was a reaffirmation of his own commitment to the demo-cratic ideal of openness and accountability. No less unique for those times was his ethical conviction that integrity of purpose and open-ness—or "transparency"—were essential in the conduct of relations between the ruler and the ruled. And between states. "He alone is a cultured man, he alone is worthy of being called a human being, whose 'yes' is a 'yes' and whose 'no' means 'no.' He who says one thing and means and intends another is subhuman."

Gobind Singh bluntly accused the emperor and his military com-manders and provincial governors of lying when they had offered the Sikhs safe conduct out of Anandpur. He warned the emperor: "Do not wantonly spill the blood of any one, for your own blood as surely will be spilt by death." Nor did he mince any words in telling him: "I have no faith in your oath . . . you know no God and you do not believe in Muhammad. He who has regard for his religion never swerves from his promise . . . If the Prophet himself was present here, I would inform him of your treachery."

A contributor to *The Sikh Review* has recently described this epic missive: "The whole of the *Zafarnamah* is full of classical Persian allusions and shows a perfect mastery of the history and literature of the Muslims and pre-Muslim Persians, whose language the Mughals had adopted for their courts. The mention of names like Kaikhusrow, Jamshid, Faridun, Bahman, Isfandyar and Iskander gives us an idea of how these non-Muslim predecessors of the Persians glorified themselves in theatres of war and upheld the cause of their country against aggressors. The mention of the name of Sher Shah Suri is more of a political nature as it was he who ousted Aurangzeb's ancestor, Humayun, from India and obliged him to take refuge in Persia where the state religion was Shiaism, of which Aurangzeb was an arch-enemy. The mention of Sher Shah's name was to make Aurangzeb realize the truth of history . . . the epistle, as a whole, is a remarkable enunciation of ethics. It is equally remarkable for its poetry and diction."

Aurangzeb, still in the South, was impressed. After receiving the letter brought to him in Ahmednagar by the Guru's emissaries, the emperor despatched two officers to Munim Khan, deputy governor of Lahore, instructing him to make peace with Guru Gobind Singh.

Dina became both the rallying point for Sikhs around their Guru and the setting for still more conversions to the faith. The rage of his followers at the recent tragedies endured by Gobind Singh could be easily perceived, even though his acceptance of the loss of his sons and loyal followers was calm and courageous.

The reassembling of the Khalsa and their resurgent mood were not lost on Sirhind's Wazir Khan, who had emerged as their most implacable foe. In anticipation of his attack, and unwilling to subject Dina to retribution for harbouring him, Guru Gobind Singh moved on to Khidrana (now called Muktsar). Here a pitched battle with the Mughals led to appalling bloodshed on both sides, Wazir Khan's force being beaten back. On the move again, the Guru and his men reached a forested terrain between Bhatinda and Kot Kapura, where, during a brief respite in the jungle of Lakhi, a sharp revitalization of the faith took place as new entrants joined it. The Sikh community was in the ascendant again.

Gobind Singh now chose to stay at nearby Talwandi Sabo, south of the Sutlej, later renamed Damdama Sahib, which means "place of calm and tranquillity." It is a milestone in Sikh history for many reasons. Not only because over a hundred thousand people in this rugged region of Malwa converted to Sikhism during the Guru's nine months' stay here, but also because the final version of the Granth Sahib was transcribed at Damdama, by Bhai Mani Singh, a childhood friend and confidant of Guru Gobind Singh. To the first copy of the Adi Granth written under Guru Arjan Dev's direction in 1603–4, the tenth Guru now added Guru Tegh Bahadur's compositions. This volume is acknowledged as the authorized version of the Granth Sahib.

Many scholars, poets and minstrels, some of whom had been with him at Anandpur, made their way to Damdama, and the Guru likened its appeal to Benares (or Kashi), the Hindu centre of learning. Damdama is often referred to as Guru-ki-Kashi. At this time the art of calligraphy there was at its creative best, and before printing techniques took over, copies of the Granth Sahib prepared in this town were much sought after.

But the Guru's stay at Damdama was coming to an end. Surprisingly, Aurangzeb, instead of being infuriated by the *Zafarnamah*, had been moved by the Guru's vigorous and incisive criticism, and by his forthright enunciation of a new ethic during a time of moral confusion. Intrigued by his courage, since most men he dealt with were craven, he invited him to the Deccan for a meeting. And even though many of his followers opposed the idea, Guru Gobind Singh agreed to go. He wanted to get the measure of the man, who was now ninety-one years of age, to see if he could persuade him to adopt a more humane approach to the social and religious turmoil he had helped create. Leaving the tranquillity of Damdama, he set out for the South in October 1706, and was in Rajputana in February 1707 when news of the emperor's death in Ahmednagar reached him.

In keeping with the unpredictable turn of events in those times,

Aurangzeb's son Prince Muazzam now sought Gobind Singh's help in his struggle against his brothers for his father's throne. Unlike his father, Muazzam was considered a liberal. Several years earlier, when Aurangzeb had sent a force under him to discipline Guru Gobind Singh and the hill rajas, he had left the Guru alone. This was not forgotten. And because of it the Guru sent a detachment of Sikhs under Dharam Singh to help Muazzam's forces against Azam, the principal claimant to the throne. In the battle of Jajau near Agra in June 1707, Azam was killed, his force routed, and Muazzam ascended the throne as Emperor Bahadur Shah.

Guru Gobind Singh and Bahadur Shah first met at Agra in July 1707. It was a cordial meeting, with the emperor extending every courtesy to his visitor, presenting him with a robe of honour and other gifts. That the Guru too was pleased with their exchange of views is obvious from a recently discovered letter written to the *sangat* at Dhaul, in which he expresses satisfaction at his talks with Bahadur Shah and his hopes of an early return to Punjab. "When we arrive at Kahlur, the entire Khalsa should come to our presence fully armed." Clearly, he was taking no chances with the deceitful Wazir Khan, though fate willed otherwise, because at this point Bahadur Shah's other brother, Kambakhsh, revolted in the Deccan and the emperor decided to deal with him personally.

Guru Gobind Singh agreed to accompany Bahadur Shah. He wanted an enduring settlement of Punjab's troubled situation and saw opportunities for fruitful discussions during the long journey ahead. Indeed, their many conversations did seem to be bringing them closer. But by the time the Mughal and Sikh contingents reached the southern town of Nander in September 1708, it was obvious that the emperor was avoiding issues that most concerned the Sikhs: Wazir Khan's violently hostile attitude, the sovereign right of the Sikhs to practise their faith and way of life in peace, and an end to the tyrannical ways of Mughal functionaries. The emperor preferred posturing to taking a principled stand on these issues. Seeing the futility of any further discussion with him, the Guru parted company with Bahadur Shah at Nander, where he once again attracted many converts. Because of this Nander would become a major centre of Sikhism in the South.

One of those the Guru converted in Nander was a man then named Madho Dass Bairagi, a *sadhu* of some standing, with a following of his own. His men and some of the Khalsa had clashed, and Madho Dass's followers had been trounced. His conversion was a momentous event for Sikhism. Banda Singh would serve the faith with exemplary dedication and valour, and in the process shake the Mughal Empire to its foundations.

Tragedy was now about to strike the peaceful camp at Nander. One evening, as Guru Gobind Singh rested on his bed after evening prayers, he was attacked by two Pathan assassins sent by Wazir Khan who, fearful of his fate if the emperor accepted Guru Gobind Singh's charges against him, had despatched the two to murder him. Ingratiating themselves into the congregations around the Guru, they had observed his movements for several days until that fateful evening. Though stabbed near the heart, Guru Gobind Singh ran the first assassin through with his sword, while the second was decapitated by his followers. Although the wound healed well, and the Guru recovered from the attempt, he overexerted himself a few days later, the wound reopened, and he died of excessive bleeding soon afterwards.

But before the end, well aware of the chaos that could follow his death and determined to ensure continuity of the faith he had nurtured with such single-minded devotion, he drew on his formidable reserves of inner strength and assembled his followers, directing them to revere the Granth Sahib as their Guru thereafter. The collective wisdom of the saints and savants, and the philosophic vigour of their work, were to be their guide from then on. Whenever decisions of consequence had to be taken, the *panjpiyare* would take them. "Wherever there are five Sikhs assembled who abide by the Guru's teachings," he said to his followers, "know that I am in the midst of them . . . Read the history of your Gurus from the time of Guru Nanak. Henceforth the Guru shall be the Khalsa and the Khalsa the Guru. I have infused my mental and bodily spirit into the Granth Sahib and the Khalsa."

This far-sighted move reflected a keen awareness of the human psyche's susceptibility to resentments, envy and conflicting pressures, and the extent to which these could endanger the cohesiveness and vitality of the movement—unless it was held together by an unbreakable bond. And what could be better for the purpose than the sacred scriptures of the Sikhs containing the divine insights of their Gurus? Who could question the logic and authority of men who had had such an impact on their times, who had founded a new faith on the bedrock of their certainties and their suffering? Whilst decisions on day-to-day matters would be taken by elected representatives, the overall framework of personal and ethical conduct would be provided by the Granth Sahib—or Guru Granth Sahib as it would henceforth be known. Guru Gobind Singh's injunction to all Sikhs has been recited each day ever since after every prayer:

> *I have established the Khalsa*
> > *by God's command*
> *To all Sikhs,*
> > *this then is the commandment:*
> *Accept the Granth as the Guru.*
> *Acknowledge the Guru Granthji*
> > *as the visible form of the Gurus.*
> *Those with disciplined minds*
> > *will find what they seek in it.*

The degree to which the Granth Sahib has since held the faith together is proof of the far-sightedness of the tenth Guru.

It is doubtful if the Sikhs could have survived their trials and tribulations without the spirit of the Khalsa to sustain and power their drive. On 17 October 1708, at the comparatively young age of 42, Guru Gobind Singh died confident that the Khalsa to whom he had given so much, and invested such high hopes, would not let him down. In his words:

> *The Khalsa is a reflection of my form,*
> *The Khalsa is my body and soul,*
> *The Khalsa is my very life.*
> . . . .
> *For the many battles won, I am indebted to the Khalsa.*
> *Sikhs owe their spirit of compassion to the Khalsa.*
> *The inspiration for my learning came from the Khalsa.*

Our enemies were vanquished by the steadfastness of the Khalsa.
Unlike countless others, we are adorned by the Khalsa.

DASAM GRANTH

The life of this exceptional man is a saga of perseverance and perfect poise. Through ceaseless personal tragedies such as few leaders face in their lifetimes, his sense of mission never faltered. The brutal murders of his father and great-grandfather, the killing of his four sons and of countless comrades-in-arms, did not deflect him from opposing rulers who subjected people to moral and physical degradation. While others were petrified of the paramount power, he publicly accused it of perverse conduct. He also handsomely acknowledged that he owed his achievements to the Khalsa's loyalty. This inspired involvement of the entire community with Sikh destiny was to show extraordinary results as an exultant Khalsa, proud of what it stood for, performed heroic deeds in the years to come.

2
Retribution and Consolidation
1708–1799

The seeds sown in Punjab's violent landscape were ripening. The rage of the Sikhs was about to take its toll of men whose disdain for human decencies had bred intolerance and hatred which would now lead to a counter-offensive the intensity of which would help bring down an empire that had flourished as few others.

Every stretch of the journey since the concept of *meeri-peeri*—that the faith must possess both temporal and spiritual authority—was first accepted had brought the Sikhs nearer the ideal of a life free of capricious feudal rule. Their insistence on military training, on spirited resistance to tyranny, on individualism, on equality and democratic decision-making, on the creation of the Khalsa itself, were milestones on the journey to a Sikh state. And Banda Singh was the man destined to lay its foundations.

Banda was an inspired choice of leader for the impending confrontation with the Mughals. Probably born in Kashmir in 1670, he had been a farmer in his early years, becoming an experienced hunter thoroughly proficient with firearms. He had then turned to the ascetic life and the practice of yoga, settling in the southern city of Nander, a centre of Hindu learning, where Gobind Singh had met and converted him a month before his death. The Guru had rekindled the intensely passionate nature that lay beneath the man's *sadhu* exterior. Once converted to Sikhism, Banda projected a sense of formidable power during the next seven years that witnessed the emergence of militant Khalsa assertiveness. When he left the South for the long journey to Punjab, however, he had only twenty-five persons with him—the five *panjpiyare*, Binod Singh, Kahan Singh, Baj Singh, Daya Singh and Ram Singh, and twenty other Sikhs.

His strength, of course, lay in Guru Gobind Singh's *hukamnamahs* (directives) to the various Sikh *sangats*, directing them to rally around Banda Singh's banner. As symbols of authority the Guru gave him five arrows from his own quiver, a *nishan sahib* (flag) and a *nagara* (war drum). Armed with these the handful of men left Nander to seek their destiny in the northern reaches of Hindustan at the end of 1708.

Cautiously making their way through Delhi after a journey of several months, Banda and his group headed for Punjab, where his emissaries had already delivered the Guru's *hukamnamahs* to the Malwa, Doaba and Majha regions, as a result of which a steady stream of Sikhs had started to join them. Even though Mughal forces had prevented reinforcements north of the Sutlej from fording the river, men from the Malwa region south of it had reached him. After several successful if small-scale military actions, Banda headed for Samana, a town of hateful memories for all Sikhs. It was home to Sayyed Jalal-ud-Din, who had executed Guru Tegh Bahadur, and Shashal Beg and Bashal Beg, executioners of Guru Gobind Singh's younger sons. A heavily defended and fortified town, Samana and its military commander were scornful of the rag-tag force they had been warned against. On 26 November 1709 they were in for a surprise.

Banda's lightning assault that morning was so sudden that the attackers were in the town before the defenders had time to close the gates. According to one account "pools of blood flowed through its drains," while another places the number killed at 10,000. What contributed to the bloodshed was the long oppressed peasantry which, seeing the citadel of their oppressors open, joined Banda's force and wreaked terrible vengeance on them.

Leaving Bhai Fateh Singh as the commander of the town and the region around it, Banda next stormed Ghuram, Thaska and Mustafabad. Each Sikh victory added to his mystique and gave the populace confidence in its own power, a discovery made possible by his fearless feats. "A will was created in the ordinary masses to resist

tyranny and to live and die for a national cause," as two Sikh historians
have it. He was also seen as a champion of the oppressed: "The example set by Banda Singh . . . was to serve them as a beacon light in the
days to come." When on his way from Mustafabad to Sadhaura, he
heard of the indecencies which Qadam-ud-din, profligate ruler of
Kapuri, was prone to inflict on the region's Hindu population, the
ascetic Banda—angered by that ruler's excesses—decided to punish
him. Kapuri was destroyed and Qadam-ud-din perished with it. The
prosperous town of Sadhaura, which had an equally infamous ruler,
Osman Khan, was Banda's next destination. This man had tortured
and killed the Muslim divine Pir Budhu Shah because he and his four
sons and several hundred men had helped Guru Gobind Singh in the
Battle of Bhangani. The Sikhs' anger was further honed by reports of
Osman Khan's atrocities against the Hindus. Ironically, Sadhaura, the
abode of *sadhus*, had once been a Buddhist holy centre. The sack of
Sadhaura was no less bloody than that of Samana.

As Banda's daring raids led to the annexation of more towns and
territories, the Sikhs' old enemy, Wazir Khan, governor of Sirhind,
fearful of the Majha and Doaba Sikhs joining up with Banda, now
ordered a pre-emptive attack on the northern contingent near Ropar
on the left bank of the River Sutlej. After a bloody battle and fearsome
slaughter, with most of the Muslim commanders being killed and their
forces routed, the memorable meeting between the northern and
southern Sikh contingents took place in the vicinity of Ropar.

Sirhind, principal town of the south-east Punjab, was the goal now.
To Banda as to all Sikhs, it represented the bestiality of its governor,
who had bricked up Guru Gobind Singh's two young sons alive there
before putting them to the sword. It was clear to every Sikh that the
time had come for Wazir Khan to render an account for this act. "Of
all instances of cruelty exercised on the propagators of new doctrines,"
observed James Browne in the pre-Independence journal *India Tract*,
"this is the most barbarous and outrageous. Defenceless women and
children have usually escaped, even from religious fury. No wonder
then, that the vengeance of the Sikhs was so severe."

Though the Sikhs were fewer in numbers, arms and ordinance, and
the well-equipped Mughal force with its muskets, heavy guns, mail
armour, cavalrymen and war elephants was far superior, Banda's force

excelled in swordsmanship and hand-to-hand combat, backed by archers and spearmen. What fuelled their drive most was their implacable sense of purpose, which their foes lacked. Wazir Khan's army in the Battle of Chappar Chiri is estimated at 20,000 men, while no clear record exists of Sikh forces. Their strength is difficult to determine since sizeable numbers of peasantry and freebooters brought up the rear—to settle scores for past wrongs or simply to loot. The core of fighting men on the Sikh side, it is generally agreed, were far fewer than the enemy's force.

The two forces, commanded personally by Wazir Khan and Banda Singh, clashed on the plain of Chappar Chiri, ten miles from Sirhind, on 22 May 1710. Not unexpectedly, the ferocity of the fighting and carnage outstripped all previous encounters between Sikh and Mughal forces. Wazir Khan and several of his commanders were killed and according to Khafi Khan, a chronicler of the time, "not a man of the army of Islam escaped with more than his life and the clothes he stood in. Horsemen and footmen fell under the swords of the infidels [Sikhs] who pursued them as far as Sirhind." The defences of Sirhind fort were breached two days later, but over 500 Sikhs lost their lives while taking the fort, mainly while trying to silence its heavy guns. Although Sirhind paid a price, it was spared total destruction after its Hindu population appealed to Banda Singh. (But its reprieve was short-lived; a little over 50 years later Sardar Jassa Singh Ahluwalia would be less forgiving of the town's past misdeeds.)

Most writers and Mughal court chroniclers have left lurid accounts of Banda Singh's "atrocities" during the seven years of his whirlwind campaigns. Yet according to a Mughal source of the period, "after the occupation of Sirhind [the Sikhs] issued such strict orders as not to permit even the killing of a single animal." On the other hand, Emperor Bahadur Shah directed Bakhshi-ul-Mummalik Mahabat Khan to issue edicts to the *fauzdars*, the officials in charge of policing country highways, "to kill the worshippers of Nanak wherever they were found," and Farrukh Siyar, Bahadur Shah's son and successor, reconfirmed the directive.

Bahadur Shah also ordered *jiziya* (tax) from Nanak-worshippers to be raised at double the normal rate. Revenue considerations, he cannily decided, could not be overlooked in case his extermination policy failed. But, to quote the same contemporary Mughal source again, "despite the anti-Sikh and anti-Hindu measures of the Mughal government, Banda Singh did not reduce his struggle to the level of a communal strife. His was a political struggle. He would not, therefore, impose any religious restrictions upon the Muslims . . . the struggle of Banda Singh was only directed against the tyranny of the local Mughal officials in Punjab, and their high-handedness was resented and opposed not only by the Sikhs and Hindus but also by the Muslims who joined his army in thousands to fight against the Mughal government."

After annexing Sirhind, and before other towns and territories fell to him, Banda appointed Baj Singh of Nander as its governor, and Ram Singh as governor of Thanessar; both these appointments were aimed at consolidation and effective administration of conquered territories. The next to fall to Banda's forces were the towns of Rai Kot, Saharanpur, Jalalabad, Ludhiana, Jullundur, Hoshiarpur, Batala, Kalanaur and Pathankot. These conquests took him to the very gates of Lahore and he was now in control of most of Punjab lying east and south of Lahore as far as Karnal and not very far from Delhi. "There was no nobleman daring enough to march from Delhi against them," comments the Mughal source.

Developments in Punjab were making Emperor Bahadur Shah uneasy. He felt that "a popular rising, such as that of the Sikhs, in a part of the Empire so near the capital, might have more serious and far-reaching consequences . . ." His concern grew as news of Banda's victories was brought to him in Ajmer, where he had stopped for a while on his way back from the Deccan after subduing his brother Kambakhsh. Distressing reports of Mughal defeats were conveyed in person by nobles from Samana, Sadhaura and Sirhind who arrived to tell him of their plight following the fall of their strongholds. Bahadur Shah, convinced it was time to lead a *jehad* in person against the Sikhs, reinforced his troops with levies from Oudh, Moradabad, Allahabad and Barha, and in August 1710 set out with a huge imperial army.

After taking Sadhaura, Banda chose the fort of Mukhlispur—built in the time of Emperor Shah Jahan and occasionally used by him as a summer retreat—as capital of the emerging Sikh state. Half-way between Sadhaura and Nahan, Mukhlispur was built on a promontory on the lower slopes of the Himalayas, surrounded by ravines and two small streams. Banda Singh restored the crumbling citadel, renamed it Lohgarh, and planted the flag of the Khalsa on its ramparts. This was the first time the Sikhs had claimed a region as their own. To give Lohgarh added authority as the administrative capital of their territories, an official seal and coins were engraved to celebrate Sikh rule. But unlike the seals and coins of the Mughals which exalted Mughal rulers, Banda's were dedicated to Guru Nanak and Guru Gobind Singh. The Persian inscription on his seal read:

Degh O Tegh O Fateh O Nasrat-i-bedirang
Yaft az Nanak Guru Gobind Singh.

The inscription eulogized the kettle (representing Sikh commitment to feed the poor), the sword (the symbol of power), victory and unqualified patronage as attributes bequeathed by Nanak to Guru Gobind Singh.

Nothing less than the annihilation of both Lohgarh and Banda, whose audacious conquests were causing extreme concern to the court at Delhi, was the aim of the vast imperial horde which an alarmed emperor was now leading into Punjab. There were 60,000 horsemen, of whom 31,000 were commanded by the emperor's eldest son, the rest being placed under three key commanders. In addition to these were the foot soldiers. Opposing them were 3,000 Sikhs on horseback and 2,000 on foot. After bloody battles at Sadhaura and Sirhind—from where cartloads of Sikh heads were sent for the emperor's edification—and despite the widely acknowledged heroism of the Sikhs— "the number of the dead and dying of the imperialists was so large that for a time it seemed they were losing ground . . ." remnants of the Sikh force had to retreat to the fort of Lohgarh.

Lohgarh was besieged by over 60,000 imperial troops on horse and foot, on whose fringes were a number of plunderers including Afghans and Bilochs. Defending the citadel were 2,000 to 3,000 Sikhs. Despite the odds, and amidst bitter hand-to-hand fighting, the Sikhs held out long enough for Banda and a few of his followers to escape. An incensed emperor who had been overseeing the siege himself saw this as a personal affront and an act of disobedience, since he had specifically ordered Banda to be brought in chains before him. He wished to climax his campaign by so sealing Banda's fate as to deter others for all time. Since Banda had escaped through the lands of some of the hill rajas, he punished them as well as his own commanders. "It matters not," said Bahadur Shah peevishly, "where the dog has fled to, whether he is drowned in the river or hiding in a cave in the hills . . . the Wazir [Munim Khan] has bound himself to produce the rebel, and produce him he must."

But Banda was in no mood to fall in with any of Bahadur Shah's wishes. Within a fortnight of his escape from Lohgarh, he issued *hukamnamahs* to the Khalsa throughout the country "calling upon them to join him at once . . . and before long he felt himself strong enough to undertake military expeditions against the offending Hindu chiefs of the Shiwaliks." The "offending chiefs" were the same rajas who had sided with the Mughals so often in the past and had also refused him help. Principal amongst them was the Raja of Kahlur, an old foe of the Sikhs. The canny raja, in anticipation of a Sikh attack, had augmented his force with those of his allies, greatly strengthening Bilaspur's defences. But to no avail. His defeat cost him over 1,300 lives and a large booty which fell into Sikh hands.

Unnerved by this convincing reassertion of Sikh power, the other hill chieftains now hastened to offer allegiance to Banda. Amongst them was the Raja of Mandi. Convinced of his goodwill, Banda visited his state, then went to call on an equally conciliatory and welcoming Raja of Chamba. Chamba also offered him the hand of a young woman of his family in marriage, and a son named Ajai Singh was born to them at the end of 1711.

Earlier that year, after establishing his power in the Kangra and Kulu hills, Banda Singh had appeared on the plains near Raipur and Bahrampur in a threatening move towards the town of Gurdaspur. A major clash with Mughal forces north-west of Raipur resulted in the defeat of the Mughals. The Sikhs killed their commanders, captured their equipment, overran the towns of Raipur and Bahrampur, and advanced on Batala. In a fierce encounter in which Sheikh Ahmed, who was leading Batala's defenders, was killed, the city fell to Banda. With characteristic audacity Banda next thought of attacking

Lahore. But with the emperor not too far away in Hoshiarpur, and many of the imperial army's generals reconnoitring for him, he decided instead to head for the mountainous region of eastern Jammu. The towns of Aurangabad and Pasrur were attacked and subdued on the way and though trapped for a while by the Mughals, the Khalsa fought their way out after inflicting heavy losses on the forces encircling them.

In February 1712 Emperor Bahadur Shah, who had moved to Lahore in August 1711, died. The usual struggle for succession took its toll and Jahandar Shah briefly ascended the throne, but was slain within months by his nephew, Muhammad Farrukh Siyar, who succeeded him in February 1713. In the year between Bahadur Shah's death and Farrukh Siyar's accession, Banda and the Khalsa emerged from their fastnesses of Jammu to recapture Sadhaura and Lohgarh. The latter, repaired and refurbished, was restored as the capital of the Sikh state, and remained so for another two years despite repeated Mughal attempts to take back this irksome symbol of Sikh power.

Emperor Farrukh Siyar's first goal was the destruction of Banda and the Khalsa and his instructions to Zakariya Khan, the new commander at Jammu, were "to expel Banda from Sadhaura or if possible to destroy him altogether." With the combined forces of the Mughals, with heavy artillery and a formidable arsenal of weapons, against the Sikhs, and with the governor of Lahore personally in command of the expedition, Sadhaura and Lohgarh fell once more to the Mughals. But not before many of their commanders and large numbers of their troops had been killed in hand-to-hand fighting. Eluding capture, Banda Singh and the remnants of the Khalsa once again vanished into the hills.

To celebrate their victory, Lahore's governor, Abdus Samad Khan, sent his son Zakariya Khan to Delhi in December 1713 to carry the good news to the emperor personally. Zakariya presented the emperor not only with his father's report, but also with a large number of Sikh heads. The emperor was delighted. Fulsomely praising Zakariya, he raised his rank and gave him several presents including a dress of honour, an aigrette, a banner and a drum. His father, who also arrived in Delhi a few months later, was similarly rewarded. But in June 1714 the two of them were ordered back to Punjab to deal with "that sect of mean and detestable Sikhs."

Within two months the Khalsa appeared outside Ropar and launched a concerted attack on it. But being heavily outnumbered by the enemy, they just as swiftly withdrew. Clearly, this was part of their war of attrition after the phenomenal losses suffered recently. Their lack of resources could be replenished only through lightning attacks on the enemy's arsenals, granaries and strongholds.

From the end of 1713 until 1715, Banda stayed in the remote hills of Jammu, about 30 miles north-west of Jammu City. Now called Dera Baba Banda Singh, it lies on a bend of the River Chenab. Whilst the Mughal commanders of Jammu, Sirhind and Lahore kept a wary eye on the Sikhs who were regrouping in the hills and taking stock of their weapons, victuals, men, money and horses, members of the Sikh community scattered across Punjab were at the receiving end of the ruling power's resentments. Then suddenly, in February 1715, Banda and his men appeared on the plains below Jammu, heading for Kalanaur. Suhrab Khan, Kalanaur's commander, who met them at the head of an impressive force of regulars, mercenaries and others, was given short shrift and the victors moved into Kalanaur to set up their own administration. Banda's next target, Batala, was also taken.

News of Mughal reverses and Sikh victories led a fuming Farrukh Siyar to deliver a stunning rebuke to the very same governor of Lahore whom he had earlier rewarded. The alarmed emperor now ordered the largest ever mobilization of his forces for the liquidation of the Sikhs. Farrukh Siyar directed that every Sikh captured should be put to the sword if he refused to embrace the Mohammedan faith, and a good price was put on every Sikh head. As the court's chronicler put it, "chopped heads of the Sikhs were often sent to the Emperor by the commanders . . . for his pleasure."

On being informed of the extensive preparations underway, Banda chose to take a stand half-way between Batala and Kalanaur. When the combined Mughal forces and their heavily outnumbered opponents clashed, Banda stood his ground to general amazement, and in the first encounter fought so heroically that he came very near to victory. Hard pressed, he made cunning use of the terrain to make constant changes of position. Khafi Khan records that "the infidels fought so fiercely that the army of Islam was nearly overpowered; they over and over again showed the greatest daring."

Inevitably, the Khalsa had to fall back again, this time to Gurdas Nangal, a village four miles from the town of Gurdaspur. They hastily built fortifications, since none existed, and cut through the banks of a nearby imperial canal to create a quagmire around their position. The Mughal horde was not long in coming. Even in the annals of those violent times, the siege of Gurdas Nangal, which lasted eight months, stands out as an epic event. Hopelessly outnumbered, starving, sick and suffering, the besieged force fought back with a heroism and tenacity which earned the grudging admiration of their enemy. As the chronicler Muhammad Qasim relates in his *Ibrat Namah:* "the brave and daring deeds of the infernal Sikhs were wonderful. Twice or thrice every day . . . when the combined forces of the imperialists went to oppose them, they made an end of the Mughals with arrows, muskets and small swords, and disappeared. Such was the terror of the Sikhs . . . that the commanders of this army prayed to God to so ordain things that Banda should seek his safety in his flight . . ."

When the end came, it was not due to unevenness of numbers, although by then there were over 30,000 Mughal troops encircling Gurdas Nangal, but to sheer privation. When the grass and leaves the besieged had subsisted on, and the bark of trees they had ground and used as flour, had all been consumed, and with men dying of starvation, Gurdas Nangal was overrun on 17 December 1715. About 300 Sikhs were executed on the spot, their heads then being "stuffed with hay and mounted on spears" and borne in the vanguard of the victory procession which headed for Lahore. Next came an elephant carrying an iron cage on its back, with Banda manacled, fettered and chained inside it. Then followed his key men and warriors in irons.

When the population of Lahore had had its fill of the "cortège of half-dead prisoners and bleeding heads," and admired this spectacle of Mughal bravery, the procession reformed for its final destination, Delhi. Zakariya Khan was again deputed by his father to take Banda and the prisoners to the emperor. The ever-eager Zakariya, convinced of the inappropriateness of presenting the emperor with only two hundred prisoners, had the countryside scoured for Sikhs so that the figure would reach a respectable count. He also included cartloads of Sikh heads. In Cunningham's words, Banda and others "were marched to Delhi with all the signs of ignominy usual with bigots, and common among barbarous or half-civilised conquerors."

According to another account, by the time the procession reached Delhi on 27 February 1716, it had in the lead "nearly two thousand heads [of executed Sikhs] stuffed with straw and a thousand persons bound with iron chains." The executions began on 5 March 1716 as a prelude to Banda's own killing. William Irvine describes the course of events in his *Political History of the Sikhs:*

"Every day a hundred brave men perished and at night the headless bodies were loaded into carts; taken out of the city and hung upon trees. It was not till June 9, 1716 that Banda himself was led out to execution, all efforts having failed to buy him off. They . . . took him away to the old city, where the red Qutb Minar lifts its proud head of white marble over the crumbling walls of the Hindu fortress. Here they paraded him round the tomb of the late emperor, Bahadur Shah, and put him to a barbarous death. First they had him dismount, placed his child in his arms and bade him kill it. Then, as he shrank with horror from the act, they ripped open the child before the father's eyes, thrust its quivering flesh into his mouth and hacked him to pieces limb by limb."

So ended the life of a man who in seven short years had so mocked the might of the Mughals with his victories that they could never again reassert their authority over the land they had once ruled with such aplomb. Though their numbers were tiny compared to the Mughal forces, Banda and his men had wrested extensive territories from the paramount power to establish the first-ever independent Sikh state complete with its royal seal, its own coins and an administrative system. In the near-absence of first-hand written accounts of that period by Sikh chroniclers, the reporting of Muslim and other observers has led to a very distorted picture of Banda, painted by men resentful of his meteoric rise.

One of Banda's little-known decisions of profound significance—the abolition of the *zamindari* system—was taken during the brief period of his governance at Lohgarh. The *zamindars* were landlords with extensive land holdings which their families had either held for a long time or which had recently been given by grateful rulers. The peasants cultivating these lands had no proprietary rights over them; they were mere tillers exploited by the *zamindars*, and their status was little more than that of slaves. In abolishing this system, Banda made the cultivators (almost all Jats) owners of the land, and the impact of his reform on agricultural Punjab is evident to this day. Since the rewards of their labour go directly to them, Punjab's farmers have excelled in the energy, endurance and diligence with which they work their land, making Punjab India's bread-basket since Independence.

Guru Gobind Singh had not only foreseen the inherent weakness of the decaying Mughal state, he had also accurately assessed Banda's potential for carrying out the Khalsa's mission of asserting Sikh authority in Punjab. Even though the brutality of the Mughal rulers and the genocide of the Sikhs would reach new levels after Banda's death, there was no longer any question of curbing the growth of Sikh power. With their rugged individualism, valorous traditions and a lively awareness of their own strength, they would found their own empire at the beginning of the nineteenth century. Much blood would be spilt before the Khalsa fulfilled its destiny, but the way ahead had been shown by Banda Singh Bahadur, or Banda Singh the Brave, as all Sikhs admiringly call him.

The years following Banda Bahadur's death were dire for the Sikhs, with the implacable hostility of the Mughals, symbolized by Abdus Samad Khan and his son Zakariya Khan, on the one hand, and on the other the Afghans, above all Ahmed Shah Durrani, who were descending like wolves on the weakening Mughal Empire. The Sikhs found themselves geographically between the two. In numbers too they were a fraction of the followers of Islam, and with inadequate weapons and little wealth. The odds they faced in their fight against the Mughals are apparent from the weapons and money recovered from them after the siege of Gurdas Nangal: "1,000 swords, 278 shields, 173 bows and quivers, 180 matchlocks, 114 daggers, 217 long knives, 23 gold mohars, 600 rupees and a few gold ornaments." But what the Sikhs did bring to the battlefield—as to their everyday lives—was raw courage, endurance, a powerful sense of kinship, and an absolute commitment to the religious ideals enunciated by the Gurus, for which they were willing to sacrifice their lives.

Guru Gobind Singh's foresight was again evident in the years between Banda Bahadur's death in 1716 and the founding of the Sikh Empire by Ranjit Singh in 1801. The unswerving acceptance of the paramountcy of the Guru Granth Sahib by every Sikh made for a cohesive bond that held the community together in adverse times, leaving no room for playing sides. The quasi-republican tradition of the *panjpiyare*, while providing collective leadership, also played an important role since respect for it was a key factor in holding the Khalsa together. No Sikh could think of flouting this tradition, and so the unparalleled violence against them was collectively and unflinchingly faced.

No one persecuted the Sikhs with greater zeal than Zakariya Khan. Eager to obey to the letter the emperor's decree that no Sikh should be left alive in the Mughal Empire, he zestfully launched a campaign of genocide, intensified when he succeeded his father as Lahore's governor. His columns combed the countryside for Sikhs, and those captured alive were brought to Lahore for daily public executions. He fixed a reward of fifty rupees for every Sikh head brought to him.

This mindless persecution only helped inflame Sikh militancy, and they retaliated by killing government functionaries and plundering Mughal posts, arsenals and treasuries. Zakariya Khan tried another tactic. In 1733 he offered the Sikhs a *jagir* (principality). The Sikhs agreed and Kapur Singh was unanimously chosen to head it. It was a wise choice. A resolute and battle-tested warrior who had carried out relentless guerrilla warfare against the Mughals, also a devout Sikh who had made an impressive number of conversions, Kapur Singh was aware that too much blood had been spilt for the truce to endure. So he set about making the most of it.

In 1734 he organized the Sikhs into *dals*, or groups. The Budha Dal was a force of veterans above forty, while the Taruna Dal consisted of men below this age. The responsibilities of these two—later known as the Dal Khalsa—included guarding places of worship, conducting conversions and baptismal ceremonies, and offering armed resistance to the Mughal state. The Taruna Dal, whose strength soon rose to 12,000, came to take especial charge of the latter, being further divided into five sections, each under a veteran and each with its own banner and drum and having administrative control of the lands conquered by it. These five sections, along with several others, would in later years become Sikh *misls* whose chiefs, like the barons of medieval times, held absolute sway over the territories ruled by them and enforced their writ with their cavalry and foot soldiers. In times of war they combined to fight their common adversary; at other times they were not averse to fighting each other. In Kapur Singh's time the *dals*, although in their early stages, provided Sikh resistance with a much-needed methodology and organization.

Within two years of granting the *jagir* to the Sikhs in 1734, the perfidious Zakariya sent a force to reoccupy it. He also arrested Bhai Mani Singh, Guru Gobind Singh's revered and scholarly companion and head priest of the Harmandir, and had him brutally cut to pieces in Lahore. He laid siege to Amritsar and after capturing it, plundered the Harmandir, filled the pool with the carcasses of slaughtered animals, and put it to the torch. An eyewitness account of these events, called the *Bansavalinama*, tells the grim story in detail. But it was a Pyrrhic victory, for the Mughals overlooked the fact that persecution and martyrdom of Sikhs invariably intensified their resolve to destroy their tormentors. Thirsting for vengeance, the Khalsa regrouped to face them.

A new element was now added to the welter of violence in the disintegrating Mughal Empire. Nadir Shah's descent on India from Persia in 1739 helped the Sikhs, although they were directly on the invader's route to Delhi. Taking advantage of the Persian's sack of the capital and the demoralized state of the imperial court, the Sikhs increased their guerrilla strikes against it. They also plundered the booty from Nadir Shah's baggage train as he returned home. The sagacious Persian assessed the potential of Sikh self-confidence and valour more accurately than the governor of Punjab was able to do. "Nadir Shah is said to have questioned Zakariya Khan about the brigands who had been audacious enough to attack his troops. The governor replied: 'They are fakirs who visit their Guru's tank twice a year, and after having bathed in it disappear.' 'Where do they live?' enquired the Shah. 'Their homes are their saddles,' replied Zakariya Khan. Nadir Shah is said to have prophesied, 'take care, the day is not distant when these rebels will take possession of your country.'"

Nadir Shah's warning made Zakariya Khan add insult to injury against the outlawed and scattered Sikhs. He encouraged Massa Ranghar, landlord of territories around Amritsar, to take over the Darbar Sahib, the Golden Temple, for his own use. Ranghar opened government offices in some of the buildings, billeted his men and horses in others, and used the Harmandir for performances by his *nautch*-girls. As he reclined on a couch one evening enjoying the revelries, two Sikhs, Mahtab Singh and Sukha Singh, walked in, and while one kept watch the other beheaded Ranghar.

This inevitably led to more reprisals, to which the Sikhs responded with even greater audacity. One such act was Kapur Singh's plan to hold Zakariya Khan hostage after a lightning raid on his stronghold of Lahore: "With a force of 2,000 strong, dressed in green, their hair hanging loosely behind in Muslim style and a green Muslim banner in the lead, he [Kapur Singh] entered the city and went to the Shahi Mosque where, according to intelligence received, the Mughal governor was expected to attend the afternoon prayer." Luckily for Zakariya Khan he missed that visit to the mosque and the Sikhs had to leave disappointed, but not before making their identity known with the resonant Sikh greeting *"Sat-Siri-Akal"* (which broadly translated means Truth and God are timeless and immortal).

Along with such collective acts of daring were those that reflected the individual's determination to uphold Sikh self-esteem. The example set by Bota Singh is particularly appealing. Determined to show one and all that his people were far from finished, he chose Punjab's busiest highway to levy a tax, in the name of the Khalsa, on everyone using it. "It amounted," as one writer has put it, "to the establishment by an individual of a State—a declaration of sovereignty which, as Sikhs sang in those grim times, had been assigned to them by God himself." Not content with the road-users' meek submission to his will, he then issued a challenge to the governor of Lahore, who promptly sent troops to overpower him. Both Bota Singh and his companion Garja Singh fell fighting them.

The persecution of Sikhs escalated further after Zakariya's death in 1745. His second son, Shah Nawaz Khan, on becoming governor, had the bellies of Sikhs ripped open, iron pegs struck into their heads, and their brains removed in his presence. It was during his governership, in

June 1746, that the first *ghalughara* (disaster)—the massacre of more than 7,000 Sikhs by a large body of Mughal troops—took place. An additional 3,000 were taken prisoner and executed publicly at Lahore.

Shar Nawaz Khan's successor, Mir Mannu, outdid him in cruelty, imprisoning, starving and torturing even Sikh women and children to death. Mir Mannu's sadism and duplicity were offered further opportunities by another predator who now appeared in India, the Afghan Ahmed Shah Abdali.

Proclaiming himself Afghanistan's ruler after the assassination of Nadir Shah in 1747, Abdali invaded India in the following year—the first of eight invasions by him between the years 1748 and 1768. If Nadir Shah had exposed the Mughals' inability to withstand a determined assault from across Hindustan's borders, Abdali provided further proof. Claiming Punjab as part of a new Afghanistan, he defeated Lahore's Mughal viceroy in February 1748. Punjab's complicated situation became even more confused in the triangular struggle for power. While Abdali dealt the Mughals deadly blows, both wanted the Sikhs destroyed, who in turn no longer saw the beleaguered Mughals as much of a threat.

Despite the ongoing devastation, Sikh control over parts of Punjab tightened. In 1748 the Darbar Sahib, which had been seized by the Mughals, was liberated by Jassa Singh Ahluwalia who had been brought up by Mata Sundari, Guru Gobind Singh's widow. He had succeeded Kapur Singh as Supreme Commander of the Dal Khalsa. In the clash of arms to liberate the shrine the Mughal commander, Salabat Khan, was killed, the holy pool—which had been desecrated and filled—re-excavated, and the sanctity of the shrine restored. A large congregation of Sikhs declared the Khalsa a state with Jassa Singh Ahluwalia as its head. A small fortress, called Ram Rauni, was built to defend Amritsar.

The respite was short-lived. Having refused to acknowledge Mughal supremacy, the Sikhs were not going to acknowledge Abdali's. To drive home the point they looted his train as he was returning to Afghanistan after his first invasion in 1748, and increased the frequency and intensity of their attacks each year. Matters came to a head in 1752 when Mir Mannu betrayed the Mughals and switched allegiance to the Afghans, his first act on reconfirmation as governor of

Lahore being to make Punjab officially an Afghan province. And in 1757 the Mughal emperor himself acquiesced in the annexation of Lahore by Abdali, along with the provinces of Multan, Kashmir and Sirhind. The Sikhs would have none of it. They had already declared their sovereignty over parts of Punjab in Banda Singh's time and had reiterated it ever since, and they were now determined to re-establish the parameters of their own Sikh state. That this was greatly resented by Abdali and his satrap made no difference to them.

During the three years of relative peace after the death of Mir Mannu in 1753, the Sikhs proclaimed the Khalsa guardians of the entire Punjab. This defiant gesture added to Abdali's anger, further fuelled by the system of *rakhi* devised by them: the word means to "protect" or "safeguard." In exchange for one-fifth of the land-rent or revenue paid to the state, the Sikhs provided people living in Punjab with full protection. In view of the instability of the times, large numbers of Hindus, Muslims and Sikhs accepted the offer since it was justly administered. This was clearly a direct challenge to Abdali's claim of sovereignty over Punjab. It helped further to define the contours of a state system, and became a substantial source of revenue for the Sikhs. It also laid the groundwork for the independent groups of Sikhs known as *misls*, which will be described later.

When during Abdali's invasion of 1757 the Sikhs not only plundered his baggage train—loaded with the wealth of Delhi and the temple cities of Mathura and Vrindavan—but also rescued hundreds of captive Hindu women and returned them to their homes, Abdali, incensed, ordered his army to repeat Zakariya's treatment of Amritsar, by demolishing the Harmandir, defiling its sacred pool, and carrying out a policy of genocide against the Sikhs. His commands were faithfully carried out. He also appointed his son Timur Shah governor of Lahore, with instructions to exterminate the "accursed infidels."

The son's task was more difficult than the father had expected. As soon as the Afghan army had finished demolishing the Darbar Sahib, a handful of Sikhs assembled at Gohalwar near Amritsar to avenge the dishonour. Electing Baba Deep Singh, who had been baptized by Guru Gobind Singh, as their leader, they fell upon the Afghan forces. The carnage that followed is recounted with awe to this day. The Sikhs fought to the last man with demonic fury, and though mortally wounded Deep Singh hacked his way through the Afghan lines to die on the *parkarma* of the sacred waters, in sight of the hallowed Harmandir. Pilgrims to the Darbar Sahib still pause in reverence at this spot.

Although periods of relative calm followed, there was no real peace. Fighting spirit being the very substance of Sikh psyche, they spurned any idea of relaxation, and relying more on morale than resources, continued to hit the Afghans when and wherever they could. By this time a new Sikh ally had materialized in the form of the Maratha people from Central India, who at this high-point in their history had swept northward to the very gates of Delhi. They were causing Abdali acute concern, disconcerted as he already was by unrelenting Sikh attacks. Then, on 10 April 1758, the Sikhs and the Marathas attacked together and briefly occupied Lahore. A large number of Afghan troops were killed, and those captured brought to Amritsar to clean the sacred pool they had earlier defiled.

A *hukamnamah* issued from the Akal Takht, Amritsar in March 1759 ordered Sikhs everywhere to send donations for the reconstruction of the Darbar Sahib. During the following year's Diwali festival, the Sarbat Khalsa, the representative council of all the Sikhs, met and passed a *gurmata* (resolution) authorizing an attack on Lahore with the aim of taking possession of it in the name of the Khalsa. The Sikhs bided their time. When Abdali returned to India in 1761 and defeated the Marathas at Panipat, he least expected the Sikhs to pick his hour of triumph to fall on him as he returned home victorious. But that is what they did, and then proceeded to attack Lahore in November of that year, Jassa Singh Ahluwalia taking possession of it. He was proclaimed *Sultan-ul-Qaum*, sovereign of the state (heralding the state which would actually be founded by Ranjit Singh 40 years later). Jassa Singh withdrew after a brief occupation but not before exacting a tribute for the Harmandir's upkeep.

Leaving Abdali in no doubt as to where sovereignty in Punjab now resided, the Sikhs decided to subdue and seize the properties of all Afghan supporters and sympathizers there. Alarmed by these developments, Abdali returned to Lahore in January 1762 fully determined to exterminate them this time.

Finding them away—the Sikhs had laid siege to Sirhind—he set out on one of his famous lightning marches to take them by surprise. And this he certainly did. Crossing two rivers and covering a distance of 110 miles in two days, he suddenly appeared before them at Kup, where a battle of unparalleled ferocity was fought on 5 February 1762. Commonly referred to as the *Wada Ghalughara* (great disaster), the Sikhs were at a disadvantage from the outset. Accompanied by a large number of women and children who were being taken to a safer region in anticipation of Abdali's invasion, they had to fight from fixed positions, quite the opposite of the high mobility guerrilla tactics they had perfected over the years. This time all odds were against them: numbers, weapons, form of warfare and the vulnerability of their families. Estimates of Sikhs killed—a great many were women and children—vary from 10,000 to 30,000.

The other item on Abdali's agenda after the massacre at Kup was the Darbar Sahib. Choosing the period of Baisakhi when thousands of pilgrims assembled at Amritsar to bathe in the *sarowar*, the sacred pool, the Afghan forces struck on 10 April 1762. Once again there was a bloodbath. Abdali filled the Harmandir with gunpowder, blew it apart and razed other buildings to the ground as well. Once again the *sarowar* was filled with human bodies, carcasses of cows and the débris of destroyed buildings, and a pyramid of Sikh heads was erected on top of it all, the latter being the customary *coup de théâtre* accompanying Afghan expeditions against the Sikhs.

If Abdali believed he had finished the Sikhs off, however, he was in for a surprise. For almost a year the Darbar Sahib remained in his hands, then, in early 1763, Charat Singh of the Sukerchakia *misl*—whose grandson Ranjit Singh would establish a Sikh empire and gild the Harmandir with gold—wrested back control of it. Once again the Khalsa gathered to celebrate the Baisakhi festival, and to pledge themselves to rebuild the Harmandir, re-excavate the pool, and punish the defilers. The pool was indeed cleared by the November festival of Diwali, and in this brief period two more battles were fought with the Afghans at Sialkot and Sirhind, in both of which the Sikhs emerged victorious.

At a gathering of the triumphant Khalsa in early 1764 in Amritsar, plans for rebuilding the Harmandir were announced and in a dramatic gesture a large sheet of cloth was spread out and all present were asked to place their offerings for its reconstruction on it. Close to a million rupees—a staggering figure for those times—was collected that day. The administration of the money was entrusted to a few trustworthy bankers of Amritsar, and work on restoring the Harmandir began.

On 1 December 1764 Abdali appeared once again outside Amritsar on his seventh invasion of India, to find only 30 Sikhs in the Darbar Sahib. In the uneven but bloody fight the defenders were killed and their bodies flung into the sacred pool, which was yet again filled with the débris of demolished buildings and slaughtered cows. This was the third and last time the fountainhead of Sikh faith was desecrated—an offence the Khalsa would avenge by hurling the Afghans out of India for all time.

Undeterred, and determined to make Abdali realize that his days were numbered, the Khalsa again assembled at the Darbar Sahib for Baisakhi in April 1765. A *gurmata* to annex Lahore, the seat of Afghan authority in India, was passed and after a swift military action the Sikhs accepted the city's surrender on 16 April 1765. This was followed by a Sikh declaration of sovereignty over Punjab. Silver coins were issued to announce their assumption of political power, and in declaring Amritsar as the mint city they underscored the fact that in the struggle for supremacy the Sikhs were establishing new institutions of state while steadily dismantling Afghan symbols of suzerainty.

The Sikhs were now in control of large parts of Punjab and present-day Pakistan, along with parts of what are now the Indian states of Jammu and Kashmir, Himachal Pradesh, and Haryana. Abdali was still not beaten, but his hold on India was broken and while his son, Timur Shah—in charge of his father's disintegrating Indian domains—scored some military successes in north-west India, he considered it prudent to coexist with the Sikhs for as long as possible. Which was not for long.

At about this time twelve Sikh *misls* had emerged as fairly well-defined entities in Punjab. By taking on state responsibilities like land administration, increasing agricultural production, land grants, revenue collection and religious endowments, the chiefs of these Sikh principalities established a structure which frequently improved upon and replaced the Mughal system of governance. The convergence of several elements contributed to the form and substance of the *misls*. Among these the Dal Khalsa, *rakhi* and the Sarbat Khalsa with its resolutions known as *gurmatas* played a crucial role in helping shape the *misl* concept and bring about the Sikhs' rise to political power in the 1750s and 1760s.

There were both feudal and democratic elements in the way in which the *misls* functioned. Whilst *misl* chiefs had absolute control of their territories, Banda Singh's land reforms had given cultivators stakes in their holdings and a reason to fight in the armies of the *misls* to which they belonged. The strength of a *misl* flowed from the contentment of its constituents. As Colonel A.L.H. Polier, a Swiss officer of the East India Company, observed in the 1770s, the possessions of the Sikh chiefs were "exceedingly well cultivated, populous and rich." Writers like George Forster commented on the "large revenues of the extensive and fertile territories of the Sikhs" and their "state of high cultivation." Other writers of the period like John Griffiths, William Francklin and John Malcolm referred to the wheat, barley, rice, pulses, sugar cane, cotton, indigo, jaggery and the variety of fruit grown in Punjab. Malcolm also pointed out that "in no country, perhaps, is the Rayat, or cultivator, treated with more indulgence."

The Sikhs also fostered manufacturing and trade in the second half of the eighteenth century. As a first step Sikh chiefs began rebuilding captured towns and cities devastated by the eighteenth century's unending wars. Lahore, badly damaged by repeated Afghan invasions, was rebuilt after its occupation in 1765. Similar importance was given to the reconstruction of other conquered cities like Sialkot, Batala, Jhang and Bhera. Among the new towns developed, the most significant was Rawalpindi. Sardar Milkha Singh (Thepuria) expanded what had been a very small village by building new fortifications and making it a major centre of trade and commerce, so that people settled there from many parts of Punjab and beyond.

Other cities developed by the Sikhs in the late eighteenth century include "Gujranwala under Charat Singh Sukerchakia, Fatehabad and Kapurthala under Fateh Singh Ahluwalia, Rahon under Tara Singh Dallewalia, Hallowal under Bagh Singh Hallowalia, Phillaur under Tara Singh Kang, Sujanpur under Amar Singh Bagga, Sayyidwala under Kamar Singh Nakkai, and Nur Mahal under Charat Singh

Nurmahilia." The patronage of the *misl* chiefs drew people of every description to these urban centres: metal-workers, gold- and silver-smiths, gun-smiths, weavers, traders in most commodities, and buyers and sellers of bloodstock.

Amritsar, already a thriving city, received a further boost after the consolidation of Sikh power. It exported goods to Yarkand, Turfan, Chinese Turkestan, Afghanistan, Bokhara, Persia, Arabia and places further afield. *Kafilas* (caravans) carried merchandise over regular routes, one such being from Amritsar to Bokhara via Kabul. Articles from Amritsar were first carried to Kabul where traders from Bokhara took delivery and sold them in Central Asia and Russia. Exports out of Amritsar included shawls, silks and woollen cloth, metalware and agricultural products, while imports included gold, raw silk, horses and arms. The trading communities of the city, each specializing in something different, imported a wide range of goods for distribution in Kashmir, Ladakh and other remote areas of the country.

Lahore too, after its revival under the Sikhs, regained its eminence in trading and manufacturing of silks, woollens, carpets, swords, leather goods, boat-making and arms. Multan, Sialkot, Batala and Phagwara, among others, reflected Punjab's spirit of entrepreneurship.

Not only did the *misl* chiefs regenerate Punjab through developing its agriculture and economy, but they also reaffirmed Amritsar's centrality by building their *bungas*, or residences, around the Darbar Sahib. Whether for spiritual sustenance, planning their unceasing campaigns against the Mughals or Afghans, receiving the Sarbat Khalsa's sanction for their major moves, or celebrating their festivals, they invariably returned to the elevating environs of the Darbar Sahib in order to experience its magnetic pull and to bow before the dignity and authority of this redoubtable symbol of their faith.

Even after the Sikhs had tightened their grip on Punjab, much remained to be done. The disciplining of the shifty hill rajas was a priority. They were duly brought to heel as was Sirhind which got its comeuppance in 1764 from *misl* forces under the command of one of the twelve *misl* leaders, Jassa Singh Ahluwalia. Zain Khan, the governor of Sirhind, was killed in battle and Sirhind was levelled to the ground in retribution for the killing of Fateh Singh and Zorawar Singh, Guru Gobind Singh's young sons. Sikh authority over several other rajas and chieftains in the region was established by Jassa Singh during this expedition.

In 1768 he overran territories around Delhi, seat of the once mighty Mughal Empire. But it wasn't until March 1783 that he entered Delhi at the head of a combined *misl* force, accompanied by a fellow chieftain, Baghel Singh and others. Crossing the river Jamuna at Burari Ghat, they took Malkha Ganj, Sabzi Mandi and Mughal Pura on the city's outskirts and entered the Diwan-i-Am, the Mughal emperor's audience hall in the Red Fort. In a symbolic gesture Jassa Singh had himself installed on the imperial throne.

The Sikh forces withdrew after the emperor agreed to pay an annual *nazrana* (tribute) to them, but returned to subjugate Delhi again in 1785 after the Mughals broke their promises. This time the ruler was made to agree to the construction of several gurdwaras in Delhi to commemorate the events with which Sikh emotions and passions were closely linked. The Mughals offered every cooperation in building them and Sardar Baghel Singh stayed on to oversee their construction on eight historic sites: Sisganj, Rakabganj, Majnu-Ka-Tila, Moti Bagh, Damdama Sahib, Mata Sundari, Bala Sahib and Bangla Sahib.

Sardar Jassa Singh Ahluwalia stood tall among Sikh chieftains for his outstanding qualities of leadership. Each of the twelve *misl* leaders, while bringing Punjab under Sikh control, carved out substantial territories for himself, capturing city after city to raise the count of Sikh conquests and provide visible proof of Sikh ascendance. Jassa Singh's domain extended from Kapurthala in the Jullundur Doab to the Majha area across the River Beas. The Bhangi *misl* included Amritsar, Tarn Taran, Lahore, all the way north to Sialkot, Gujrat and Multan. The Ramgarhias, named after Ram Rauni, the fortress built for the defence of Amritsar, had Qadian, Batala and Sri Hargobindpur in the Bari Doab as well as further towns in the Jullundur Doab.

The Nakkais held sway over lands south of Lahore between the Rivers Ravi and Sutlej. The Dallewalia possessions in the Jullundur Doab included Nawanshahar, Phillaur, Rahon and Mahatpur. The Karorsinghias had Hoshiarpur and the territories around it, whilst the Nishanwalas, flag-bearers of the Sikh Army, possessed Ambala. The Shahids, family of the martyr Baba Deep Singh, possessed territories around Ambala and Saharanpur. The Phulkians controlled Patiala, Sirhind, Nabha and Jind. The Singhpurias possessed Jullundur and many villages in the Malwa region whilst the Kanhaiyas owned territories in the Batala region. The Sukerchakia possessions ranged from Gujranwala to parts of Pothohar and further north.

Motivated as each chieftain was by his own agenda of conquest and consolidation, and despite clashes between them over territory or due to plain greed, the thread that bound them together—besides their unchanging commitment to their faith—was the sense of shared destiny enunciated by the Gurus. Some other aspects of their conduct have been frequently commented upon. "In all contemporary records, mostly in Persian, written generally by Muslims as well as by Maratha agents posted at a number of places in Northern India, there is not a single instance either in Delhi or elsewhere in which the Sikhs raised a finger against women . . ." (Hari Ram Gupta). Nor were Muslims, Afghans or others under them mistreated. Writing of the *misl* period, the distinguished historian Sir Jadunath Sarkar notes that "the Sikhs had now established their rule over much of the Punjab and given to the people of that province internal security and the promotion of agriculture to a degree unknown for sixty years past."

But the tyrant would still show a spasm or two before the gateway to India was slammed in his face by the Sikhs, who ended "the stream of immigration of needy adventurers from Turkistan, Iran, Afghanistan and Baluchistan which had supplied to various Muslim kingdoms in this country nearly all of their distinguished statesmen, eminent politicians, illustrious administrators and celebrated generals . . ."

The two men who couldn't get India out of their system were Ahmed Shah Abdali's son, Timur Shah, and his son Shah Zaman. Timur was married at the age of ten to the Mughal emperor Alamgir II's daughter. His relations with the Sikhs were embittered at the very outset when they plundered his train as he was returning home after his marriage in early 1757. Appointed governor of Lahore by his father shortly thereafter, Timur Shah was driven out of Punjab in April 1758 with the help of the Marathas.

After ascending the Afghan throne on Abdali's death in 1772, Timur spent the first three years tightening his grip on Afghanistan before setting out in January 1775 on the first of five invasions of India. The first did not get him very far into Punjab. And despite Shah Alam II's urgent invitation to his son-in-law to visit Delhi—he had little power by then—it was not till 1779 that Timur returned to India, alarmed by reports "that a strong army of 60,000 Sikhs . . . intended to seize Derah Ismail Khan, Derah Ghazi Khan and Sind." To foil this move, Timur concentrated his forces on recovering Multan from the Sikhs in February 1780, which he followed up by building twenty forts along the line separating Multan from Sikh territories.

Even though the aim of the next invasion in the winter of 1780 was to punish his recalcitrant satraps in Sind, Bahawalpur and elsewhere, the Sikhs, numbering about 20,000 horsemen, attacked Timur Shah's post near Multan and the Afghans sued for peace. The Sikhs realized *rakhi* before returning to Lahore. Five years later, in December 1785, Timur again entered India on the entreaties of Shah Alam II, who wanted him to shore up his declining fortunes, although he knew it was impossible to reach Delhi since the Sikhs held the lands that lay between North-West India and Delhi. This view was endorsed by James Anderson, British Resident at the Scindias, who believed the Shah's advance on Delhi was "impossible . . . as the Shah was not prepared to fight the Sikhs, and the Sikhs will not make peace with him." So Timur returned to Kabul in May 1786 without making any inroads into Punjab.

But the lack of self-esteem of India's people was pitiably evident in the raja of Jodhpur's invitation to Timur urging him to send his forces to Delhi to "defeat the Marathas." The alternative he offered Timur was that "if the Sikhs would not allow him an easy passage through the Punjab, he should march across Multan, Bahawalpur and Bikaner and the Rajput rajas would accompany him to Delhi." When after his last invasion Timur Shah wished to place his son Humayun on the throne of Delhi, he was supported by the rajas of Jaipur and Jodhpur. During his fifth and last invasion in January 1788, Timur again stayed clear of Punjab: "The Sikhs, whom he had known from his childhood, were avoided by him as far as possible, and he never summoned up the courage to attack them in the heart of their country."

Shah Zaman, who succeeded his father Timur in May 1793, was even more keen to restore the Afghan hegemony in Punjab that had been imposed by his grandfather, Ahmed Shah Abdali. But he too failed to take into account the power now wielded by the Sikhs. Despite Zaman's four invasions between 1794 and 1798 and some successes including brief occupations of Lahore, his dreams of conquest came to a sorry end. He enjoyed many advantages over the Sikhs, especially the support of India's Muslim rulers who were willing to rally around him to help restore Muslim pre-eminence in the country. The Mughals of Delhi, Tipu Sultan in the south, the Rohillas of Rampur, the non-Muslim turncoats of India, all offered him every form of assistance ranging from money and materials to men and equipment.

Even the British, propelled by their own ambitions in India, and aware of the promise Hindustan's internal conflicts held for them, were opening their lines of communication to Shah Zaman. They had established their hold up to the Indo-Gangetic plain, with a British Resident at Lucknow, and were fearful of the combination of forces that might be formed against them on Shah Zaman's arrival in India. So the British Governor-General, the Marquis of Wellesley, sent his agent to Shah Zaman's court in Kabul with letters and "presents of precious commodities of China and Europe, some lacs of Gold Mohars [gold coins] and rupees without number." His spies too—or "intelligencers" as they were called—were gathering information on events beyond the Sutlej. The British were keen to form their own alliances in case Shah Zaman should break through Sikh territories and reach Delhi. They were greatly helped in their desire to prevent India slipping out of their hands by the immense scope for intrigue offered by the ceaseless infighting amongst Indians.

Since diplomacy and treachery were two sides of the same coin, the British also used Mehdi Ali Khan, an Iranian adventurer in their service in India, to create a diversion in Afghanistan with the help of Iran's king, Fateh Ali Shah. Mehdi Khan not only successfully prevailed on the Iranian monarch to march into Afghanistan but also persuaded Prince Mahmud of Herat to revolt against Zaman. These developments forced Shah Zaman to cut short his fourth and last invasion in January 1799 and Mehdi Khan received a reward of 300,000 rupees from the British for his efforts. The British, of course, were biding their time for the eventual takeover of India. Since consolidation of Sikh power was at variance with British goals, their strategy called for preventing inroads into India by other powers, while waiting for an appropriate opportunity to destabilize the Sikhs.

The British were not the only ones making overtures to Shah Zaman. Some of the Sikh rajas too, south of the Sutlej and especially of Patiala, were willing to side with him. In a letter to the Governor-General dated 27 December 1796, J. Lumsden, British Resident at Lucknow, reported that "Sahib Singh, the Patiala Sardar, seems to be disposed to unite his interests with those of the Shah . . . [he] is in the habit of maintaining friendly correspondence with the Ministers of the Shah . . ." An accurate assessment, because when Ranjit Singh of the Sukerchakia *misl* wrote to Sahib Singh urging him to join him after a bloody encounter with the Afghans near Amritsar, Sahib Singh sent no reply, but is reported to have said: "I am a Zamindar. I cannot do without meeting the Shah." Even more than that, he seemed to be in awe of the invader. When his messengers returned after offering Sahib Singh's submission and homage to Zaman at Peshawar, and brought with them letters from the Shah, "Sahib Singh received these letters in full court and after applying them to his forehead [signifying profound respect] delivered them to his Munshi to be read out." It was Ranjit Singh who was now emerging as a consistent foe of the Afghans.

The eighteenth century had taken a cruel toll of the Sikhs. According to one "modest" recent estimate: "Guru Gobind Singh, in several battles fought . . . [with] the Mughals, lost about five thousand of his newly created Khalsa. Under Banda Singh, at least twenty-five thousand Sikhs laid down their lives in their fight against the Mughals. After Banda Singh's execution, Abdus Samad Khan, governor of Punjab (1713–26), killed not less than twenty thousand Sikhs. His son and successor, Zakariya Khan (1726–45), was responsible for the death of an equal number. Yahiya Khan (1746–47) destroyed about ten thousand Sikhs in a single campaign after *Chhota Ghalughara*. His brother Shah Nawaz Khan, in 1747, assassinated nearly one thousand Sikhs. Yahiya Khan's brother-in-law, Muin-ul-Mulk (1748–53), slaughtered more than thirty thousand. These rulers were all Turks from Central Asia. Adeena Beg Khan, a Punjabi Arain, put to death at least five thousand in 1758. Ahmed Shah Abdali and his Afghan governors killed around sixty thousand from 1753 to 1767. Abdali's deputy, Najib-ud-

Daulah, also an Afghan, slew nearly twenty thousand. Petty officials and public must have killed four thousand." This total of over 200,000 killed does not include those who fell fighting Timur Shah and his son Zaman.

Notwithstanding the long years of savage persecution, the Sikhs emerged triumphant at the end of the eighteenth century. What of their persecutors? On returning to Afghanistan in 1799 after his last abortive invasion of India, Shah Zaman had to face a revolt by his brother Prince Mahmud. Betrayed by his trusted supporters, he was captured and blinded whilst in custody, ending his days in misery as a pensioner of the British.

As for the Mughals, the countdown to their end, which had begun after Nadir Shah's sack of Delhi in 1739, was hastened by the Sikhs in the north, and by the Marathas and the British to the south, east and west of Delhi. With the British gaining the upper hand, Emperor Shah Alam became their virtual pensioner until he too was blinded by an adventurer, Ghulam Kadir, in 1788. He spent his last years under British protection after the Maratha defeat in 1804. The Mughals continued to survive as British puppets until 1857 when the Indian Mutiny put an end to that pretence. Bahadur Shah, the last Mughal, was exiled to Rangoon where he died as a prisoner of the British.

The British had come a long way. As an Englishman put it in a letter written in 1783: "In the year 1707 when Aurung-Zebe died it may be said without any violation of the truth that Hindostan, whether for its Military Resource, its Wealth or Magnitude, was the most distinguished Empire in the World, and at that period, it is to be noted, that the English were known, only on the Sea Coasts of that Country, and occupied, under many restrictions, merely the Profession of Merchants."

This situation changed dramatically in the nineteenth century, which witnessed Sikh efflorescence under Ranjit Singh, two decisive wars with these ambitious British "merchants" after his death, and the inevitable sunset of the magnificent Sikh Empire thereafter. Not because of its adversary's superior fighting qualities but because of betrayals and bitter infighting within Sikh ranks, all too frequently engineered by the British.

3
Empire of the Sikhs
1801–1839

Not only was the Sikh monarchy "Napoleonic in the suddenness of its rise, the brilliancy of its successes and the completeness of its overthrow"; equally striking were the physical similarities of the two key figures. Both were small and slight. Ranjit Singh had the added disadvantage of a face scarred by an early bout of smallpox which had blinded his left eye, earning him the nickname of Kaana, or "the one-eyed," while Napoleon was known as "the little corporal." They were contemporaries. Astonishingly, their countries also fleetingly figured in each other's calculations despite the 5,000 miles or more that separated them.

Ranjit Singh was born on 13 November 1780, and became chief of the Sukerchakia *misl* after his father Mahan Singh's death on 15 April 1790. At nine years and five months, by a strange coincidence, he was roughly the same age as his father had been when he had become *misl* chief.

His lineage was impressive. His great-grandfather, Budh Singh, had been a legend in his lifetime. He was a giant of a man and a fighter all his life and his body bore over thirty sword and gunshot wounds. He and his beloved piebald mare Desan had swum each of Punjab's five rivers in flood. Budh Singh's feats are a part of Punjab folklore.

Ranjit Singh's grandfather, Charat Singh, had founded the Sukerchakia *misl*, and through deft campaigns brought extensive territories and towns under his control, including Gujranwala, Wazirabad, Pind Dadan Khan, Dhani, Pothohar, Rohtas, Jhelum, Sialkot, Ahmadabad and the salt mines of Kheora. Within less than fifteen years the entire region between the Jhelum and the Indus was in the possession of Charat Singh and the chiefs of the Bhangi *misl*, although the Bhangis would soon be ousted.

On Charat Singh's death in 1770, due to an accidental matchlock burst, his ten-year-old son Mahan Singh succeeded him. He was cast in his father's mould. Mahan Singh's feats of arms won him "so great a reputation that many influential independent Sardars joined his banner. His rapid successes gave him an ascendancy over all the Sikh Chiefs." It was also felt that "if he had lived ten years longer [he was twenty-seven at the time of his death after being taken ill during a battle] he would have become the sole monarch of the whole of modern India from the Khyber Pass to the Ganges and from the Himalayas to the Arabian Sea."

The young Ranjit Singh received no formal education. His passion was horse-riding, and from early boyhood he would spend whole days in the saddle. In adulthood he was to perform prodigious feats of horsemanship, such as riding over a hundred miles in one day, from Lahore to Jhelum, when he heard the news of a favourite general's death, or at full gallop (at fifty years of age) halving a lemon held by a soldier in his palm with his sword without harming him. He had a thorough professional training in musketry and swordsmanship. From an early age he rode into battle with his father and was often in the thick of the fighting. He was completely fearless. His style was one of rustic simplicity; he disliked sitting on a throne, preferring the carpeted floor, or squatting Punjabi-style on a chair. Throughout his life he was most at home in the saddle, and K.S. Duggal thus describes the impression he is said to have made: "The moment he sat on horseback, his ill-looking countenance was completely transformed. Every muscle of his body seemed to vibrate. There was a glow on his face . . ."

There are many accounts of Ranjit Singh's fearlessness. At the age of seventeen, for example, laying siege, with other *misl* chiefs, to Lahore which had just been taken without a fight from the Bhangi *misl* by the powerful forces of the Afghan ruler Shah Zaman, Ranjit went and stood below the tower in which the Afghan usually sat and in a loud voice announced: "Behold, grandson of Ahmed Shah. Here is a grandson of Sardar Charat Singh come to meet you. Come, if you dare, and accept his challenge." Zaman declined. On another occasion Ranjit Singh's reply to a message from Zaman asking for gifts was that the "presents would be delivered to the invader on the field of battle."

Ranjit Singh saw the unification of the *misls*, by force or whatever means possible, as his foremost priority, and the first, very agreeable opportunity towards this end was provided by his marriage to Mehtab Kaur, daughter of Sada Kaur, widow of the Kanhaiya *misl* chief. By engaging her daughter to him, Sada Kaur skilfully created conditions for taking control of the Kanhaiya *misl* herself. In the words of the historian Syad Muhammad Latif: "The wisdom and energy of this extraordinary woman, one of the most artful and ambitious of her sex that ever figured in Sikh history, contributed materially to the success of Ranjit Singh in his early exploits . . . she was the ladder by which Ranjit Singh reached the summit of his power." Ranjit Singh's own statesmanlike moves, even at his young age, also helped him win over further *misl* chieftains. Others had to be subjugated—and this he would do at the beginning of the new century.

Although it brought a successful political alliance, the marriage to Mehtab Kaur did not, in fact, work for either side, and in 1798 Ranjit Singh took the opportunity of securing another *misl* alliance by marrying the Nakkai chief's sister Raj Kaur.

In 1799 the Sukerchakia chief turned his attention to the Bhangi *misl*, which had retaken Lahore from the weakened Afghans. On 6 July he entered the city by a swift military move, to be greeted by a populace fed up with the repressive ways of the dissolute Bhangis. The Bhangi chiefs were irked by the dynamic presence of the ambitious young Sukerchakia chief in their citadel, but there was no stopping him, and within days of entering Lahore he had brought it under his control. Not yet nineteen, he was now undisputed overlord of Lahore, for centuries a symbol of Islamic power.

The palpable hostility of the other Sikh chiefs and leaders of the Pathan principalities—remnants of Afghan rule—notwithstanding, Ranjit Singh set about establishing his Darbar (court) and his authority in the countryside and the city that was to become the capital of his empire. He forbade his soldiers from harassing, molesting or robbing citizens, and for the first time in decades the people of Lahore enjoyed peace and security.

Since the new young ruler of Lahore did not decapitate his defeated adversaries as was the custom of those times, but treated them with magnanimity, the Bhangis were allowed to leave the city unscathed. But they were smarting from their humiliating defeat, and it wasn't long before they combined with others equally hostile to Ranjit's rising star. Early in 1800 they marched on Lahore. In their ranks was Niza-muddin Khan, nawab of Kasur, who, seeing himself as the leader of Punjab's Muslims, had helped Shah Zaman in his efforts to restore Afghan rule over Punjab; his own secret ambition was to become governor of Lahore. So he too was concerned by the Sukerchakias' annex-ation of Lahore, as was Jassa Singh Ramgarhia, whom the Bhangis also invited to join them. The combined force which set out from the Bhangi stronghold of Amritsar was routed by Ranjit Singh ten miles from Lahore. But it was not to be until 1809 that he took over the Bhangi territories, to be followed by the Ramgarhia lands a few years later.

At this stage Ranjit Singh's empire was no more than a distant dream. However, on Baisakhi Day in April 1801, at the age of 20, he had him-self crowned Maharaja of Punjab. The proclamation was proof of his confidence and élan, qualities that contributed to his successes during the 38 years he occupied the throne—the age of Sikh ascendance.

In the early style of the young ruler his mature hallmarks—the lib-eralism and breadth of vision that went along with a sure grasp of pre-vailing political realities—are already apparent. Keenly aware that the overwhelming majority of his new subjects were Muslims, he did noth-ing to upset or alienate them. He continued to grant state support to the leading mosques in Lahore and confirmed the jurisdiction of Islamic law over Muslims. He appointed Muslim and Hindu officers in his army. His home minister and his foreign minister were Muslims—the brothers Nur-ud-Din and Aziz-ud-Din, sons of an eminent physi-cian who treated Ranjit Singh's eye after the conquest of Lahore; and he relied on a third brother, Imam-ud-Din, to carry out important tasks.

The coin minted on the occasion of the Maharaja's coronation bore a verse in Persian:

My largesse, my victories, my unalloyed fame
I owe to Guru Nanak and Guru Gobind Singh

It did not bear the name of Ranjit Singh. In the same spirit he ensured that in his régime there would be no discrimination against any faith. To Aziz-ud-Din he once said: "God intended that I look upon all religions with one eye; that is why I was deprived of the other eye."

As for his personal style, the Maharaja soon developed an incredible capacity for bacchanalian revelries, which often lasted throughout the night. And yet early the next morning he would go on long and furious gallops across the countryside on his favourite steed. He was no less zestful where women were concerned. He was to be married twenty times (although there is disagreement on this number), and in addition acquire a harem of enviable size and variety. He was a driven man, propelled by his own personal agenda of conquest and consolidation, and during the periods he had time to indulge himself, his indulgences were prodigious.

The Sukerchakia *misl* that Ranjit Singh had inherited lay on the direct route of invading armies from Afghanistan and beyond. Enlarged into a formidable kingdom, it attracted the attention of several European powers including France, Russia and of course Britain, intent on her own agenda of conquest and consolidation in the subcontinent. With the Marathas in the south-east and the Kangra chieftains and the Gurkhas in the north and north-east also eyeing Punjab's territories, in addition to the Afghans in the north-west, and encouraged by fratricidal conflicts between *misl* chiefs, the challenges that Ranjit Singh faced, when he crowned himself Maharaja of Lahore in April 1801, were considerable. But he was unfazed.

Besides securing alliances with the Kanhaiya and Nakkai *misls* through his marriages, Ranjit also formed a close friendship with Fateh Singh Ahluwalia, grandson of Jassa Singh Ahluwalia who was universally admired by the Sikhs. Becoming *misl* chief in 1801 at the age of twelve, Fateh Singh quickly realized that the powerful Sukerchakia ruler and new-crowned Maharaja represented the future and that an alliance with him was the only sensible course that the Ahluwalias could take. So in 1802 the two chiefs exchanged turbans as a sign of lasting friendship, pledging their brotherhood before the Guru

Granth Sahib. The Sukerchakia, Kanhaiya and Ahluwalia coalition, writes one biographer of Ranjit, "based on kinship and political friendship, served as the ladder by which Ranjit Singh climbed to political supremacy." As was evident to all, "the initiative always rested with the Lahore chief."

Ironically, even the marriage ties that linked the Nakkais and Kanhaiyas to Ranjit Singh did not prevent their absorption by the Lahore Darbar. The Nakkai territories were annexed in 1811, but the Kanhaiya lands took longer because of Sada Kaur's powerful personality and matching ambitions. In the early years of Ranjit Singh's struggle to establish himself, his mother-in-law had proved a formidable ally, helping galvanize support for him from other chieftains and taking to the battlefield whenever necessary. But her driving ambitions led to their estrangement, which increased with her daughter Mehtab Kaur's death in 1810.

The final break came when Sada Kaur crossed the Sutlej to seek British help. An incensed Ranjit Singh induced her to return to Lahore, then promptly confined her to the Lahore Fort. He took over the Kanhaiya territories, and kept her in Lahore—except for time spent in Amritsar—from 1821 until her death in 1832. "The high-spirited Sada Kaur" has been called "one of the most remarkable women in the history of the Punjab."

Ranjit Singh's consolidation of his control over Punjab continued with the annexation of the Karorsinghia, Singhpuria and Dallewalia *misls*. The circumstance of each of these differed: one was absorbed on the death of a chief, another through conquest, yet another through negotiation. But Ranjit Singh was not vindictive to the vanquished and settled handsome estates or stipends on those whose territories he took over. "While those of the royal blood are all but begging their bread at Delhi and Kabul, he almost invariably provides for the families of his conquered enemies," noted Major H.M.L. Lawrence, Political Agent in charge of British relations with Lahore.

Since the fate of some of the *misls* had to do with their location in the Majha or Malwa regions of Punjab, some explanation of these is called for. Majha is the southern stretch of the Bari Doab between the Rivers Beas and Ravi—*doab* meaning the tract of land that lies between two rivers. Lahore and Amritsar lie in the Majha region. Malwa on the other hand is the territory south of the Sutlej, and the Sikhs of this region, which at one time bordered on Delhi, are known as Malwa Sikhs. The principal constituents of the Phulkian *misl*, the foremost in the Malwa region, were Patiala, Nabha and Jind, and their leader was Patiala.

The Patiala chiefs were no great exemplars of the sense of self-esteem that had fuelled the Sikhs' drive towards a distinctive disposition and character. They were prone to relegate pride to a secondary position, and their prime concern had been survival—often at the cost of self-respect. It is scarcely surprising that after the *Wada Ghalughara*—great disaster—of February 1762, when Ahmed Shah Abdali had slain thousands of Sikhs, including women and children, he had "embraced Ala Singh [of Patiala] and bestowed on him a dress of honour with the title of Raja." That the Patiala chief, taken prisoner in the battle preceding the *Wada Ghalughara*, had paid a ransom of half a million rupees for his freedom might also have contributed to his subsequent lack of pride and spirit.

The same pattern is seen when the Patiala Chief Sahib Singh's emissaries offered his submission and homage to Shah Zaman at Peshawar, at a time when Zaman was planning to invade India, and *after* Sahib Singh had turned down Ranjit Singh's request for assistance in fighting the Afghan invader. So, true to form, Patiala and the other Phulkian chiefs turned to the British for protection after Ranjit Singh had taken care of the Afghans. They preferred outsiders—by the end of the eighteenth century a powerful presence on the subcontinent—to Ranjit Singh.

This craven submission to Delhi's rulers went back a long way. In a memorandum—which "ultimately shaped British policy towards the *cis*-Sutlej region"—a deputation from states south of ("*cis*," "on this side of," from the British point of view) the river met Archibald Seton, the British Resident in Delhi, and assured him "that if protection were granted to them, they would remain loyal to the British forever." Chain Singh, the Patiala *diwan* or chief minister, was at particular pains to trace the history of the Patiala family's loyalty to Delhi's rulers. For much of the eighteenth century, from Muhammad Shah's reign through the Abdali (Durrani) invasions to the time Nawab Najib-ud-

Daulah became Delhi's master on behalf of the Kabul king, the Patiala chiefs had given their loyalty to whoever was in power. So it had continued. "When the British became masters of Delhi, they [the Patiala chiefs] placed their services at Lord Lake's orders," and the latter responded by announcing that "Puttealeh, Jeend, Kheytul and the Nabeh, with all the country belonging to them, were under the protection of the British."

The East India Company's representatives saw the potential of the emotional and physical divide offered by the Sikhs and the Sutlej. Although in 1803 Ranjit Singh had himself suggested to Lord Lake, commander-in-chief of the Company's forces, that the Sutlej should be treated as the boundary between the Sikh and British spheres of influence, privately the British, after defeating the Marathas who held sway north of Delhi and up to the Sutlej, looked upon the Jamuna—the great river which rises in the Himalayas and flows down to the plains and after passing Delhi, Agra and other towns joins the River Ganges near Allahabad in the State of Uttar Pradesh—as the natural frontier between them and India's unconquered territories north of it. There was an ongoing clash about this within the Company between the expansionists and the moderates, with the former favouring a forward policy of conquest and annexation, and viewing the *status quo*–ists as "cold and servile formalists." Even the paterfamilias of the expansionists, the Governor-General, Lord Wellesley, was "growing thoughtful of late" because territorial expansion was driving the Company to financial bankruptcy. Whilst he had earlier favoured defensive alliances with those on its border whom the Company could not defeat, the shortcomings of this policy where the Marathas were concerned, especially the ruler of Gwalior State, Scindia, had confirmed him in his view that the answer lay in total subjugation.

So when Ranjit Singh offered the Sutlej as a boundary in 1803, Wellesley was undecided, which suited Ranjit Singh. Invited to mediate in a tiff between the raja and rani of Patiala in 1806, he happily crossed the Sutlej and did so again in 1807 and 1808. Each visit brought with it further annexations, some of the lands from which he kept, whilst others were redistributed to win allies.

Inevitably, as Ranjit Singh's hold south of the Sutlej increased, so did a sense of alarm in the Sikh chiefs of the area. They called on the

British Resident in Delhi in March 1808 to seek the Company's protection but "were sent away with courteous words but no more." In 1808, according to one assessment, the British were still "not conscious that behind the bold, bad barons of the Doab lay the primitive energies of the Khalsa." What they were in no doubt of, however, was "that in the Punjab one of the Sikh Chiefs was rising to an authority that might make him worthy of diplomatic considerations." Indeed, Britain was feeling a pressing need for some deft diplomatic manoeuvring.

Her continuing wars with Napoleon during this period had led to a realignment of forces in the wake of successive French victories, the most worrying for Britain being the treaty signed by Napoleon and Tsar Alexander I at Tilsit in 1807. The British saw a danger to India in the reconciliation of these two since French agents were already active in Turkey and Persia, and London was apprehensive of a possible Franco-Russian thrust against India. France and Persia were, in fact, allies following the Treaty of Finkenstein, one of the principal articles of which required the Shah of Persia to break diplomatic and commercial relations with Britain and to give passage to a French army should Napoleon decide to attack India. But by the time Lord Minto, the Company's Governor-General in India, sent an envoy to Persia, the Persians were already disillusioned with Napoleon. They felt he had sacrificed their interests in his talks with the Tsar at Tilsit.

Against the backdrop of these concerns, the view that eventually prevailed within the Company was that while the Jamuna as a boundary between them and their Indian adversaries was perfectly acceptable, it would be inadequate if the French and Russians appeared on the scene. The danger to Delhi and other British territories would then be grave. Thus the decision was taken to send four diplomatic missions to Lahore, Sind, Kabul and Persia, in order to find ways of stopping the invaders as far as possible from the Company's territories.

Was this really the *raison d'être* for these four missions? Or was "the fear of French intrigue, which had operated so powerfully in extending the red line of British dominion on the map of Southern India, to exercise a similar influence in a new direction?" Was the Francophobia which so affected statesmen in London used by the young adventurers in the Company's pay in India to make their fortunes through acquisition of new territories, and the power, status and wealth which flowed from that? In the context of the mission to Lahore, "the negotiations with Ranjit Singh were in fact to turn so little on French affairs, that it might be permissible to suspect Napoleon of being in this case a mere red herring, and the mission of being sent to initiate a penetration of the Punjab."

The man chosen for the Lahore mission was Charles Theophilus Metcalfe, aged 23. Ranjit Singh was now 28. Born in 1785 in Calcutta, where his father had prospered before returning to England to become a director of the East India Company, Metcalfe returned to India in 1801 to seek his own fortune in the Company's service at the age of sixteen. "A stripling from the fifth form at Eton was suddenly converted in his teens into an Indian administrator, and launched at once into a sea of temptation . . . ," a nineteenth-century writer comments. Although he hated India at first and was keen to go back to England, Metcalfe was soon won over, if not converted to Wellesley's hawkish policies. He was Assistant to the Resident of Delhi—where the British writ over the blind and infirm Mughal Emperor Shah Alam now prevailed—when he was asked to head the Lahore mission. In time he would mature into an able British administrator, but at this stage of his career he had a lot to learn.

Metcalfe crossed the Sutlej on 1 September 1808 and was received by Ranjit Singh at Kasur on 12 September. The next eight months were by all accounts stormy, given the stated purpose of the Metcalfe mission: to alert Ranjit Singh to the French threat and to the danger of European invaders from the north. Its covert purpose, however, was to probe, assess and evaluate Ranjit Singh's strengths and weaknesses. Archibald Seton, the British Resident at Delhi, in a letter dated 17 October 1808 to his Foreign Secretary, N.B. Edmonstone, described Ranjit Singh as "an ambitious, restless and warlike character . . . whose conduct and growing power it is necessary to watch with a jealous and vigilant attention."

Another important part of Metcalfe's brief was to persuade Ranjit Singh to accept Britain's suzerainty over territories south of the Sutlej. When the matter came up the Maharaja was understandably exasperated by the impudence of this demand. Proving himself more than a match for Metcalfe in the art of negotiation, he was not as naïve or new to diplomacy as the British had hoped. Easily seeing through the Napoleon ploy, he expressed his complete willingness to side with the British in the event of a French invasion. But English suzerainty south of the Sutlej was a different matter altogether. A rueful British comment on Metcalfe's inability to play the French card to the hilt aptly summed it up: "In this wild encampment the bogey of Napoleon could not look so convincing as in the dining rooms of Calcutta and Delhi."

Brushing aside Metcalfe's bluster about British commitments to the various chiefs south of the Sutlej, Ranjit Singh startled the envoy, who after going to bed on the evening of 24 September following prolonged discussions with Ranjit's advisers, arose the next morning to find the Sikh army moving off. The Maharaja was on his way south and had left word for Metcalfe to follow. The indignant envoy, little relishing this diplomacy "on the run," sat in his tent and vented his feelings in a warm dispatch to Calcutta. With no option but to follow, Metcalfe too left Kasur on 27 September and caught up with Ranjit Singh and his army the next day. The renewed talks were affable but that was about all, although Ranjit Singh seemed to be greatly enjoying the cat-and-mouse game of diplomacy.

Not that he allowed it to come in the way of his immediate objective of crossing the Sutlej and marching towards Faridkot, one of the Phulkian states. It surrendered on 1 October. Metcalfe followed him the next day. As the negotiations continued, this time over the first draft of a treaty, Ranjit Singh kept moving and so did Metcalfe. Clearly, Ranjit Singh's strategy was to have the entire region witness Metcalfe's presence alongside the Sikh forces so that the message would be clear: the British were acquiescing in the disciplining of the Phulkian chiefs. The British of course were far from approving of Ranjit Singh's actions, but Metcalfe was being carried along by the sheer momentum generated by the Maharaja.

The despondent British Resident in Delhi, finding it difficult to keep track of Metcalfe's movements, found Ranjit Singh "so very restless and unsteady that it is almost impossible to form a true judgment as to his real plans or probable movements." Which is precisely what Ranjit Singh wanted. Far from being unsteady, Ranjit Singh was quite clear about his plans and movements, but just as the British were not ready to disclose their plans, neither was he. Seton was also worried about the Patiala chief, who he said "labours at this moment under the most cruel anxiety and alarm less Ranjit Singh attack him." By the end of October, Metcalfe, realizing that his presence by Ranjit Singh's side during the annexation of territories by him was compromising Britain's territorial aims south of the Sutlej, decided to return to a place called Gongrana to await the Maharaja there, while continuing to be in energetic contact with his headquarters in Calcutta. Ranjit Singh continued with his conquests.

The Company's policy was about to change. The Governor-General, Lord Minto, who had once inclined towards "imperturbable forbearance and scrupulous non-intervention," now "could not resist the conviction that the interests and security of the British Government would be best promoted by the reduction, if not the entire subversion of his [Ranjit Singh's] power." Since the danger of a French invasion of India was receding—assuming it had existed in the first place—the British were no longer willing to trade their territorial ambitions south of the Sutlej for an alliance against an ambiguous threat from the north. So whilst Metcalfe was instructed to drag out his negotiations with Ranjit Singh, Lieutenant-Colonel David Ochterlony was asked to proceed from Allahabad to Delhi and assemble an expeditionary force there, then advance to the Sutlej to establish a British protectorate over territories lying between the Jamuna and Sutlej.

The Sikhs, once strenuously wooed as prospective allies, would if necessary be met with force of arms since the circumstances had changed. The British now projected themselves as successors of the Marathas whom they had defeated, and since they had held sway over these lands for a while, they claimed them as British—somewhat con-voluted reasoning, but quite justified in the heady days of conquest and expansion, and especially if cloaked with a nobility of purpose. In this case, Ranjit Singh's dominance of the Phulkian chiefs—Patiala fore-most amongst them—provided the necessary legitimacy, although the British had clearly decided that as an internal report put it, their "troops would advance with or without the consent of those chiefs."

Ranjit Singh's return to Lahore towards the end of 1808 coincided with the British decision to send the Ochterlony expedition to the Sut-lej, although the Maharaja was unaware of it. During the two months or so of his trans-Sutlej campaign he had annexed Faridkot, Ambala, Shahbad, imposed levies on Malerkotla and Thanesar, and taken over and redistributed several other estates. He heard of the British military moves on returning home, and from Metcalfe as well, at their meeting on 21 December 1808. What the envoy conveyed was that even if the chiefs wanted to side with Ranjit Singh, "the British Government would not admit that they had any right to throw off their allegiance and to subject themselves to another power without its permission." British intentions were now becoming clearer.

Seeing that negotiations to establish his right to territories south of the Sutlej were pointless, Ranjit Singh ordered General Mohkam Chand, one of his finest commanders—and a man who had very little time for the British—to march with an adequate force on Phillaur, which faced Ludhiana across the River Sutlej. The British response was to order Ochterlony to Ludhiana. Whilst en route, he passed Patiala and Nabha and was enthusiastically received.

These warlike moves led Metcalfe to wonder, in a communication to the Commander-in-Chief, whether it wasn't time for him to leave. The C-in-C suggested he "delay his departure." Towards the end of January 1809, as British troops advanced on Ludhiana, the detachment left by Ranjit Singh at Ambala withdrew to a point south of the Sutlej. At this stage British intelligence again indicated the possibility of a renewed French threat, so on 23 January 1809 the British C-in-C was confidentially told to withdraw his military force from its advance position, because Ranjit Singh had again become important as the indomitable defender of India's northern reaches. More eager than his peers, Metcalfe, as officially reported, "did not judge it expedient to acquaint the Rajah with the intention of the British Government to withdraw the detachment from Ludhiana."

After months of negotiations Ranjit Singh agreed to the terms of a treaty which, whilst stipulating the return of his recent conquests south of the Sutlej, would not require his relinquishing sovereignty over those acquired earlier, from 1806 onwards. The Sutlej Treaty was signed at Amritsar on 25 April 1809. It had three main points: "perpetual friendship"; that Ranjit Singh would not maintain "more troops than are necessary for the internal duties" of his territories on the left bank (i.e., south) of the River Sutlej, "nor commit or suffer any encroachments on the possessions or rights of the Chiefs in its vicinity"; that if these articles were violated, or if there was a "departure from the rules of friendship" the Treaty would be considered null and void.

Why did Ranjit Singh undertake his successful expedition south of the Sutlej only to acknowledge British suzerainty over the lands between the Sutlej and Jamuna? Why didn't he engage the British and push them beyond the Jamuna? What accounts for his eight months of constant activity from Metcalfe's arrival till the Treaty's signing? In the answers to these questions lies the key to Ranjit Singh's character and vision. No person could have built an empire on the foundations of a small *misl*, as Ranjit Singh did, unless he was able to judge his own limitations and the adversary's advantages objectively. Some critics suggest that the Treaty's "weakness lay in the fact that it forever put an end to the pretensions of Ranjit Singh to exclusive sovereignty over the entire population of the Sikhs living between the Jamuna and Indus" and that it was "tantamount to a confession of defeat . . . in the game of diplomacy as well as of war."

Such assessments show ignorance of Ranjit Singh's make-up. More than a canny observer of the war-torn subcontinent, he was also a military general, political leader, diplomat and arbiter of his kingdom's destiny. His moves were based on a clear-headed perception of his adversary's potential; on his knowledge of British artillery, ammunition, equipment and other hardware, and the drill and discipline of the Company's troops. He was equally aware of the advantages Britain's hold on India gave her, in the form of limitless resources to back up a war; resources far more than his own. In keeping himself informed about them he did not rely only on reports brought to him. Knowing that the British could not have succeeded to the extent they had without trying every means of cajolery, coercion, trickery or bribery against their adversaries, he chose to take a calculated risk by personally assessing the extent to which the British would accept his territorial ambitions. His sagacity and "sense of limits" played a key role in his successes both on the battlefield and in diplomacy, as did his clear understanding of his adversary's strengths and weaknesses. This is illustrated by his reaction when, on seeing a map of India with areas under British control tinted in red, he is said to have remarked: "The whole map will be red one day." According to H.M.L. Lawrence, who served in Ranjit Singh's army, "his whole conduct showed that he had from the outset penetration enough to estimate justly his own power and that of the English."

In a sense, he was more successful than Metcalfe in his mission. Sir Lepel Griffin, writing sixty years or so later, felt that despite Ranjit Singh's warlike moves in early 1809, he was not seriously contemplating war even if "Mr. Metcalfe certainly believed him to be so." Griffin's view is that at that time "the great sagacity and shrewdness of the Maharaja were only imperfectly known and it was more probable that he was only playing a game of brag to the last, in the hope that the British Government might withdraw a portion of their demands." To this end the Maharaja was partially successful, because whilst ceding recent conquests he did retain his earlier ones. It has been suggested that had Ranjit Singh's successors only followed "in his footsteps and kept firm control of the army and over the administration . . . the boundary of the British Empire in India might well have been the south bank of the Sutlej still, as fixed by the Treaty of 1809." (This was written prior to 1947.)

Ranjit Singh had no illusions about the British. Nor they about him. He knew he had to secure his southern boundary if other more important matters were to be attended to, such as the conquest of Multan, Kashmir, Attock, Peshawar and Derajat and the expulsion of Afghans from these territories of Punjab. He also had his eyes on Kabul, but before that he had to discipline the hill states, and eject the Afghans from Jammu and Kashmir. He could not attend to any of these if he was constantly threatened on his southern flank. Accordingly, even before the end of 1809 he moved to give shape to his blueprint of future conquests.

Kangra was the first on his list. Its wily chief, Sansar Chand Katoch, a one-time ally of the Afghans, who had some years earlier nursed his own ambitions towards Punjab and had twice invaded its fringes, was now in trouble. Besieged by the Gurkhas—who had emerged from Nepal in search of new territories and were now at Kangra's doorstep—he desperately needed help against them and their charismatic general, Amar Singh Thapa. Sansar Chand's appeal for help offered the opportunity Ranjit Singh was waiting for.

After making the shaken Sansar Chand accept Kangra as a part of Punjab, and on his agreeing to surrender Kangra fort, the Maharaja's forces arrived to find Sansar Chand trying to wriggle out of his pledge. But he hadn't reckoned on his adversary. Ranjit Singh had the Kangra chief's son taken hostage, to be released only when the fort was opened to Sikh troops; which was on 24 August 1809 after their decisive victory over the Gurkhas at Ganesh Ghati. Exactly four months later, on 24 December 1809, the Maharaja himself paid a ceremonial visit to receive homage from the various hill rajas including those of Kangra, Kulu, Nurpur, Chamba and others.

On his next visit to select a bride for his adopted son Hira Singh, Ranjit Singh acquired two more for himself. Rani Mehtab Devi (also known as Guddo) and her sister Rani Raj Banso, both daughters of Raja Sansar Chand, became his favourites and exercised enormous influence on him. They were fifth and sixth in an impressive number of wives!

After he had witnessed hand-to-hand fighting between the Sikhs and Gurkhas at Ganesh Ghati, Ranjit Singh's admiration for their fighting qualities resulted in the raising of a Gurkha contingent for his own army. He also took Bhopal Singh Thapa, son of the Gurkha commander Amar Singh Thapa, into his service, paving the way for the possibilities of close ties with Nepal—a kingdom which would not be too far from his territories after the Sikh conquest of Ladakh in 1834.

Ranjit Singh's annexation of the Kangra and Kulu regions led to a flowering of his love for Pahari paintings (hill artists' miniatures). His increasing patronage of artists from the Jammu, Kangra and Kulu areas of the Punjab hills provided a powerful stimulus to the region's Guler, Basholi, Mandi and Bilaspur schools of painting. In the style of Mughal and Rajasthani miniatures, small in size with fine and sensitive details, these paintings covered everything from religious art to lyrical renderings of different seasons of the year, landscapes to courtly glamour and portraits.

The arrival of the Sikhs in these parts was resented both by the former princely patrons of the arts and for a while by the artists also, who viewed them as a cultural intrusion. But their attitude changed with the enthusiastic patronage of Ranjit Singh and his son Sher Singh, governor of Kangra state, and Desa Singh Majithia, governor of Guler. The mutual regard between the painters and their Sikh patrons grew from 1810 to 1830, when many of them moved to Lahore and Amritsar. A Kangra artist's mural adorns the Harmandir in the Darbar Sahib.

With Kangra secured, Ranjit Singh's thoughts turned to other conquests. Not that his generals had been idle during this time. There had been rapid and sizeable gains in territory: Jullundur, Jammu, the hill states of Mandi and Suket, the salt mines of Kheora, the town of Gujrat on the River Chenab, and Hallowal, Daska and Mangla on the River Jhelum had been brought into the Kingdom's fold within less than two years of the signature of the Sutlej Treaty.

Multan, next on the Maharaja's agenda, was a western city still controlled by the Afghans. Its governor, Muzaffar Khan, respected for his courage and fighting qualities, had repulsed many attacks against his state by Sikh chiefs and Afghan tribes hostile to him. Amongst those who coveted Multan was Shah Shuja, who had ascended the Afghan throne after his brother Shah Zaman was blinded by their third brother Mahmud. Not long after coming to power, Shuja had himself been thrown out to make way for Mahmud. He had escaped to India and now sought a meeting with Ranjit Singh to seek his help in getting back his throne.

Ranjit Singh, while receiving Shuja with ceremony, understood the danger of allowing an aspirant to the Afghan throne to establish a base in Multan, which he saw as a natural part of Punjab. Considering it prudent to invest Multan himself, he arrived outside the city in February 1810 and soon annexed it. But the formidable fort under Muzaffar Khan held out, and the Sikh forces withdrew after receiving tribute from him.

Since other things now occupied Ranjit Singh, Multan had to wait for a while. Shah Shuja, who had returned to Afghanistan for a short spell on the throne, was back in India after being thrown out again. This time he arrived in Attock as a guest of its governor, Jahan Dad Khan. The latter, learning that Shuja was in contact with the power behind the Afghan throne, Wazir Fateh Khan, whom Dad Khan detested, manacled and despatched Shuja to his brother, Ata Mohammed, governor of Kashmir.

This was only a part of the Afghan problem. Another former Afghan ruler and frequent invader of India, the blinded Shah Zaman, was now a resident of Rawalpindi, living—like members of Shuja's family—on a pension provided by Ranjit Singh. After reports reached Ranjit Singh that the irrepressible Zaman was in touch with outside powers for help to regain his throne, he had both the families brought to Lahore to be kept under observation, though they were received with honour as state guests.

Shuja's wife, Wafa Begum, now entered the scene. Frantic over her husband's fate, she begged Ranjit Singh to get him out of Ata Mohammed's clutches in Kashmir before the latter dispatched him, in the style of her fellow Afghans. She also offered Ranjit the Koh-i-noor Diamond in return for sending a military expedition to Kashmir.

This fabled diamond embodied both the romance and the violence of India, Persia and Afghanistan—the three countries it travelled to before being taken to Britain. Its origins are obscure. The Persian diplomat and scholar Iradj Amini raises interesting questions in his excellent book on the diamond: "Was it the same as the Samantik Mani, the diamond that adorned the bracelet of Kama and Arjuna, legendary heroes of the *Mahabharata*? Or was it 'Babur's diamond' as most historians and mineralogists seemed to think? It might even be the 'Great Mughal,' the enormous stone that the French traveller and jeweller Jean-Baptiste Tavernier saw in the court of the Emperor Aurangzeb in 1665."

The Koh-i-noor Diamond was seized around 1306 by Ala-ud-din Khilji, Delhi's ruling Sultan, from Rai Mahlak Deo, ruler of Malwa in the Deccan. It then fell into the hands of Babur, via Emperor Ibrahim Lodhi of the Lodhi Dynasty (1517–26). Babur recounts in his memoirs that "every appraiser has estimated its value at two-and-a-half days' food for the whole world. Apparently it weighs eight misqals [approximately 188 carats]. Humayun [his son] offered it to me when I arrived at Agra; I just gave it back to him." After Babur's death in 1530, the diamond seems to have changed hands by gift, from motives of gratitude for services rendered and proselytism, from Babur's son Humayun to

Shah Tahmasp of Persia to the ruler of a petty kingdom in the Deccan before disappearing for a hundred years and reappearing at the court of the Mughal Emperor Shah Jahan (great-grandson of Humayun) in 1656. It remained with the Mughals until the sadistic Persian Nadir Shah made off with it when he sacked Delhi in 1739 (slaughtering 100,000 Muslims and Hindus in eight hours); it was he who gave the diamond its name, which means "mountain of light." When Nadir was hacked to death in a savage family coup in 1747, the Afghan Abdali took the Koh-i-noor from his body; it then passed to his son and successor Timur and next to the latter's son and unsuccessful successor Zaman who, though imprisoned and blinded, managed to save the diamond for his brother Shuja who had stood by him and who eventually occupied the Afghan throne for the customary short time.

Shah Shuja and his wife Wafa Begum, having pledged the Koh-i-noor to Ranjit Singh in return for Shuja's rescue, were reluctant to part with it once the former Shah was safely back in Lahore. But Ranjit Singh was having none of it, and his will prevailed when the diamond was handed over to him on 1 June 1813. Two years later Shuja left for Ludhiana on the south bank of the Sutlej, to become a pensioner of the British at 48,000 rupees per year. Shah Zaman was given 24,000 rupees annually. Even though both brothers left India for about three years to try to regain the throne of Kabul, they were back under British protection by 1821, their dreams of empire extinguished forever.

Ranjit Singh's other unfinished business included Kabul's continuing control of Kashmir, Attock, Multan and Peshawar. There was also the meddlesome Afghan Wazir Fateh Khan, head of the Barakzai tribe, to be dealt with. His writ ran large in Afghanistan and his burning hatred of Shah Zaman—who had executed his father—had been the cause of Zaman's blinding. Fateh Khan was keen to find Shah Shuja too, currently languishing in the dungeons of the governor of Kashmir. Fateh Khan first tried to get to Kashmir with his own forces but finding himself face to face with a Sikh army near Attock—proof of the Maharaja's determination to keep all aliens out of Punjab—he realized that the invasion of Kashmir could succeed only with Ranjit's collaboration. So he proposed a joint expedition. Once the modalities—to the Lahore Darbar's advantage—were settled, a combined force set out for Shergarh, where Shuja was imprisoned, to take him into custody and bring its governor to heel.

Diwan Mohkam Chand, the commander of the Sikh army, saw through the wily ways of the Afghan within days and informed his master accordingly. Ranjit was unperturbed. He directed Mohkam Chand to give no indication of his doubts to Fateh Khan, who would be dealt with if he double-crossed them. Which he soon did. He tried to steal a march on the Sikhs and reach Shergarh first so that he could lay his hands on Shuja and the treasury. Mohkam Chand, however, took a shorter, more precipitous and little-known route to reach Shergarh first, and the Afghans arrived after the Sikhs had already mounted their assault on the fort. When its resistance caved in the Afghans spent their time in ransacking the treasury whilst the Sikhs searched the fort for Shuja. He was spirited away to the Sikh encampment despite the danger of an armed showdown between the Sikh and Afghan forces.

To show an infuriated Fateh Khan that he did not take kindly to deceit, Ranjit now convinced Jahan Dad Khan, Attock's governor, that the only course open to him was to hand over Attock and its fort to the Sikhs. This made sense to Jahan Dad, who had no illusions about how long he would last if Fateh Khan laid hands on him. He was offered a *jagir* (tenure of land) in compensation by Ranjit Singh, and Attock was handed over to the Sikhs in 1814. The Afghans had held it for over 800 years, ever since the days of Raja Jaipal's defeat by Mahmud of Ghazni.

Fateh Khan was incensed at this loss of control of a major invasion route into India, located at the confluence of the Rivers Indus and Kabul. Reaching Peshawar, he assembled the tribal leaders of the region and whipped up a *jehad*-like frenzy against Ranjit Singh, at the same time sending an ultimatum to Lahore asking for Attock's return. Ranjit shrugged it off. As it happened, he had long nurtured a wish to smash the Afghan hold on Peshawar, and with it the Afghan reputation for military prowess. He wanted to turn Peshawar round and make it the gateway to Kabul and beyond, not the gateway to India as it had been for centuries.

But before Peshawar, Multan—which had tenaciously held out for four years despite several Sikh attempts to invest it—had to be subdued. Its doughty commander, Nawab Muzaffar Khan, a brave Afghan warrior, was determined to fight to the bitter end along with his many sons when a do-or-die assault was mounted against him early in 1818. He fought with courage, and a deep conviction that this was a holy war in which the believers must prevail over the infidels. But the infidels too in this case had their own beliefs to sustain them, and when Multan fell after a siege which lasted over three months, its gallant commander died fighting in hand-to-hand combat.

Two key factors contributed to the fall of Multan: Zam Zama, the great cannon which Abdali had brought to India, and the Nihangs—the legendary and fanatical fighters who had, with utter disregard for life, spearheaded many Sikh victories since Guru Gobind Singh's time. The Zam Zama, one of the most formidable cannons in that part of the world, which had helped Abdali win the battle of Panipat against the Marathas, was sent from Lahore to clinch the siege of Multan. True to its reputation, it tore gaping holes in the walls of the great fortress through which bands of Nihangs launched their suicidal attacks. Nawab Muzaffar Khan and two of his sons fell in battle while another two sons were taken prisoner.

When the nawab's captive sons were brought to Ranjit Singh, who was kept informed of their father's feats, he embraced them warmly and honoured them with a large *jagir*. He found time also to pray in Lahore's Shah Abdul Malli Masjid for the soul of his commander Mian Ghausa, who had helped establish the artillery formations of the Maharaja's army. By an ironic coincidence, Wazir Fateh Khan was put to death in Herat about the same time, by the son of Mahmud, the man he had placed on Afghanistan's throne.

At the end of 1818, the year of the annexation of Multan, Peshawar—a city he had conquered many times in his childhood fantasies—was occupied by Ranjit's forces. This traditional gateway to Hindustan, which had witnessed central Asian hordes pouring into India for over eight hundred years, now saw the victorious Ranjit Singh riding through its streets on his elephant. The last non-alien ruler to have done so was Raja Anang Pal around the end of the tenth century.

Like others before him, Ranjit Singh was enchanted by the stories he had heard of the spectacular stretch of land with its rushing rivers, magnificent lotus-covered lakes, valleys and pine forests against the backdrop of the Himalayas that lay to the east of Peshawar—Kashmir. Nestling in the northernmost reaches of Hindustan, and ringed by snow-covered mountains throughout the year, Jammu and Kashmir (the name of the present Indian state) is the size of Britain. In its three main constituents, Jammu, Kashmir Valley and Ladakh, Hindu, Islamic and Buddhist beliefs, skills and scholarship have contributed to the richness of its texture.

The creativity of the Valley's people has been reflected for centuries in their extraordinary skills in the making of hand-woven shawls, silks, carpets, walnut-wood furniture and papier mâché. Kashmir shawls, the tradition of their manufacture dating back to Babur, owe their special quality to the material of which they are made, the fine winter down of the animals found in this region—the Kashmir goat, the wild sheep and the Tibetan yak—which far surpasses merino wool in length and fineness. The Persian influence in Kashmir, with its ancient traditions of arts and crafts, is everywhere to be seen. The Kashmiris have also long worked their land with imagination and diligence to produce saffron, almonds, walnuts, apples and pears.

Kashmir exercised a magnetic hold on the Mughal rulers of the time; the Emperors Aurangzeb, Akbar, Jahangir and Shah Jahan made regular visits to its pleasant valleys with their entire courts. With the twilight of the Mughals, the Afghans took over Kashmir as they did many other parts of India.

After several attempts to loosen Kashmir from the Afghan hold, some successful and some less so, Ranjit Singh was ready to annex it once Attock and Multan—which had facilitated the Afghans' access to it—were in Sikh hands. With Azim Khan, Kashmir's governor and brother of the slain Wazir Fateh Khan, in Kabul, he felt the time was right. Jabbar Khan, Azim Khan's younger brother, was in charge but his brutal treatment of the Hindu population had so alienated the people that even his own revenue minister, Pandit Birbal Dhar, had fled the valley. When Dhar arrived in Lahore, his advice in favour of an immediate invasion helped Ranjit Singh make up his mind.

Three formations of the Sikh army headed for Kashmir in April 1819. Whilst one formation under Ranjit Singh stayed at the base camp, two others advanced in a pincer movement on the Valley. The

Maharaja had shrewdly arranged for one of his columns to take a route through little-used mountain passes and this gave the Sikh forces a much-needed element of surprise. The pincer strategy worked admirably, both columns arriving in sight of each other at Supaiya, where 12,000 Afghans under Jabbar Khan awaited them. The decisive battle for Kashmir was fought on 3 July with the victorious Sikh army entering Srinagar on 4 July 1819. The fighting was bitter and what decided the day was the charge against the Afghan horsemen and infantry by Akali Phula Singh and his Nihangs. The Afghans recoiled from the shock of the Nihang charge and fled into the hills. Jabbar Khan was severely wounded and only just managed to escape with his life.

Within a few months, Ranjit Singh was once again in the saddle, leading a force across the Indus to Dera Ghazi Khan, then under the vassalage of Kabul. As with Peshawar and several other earlier acquisitions, once Dera Ghazi Khan was annexed, it was placed under the tutelage of the nawab of Bahawalpur who, though his main territory was located south of the Sutlej, paid tribute to the Maharaja for his lands that lay north of the river. Ranjit's initial preference was always to have friendly vassals administer territories conquered by him, rather than burden the Lahore Darbar with their direct administration. Only if the chiefs of these dependencies proved unreliable—an all too frequent occurrence—was direct control exercised.

After the year 1820 had been spent on taming the warlike Muslim tribes south-west of Kashmir, the following year witnessed the subjugation of Dera Ismail Khan, a key outpost on the central Indus. The fall of Mankera fort, lying between the Indus and Chenab, Punjab's westernmost rivers, was the key to Sikh domination of the Derajat region, and its Afghan governor was also made a feudatory.

But Peshawar was proving troublesome. Azim Khan, Kashmir's former governor and brother of Fateh Khan, who now had the power his brother once exercised in Kabul, was still smarting from the loss of Kashmir. He left Kabul for Peshawar and Attock in 1822 but withdrew without engaging the Sikhs. Returning in January 1823, he committed the region's entire tribal belt to a *jehad* against the Sikhs. The strength of the tribal forces assembled against Ranjit Singh has been estimated at 20,000 in addition to the troops under Azim Khan. On 14 March Ranjit Singh's personal command of his troops in battle, especially the deployment of his artillery and cavalry, won the day despite initial set-backs. Advance Sikh columns reached the Khyber Pass but once again the "prudent Maharaja" chose to make an Afghan, Yar Muhammad Khan, his vassal rather than occupy his lands and assume direct admin-istrative control of them. He was all too aware of the restlessness and volatility of the tribesmen. Moreover, like many outstanding generals, Ranjit Singh was more excited by conquest and expansion than by administration. The idea of striking terror into Afghan hearts was more exhilarating than acquisition of Afghan territories.

But the problem of Peshawar, indeed of that entire frontier region, was not easily resolved. This time the arch-instigator of the tribesmen was Sayed Ahmed Barelvi, who by 1827 had whipped up a revolt with the support—or so he claimed—of the rulers of Turkey, Afghanistan, some countries of the Middle East, and the chiefs of several Indian Muslim states. *Jehad* was the rallying cry and recruits responded by pouring into the region via Sind. Seeing the odds mounting against him, the Lahore Darbar's vassal, Yar Muhammad, took to his heels, leaving Peshawar to Barelvi's tribesmen-fighters, the *mujahids*. Sikh forces under Budh Singh Sandhawalia, however, soon reconquered Peshawar. But Sayed Ahmed Barelvi's passionate oratory rekindled old fires and led to an armed uprising and reoccupation of Peshawar by Afghan and tribal forces, culminating in the installation of Sayed Ahmed Barelvi as its caliph. "Coins were struck, inscriptions were issued in his name, Muslims from Kashmir, Sind, Delhi and UP rallied around him and he assumed the air of a king of the whole Muslim world." Although heavily outnumbered by the zealots in the area, the Sikhs struck back as soon as reinforcements reached them. Led by Ranjit's son Sher Singh, the Sikhs retook Peshawar in October 1829. Barelvi fled to the hills, still fanatically focused on his idea of *jehad*, still determined to retake Peshawar, until he was tracked down by Sher Singh and finished off with a single stroke of the sword. He was buried with full honours, draped in a shawl personally presented by Sher Singh.

Metcalfe's suave remark to the Maharaja at the time of signing the Sutlej Treaty with the British in 1809: "Your Excellency will reap the

1. Aerial view of Anandpur. On 30 March 1699, on the site of Gurdwara Keshgarh—the white domed building seen above the far edge of the pool—Guru Gobind Singh initiated the first five persons, the *panjpiyare*, or "beloved five," into the new Order of the Sikh Faith, the Khalsa.

2. The Akal Takht. A watercolour by William Simpson, 1860

3. The *panjpiyare* during the festival of Hola Mohalla in Anandpur

4. Nihangs, the traditional Sikh warriors, continue to show their fighting skills during the festival of Hola Mohalla every year

5. Maharaja Ranjit Singh listening to the Guru Granth Sahib being recited near the Golden Temple, Amritsar. Oil painting by August Schoefft, Vienna, *c.* 1850, based on sketches made earlier in Amritsar

6. Ranjit Singh's favourite horse, Laili, in emerald trappings, with his syce. Lithograph by Emily Eden, *c.* 1838

7. *The Court of Lahore*. Oil painting by August Schoefft, Vienna, *c.* 1850–55, based on earlier sketches made in Amritsar

8. Detail from Schoefft's *The Court of Lahore*, showing Ranjit Singh with prominent members of his family and court

Key
1. Ranjit Singh
2. Kharak Singh
3. Nau Nihal Singh
4. Udham Singh
5. Gulab Singh
6. Bhai Ram Singh
7. bodyguards

9. Maharaja Sher Singh, a son of Ranjit Singh, setting off on a hunt near Lahore. Lithograph by Prince Alexei Soltykoff, 1842

10. Men of the 47th Sikhs take part in the Victory Parade on The Mall, London, after the Armistice, 1918

11. Sikh fighter pilot of the Indian Air Force with his Mirage 2000 bi-sonic fighter, 1990s

12. In 1947 Pakistani-sponsored tribesmen and irregulars took the 11,000-foot Zoji La, the only pass from the Kashmir Valley into Ladakh, where they overran the Kashmir Maharaja's forces. The Indian Army made a crossing of the Zoji La, unprecedented at that height with tanks, to liberate Ladakh. This photograph, taken on 2 November 1948, shows men of the 1st Patiala Infantry crossing the Zoji La. In the foreground are Major Daljit Singh and the war artist Serbjeet Singh.

fruits of the alliance with the British in a period of twenty years," was proved right by events. In less than twenty years, the vastly expanded Sikh Kingdom came to include Kangra, Attock, Multan, Kashmir, Derajat and Peshawar; its flag would fly in Ladakh, and weeks before his death, Colonel Shaikh Basawan would plant the Sikh ensign on the fort of Kabul. Last but not least, there was the consolidation of the many *misls*, principalities and feudatories within Punjab.

It will be appropriate here to assess the extent to which Ranjit Singh's aim of establishing the Sikh Empire was served by the Sutlej Treaty. Its advantages were evident from the outset: within months of its signature the appeals of both Sansar Chand of Kangra and the Gurkhas for British intervention were refused, and Sansar Chand's further appeals even after his subjugation by Ranjit Singh were also rejected. When during the first unsuccessful siege of Multan in 1810 by the Lahore Darbar, its doughty governor Muzaffar Khan also asked the British for help, he was told that in view of the Treaty there was little they could do.

In 1819, another man who pleaded vainly for British help was the Afghan governor of Kashmir, Azim Khan. Despite the persuasiveness of his envoys who met Colonel David Ochterlony in Delhi, urging him to take Kashmir under their "protection," the British stood by the terms of the Treaty. Many others similarly sought British help, amongst them Shah Zaman and Shah Shuja. But even though Afghanistan lay outside the Treaty's purview, to accede to their designs would have earned Ranjit Singh's ire because of the implications of the Afghans' hidden agenda, which included claims on Peshawar, Attock, Multan and Kashmir.

Indeed, in 1837 Kabul's claim on Peshawar surfaced once when its ruler Dost Muhammad Khan held talks with the British. This time Russia's revived interest in India was again seen as a danger to British imperial interests in the subcontinent. So in order to stiffen Afghanistan against the Russians, a mission under Alexander Burnes was sent to Dost Muhammad, who seized the opportunity of asking the English for a guarantee against Ranjit Singh and assistance in winning back Peshawar. The British decision to turn down Dost Muhammad's demand, and opt for Ranjit Singh instead, was not so easily taken. Nor did the Treaty and its clauses have anything to do with it. With two senior functionaries taking diametrically opposite stands—Burnes for promising Peshawar to Dost Muhammad in return for an anti-Russian alliance, and Captain Claude Wade, British Political Agent at Ludhiana, against a move which would seriously destabilize Anglo-Sikh relations—pragmatic considerations prevailed. The British refused the Afghan ruler since "the friendship of the Maharaja was valued more by Auckland [the British Governor-General in India] than that of Dost Muhammad who he thought *was not to be trusted.*"

If the Treaty had helped Ranjit Singh secure his borders with the British and concentrate on conquests in the north and north-east, how did the British view the Treaty? Writing in 1837, Wade felt that "Ranjit Singh has hitherto derived nothing but advantage from his alliance with us. While we have been engaged in consolidating our power in Hindustan, he has been extending his conquests throughout the Punjab and across the Indus, and as we are now beginning to prescribe limits to his power, which it cannot be supposed he will regard with complacency, he is now more likely to encourage than to withdraw from an alliance, which may hold out to him a hope of creating a balance of power." As good an assessment as any.

The sprawling territory of Sind was now set to strain Anglo-Sikh relations. Wade's mention of a shift in British policy—"we are now beginning to prescribe limits to his power"—would be evident soon enough, with Sind as the bone of contention. Roughly 58,000 square miles in area, Sind lies south-east of Baluchistan and south of Punjab. Excavations early in the twentieth century revealed Sind's historic past with the discovery of the lost city of Mohenjo Daro, lying about 180 miles north-east of Karachi. Here was evidence of the existence of a civilization going back to 3000 BC, contemporaneous with the Sumerians. Sind was occupied by Alexander the Great in 325 BC, and after him came various Buddhist, Brahmin and Islamic rulers. It remained semi-autonomous until the Mughal Emperor Akbar incorporated it into his empire in 1583. With the decline of the Mughals, local dynasties again took over, first the Kalhoras and after them the Talpurs. Parts of Sind are watered by the Indus, the Thar Desert also claiming portions of it. Overlooking the Arabian Sea—a major attraction for land-locked

Punjab—the town of Karachi would become a thriving port in the years ahead.

With the conquest of Multan in 1818, of Dera Ghazi Khan a year later, and of Dera Ismail Khan after that, the Sikhs established a powerful presence on Sind's borders. The British, in a sense, were already there. In 1758 an English merchant, Mr. Sumption, had been given trade and manufacturing facilities and three years later the East India Company had been permitted to post an agent in Sind, although they were thrown out in 1775 by the isolationist Sind amirs. In 1798 Nathan Crowe, a Bombay servant of the Company, was again allowed in, but within two years was asked to leave. After several years of visits by emissaries and missions and the signing of two treaties, the British arrived on Sind's border with their annexation of Cutch on the Indian side. A flexing of muscles to overawe the amirs was now clearly in order, and this was accordingly done in 1825.

Sikh appetites, like British, were whetted by prospects of the conquest of Sind: the British for reasons of strategy, the Sikhs for reasons of revenue and commerce. Ranjit Singh also believed that since he had divested the Afghans of all their Indian conquests, the remnants of Afghan tributaries in India—like Sind—should rightfully come under Lahore's suzerainty. The British thought otherwise.

The game of who would outmanoeuvre whom soon started. Britain made the first move by sending Alexander Burnes to reconnoitre the Indus. Whilst the ostensible purpose of this "spurious mission" was to study the prospects of commercial navigation on the river, its real aim was to obtain a first-hand report on the land of the amirs and on the Indus's military potential. The expansionist Burnes's report, *Geographical and Military Memoirs*, was to influence Britain's future Sind policy. Burnes ardently advocated a defensive alliance between the British and the amir of Hyderabad to check the Sikhs, and a treaty to open up the Indus to British navigation.

Navigational study is often presented as the more acceptable face of colonial enterprise—a seemingly honourable way of spying out the land for the movement of military men and material under the guise of commerce. This was the case with the Indus scheme. From the British point of view, control of the Indus was necessary if the southern and westward Sikh advance was to be checked. With only Sind and the

Sikh Kingdom outside British control at the beginning of the 1830s, the first step to remedy this state of affairs was the Indus Treaty with the amirs.

Lord William Bentinck having fully briefed London on the political and military advantages of the Indus move, the Governor-General now sought a meeting with Ranjit Singh to allay his suspicions with regard to British intentions. Wade was also sent to Lahore to reassure the Maharaja that, as Cunningham was to put it, "by the extension of British commerce, was not meant the extension of British power." Why were the British keen to keep Ranjit Singh in good humour? Because, though confident of their own power, they were wary of his. It was necessary to maintain his trust until they were ready to face him with a *fait accompli*.

Ranjit Singh readily agreed to a meeting with Bentinck, and a spectacular "Field of the Cloth of Gold" oriental-style was arranged at Ropar on the Sutlej, the boundary between the Maharaja's domains and British-held territory. Each side vied to impress the other, Ranjit Singh with pavilions of fairy-tale splendour and the British with the pomp and panache of colourfully dressed and meticulously drilled soldiers. Ranjit Singh gave a masterly personal display of tent-pegging. Five days of feasting and ceremony resulted in no formal agreement, and there is no evidence that there was any serious discussion of Sind, but the cordiality of the whole affair was a pleasant smokescreen for both sides to gauge each other's intentions.

Even though he was not privy to the secret records of British agents—"*the Government of India is bound by the strongest considerations of political interest to prevent the extension of Sikh power along the whole course of the Indus*"—Ranjit Singh was fully aware of the British game plan. Aside from his remarkably efficient intelligence network which brought him daily reports through special messengers from "Kashmir, Kabul, Sind, Ludhiana, and the *cis*-Sutlej British-protected principalities of Patiala, Nabha, Jind, Kaithal and Kalsia," the brisk activity of the British in Sind and Kabul, and the tenor and tone of the many English emissaries sent to Lahore, were not lost on him. Despite two Sikh armies poised along the Indus, and his military commanders urging him "not to yield to the demands of the English, for to their understanding it was not clear where such demands would stop," Ranjit

Singh would not be hustled into a hasty decision. His caustic response to his generals who urged him to fight the British was to tell them to jog their memories about the fate of the 200,000 men the Marathas had fielded against the British not so long before.

There was a parallel between Ranjit Singh's present dilemma and that he had faced before the signing of the Sutlej Treaty. This time the problem was not of Sind alone, which he could have taken in a lightning operation given the amirs' lack of military muscle, but of the British opening a second front across the Sutlej, and of the encouragement they would extend to the Afghan ruler, Dost Muhammad, desperate to retake Peshawar after his unsuccessful attempts in 1835 and 1837. Burnes, the duplicitous British envoy to Kabul, was also trying to impress on his superiors that Dost Muhammad "could scarcely be expected to resign all pretensions to Peshawar," and that "he should be protected from Sikh attacks, and Peshawar should be restored to him."

Once again, as in 1809, Ranjit Singh was clear about the scale of his resources as compared to those of the British. He was in no doubt about the fighting qualities of the Sikhs, or of their courage and valour, or that they could take on the British and anyone else. He was more concerned about weaponry of every kind that the British had and he did not. He could still remember when in 1812 he had asked them for 500 muskets, and they had readily obliged; but not when he had later asked for 50,000. The British had these weapons and would use them whenever needed. He was equally clear that he did not have ready access to weapons in quantities needed to wage a war against the British.

Yet another event had left its mark on him: the visit of Sir Henry Fane, Commander-in-Chief of the British Indian Army, who had come to Lahore in 1837 to attend the wedding of his grandson, Nau Nihal Singh. Whilst Ranjit Singh carefully observed the quality of the British lancers and horse artillery that had accompanied the C-in-C, Fane, as a modern historian puts it, "made a detailed appraisal of the Sikhs' military power which, according to him, consisted of 67 regiments of infantry, 700 pieces of artillery and innumerable cavalry. His confidential report to Lord Auckland, the Governor-General, contained speculations on the ability of the British to destroy the military might of Ranjit Singh." The same writer comments that "a young

British Officer prepared during Sir Henry's visit a map of the Punjab which formed the groundwork of all maps used during the first Anglo-Sikh war."

To put beside the refrain of British chroniclers on oriental duplicity, a passage in Cunningham's *History of the Sikhs* (1849) reveals the Anglo-Saxon way of doing things. Writing of Fane's visit to Punjab, Cunningham says that during his social visit to Ranjit Singh as a wedding guest, "he formed an estimate of the force which would be required for the complete subjugation of the Punjab . . ." but in the next sentence observes that "the prospect of a war with the Sikhs was then remote, and hostile designs could not with honour be entertained by a guest!"

Many Western historians have given undue credit for his military victories to Ranjit Singh's European officers. But Cunningham thinks otherwise. In 1837 Cunningham was assistant to Colonel Claude Wade, British Political Agent on the Sikh frontier. He later served as political officer for several years and in all spent eight years dealing with Sikh affairs. Publicly disgraced after the publication of his book for his temerity in exposing the truth about British conduct in the First Sikh War, he "died of a broken heart" because of his government's unjust action against him. Of Sikhs as soldiers, Cunningham wrote: "It has been usual to attribute the superiority of the Sikh army to the labours of these two officers [Generals Jean-François Allard and Jean-Baptiste Ventura], and of their subsequent coadjutors, the Generals Court and Avitabile; but, in truth, the Sikh owes his excellence as a soldier to his own hardihood of character, to that spirit of adaptation which has distinguished every new people, and to that feeling of a common interest and destiny implanted in him by his great teachers."

Writing in 1818, well before a number of French and other officers were brought into the Sikh army, Captain A.H. Bingley reported that Ranjit Singh's "battalions were a formidable body of troops, well-disciplined and steady. Their endurance was remarkable and it was not unusual for whole regiments to make 30-mile marches often for days at a time."

The British Governor-General Lord Auckland's observation, after his visit to Ranjit Singh's kingdom in 1838 and his inspection of the

Maharaja's battalions, was that "in equipment, in steadiness, and in precision of manoeuvres, the Punjab armies seemed in no way inferior to our own army." H.M.L. Lawrence, a British army officer, felt that the white officers' most singular contribution was improvement of the Sikh military band!

A present-day French historian, Jean-Marie Lafont, on the other hand, feels that because of British dominance in historical writing on India, the contribution of continental European officers to the Sikh army has been consistently downplayed and "whenever noticed, their work seems to have had the result only of enhancing the valour of British arms" at the expense of their French adversaries. But in fact most of Ranjit Singh's military victories were won before he introduced European officers into his army. It is equally true that these officers did instil a strong sense of discipline into Sikh forces and ensure effective and efficient use of firearms.

Allard and Ventura had arrived in Lahore in 1822. Both appeared to have served in Napoleon's army with distinction—a fact Ranjit took the precaution of checking out—and both stood up well before his insatiable curiosity and barrage of questions. He did other checks on them as well, aware of the ever-present danger of moles. Satisfied as to their integrity and ability, he gave them responsible positions and generous terms with Allard training Sikh cavalry and Ventura the infantry.

Allard was 37 when he arrived in Lahore with an impressive military career behind him which had abruptly ended with Napoleon's defeat at Waterloo. As *aide-de-camp* to Marshal Brune, he had barely escaped with his life when Brune was assassinated at Avignon. He had fought at Naples and in Spain and Portugal before joining the Imperial Guard in the French army. Officers who had served with Napoleon were not very favourably looked upon by the royalists after his defeat, and Allard was no exception. He was kept under police surveillance after his return to Saint-Tropez, his birthplace, with the army neither reinstating nor discharging him. Kept on half pay from 1815 to 1820, he was finally given three months' leave to go to Italy—a journey that eventually landed him in Lahore on leave that lasted seventeen years.

Allard was single when he arrived in Lahore but within four years married a twelve-year-old girl, Bannou Pan Dei from Chamba. Of their six children, five survived, in addition to an adopted boy from Multan. Allard adored his family. Ranjit Singh gradually developed a great affection for Allard and respect for his professional qualities and when news of the honours bestowed on him by the Lahore Darbar travelled to France, Allard was given a hero's welcome on arriving home on leave in 1835. When he died of a heart attack in Peshawar in January 1839—less than five months before Ranjit Singh's own death—the ailing monarch's attendants were afraid to inform him for fear of the medical effect the news might have on him.

Jean-Baptiste Ventura was both a colourful man and a good professional soldier who, as Jean-Marie Lafont tells us, "had been in the bodyguards of Prince Eugene, and all available evidences show that he was with Napoleon in Russia." A few years younger than Allard, he had a more free-wheeling life-style: married to a Muslim woman, he still maintained a sizeable harem, and had a roving eye. While Allard settled his family in France during his lifetime, Ventura took only his daughter to Europe, leaving the rest of his family behind him.

Although figures vary, there were perhaps 42 non-Indians in Ranjit Singh's armed forces: twelve Frenchmen, four Italians, four Germans, three Americans, two Spaniards, one Russian, one Scot, three Englishmen, seven Anglo-Indians and five others. When a British officer asked General Avitabile why Europeans preferred service with Ranjit Singh, he said that it was because the Sikhs "have no religious prejudices as the Persians and Afghans have."

So over Sind as over the Sutlej in 1809, Ranjit Singh decided against clashing with the British. It was a pragmatic decision based on his sense of limits and human mortality. For his own health was deteriorating. He had been seriously ill with malaria in 1825, but had made an excellent recovery. In good health for the next ten years, he had a paralytic stroke in August 1835. A second stroke in January 1837 took a greater toll of him, affecting his speech and his entire right side. Although he still insisted on riding, his life-long passion, he had to be lifted onto the saddle after his second stroke. The third, nearly fatal attack came in the midst of festivities on Christmas Eve during Auckland's visit to Lahore in 1838. It was becoming clear to him, as also to those around him, that the Maharaja's health was failing and the unthinkable would soon have to be faced.

It is not too far-fetched to assume that Ranjit Singh's declining health influenced his stand on Sind. Throughout his life he had taken all big and small decisions himself, and had personally led his armies into many major campaigns. At other times he had ridden out at the head of relief columns to help his commanders in battle. This had been the pattern of his life from the beginning, whether in subduing the *misl* chiefs or each of the many Muslim principalities, or in the critical battles over Attock and Peshawar, or in subduing Mankera Fort in the Derajat region. It couldn't but be obvious to him now that any new and extravagant military enterprise, with his own health failing, would prove critical to the kingdom he had established with enterprise and élan. For the Maharaja had always reconciled his own individual urges with the inescapable political and military realities facing him, and taken decisions accordingly.

That a man as astonishingly fit as he was, who at the age of 50 had stunned the British Governor-General, at the ceremonial meeting at Ropar in 1831, by competing with his best horsemen in tent-pegging, should be felled by a series of strokes in the last three years of his life seemed a cruel irony. How could a man with an iron constitution like his die at the age of 58? Could the only answer to that be his sheer zest for life? A doctor sent by the East India Company to attend the Maharaja in 1826 was of the opinion "that Ranjit Singh's soundness of mind and body would enable him to live for thirty more years"—provided that he controlled his intake of liquor.

But quantity was not the only problem. The composition of his favourite drink was another. He favoured a brandy "in which were the strongest sauces, compounded from the flesh of every animal, beef excepted, pearls and jewels, musk, opium, plants of various kinds, all mingled together into a beverage," wrote Baron Charles Hugel, adding that having tasted it the evening before, "the following morning my spirits were exceedingly depressed." When the British presented Ranjit Singh with port, claret, hock, champagne and the like, the only thing that caught his fancy was whisky.

The relentless pace he had set since the age of ten, when he had become head of the Sukerchakia *misl*, caught up with him at last. In June 1839 his condition worsened. From 20 June, as he neared his end, he reiterated his wish that his eldest son Kharak Singh should succeed him, assisted by Raja Dhyan Singh as his chief minister. Immense quantities of money and jewels, in addition to a hundred caparisoned horses with bejewelled saddles, four elephants with golden howdas and swords, shields, weapons, gems and other alms, were given away to shrines and places of worship. "But so deep and sincere were the feelings of respect and attachment with which he was universally regarded," writes a contemporary English chronicler, "that to the last the most implicit obedience was paid to his commands, and (when he could no longer speak) to the signs by which his will was expressed."

Ranjit Singh became unconscious on 26 June, and died on the evening of 27 June 1839. The next morning, after traversing the capital crammed with mourning crowds, the cortège arrived at the cremation ground where, in a surprisingly un-Sikh act, four of his wives and seven maids burned themselves on his funeral pyre. Rani Guddo, daughter of Raja Sansar Chand of Kangra, placed Ranjit Singh's head in her lap and according to all accounts she and her companions willingly consigned themselves to the flames.

The paradox of Ranjit Singh's life, and the tragedy that overtook his kingdom after him, was the contrast between his own formidable charisma and capacities and the inadequacies of the seven sons who survived him. That a man of such exceptional and versatile brilliance, who had commanded the unswerving loyalty of men from such diverse backgrounds, was unable to establish his kingdom on more enduring foundations will always remain—despite countless explanations—a puzzle.

A Sikh scholar and civil servant of impressive credentials once offered an explanation. Kapur Singh felt that Ranjit Singh's first mistake was to assume "the un-Sikh title of Maharaja" because by doing so "he was sabotaging the very basis of the Sikh polity . . . within a few years after his coronation, he reduced to desuetude the supreme authority of the Sikh polity, the *gurmata*, and entrusted the control of the government of his expanding territories to a cabinet of his own choice, in accordance with the ancient Hindu monarchical tradition, but *qua* his own person, in whom he had gathered all the power of authority of the state in accordance with the un-Sikh, Hindu doctrine . . ."

Each time that major decisions had to be taken in the past, the Sarbat Khalsa—the widely attended gatherings of Sikhs which accorded collective sanction to all major initiatives—had taken them by passing a *gurmata*, or resolution, on the course of action to be taken. This was done in 1760 and in 1765, when the Khalsa, assembled at the Darbar Sahib, had decided to annex Lahore, the seat of Afghan authority in India. The point Kapur Singh makes with some justification is that by vesting all authority in the monarchy, Ranjit Singh weakened the republican tradition established by Guru Gobind Singh: "It is the self-respect, the awareness of his own ultimate significance in the creation of God, which imparts to a Sikh of Guru Gobind Singh that Olympian air and independence which fits ill with any totalitarian or autocratic monarchical system of organization of power."

Whilst in Ranjit Singh's lifetime his charismatic presence and personal skills, both in warfare and matters of state, kept the Khalsa totally loyal to him, the erosion of republican traditions could well have had an alienating effect, which became evident only after his death. Since the commonwealth of the Khalsa "was a creation of the Khalsa arms, and could not otherwise be maintained except through the cooperation and devotion of the Khalsa," Kapur Singh feels that Ranjit Singh's policy of bringing in so many untried persons in senior civil posts in his government was bound to prove fatal. "In pursuance of this policy of his, he raised the alien hill dogras,* Dhyan Singh and Gulab Singh, almost from the gutter to positions of supreme authority in the civil apparatus of his government, and Tej Singh, an insignificant Brahmin of the Gangetic-Doab, and Lal Singh, another Brahmin from Gandhara Valley, were granted such influence that eventually raised them to the supreme command of the Sikh army, and thus he dug his own grave, the grave of his descendants, and paved the way for the eventual enslavement of the Sikh people."

These men were never out of step with his wishes during Ranjit

---

* Hill dwellers in the Dogra region of Kashmir; despite the surnames of these two men, the dogras were not Sikhs.

Singh's lifetime. Even when his end was near, none dared question the authority of the dying Maharaja. But they did help dismantle his kingdom after his death, especially Dhyan Singh who, adds Kapur Singh, "embarked upon a conspiracy to destroy the entire line of Ranjit Singh's descendants to clear the way for putting his [own] son, Hira Singh on the throne of Punjab."

In assessing Ranjit Singh, the almost ungovernable complexity of Punjab in his day must be kept in mind. In consolidating his hold on it, he had to face numerous problems head-on, and while doing so he could not refuse non-Sikhs involvement in his government, for the Sikhs accounted for only 7 per cent of a population in which the Muslims were over 50 per cent and the Hindus around 42 per cent.* To get the support of all his constituents, he had to give them a sense of participation, make them feel secure, give them a stake in the kingdom. Ranjit Singh's policy of benign rule was based as much on self-interest as on his kindly and non-vindictive nature. If he exercised paternal control and allowed freedom of religion to ensure plurality in his kingdom, it was a policy which made sense to him, because he was above all a pragmatist.

In making Dhyan Singh chief minister to his heir Kharak Singh, however, Ranjit Singh does seem to have misjudged the man's treacherous bent. Possibly because this wily courtier had served him faithfully, Ranjit Singh did not anticipate his *volte-face* after his death. But had he acknowledged the central importance of the Sarbat Khalsa and the *gurmata* and established an assembly of people representing Sikh traditions who would speak fearlessly on key issues at critical times, the subsequent tragedies of Sikh history might have been averted, and the vitality of the body politic maintained by isolating dangerous elements within it.

There is no end to the what-might-have-beens of history. The historic fact is that Ranjit Singh's life was one of towering achievements, attained not through tyranny but through the lubricants of decency and civility. Even though besieged on all sides, he pushed back the frontiers of Punjab, established borders which others could not have dreamt of, broke the stranglehold of the Afghans, and established his

---

* Based on 1881 census figures which placed Punjab's population at 22 million.

capital in Lahore, long considered a legacy of the Timurids from Central Asia. A study of the forces that were unleashed against Punjab after his death—as we shall see in the following chapter—will provide a greater awareness of the achievements of this man who was able to keep them in check in his lifetime, yet lived a life of courage, magnificence and generosity, as few others have done.

4

Grievous Betrayals
1839–1849

The Sikhs entered the tragic, unsparing and destructive 1840s with blinkers on. Heedless of the menacing forces against them, Ranjit Singh's successors destroyed the promise of the Sikh State through self-destructive moves and betrayals. In the end they not only tarnished a noble heritage, but destroyed themselves as well. The witnesses of the manner in which Ranjit Singh gave shape and substance to his dreams learned surprisingly few lessons from his leadership. Little thought was given to the spectacle of India's gradual colonization by the British.

Perhaps it was too much to expect the Maharaja's successors to understand—as he did—that a power collapses, as Umberto Eco tells us, because of "'barbarians' pressing at its borders." The barbarians, though, "not necessarily uncultivated," brought in "new customs, new views of the world." And given their own ways of establishing dominance, "barbarians may burst in with violence, because they want to seize a wealth that has been denied to them, or they may steal into the social and cultural body of the reigning Pax, spreading new faiths and new perspectives of life." Kharak Singh was a disastrous successor to an illustrious father. What little faculties he ever had were ruined by a dissolute life and he was totally incapable of dealing with external or internal threats. He has been described as a man who "had nothing to attract or attack." A web of intrigue was soon woven around him, even before the thirteen days' mourning period after his father's death was over. His half-brother Sher Singh, a key aspirant to the throne, represented one line of danger. Another was his own son, Nau Nihal Singh. Whilst the latter was "intolerant of the English and hated his minister Dhyan Singh," Sher Singh was favoured by the British.

On 2 July 1839, within five days of the Maharaja's death, Sher Singh had sent a secret message to the British Political Agent at Ludhiana, drawing the Governor-General's attention to his own superior merits as an aspirant to the Sikh throne. Whether his haste in communicating with the British was a result of their subtle encouragement is not known. But he was certainly well thought of in the camp of the Governor-General, Lord Auckland. Referring to him as "our dear friend," Auckland's sister, Emily Eden, after their visit to Lahore in 1838, touchingly expressed her concern about him during the regime of the "foolish Kurruck Singh," and felt "it is just possible his dear fat head will be chopped off, unless he crosses to our side of the river."

Nau Nihal Singh was in Peshawar at the time of Kharak Singh's investiture on 1 September 1839, and as the ceremonies were carried out without him, it was obvious all was not well between father and son. Matters were further aggravated by the father's closeness to Chet Singh, a self-important courtier, who ranked higher in Kharak Singh's estimation than Dhyan Singh or his own son. Within weeks of Nau Nihal Singh's return to Lahore, Chet Singh was killed by Dhyan Singh in the Maharaja's personal quarters, on 8 October 1839. Nau Nihal Singh evidently concurred with the killing; some accounts suggest he was even present at the time. Within weeks Nau Nihal Singh assumed all his father's powers when in December 1839 Kharak Singh was stricken by an illness from which he never recovered. "It was suspected by the royal physicians," writes one modern historian, "that slow poison was being administered to him . . . that he was either poisoned under Dhyan Singh's direction with the connivance of Nau Nihal Singh or his already shattered constitution was allowed to break down under ill treatment and neglect."

During the year or so that Nau Nihal Singh ruled the Kingdom whilst his father was dying a slow death, he handled a number of crises with considerable confidence. Though only nineteen, he had an impressive record of experiences thanks to the encouraging support of his grandfather, Ranjit Singh. He had fought with the Lahore forces in the conquest of Peshawar and the trans-Indus regions, and seen active service in other parts of the kingdom. He had also gained experience in the administration of Attock and Peshawar and was equipped to handle at least some of the many problems created by Ranjit Singh's death. He was said to combine "the discretion of a statesman with the best virtues of a soldier."

Both these sets of qualities were needed to deal with restless regional chieftains, especially those in the north-west around Attock, Rawalpindi and Peshawar—in that entire territory where the turbulent Pathans were again champing at the bit. There were attempts at assertiveness elsewhere too. Some had to do with defiance of the Lahore Darbar, others with a reluctance to pay revenues, still others with petty chieftains taking the law into their own hands. Nau Nihal Singh dealt with each promptly and judiciously.

He was ill-equipped, however, to deal with the rampant court deviousness; with those who were subverting the kingdom from within. He was also disadvantaged both by his unprincipled role in Chet Singh's murder and his father's incarceration, aside from his inability to match the intrigues of the wily dogra Dhyan Singh, whom he detested, and the latter's brothers Gulab Singh and Suchet Singh. These Jammu dogras* had sought employment in the Lahore Darbar and, having found favour with Ranjit Singh, risen in office, especially Dhyan Singh and his son Hira Singh, who was Ranjit Singh's favourite. Dhyan Singh hatched a conspiracy soon after the Maharaja's death in which hatred, mistrust and violent deaths would help clear his son's way to the throne. As prime minister he could effect the bloodbath needed to attain his ends.

As if the dogras' intrigues weren't bad enough, the British too were far from idle. With conditions becoming increasingly favourable for their expansionist agenda because "Kharak Singh's rule appeared unpromising," they took the stand that "the drift of Court politics had to be watched with an eye on operations in Afghanistan." To "watch" is one thing, but to actively instigate events quite another. Which is what

* See footnote on page 129.

George Clerk, officiating Political Agent at Ludhiana, proceeded to do. On being told when he arrived in Lahore that Kharak Singh's confidant, Chet Singh (while still alive), was opposed to the British demand for passage of troops, Clerk advised some of the key men in the Lahore Court to get rid of the Maharaja's favourites. "I proved to them that they might be effectively removed," wrote Clerk in a confidential dispatch to Auckland. According to one historian, "Clerk gave encouragement to rival parties against each other." The classic British policy of divide and rule.

What was the "passage of troops" all about? Before Ranjit Singh's death the Company—on the well-worn plea of an impending Russian threat to Afghanistan and India—had got the Maharaja to agree to a double invasion of Afghanistan. One component was to be led by the puppet Shah Shuja with British support, and the other through Peshawar by troops provided by the Lahore Darbar. The idea was to put Shah Shuja on Kabul's throne. Ranjit Singh was informed of Kandahar's fall in April, but news of the capture of Kabul and Ghazni and the storming of the Khyber Pass by his troops came after his death on 27 June. So what Clerk was referring to was right of passage through Punjab for British troops returning from Afghanistan. This proposition found disfavour with many in the Lahore Court, including Chet Singh, whose effective removal Clerk had advised. Obviously duplicity was not the prerogative of Orientals only! But more was to come.

Taking advantage of every opportunity to subvert the Sikhs—even if it meant abusing their ally's hospitality—the British formed estimates of the force "required for the complete subjugation of the Punjab." When Colonel Claude Wade, Political Agent at Ludhiana, considered a "good friend" of Ranjit Singh, was returning from Afghanistan through Punjab—by courtesy of the Maharaja—detailed information on Sikh territories was collected for the British high command, just as had been done for Fane during his 1837 visit. When the Lahore Darbar, in response to a British request for help after the rout of their forces in Afghanistan in November 1841, sent troops under the command of Gulab Singh, the Jammu dogra, the British tried to buy them over. According to the assessment of Henry Lawrence, who later played a key role in Punjab, "we need such men as the Raja

[Gulab Singh] . . . and should bind them to us, by the only tie they recognize—self interest." Which the British, of course, well recognized too.

Gulab Singh responded to British overtures readily enough. Other Darbar officers who also did so were the Brahmins Lal Singh and Teja Singh, who eventually became prime minister and commander-in-chief of the army respectively—the same Lal Singh and Teja Singh who, in Kapur Singh's words, "paved the way for the eventual enslavement of the Sikh people." Their sell-out, as will be soon evident, ranks high in the annals of treachery and deceit. While the British would have shot their own wartime traitors out of hand, they were perfectly agreeable to having Teja Singh help them win against the Sikhs by betraying his troops. British victories in the two Sikh Wars were not won by valour on the battlefield but by persuading their adversary's key men to betray their side. Though this was still in the future, even in Nau Nihal Singh's brief span of life he had begun to understand the ways of expansionists.

The rather hawkish William Macnaghten, British envoy in Kabul, was prone to lose sight of the overall picture while favouring the Afghans. And so he had been urging his government to arm-twist the Sikhs into making concessions to the Afghans in the Peshawar area, just as his predecessor, Burnes, had done before him. Coincidentally or otherwise, Macnaghten managed to unearth a plot in which a letter purportedly written by Nau Nihal Singh indicted the Sikhs for helping the enemies of Shah Shuja, who enjoyed British support. The letter was proved a forgery, but it did create a degree of bitterness all round. No evidence is on record on whose instructions the forgery was perpetrated: whether by the enterprising Macnaghten in a bid to strengthen his case against the Sikhs, or by Dhyan Singh in his efforts to subvert Sikh rule.

Despite Macnaghten's efforts to inflame Pathan passions against the Sikhs and to implicate Nau Nihal Singh as a man of bad faith, the young prince weathered the crisis well, and his statesmanship was widely acknowledged. His stature remained high at court and with the Sikh army, as also with the British (despite Macnaghten's machinations). But relations with Dhyan Singh—given the divergence of aims—were uneasy. Then suddenly the countdown to another major tragedy began in September 1840. The ailing Kharak Singh's condition took a turn for the worse and he died on 5 November 1840, at the age of 38. The very next day, as Nau Nihal was returning to the palace after performing the last rites for his father, a gateway he was passing under collapsed, and his injuries proved fatal.

Historians cannot agree on what caused his death: was it engineered by Dhyan Singh to prevent him from ascending the throne, or was it an accident? Each view in this controversy has its emphatic adherents. However, the extraordinary steps taken by Dhyan Singh immediately after the event point to murder. He sealed all the gates to the fort and palace and allowed no one to see Nau Nihal Singh; neither senior chiefs, nor ranking members of the court, nor even his mother or wife. He put out that the prince was being treated well for his injuries. Whether he died in the accident or was killed in the palace later, no news of his death was given out for three days. Dhyan Singh is also reported to have urged Chand Kaur, Kharak Singh's widow, to make his own son, Hira Singh, Maharaja of Punjab.

Chand Kaur refused, and in turn claimed the throne for herself as the legitimate heir of Kharak Singh, which set her on a collision course both with Dhyan Singh and Sher Singh. She presided for a while over affairs of state as regent, but inevitably she too was done to death by her maids on 9 June 1842, victim of a conspiracy hatched by Dhyan Singh with the concurrence of Sher Singh. The maids are said to have poisoned her, and after she lost consciousness, to have killed her by stoning her head.

The resort to assassination of political rivals—in contrast to Ranjit Singh's policy of non-violence even against the vanquished—was assuming menacing proportions. By conniving with the dogra brothers in such crimes, Nau Nihal Singh and Sher Singh had encouraged events whose repercussions would prove fatal for them. They provided legitimacy for political murders, and set court intrigues on a dangerous course which would inevitably invite attention to their own vulnerability. The portents for the future were ominous. The invitation to the British to become involved in the infighting in Lahore was another reckless move made with complete unconcern for the consequences. Sher Singh, in his bid for the throne, was more guilty of this than the others even before Nau Nihal Singh's death, but more so after it. He also made the army take sides in palace intrigues.

Having won over sections of the army to his side during Chand Kaur's regency, Sher Singh attacked Lahore on 14 January 1841 and was declared the new ruler on 18 January. With this move he cast the army in the king-maker's role. It was a serious development, because even though "Sher Singh's accession was unattended by any acts of violence, the army which had enthroned him, had also become his master. It began to wreak vengeance on those whom it considered traitors to the Khalsa. It plundered the houses of several chiefs, dismissed foreigners from state service, and declared its determination to punish those who sought foreign interference." Compounding these problems and those of the Lahore Darbar was the fact that Sher Singh had also been in frequent touch with the British.

According to the Governor-General, Lord Auckland, "while he did not write to me, at my suggestion or perhaps without it, he would write away half of the Punjab to the British government to obtain interference in his favour." Another report has it that Sher Singh offered territory to the British north of the Sutlej in return for their help. How far these allegations are based on fact is unclear. But in February 1841 Auckland did decide to support Sher Singh with military force. This indicates a request by Sher Singh, even though the intervention came to nothing because of the violent reaction of the Sikh army which was not well disposed towards the British.

Unwittingly, Sher Singh, by bringing the army into the political decision-making process, gave it the right to contribute to decisions affecting the state. Such a right is not inherent in the concept of the Khalsa. Furthermore, whilst Ranjit Singh's leadership qualities had kept the army in line, its restiveness against his weak successors was now evident, and when it spilt over a major shift occurred from the political system created by the Gurus, in which rights had been invested in the entire Khalsa community, and not just the army. The manner of the army's assertiveness, though not directed at the state, damaged the state's cohesiveness since it lacked the discipline with which the Khalsa had closed its ranks against all adversaries in the past. This time it was divided both against itself and against others; an antithesis to the concept of a united Khalsa. Quite naturally the British misunderstood both the impulses behind the disorders and the fact that the army's ire was not directed against the Darbar but against foreigners who were trying to impose their will on it.

Even Sher Singh, while wooing the British, was unable to see the signs of a resurgent Khalsa. A bitter price would be paid for this oversight: by the British for alienating the Sikh army through their actions, and by Sher Singh for failing to earn its respect and continuing support. Two other developments further diminished the standing of the British in the army's eyes: their devastating rout in the Kabul insurrection in November 1841—in which Macnaghten too was killed—and British efforts to subvert Gulab Singh's loyalty to the Sikh Darbar.

To relieve their beleaguered troops, the British appealed to the Lahore Darbar for help. Even as Sikh troops assembled around Peshawar to help the British, mutual suspicions between the two continued to muddy their relations, with several unwise moves exacerbating them still further. Major Mackeson, a key British official, made the absurd suggestion—considering he was desperately casting about for Sikh help—that Peshawar should be taken over from the Sikhs. He also tried to bribe the Muslim Auxiliary Battalion of the Sikhs, but was rebuffed. Pressure on Gulab Singh too was kept up. Those trying weeks and months led to rising resentments of Sikh soldiers against the British, and against Sher Singh for trying to involve them in Punjab's affairs.

Despite his varying moods, Auckland's private papers reveal a more moderate approach than the bluster and deceit of his successors Ellenborough, Hardinge and Dalhousie. Two of his letters are particularly interesting. To Clerk he wrote: "I am always a little surprised at your warlike tone in regard to Lahore, and I should find it more difficult, than you seem to think it would be, to frame a declaration of war with the Sikhs . . . every demand made upon the Darbar has been complied with. Our convoys and our merchants continue to traverse the Punjab frequently under Sikh escorts with stores and treasures of immense value. But nothing justifies our interference."

To Sir John Hobhouse, President of the Board of Control of the East India Company, he wrote: "I thought that Clerk made a false step when he proposed through Faqueer Azeezood Din [Aziz-ud-Din, Ranjit Singh's foreign minister] to the Maharaja that for a consideration he would march with the British force for the restoration of order, for I thought it likely that such a proposition would have the effect of combining parties in a manner and upon grounds which would be very unfavourable to us." Which was precisely what happened. Even though the British force never materialized, the mere suggestion—which soon became known—compromised Sher Singh's popularity still further, especially with the army. Since it had brought him to power, its disenchantment with him made him more vulnerable to the shifty Dhyan Singh. The fact that this man was detested by the army did not help either.

Another threat to Sher Singh, at the instigation of Dhyan Singh, now materialized in the form of the chiefs of Sandhanwalia, Attar Singh and Ajit Singh along with their uncle Lehna Singh. Remotely related to Ranjit Singh, the Sandhanwalia chiefs had first befriended Chand Kaur, widow of Ranjit Singh's eldest son, and after her eclipse, fearful of Sher Singh's anger, had crossed the Sutlej to seek British protection. On the latters' intervention, Sher Singh had allowed them to return to Lahore where, in connivance with Dhyan Singh, they assassinated Sher Singh and his young son Pratap Singh on 15 September 1843. Within hours they also killed Dhyan Singh, whose son Hira Singh now shrewdly appealed to the army to rally around Ranjit Singh's youngest son, Dalip Singh. Ajit Singh and Lehna Singh died in the army action, while Attar Singh fled back to the British camp across the Sutlej. Dalip Singh became Maharaja on 18 September 1843, and Hira Singh his prime minister.

Vengeance was in the air. With a five-year-old on the throne, and an inexperienced, petulant young man as the head of government, the air was rife with rumours and intrigue. Hira Singh's first act was to murder those who had opposed his father's move to make him king after Nau Nihal Singh's death. He then turned on Jawahar Singh, brother of Dalip Singh's mother, Rani Jind Kaur, and threw him in jail. He next confiscated the *jagirs* of Kashmira Singh and Peshaura Singh, sons of Ranjit Singh. But the army refused to accept this slight on Ranjit Singh's sons and their *jagirs* were restored. Having fallen out with his father's brother Suchet Singh, he had him killed when he was returning to Lahore from Jammu. Others to be killed at his behest included Prince Kashmira Singh, Attar Singh Sandhanwalia and a Sikh divine, Baba Bir Singh. His attempt to get Rani Jind Kaur poisoned proved his undoing, and Hira Singh was killed by the army on 21 December 1844.

If any hopes were entertained for an improvement in the situation, they were ill-founded. Jawahar Singh, Rani Jind Kaur's brother, who now became prime minister, was no better than his predecessors. After bringing Gulab Singh, the Jammu dogra, to heel for not paying tribute to the Lahore Darbar, he then sent a force to Attock which Prince Peshaura Singh had occupied, and when the prince agreed to come to Lahore, he was waylaid, taken back to Attock and killed. This was too much for the army, already mistrustful of Jawahar Singh's intentions with regard to the British. He was shot to death by Sikh soldiers on 12 September 1845. With only Gulab Singh of the many conspirators left, things might have settled down but for the appearance of two other arch-villains: "Teja Singh, an insignificant Brahmin of the Gangetic Doab, and Lal Singh, another Brahmin from Gandhara Valley . . ." They had risen in the Lahore Darbar through devious means. In November 1845 both were chosen to succeed Jawahar Singh, Lal Singh as prime minister and Teja Singh as commander-in-chief of the Sikh army.

Why did Gulab Singh not become prime minister? The choice of leadership, according to some accounts, was reached through lots drawn by the infant Maharaja Dalip Singh. Not that Gulab Singh had done too badly for himself since joining the Lahore Darbar. By playing people against each other over the years he had amassed immense wealth, and by courtesy of the Darbar acquired lands in Jammu while continuing to nurse ambitions of becoming a key player in Punjab. His aspirations left no room for pangs of conscience or purity of ideals, and because he was wilier even than his brothers Dhyan Singh and Suchet Singh, he had outlived them both.

In April 1841, less than two years after Maharaja Ranjit Singh's death, he was sent to Kashmir to restore order after some disturbances, but as Cunningham comments, "it was soon apparent that Gulab Singh had made the governor, whom he was aiding, a creature of his own, and had become a virtual master of the valley," though no more than that. In November 1841, on a mission to help the British after their abortive expedition to Afghanistan, he was identified by them "as a most likely instrument of British policy and plans, so far as a Sikh dominion was concerned." Given his habitual tendency to help himself, it was more than likely he struck a deal with the British, despite their mistrust of his "troublesome ambitions"; based on the old adage of there being no permanent friends or enemies but only permanent interests, they continued to deal with him. This relationship was to be of enormous help to the British in the First Anglo-Sikh War.

That Gulab Singh took to feathering his nest whenever he could after Ranjit Singh's death was evident during his July 1840 mission to subdue Iskardo Fort: he looted the treasury in Jeswareh Fort and despatched all its contents to his home in Jammu. After the deaths of Kharak Singh and Nau Nihal, and with the decline of Chand Kaur's fortunes, although he was the custodian of her *jagirs*, he "carried off the accumulated treasures of Ranjit Singh [now her property] which were in the [Lahore] Fort. Sixteen carts were filled with rupees and other silver coins, while 500 horsemen were each entrusted with a bag of gold mohurs and his orderlies were also entrusted with jewellery and other valuable articles. The costly *pashminas*, and rich wardrobes, and the best horses in Ranjit Singh's stables, were all purloined by Gulab Singh . . ."

He also misappropriated the revenues of 22 districts under his administration and usurped several of the hill states' tributary to the Sikhs. He was by no means hard-up because Ranjit had all too often made him gifts for services rendered. Besides owning large tracts of land in the hills, Gulab Singh also owned farmlands between the Chenab and the Jhelum, his various *jagirs*, and a monopoly of the salt mines at Kheora.

Although Gulab Singh's sense of self-interest and his betrayal of the Darbar would be rewarded by the British, the centre-stage for a while was occupied by Lal Singh and Teja Singh. Their coming to power was a prelude to the Darbar's showdown with the Company, for a hawkish Governor-General, Lord Ellenborough, who had replaced the comparatively reasonable Auckland, was set on assembling a sizeable British force south of the Sutlej, of a strength needed to invade Punjab. In a letter to the Duke of Wellington on 20 April 1844, he wrote: "We can only consider our relations with Lahore to be those of an armed truce. I earnestly hope nothing may compel us to cross the Sutlej, and that we may have no attack to repel till November 1845. I shall then be prepared for anything. In the meantime we shall do all we can in a quiet way to strengthen ourselves." Almost as if working to a time-table, the British did declare war on the Sikh State on 13 December 1845. But since appearances had to be kept up, and the British had to be shown as responding to unprovoked aggression, their moves must convey a sense of *noblesse oblige.*

With Ellenborough's recall in July 1844 his successor, Lord Hardinge, felt that events in Punjab might favour British plans: "In the hills Gulob Singh has succeeded in raising a religious war against the Sikhs. At Peshawar, the symptoms of disaffection are equally averse to Sikh ascendancy—the insurgents are Musalmans; at Mooltan, the governor threw off the Sikh yoke. There is, therefore, every sign of a dismemberment of the conquests of the old Punjab." This was obviously the right time to intervene.

Writing on 23 January 1845, Hardinge observed: "even if we had a case for devouring an ally in his adversity, we are not ready . . . moderation will do us no harm, if in the interval the hills and the plains weaken each other; but on what plea could we attack the Punjab, if this were the month of October and we had our army in readiness?" There were hopes that Gulab Singh's "religious war" and Punjab's "dismemberment" would provide the "plea" for British intervention. Of course Gulab Singh too would be encouraged to do everything he possibly could to embarrass the Darbar. But there were some qualms of conscience as well: "how are we to justify the seizure of a friend's territory, who in our adversity assisted us to retrieve our affairs?"

By October 1844 the British had 17,000 infantrymen and 60 pieces of artillery south of the Sutlej with 10,000 more men expected within a month. By 8 January 1845 Hardinge confidently stated: "we have 200,000 men pretty well up for defensive objects, and 36,000 for offensive operations." The build-up of troops was unrelenting. Mobilization of an increasing number of European and Indian regiments was augmented by more field batteries, heavy ordnance and over 600 elephants to haul them. Components of pontoon bridges at strategic locations along the Sutlej were assembled, construction of cantonments at Ambala, Ludhiana, Ferozepur and Kasauli completed, and exercises conducted under the very eyes of Sikh troops stationed in the *cis*-Sutlej area. The instigator of this provocative act was Major George Broadfoot, British Agent at Ludhiana, whose hostility towards the Sikhs dated back several years. His deputy, Robert Cust, viewed him as "the prime mover, by many considered the cause of this [the First Sikh] war."

Ellenborough had supported Broadfoot with assurances that "I will not fail to make him [Hardinge] acquainted with your merits and services." Broadfoot's principal "merit" was that as a willing instrument of his superiors' Punjab policy, he could be trusted to play the role of *agent provocateur*. Since he was aware of the Sikh army's antipathy to the British, his provocations were aimed at goading them into precipitating matters. One of his more audacious acts on taking over at Ludhiana was, as Cunningham observes once more: "to declare the *cis*-Sutlej possessions of Lahore to be under British protection equally with Patiala and other chiefships, and also to be liable to escheat on the death or deposition of Maharaja Dalip Singh." No wonder Hardinge was approving: "Broadfoot is in his element on the frontier."

Even though the major's impertinence was not officially communicated to Lahore, news of it infuriated the Sikhs. During Ranjit Singh's reign "British suzerainty over his *cis*-Sutlej possessions had never been claimed, and questions of jurisdiction that arose were dealt with by mutual understanding and goodwill." So the "escheat" idea, that the Sikh Darbar's possessions south of the Sutlej which had been administered by Lahore since 1809 could revert to the British in the event of Dalip Singh's death, was obviously designed to provoke a Sikh retaliation. Broadfoot's crude move had a sobering effect on Patiala, Nabha, Jind and Faridkot, the *cis*-Sutlej states which had embraced the British but now felt diminished by a major's decree. The major's two subsequent actions finally helped him achieve his aim. The first was his offensive behaviour towards a judge of the Lahore court who was crossing the Sutlej in the course of his duties without British permission. According to a British observer Broadfoot's intervention "was wholly unjustifiable"; another felt that had the judge acted with less restraint, the shot that killed one of his followers in the scuffle "would have turned out to be the first shot of the great Sikh war." The major's second provocation in early November 1845 was confiscation of two villages of the Sikh State near Ludhiana on the patently false ground that they were harbouring criminals. According to Cunningham "every act of Major Broadfoot was considered to denote a foregone conclusion, and to be conceived in a spirit of enmity rather than goodwill."

Broadfoot's actions, combined with British troop movements south of the Sutlej towards which the Governor-General was himself heading, left the Sikhs in no doubt of British intentions. Cunningham again: "Had the shrewd committees of the [Sikh] army observed no military preparations on the part of the English, they would not have heeded the insidious exhortations of such mercenary men as Lal Singh and Teja Singh, although in former days they would have marched unenquiringly towards Delhi at the bidding of their great Maharaja . . . [so] when the men were tauntingly asked whether they would quietly look on while the limits of the Khalsa dominions were being reduced . . . they answered that they would defend with their lives all belonging to the commonwealth of Gobind and that they would march and give battle to the invaders on their own ground."

As was bound to happen, units of the Sikh army under the command of Teja Singh crossed the Sutlej on 12 December, and the British Governor-General declared war on the Lahore Darbar on 13 December 1845. The home-grown provocations of a major proved more successful in providing the British with a raison d'être for war than the hoped-for "religious war" of Gulab Singh or the eagerly awaited "dismemberment" of Punjab.

Cavalry units of the army under Lal Singh also assembled north of the river in support of Sikh troops who had already crossed the Sutlej. Ferozepur, where in February 1845 the British had assembled a fleet of 60 boats built in Bombay for transporting 6,000 troops in a single crossing, was chosen for attack. It was stocked with military equipment and stores. The decision to attack Ferozepur began to unfold a sordid drama of deceit by Teja Singh and Lal Singh. The latter at first refused to cross the river to reinforce Sikh formations, but his troops compelled him to do so, although this in no way changed his personal agenda. He "had not come to gain a victory over the British; his object was to solicit their goodwill and continue as minister in a dependent Punjab." With foresight he had already informed the British of this.

Lal Singh and Teja Singh both desired this goal. They urged on their troops "the necessity of leaving the easy prey of a cantonment

[Ferozepur] untouched," and to take on the main body of the British army further south so that "the fame of the Khalsa [could be] exalted by the captivity or death of a Governor-General." An assurance to the British that despite the small numbers of their garrison force, Ferozepur would not be harmed was secretly sent on 16 December in spite of the fact that Ferozepur would have been easy game with only 7,000 defenders against the Sikh force of 35,000 or more. According to a British historian, had the Sikhs—after crossing the Sutlej—captured Basian, a major supply base of the British, and then attacked Ferozepur, it "would almost certainly have fallen, lacking fortifications capable of withstanding their heavy artillery."

In keeping with Lal Singh and Teja Singh's plan of not attacking the Ferozepur garrison under Sir John Littler, the Sikh army moved towards Mudki where advancing British divisions from Ambala were rumoured to have arrived. Here, on 18 December, a detachment of the Sikhs consisting of "less than two thousand infantry, supported by about twenty-two pieces of artillery, and eight or ten thousand horsemen" launched an attack on the British force. As soon as the enemy was engaged, Lal Singh deserted his men. Though the Sikh attack was repulsed, "the success of the English was not so complete as should have been achieved by the victors in so many battles." A modern English view is that "the whole action was unsatisfactory and unduly costly." Instead of continuing the engagement, the British "wisely determined to effect a junction with the division of Sir John Littler before assailing the advance wing of the Sikh army which was encamped in a deep horseshoe-form around the village of P'heerooshuhur about ten miles both from Mudki and from Ferozepore." Had Littler's force been neutralized at Ferozepur, the course of the Ferozeshahr battle would have favoured the Sikhs.

Even so, the ferocity of the fighting at Ferozeshahr is the stuff of legend. On the other side of the coin, the perverse persistence by Lal Singh and Teja Singh in betrayals is of a kind that makes men hang their heads in shame. The testimony of British participants and military historians is interesting. At Ferozeshahr "the confident English," writes Cunningham, Political Agent of the East India Company turned historian, "had at last got the field they wanted . . . [but] the resistance met was wholly unexpected . . . Guns were dismounted, and their ammunition was blown into the air; squadrons were checked in mid career; battalion after battalion was hurled back with shattered ranks . . . the obstinacy of the contest threw the English into confusion; men of all regiments and arms were mixed together; generals were doubtful of the fact or of the extent of their own success, and colonels knew not what had become of the regiments they commanded or of the army of which they formed a part."

This was the scene on 21 December. "On that memorable night the English were hardly masters of the ground on which they stood . . ." According to Sir Hope Grant, a British general, the night of 21 December "was one of gloom and never perhaps in our annals of Indian warfare, has a British army on so large a scale been nearer to defeat which could have involved annihilation. The Sikhs had practically recovered the whole of their entrenched camp; our exhausted and decimated divisions bivouacked without mutual cohesion over a wide area . . ." As day broke on 22 December, the opposing forces once again joined battle in the midst of which the reserve Sikh army under Teja Singh arrived on the scene: "The wearied and famished English saw before them a desperate and, perhaps, useless struggle." On this day, had the Sikhs been led by commanders of integrity, they would have emerged triumphant at a time "when the fate of India trembled in the balance."

But Teja Singh refused to attack the dispirited British, although urged by his seasoned commanders to fall upon them, according to the analysis of one modern historian, "at daybreak on the 22nd when they were entangled in the entrenchments. This he would have done had he been as loyal as the last of his followers. He delayed until Lal Singh was everywhere put to flight, until the British line had had time to reform—and ranged themselves around their colours. At no time did he do more than skirmish with the British, making feints rather than sending in his men in a resolute attack." General Sir Henry Havelock, who took part in the battle, felt that "India has been saved by a miracle." Quoting from a letter by Hardinge, the Governor-General, the British Prime Minister, Sir Robert Peel, told the House of Commons of the mournfully large losses sustained by his officers and men in fighting with "the most warlike [men] in India."

What these accounts reveal is the manner in which victory was won

THE SIKHS

by a mere whisker, and the means by which a British defeat was averted in the opening battle of the First Anglo-Sikh War. They place in perspective the role of Teja Singh and Lal Singh, and the extent to which their treason determined the outcome of this crucial battle. Even then victory was not decisive: the precipitous retreat of the British cavalry, which should have been a sign for Teja Singh to attack the remaining enemy troops, was deliberately misinterpreted by him to his men as indicative of the enemy's intention to attack them in the rear. And so "his largely untouched force began slowly to follow Lal Singh's discomfited units which were making their way back towards the Sutlej."

Modern British assessment of this astounding withdrawal of largely "untouched" Sikh forces is that "The Sikh leader had only to continue to fire from his heavy guns to win an easy victory, for even the British found the trial almost unendurable. Perhaps Teja Singh did know this, for his . . . failure to press home his obvious advantages on the 22nd point[s] to his reported reluctance to see the Khalsa beat the British." Remarking on the courage and valour of the Sikh soldiers so badly led and betrayed, Peel remarked: "we are astonished at the numbers, the power of concentration and the skill and courage of the enemy."

Even as deceit paved the way for British victory, their losses at Mudki and Ferozeshahr were very high. The killed included senior British officers Sir Robert Sale, Sir John McCaskill and Brigadier Wallace, two staff officers Herries and Munro, Major Broadfoot, who had figured prominently in Punjab's affairs, and many others. In all they lost 215 officers and men killed and 655 wounded at Mudki, and 2,415 killed or wounded at Ferozeshahr. As for Sikh losses in the former engagement, one British account "claims that it is possible that their casualties did not exceed those of the British." At Ferozeshahr they have been placed at 2,000 in all.

The initial excitement in Britain over Punjab events was soon replaced by the realization that a high cost had been paid for a victory that was "not very far removed from failure." Over a fifth of the British force had either died on the field of battle or been wounded. And the largest body of armed men ever assembled by the British in India still faced the Sikh army on the Sutlej. High casualties and uncertain "victory" also resulted in a flurry of secret correspondence between the Governor-General, Commander-in-Chief, Prime Minister and others over the conduct of military operations, strained relations between Hardinge and the army chief, Sir Hugh Gough, and conferment of commissions on non-commissioned officers following exceptionally heavy losses of British officers. These agonizing reappraisals eventually resulted in the Commander-in-Chief's resignation. But whilst these acrimonious exchanges would stretch over months, the immediate strategy of the British was to reinforce their badly depleted forces.

On Christmas Day 1845, in a very unworthy move, "the Governor-General issued a proclamation encouraging desertion from the Sikh ranks, with the assurance of present rewards and future pensions . . ." This was doubly disgraceful because of the moral high ground Hardinge liked to flaunt. (He would be guilty of even more unbecoming conduct in the next two months, after the third battle at Aliwal.) In a series of moves and counter-moves centred around the fortifications and supply routes in the Ludhiana region—during which the British suffered a disconcerting reverse at Badowal on 21 January—the battle-lines were finally drawn on the left bank of the Sutlej. The British positions faced Sikh entrenchments between the villages of Aliwal and Budri, both in the Khalsa's possession. The battle took place on 28 January 1846, with 12,000 British troops facing a Sikh force of similar strength, although some British estimates place it at 15,000 men.

It was a fierce battle: "Even our Peninsular heroes say they never saw more severe fighting." But in the end the Sikhs lost, in large part because of the river behind them which left them no room to manoeuvre. Prevented from retreating to more advantageous positions when they were outflanked, they had to jump into the river and swim across "under a tempest of shot and shell from the British guns." The casualties on both sides were high, and according to unconfirmed estimates 3,000 Sikhs were killed. The British lost 598 killed and wounded. One reason for Sikh losses was the ferocity with which they fought: "they knelt to receive the dashing charge of the British Lancers and their Indian comrades; but as these approached, they instinctively rose and delivered their fire. Beneath the charge that followed, they did not yield, nor was it till they had three times been ridden over, that they gave way. After the battle it was found that the ground was more thickly strewn with the bodies of the victorious horsemen than of the beaten infantry."

Sobraon, the remaining Sikh redoubt south of the Sutlej, was the setting for the fourth and last battle of the First Anglo-Sikh War. As at Ferozeshahr, far from being a clean battle between worthy adversaries, it was tainted by secret deals to facilitate a British victory on the battlefield. The parties to the deals were the Governor-General and the avaricious Gulab Singh. In February 1846, the former disclosed to the Secret Committee that Gulab Singh had been in touch with him. Whilst they were ostensibly in contact to discuss the Darbar's affairs after its defeat, the reality was different. Gulab Singh had become prime minister at the Lahore Darbar. Having inveigled himself into the good books of Maharaja Dalip Singh's mother, Rani Jind Kaur, he had replaced the perfidious Lal Singh. In the public and secret despatches of the Government of India, which include Gough's despatches and Hardinge's papers, "the latter refer with staggering frankness to . . . the open and avowed treachery of Gulab Singh." But some historians feel that Lal Singh and Teja Singh are less culpable, although their stand, in light of evidence available, is unconvincing. "[Hardinge] knew that time was pressing, that the speedy dictation of a treaty under the walls of Lahore was essential to the British. A remedy had to be found that would accomplish this and, at the same time, suit the ends of Gulab Singh, Teja Singh, and Lal Singh. It required a policy of discretion allied to shameless treason." Treasonable acts began soon thereafter.

Astonishingly, Lal Singh and Teja Singh were again assigned military commands and this time their subversion of the Sikh army from within was under the direction of Gulab Singh. To begin with, the thirteen days between Aliwal and Sobraon were wasted through deliberate inaction. They should have been utilized to attack the British both at Ferozepur—whose defenders were too few to defend themselves—and Aliwal where the depleted British force was desperately awaiting reinforcements and supplies. When battle was finally joined at Sobraon on 10 February, the diversionary opportunity offered by Ferozepur was lost, and the main British force at Aliwal had been augmented. It was hardly surprising that the British won.

The battle was fought with daring and incredible determination, and blood was shed with utter disregard for life. The intensity of the fighting can be judged from this single engagement as described by a British historian: "The Sikhs, seeing their right had been broken into, commenced a rush from all parts of their position to retake it in a strong counter-attack delivered with determination. In vain Stacey's brigade tried to withstand the mass of enemy; Wilkinson's brigade was forced back, and even the addition of Ashburnham's reserve failed to restore the earlier successes. Gradually the three brigades were driven back, disputing every inch of ground but unable to maintain themselves, until the Sikhs finally drove them from the batteries and recaptured the guns." Characteristically, "Teja Singh, the Sikh Commander-in-Chief, had fled soon after the first assault . . . Lal Singh and his cavalry force were nowhere to be seen. He had taken the road to Lahore."

He opened the road to Lahore for the British as well. As if to compound the tragedy still further, Teja Singh, whilst fleeing across the bridge of boats, destroyed it behind him to prevent an orderly Sikh retreat and regrouping on the northern bank. This, no doubt, was in the spirit of the *entente cordiale* between the Governor-General and Gulab Singh. The latter's twofold aim was to ensure the defeat of his own side and facilitate the adversary's victory. As a footnote to this deceit was the decency shown by an additional aide-de-camp to the Governor-General during the Sobraon battle. Captain Joseph Davey Cunningham, who openly expressed his disgust at this "understanding" in his *History of the Sikhs*, earned the severe displeasure of his superiors and as punishment was removed from political office and returned to his regiment in disgrace. He died within two years—of a broken heart, it is said—at the age of thirty-nine.

What was the "understanding" this upright officer found distasteful? As he put it: ". . . that the Sikh army should be attacked by the English, and that when beaten it should be openly abandoned by its own government; and further that the passage of the Sutlej should be unopposed and the road to the capital laid open to the visitors. Under such circumstances of discreet policy and shameless treason was the battle of Sobraon fought."

Nor was there any grace in British conduct after the road to Lahore was open. Aside from acquisition of territory, dismemberment of the Sikh State and disbanding of the Sikh army—which were to be expected despite the verbal nobility of the victors—the degree of British arrogance from the outset was odious. Within four days of entering Punjab, Hardinge issued a proclamation which stated that the entire exercise had been forced on the British for "effectually protecting the British provinces and vindicating the authority of the British Government, and punishing the violators of treaties and the disturbers of the public peace."

This was of course laughable to those who had witnessed the provocations, intrigues, military preparations and territorial aims of the British prior to their war with the Sikhs. In continuation of the tenor and tone he had adopted, Hardinge curtly received the dignitaries of the Lahore Darbar, and as further humiliation required that the young Maharaja should come to him in person, which he did on 18 February. To Hardinge's credit is the manner in which he responded to Gulab Singh's invidious suggestion when Dalip Singh was brought before him: "that the Maharaja should not be allowed to return to the Rani, intimating plainly that it was for the Governor-General to dispose of the young Chief as he pleased! Hardinge incredulously looked at the functionary of the Sikh Government: he praised him for his neutrality but discreetly ignored his ignominious suggestion."

By the Treaty of Lahore of 9 March 1846, the British acquired the Darbar territories south of the Sutlej; they took the entire territory (11,408 square miles) lying between the Sutlej and Beas; the Sikh army—except for a few battalions—would be disbanded; the Sikhs would also pay an indemnity of a million and a half pounds for war expenses; Jammu and Kashmir were taken under British control; Gulab Singh was declared an independent sovereign of the territories already in his possession—*and also those which the British might reward him with.*

Article 12 of this Treaty deserves to be reproduced in full.

IN CONSIDERATION OF THE SERVICES RENDERED BY RAJA GOLAB SINGH OF JAMMU TO THE LAHORE STATE, TOWARDS PROCURING THE RESTORATION OF THE RELATIONS OF AMITY

BETWEEN THE LAHORE AND BRITISH GOVERNMENTS, THE MAHARAJA HEREBY AGREES TO RECOGNIZE THE INDEPENDENT SOVEREIGNTY OF RAJA GOLAB SINGH, IN SUCH TERRITORIES AND DISTRICTS IN THE HILLS AS MAY BE MADE OVER TO THE SAID RAJA GOLAB SINGH BY SEPARATE AGREEMENT BETWEEN HIMSELF AND THE BRITISH GOVERNMENT, WITH THE DEPENDENCIES THEREOF, WHICH MAY HAVE BEEN IN THE RAJA'S POSSESSION SINCE THE TIME OF THE LATE MAHARAJA KHARAK SINGH; AND THE BRITISH GOVERNMENT, IN CONSIDERATION OF THE GOOD CONDUCT OF RAJA GOLAB SINGH, ALSO AGREES TO RECOGNIZE HIS INDEPENDENCE IN SUCH TERRITORIES, AND ADMIT HIM TO THE PRIVILEGES OF A SEPARATE TREATY WITH THE BRITISH GOVERNMENT.

In a later treaty with Gulab Singh signed on 16 March 1846:

THE BRITISH GOVERNMENT TRANSFERS AND MAKES OVER, FOR EVER, IN INDEPENDENT POSSESSION TO MAHARAJA GULAB SINGH, AND THE MALE HEIRS OF HIS BODY, ALL THE HILLY OR MOUNTAINOUS COUNTRY WITH ITS DEPENDENCIES SITUATED TO THE EASTWARD OF THE RIVER INDUS, AND WESTWARD OF THE RIVER RAVI, INCLUDING CHAMBA AND EXCLUDING LAHUL, BEING PART OF THE TERRITORY CEDED TO THE BRITISH GOVERNMENT BY THE LAHORE STATE . . .

Thus was treason rewarded by the grateful British.

Prior to the transfer of the above lands to Gulab Singh, another quiet transaction had taken place. Since the Lahore Darbar could not pay the indemnity imposed on it, and the Company had to balance its books, the State of Kashmir was sold to Gulab Singh for a million pounds. It was a deal Hardinge was proud of, as came through in his communication to Ellenborough while submitting the Statement of War Charges. "Half a million, the total expenses of the war to the E.I. Co." How was the figure arrived at? The cost of the sixty days Sutlej campaign came to two million pounds, of which a million was earned by selling Kashmir and another half a million realized as indemnity from the Lahore Darbar. "From a financial point of view, the First Sikh War was one of the cheapest . . ." But the Company's profits were higher than this arithmetic indicated. The Treaty took away more than one-third of the Sikh Kingdom's territory, while adding an annual revenue of three million rupees to the Company's revenues. It would prove a steady source of income—which was what the Company was in India for.

Hardinge's sordid deal with Gulab Singh did not go uncommented upon in London. In some quarters it was considered a disgraceful bargain unworthy of the British, and when reminded of it by his predecessor Ellenborough, Hardinge's reply was revealing: "Golab Singh's neutrality was most valuable before I crossed the river. He was informed that his good conduct to us would be appreciated. And yet, after recommending me to bribe the chief of Mooltan by the offer of his independence you consider it treacherous to make Golab Singh the purchaser of Cashmere and the independent prince of the Hills?"

Punjab's administration under the Treaty's terms now rested with Henry Lawrence, the British Resident at Lahore, and not surprisingly, he reinstated Lal Singh and Teja Singh as prime minister of the Sikh Kingdom and commander-in-chief of its army. But Hardinge and others held them in contempt. Lawrence even ignored Lal Singh's new shenanigans, such as confiscating several Khalsa *jagirs* and transferring them to his brother and himself, trying to replace the Multan governor with his own brother, and so on. Only after he over-reached himself and instructed Lahore's representative in Kashmir to refuse to hand the state over to Gulab Singh did the British depose and expel him from Punjab. As for Teja Singh, he was made the raja of Sialkot despite the veto of the eight-year-old Maharaja of Lahore.

Gradually but relentlessly, British control of Punjab was tightening. In addition to their 10,000 troops in Lahore, British interference in every sphere of administration entrenched them still further. And even more so after the signing of the Second Treaty of Lahore at Bhyrowal on 22 December 1846. Powers under this new treaty made the Sikh Kingdom—although independent in name—a virtual protectorate of the British. The regent, Rani Jind Kaur, was exiled from Lahore, and the young Maharaja Dalip Singh came under the guardianship of the British. All civil and military matters were now decided by the Resident; a council of ministers with eight members (six Sikhs, one Hindu and one Muslim) existed only in name.

Having taken large slices of the Sikh Kingdom for themselves and Gulab Singh, the British buckled down to tightening their hold on what was left of Ranjit Singh's sprawling domain. The reduction of his formidable army—except for a token force—was first on the agenda. Then came moves to boost revenues, since these would eventually find their way to the Company under the new treaty's terms. In matters of administration, British commissioners were sent to different regions, as were companies of troops. But it was not easy to exercise control over a region with vastly different customs, diverse constituents and simmering resentments. This became evident when a small fracas in Multan at the end of 1847 turned into a major rebellion by April 1848.

This development coincided with a change in the key personae in Punjab's unfolding drama. In January 1848, Hardinge made way for the new Governor-General, the Marquis of Dalhousie. Henry Lawrence took leave and returned to Britain, as it happened, on the same boat as Hardinge. Dalhousie, known for his "wild outbursts" and "overstrung" nature, was hardly the man to find a statesmanlike way out of the conflagration which was about to occur; especially as he had come committed to Punjab's annexation to the rest of India.

The easing out of Mulraj, Multan's governor, by the British and the murder by mutinous soldiers of two British officers accompanying his replacement, rapidly escalated into a full-scale mutiny. The new Resident, Sir Frederick Currie, held the Lahore Darbar responsible for the mutiny which British ineptness had precipitated, and demanded that it should be put down with Sikh troops. A mindless order as it turned out.

The Lahore troops accompanying the two unfortunate British officers joined the disaffected Multan soldiers, and the uprising soon spread, with Mulraj, the ousted governor, becoming the rather reluctant rallying point of the riled soldiery. As word got around, men disbanded from the Sikh army also started trickling towards Multan. But despite the seemingly ominous signs, these events were not precursors of a national Sikh uprising, even if the ever-excitable Dalhousie thought otherwise. Determined to "exact a national reparation from the State of Lahore," he vowed that that day would soon come and "the reckoning shall be a heavy one." A considerable amount of bungling helped exacerbate matters still further. With Dalhousie and Gough, Commander-in-Chief of the British army, in favour of a full-scale invasion of Punjab in the cold weather—still five months away—and Currie favouring immediate action to deal with what he considered was only a local affair, an impetuous young subaltern, Lieutenant Herbert Edwardes, took it upon himself to march on Multan with a force of about 14,500, consisting largely of Pathan and Baluch mercenaries and freebooters. As news of British-inspired cries of a *jehad* against the Sikhs spread—understandable in view of past Afghan defeats at Sikh hands—this action evoked religious passions throughout Punjab. Edwardes' action was seen as a deliberate assault on Sikh sensibilities.

Another young officer, a political assistant by the name of Captain James Abbott, added greatly to the worsening situation. Variously described as a "suspicious little autocrat" and a man in "a state of perpetual excitement," Abbott took it into his head to fall out with Sardar Chattar Singh Attariwala, governor of Hazara and a man highly respected both by the Sikhs and the British Resident. Suspicious to the point of paranoia, Abbott convinced himself that Chattar Singh was not to be depended upon, despite all evidence to the contrary. Despite Chattar Singh's initial reluctance to react to the upstart captain's provocations, he finally felt that things had gone far enough when this excitable young man started inciting Muslim levies and peasants against the Sikhs. Not content with this, Abbott then marched on Hazara to subdue Chattar Singh with the help of Muslim mercenaries. Chattar Singh naturally chose to offer armed resistance. In fact, Abbott's tactic of inciting Muslims against the Sikhs was no different from what Edwardes was doing at Multan. Even Currie believed that such attempts to excite religious passions against them was one of the causes of increasing Sikh anger.

But despite Currie's rejection of Abbott's "ready disposition to believe in conspiracies, plots and treason," Dalhousie supported the captain's action. Things now took a dangerous turn. The commander of the Darbar troops who was sent to quell the Multan rebellion, Raja Sher Singh Attariwala, was Chattar Singh's son. Greatly upset by the malicious attempts to tarnish his father's reputation, he first tried to get saner British counsels to intercede, then finding this futile he and his men joined Mulraj in September. This suited Dalhousie. Instead of regretting the runaway situation which allowed the Company's junior officers to take matters into their own hands, he announced that "we have without hesitation resolved that Punjab can no longer be allowed to exist as a power and must be destroyed!"

On 8 October, in a letter to London, he took his customary crudeness still further. "I have drawn the sword and have this time thrown away the scabbard. If the Sikhs, after this is over, arise again, they shall intrench themselves behind a dunghill, and fight with their fingernails, for if I live twelve months they shall have nothing else to fight with." Dalhousie nearly landed on a dunghill himself in the Second Anglo-Sikh War.

The pace of events was quickening. On 16 November 1848, Gough crossed the Ravi to confront Sher Singh who had been joined by several small contingents of the Sikh army. Gough headed a force of 24,000 men and 66 guns. In addition, British forces already in Punjab totalled 26,000 men with several cavalry units. There were also 38,000 Muslim, Afghan, Baluchi and tribal mercenaries, along with 5,000 horse and a camel corps. Out of this astonishing total of over 104,000 men, about 60,000 supported by 145 guns converged to give battle to the Sikhs, whose strength was around 23,000 men, drawn from the Hazara, Peshawar, Tank and Banu garrisons, and including Sher Singh's own contingent. Because the British had for over two years systematically dismantled the Sikh army, sending some of its finest fighting men back to their villages, disbanding its generals and appropriating or destroying its guns, a force of 92,000 men, 31,800 cavalry and over 384 guns was now reduced to a few thousand. Moreover, unlike the British, the heavily outnumbered Sikhs had no reinforcements to fall back upon, as even their unarmed comrades from the Majha and Malwa regions were stopped at river crossings and fords and prevented from joining them. After the British—helped by Pathan horsemen—had taken over the lightly defended fort at Attock, the prospects of Sikh troops from Peshawar joining Chattar Singh's force at Hazara were also slim.

In London "eyebrows were raised at his [Dalhousie's] determination to prosecute an illegal war to end rebellion." Gough, the Commander-in-Chief, "appears to have been in some doubt as to whether he was carrying out operations to suppress a rebellion on behalf of the Durbar, or whether the Durbar in Lahore was itself to be regarded as an enemy." But Dalhousie was undisturbed by these niceties. "Our acts," he said, "require no explanation." He was untroubled by going to war on the pretext of putting down a disturbance *his side had helped create.*

On 22 November 1848, in the first battle of the Second Anglo-Sikh War at Ramnagar on the River Chenab, the British defeat was decisive. The outnumbered Sikhs under Sher Singh, fighting with the river in front and not behind their positions, took a heavy toll of the enemy and amongst those killed were the two cavalry commanders, Brigadier Cureton and Colonel Havelock. To Dalhousie, Ramnagar was "a sad affair with distressing results," the net gain from which was the capture of a handsome Sikh silk standard. The Muslim trooper who secured it was recommended for one of the most distinguished awards. On 3 December the regrouped British forces tried to engage the Sikhs at Sadulpur, a few miles upstream of the Chenab, on its right bank. As two British columns moved from opposite sides to outflank the Sikhs and threaten their rear, Sikh cavalry barred their movement. Under cover of fading light Sher Singh marched to the left bank of the River Jhelum and thus made it possible for Chattar Singh's force to join him later.

Gough viewed Sher Singh's brilliant tactical move as a "victory" for the British, his net gain from it being 60 boats abandoned by the Sikhs. To his disappointment neither Parliament nor Dalhousie was impressed. The Governor-General rather caustically remarked that he would "reserve salutes for real victories which this is not." The President of the Company's Board felt "it is no wonder that all confidence in Lord Gough, if it ever was entertained, should have been entirely lost."

On 13 January 1849 began the battle of Chillianwala, in which a Sikh force of 10,000 faced a much bigger army whose casualties alone came to 2,446 men, which included 132 officers killed. For the British, Chillianwala was a disaster. As a British historian describes: ". . . advancing British infantrymen were mowed down by the terrific fire of the Sikh musketry. The Sikh *ghorcharas* ... in successive onslaughts broke up the British cavalry line and cut down their horsemen ... suddenly to their amazement the enemy took to their heels ... galloping over their own horse artillery and turning it topsy-turvy leaving their comrades to be slaughtered by the Sikhs." At another site "from within the jungle the guns opened up with devastating effect. Lieut. Col. Brookes leading the 24th Foot was killed between the enemy guns. Trapped, the brigade turned to flee in the face of destructive fire of shot and shell." In yet another engagement "a large body of Sikhs surrounded the second Infantry Brigade. Now Gilbert's Force [Sir Walter Gilbert was divisional commander] had neither the cover of guns nor the support of cavalry. In the hand to hand fight, the brigade was repulsed and driven back with heavy loss."

With the onset of darkness Gough ordered his men to retreat to the village of Chillianwala, whilst the Sikhs carried away 40 guns which the British later claimed to have captured themselves. Characteristically, Gough claimed Chillianwala as a victory over the Sikhs, but Dalhousie dismissed the claim as "poetical." As he put it: "we have gained a victory like that of the ancients: it is such an one that 'another such would ruin us.'" London was shocked by the outcome of the battle, and Gough's immediate replacement was demanded. Even the eighty-year-old Wellington volunteered to go to India.

Dalhousie now set about using the Chillianwala disaster to strengthen his case for annexation, even while Auckland, Ellenborough, Hardinge and Henry Lawrence were advising the Cabinet against it. So as not to discourage Dalhousie—expansion being very much the mood of the times—it was delicately suggested that short of annexation, "subjugation without the name" would be appropriate. But London's views mattered little to an unrelenting Dalhousie convinced that "the preservation of our own power upon the spot, and the necessity of maintaining its reputation in order to render secure our positions in India, compel us at once to declare war and prosecute it to the entire subversion of the Sikh dynasty and the absolute subjection of the whole people."

All British resources in India were geared to this end, for the Battle of Gujrat. "Never perhaps had the British amassed so many guns and men in any single battle." The strength of the army assembled for it, including the British force at Lahore, was 56,636 infantry, 11,569 cavalry, 96 field guns and 67 siege guns. Facing them was a Sikh force of about 20,000 men. The Gujrat battle was joined at 7:30 on the morning of 21 February 1849. As in the case of previous battles, this too was fought with ferocity and valour by both sides, but the odds were loaded against the Sikhs, the decisive factor being the artillery strength of the British. After two hours of a sustained cannonade by both sides, the Sikhs were outgunned even though "Fordyce's battery, which came up against the heavy Sikh guns around Bara Kalra, twice had to draw back to replenish men and horses . . . At first the artillery contest appeared to be fairly even, but gradually the British guns got on top and battery after battery of the Sikh artillery was silenced." When Bara Kalra, a village held by the Sikhs as a forward position, was finally stormed by the brigade of 2nd Europeans, "the Sikhs fought desperately and held out to the last man in some of the mud houses in the village." It was the same story elsewhere and when the battle ended Sikh losses were exceptionally heavy: around 4,000 men, as against British casualties of 96 killed and 700 wounded. Suffering from a severe shortage of supplies, the Sikh army fell back on Rawalpindi, which it finally surrendered to the British on 14 March. As its regiments, 16,000 strong, trooped out and laid their weapons before the British, "observers who watched the surrender greatly admired the bearing of the Sikh soldiers, who still carried themselves with pride. They were tired and hungry, but their spirit was by no means broken. It was noticed that many of the older men threw down their talwars [swords] with a gesture of disgust . . ."

Thus ended the Second Sikh War, and with it the curtain came down on Ranjit Singh's proud empire. Even though the absorption of Punjab into the rest of India was a foregone conclusion, clashes between Dalhousie and Henry Lawrence, who had rejoined as Resident, continued. Dalhousie, wedded to the idea "that the British Empire was God's gift to the people of Asia," was all for annexation. He was convinced "that the Sikhs had risen in rebellion against a benevolent government, which had treated them leniently after their first offence, and that it would be unsafe to trust them again." Lawrence's view was quite the opposite. In the end Dalhousie prevailed and the proclamation of complete annexation was issued on 30 March 1849, placing all the Darbar territories under British sovereignty. Dalip Singh was told he could live wherever he wished—except in Punjab—with a pension of 120,000 rupees a year. Since the Punjab campaign cost the Company £1,500,000, it confiscated Maharaja Dalip Singh's property estimated at 15 million rupees. The Maharaja was also forced to surrender the Koh-i-noor Diamond to the Queen of England in a symbolic gesture of his submission. The egotistical Dalhousie sanctimoniously told London: "I do not recollect any subject has fallen on the good fortune of sending so precious and so storied a trophy of war as the Koh-i-nur."

As a requiem to the Sikh Wars, these words of a British military historian aptly sum up the tragedy. "The Sikh Army fought valiantly and stubbornly in spite of poor generalship from commanders who, for political reasons, did not want to win the war and who were constantly in touch with the British commanders to assure them of that fact!" Whilst acknowledging the extent to which treachery was encouraged to turn the tide in Britain's favour, very few British writers have criticized the complicity of their countrymen who encouraged traitors to betray their soldiers and their state. Cunningham, who dared to expose the sordid deals by which these wars were won, paid the price for it. But for his premature death, Broadfoot, the *agent provocateur* who was given the task of provoking the Sikhs into crossing the Sutlej, would no doubt have been honoured for his dishonourable role.

Dalhousie's own actions were no less dishonest than those of Broadfoot. He engineered the invasion of Punjab on the false pretext of dealing with a fracas in Multan. And later, when Punjab was finally annexed—which is what the invasion was designed for—the annexation was carried out without the home government's authority. The exiled Dalip Singh, last of Ranjit Singh's sons, was converted to Christianity at Fatehgarh on 8 March 1853. He was then fifteen. In a letter to him, Dalhousie wrote: "I earnestly hope that your future life may be in conformity with the precepts of that religion, and that you may show to your countrymen in India an example of a pure and blameless life, such as is befitting a Christian prince." As for "pure and blameless" lives, although Dalhousie was at pains to stress that Dalip Singh's conversion to the Christian faith was by his own free will, in a letter to

THE SIKHS

Sir George Couper he wrote: "Politically, we could desire nothing better, for it destroys his influence for ever!" Significantly, the two men
who closely attended on Dalip Singh during those years—Purohit
Golab Rai and Bhagun Lal—were Brahmins.

The ultimate blame for what happened to the Sikh State rests neither with the dogras, nor with the Brahmins, who subverted it from
within, nor with the British who triumphed with the help of traitors. In
the end the Sikhs themselves are responsible for failing to protect the
magnificent legacy of an exceptional man. And to an extent Ranjit
Singh himself also contributed to the tragedy by ignoring the republican temper of the Khalsa and leaving its fate to monarchical whims.
While he handled his followers with élan during his lifetime, he failed
to foresee that if the tenets and traditions of the faith that held the state
together continued to be overlooked, the state would crumble. And
under his successors it did so. Lacking his powerful personality and
charisma, incapable of providing inspiring leadership, blind to the
betrayals around them, and unable to understand the dynamics of the
Khalsa, Ranjit Singh's successors mindlessly destroyed a distinctive
moment in Sikh history.

5

From Annexation to Partition
1849–1947

Sikh loss of sovereignty underscored the recurring ironies of history, since Britain herself had lost America 66 years earlier through irresponsible leadership. If the leading British figures of the time "had been other than they were, there might have been statesmanship instead of folly, with a train of altered consequences reaching to the present." So also in the case of the Sikhs, but with a significant difference. The Sikhs, unlike the British, were not just let down by irresponsible political leaders, they were continuously subverted even on the battlefield by the treachery and amorality of those who had risen to powerful positions under them.

". . . despite the deceitfulness of courtiers such as Lal Singh and Tej Singh, they [the Sikhs] had fought the *ferringhi* [white foreigner] squarely, and maintained their manly demeanour even in defeat." In the ominous silence that descended on the vanquished Punjab, no Sikh voices were raised in supplication, though this fact was rarely recorded either by Western historians or Sikhs themselves since they were not great communicators. The adversaries of the Sikhs, more often than not, depicted even their victories as defeats. The British, for their part, understood all too well the power of the written word; the art of skilfully manipulating facts to enthral audiences at home and abroad. "No nation has ever produced a military history of such verbal nobility as the British," observes Barbara Tuchman. "Retreat or advance, win or lose, blunder or bravery, murderous folly or unyielding resolution, all emerge alike clothed in dignity and touched with glory . . . Other nations attempt but never quite achieve the same self-esteem. It was not by might but by the power of her self-image that Britain in her century dominated the world."

When the Sikhs' climactic moment in history was at an end, the British improved on the brashness of men like Dalhousie. After their annexation of the Sikh Kingdom, British self-interest was served by a more flexible and far-ranging policy. Its foremost priority was the dismantling of the Sikh army, followed by the establishment of an elaborate governmental structure which included executive, judicial, revenue-collection and developmental functions. The administration of the Province of Punjab was entrusted to a Board of Commissioners, of whom there were three: Sir Henry Lawrence, his brother John Lawrence, and Charles Mansell. The Punjab was divided into seven Commissionerships and 27 Districts, and by 1 June 1849 the new administrative system had been set up in most areas.

The District Officer's job was collection of revenue, keeping the peace, the dispensation of justice, and the economic development of his District. Revenue in Punjab was collected from water rates, land revenue, *malikana* (fees for recognizing proprietary titles), and various other forms of duties, rents and taxes. When it came to constructing canals, however, the cost of their development was largely financed by the Punjabis rather than the colonial administration although the revenue collected went to its treasury, and from there to the British exchequer as charges for administering India. Dramatic increases in agricultural production were high on the agenda, alongside construction of metalled roads, post and telegraph systems and, later, railways. These sectors had clear goals: the creation of stable conditions in which the high-voltage human energy of Punjab could be harnessed to generate wealth which British trading houses, banks, shippers and others could exploit. Which is what the colonial age was about.

The Mutiny of 1857 is not part of the story of the Sikhs. No account of it, therefore, is given here, nor of its principal cause in Dalhousie's insensitivity to Hindu and Muslim sensibilities, nor even of Sir Henry Lawrence's sensible handling of the situation in Punjab which prevented any disturbance in the province. After the Mutiny had finally been put down by the British, with much bloodshed on both sides, the government of India was transferred, on 1 November 1858, from the East India Company to the British crown. Pax Britannica had arrived in India.

An apparent paradox, which has prevented understanding of the Sikhs' attitude to the 1857 Mutiny, now needs explanation. Though the Sikhs are often accused of failing to support an uprising aimed at ending British rule in India, their reasons for not doing so are seldom mentioned. The most important of these is that the Sikhs did not view the Mutiny as an attempt to force the British out of India, since the *poorbias*—sepoys of the Company's Bengal Army—were unlikely representatives of nationalist aspirations. They had served the British Indian Army for the preceding hundred years, and had helped the British bring India under their dominance. So the Sikhs found the *poorbias'* nationalist pretensions unconvincing. Nationalism, in fact, did not exist then. It began to flower almost half a century later and that too after the British integrated India, thus making it easier for Indians to think in national terms.

The distinguished historian R.C. Majumdar places events in perspective. "The Punjab was conquered by the British with the help of the sepoys less than ten years before the outbreak of the Mutiny. The battle of Chillianwala, which proved the valour and heroism of the Sikhs and their ability under more favourable circumstances to defeat the English, was fought in 1849, only eight years before the Mutiny." And yet these sepoys "who are supposed to have sacrificed their all for the sake of their country in 1857, had not the least scruple to fight the Sikhs who were the last defenders of liberty in India." He then points out that "It is difficult to resist the conclusion that the attitude and activities of the sepoys in 1849 certainly did not correspond to the patriotic fervour with which they are supposed to be endowed in 1857." Which just about sums it up. The Sikhs refused to be taken in by men who had been fighting them under the British colours a few years earlier.

Another fact often overlooked is that the idea of placing the Mughal emperor, Bahadur Shah II, on the throne of Delhi was anathema to the Sikhs. Until recently they had always opposed Mughal tyranny, and had carved their empire out of what had once been Mughal territories. To expect them to help restore Mughal rule over India would have been unrealistic. The rapacity of the mutineers; the frequent and bloody clashes between Hindu and Muslim units; their murderous attacks on British men, women and children and on Christians—Dr. Chamanlal, an Indian Christian, was the first to be killed in Delhi; the widespread looting and pillaging in which everyone from the emperor's sons and relations down to the sepoys was involved, was not the stuff of which idealistically inspired wars of independence are made. Shorn of all subsequent hype, the uprising was a very limited affair, and by no means a concerted attempt at ending British rule. This is further borne out by the fact that neither the Company's Madras nor Bombay Armies was affected by it, nor even the Bengal Army as a whole, except for the *poorbia* sepoys in it. Had the Mutiny been more than a mutiny, the Sikhs would have played a key role as they did many times in later years when the countdown to India's independence actually began.

The new dispensation certainly helped the people of Punjab, even though they shared only a fraction of the imperial power's earnings. Amongst the innovative schemes conceived was the development of canal colonies in the province's largely arid western territories and in some other regions. With no access to regular irrigation, the development proposals for these vast and unproductive lands envisaged a major network of canals to provide constant irrigation. Designed to draw water round the year from rivers via permanent weirs and headworks, this scheme was one of the most successful ever seen in India, and its benefits were far-reaching for the people of Punjab as well as for British rule in India. The first major canal, the Lower Bari Doab irrigating the densely populated Amritsar and Lahore districts, was opened in 1861, and the lower Jhelum and Chenab canal systems in the 1880s. These canals "transformed the endless waste and scrub of the Jhang, Lyallpur and Shahpur districts into flourishing Canal colony regions." A million Punjabi peasants—mostly Sikhs—emigrated to the nine canal colonies.

The results of all this were both obvious and impressive: "By the 1920s," writes a modern historian, "Punjab produced a tenth of British

India's total cotton crop and a third of its wheat. Whilst other regions such as Bengal, Bihar and Orissa were experiencing a growing agricultural crisis, the Punjab had emerged as the pace-setter of Indian agricultural development." The agricultural breakthroughs of Punjab were also helped by a far-ranging piece of legislation: the Punjab Alienation of Land Act of 1900 which prohibited transfer of land from agriculturists to non-agriculturists. Aimed at preventing urban money-lenders from taking over agricultural lands, this Act did much to place Punjab's agriculture on a solid footing. Not surprisingly, it also generated communal resentment between Hindu money-lenders and the Sikh/Muslim peasantry.

By giving land to ex-soldiers and servicemen on a preferential basis in the canal colonies, a powerful incentive was offered to a warlike people to join the military. The move, it was hoped, would also help pacify the Sikhs. The colonial power needed them as the backbone of its army and for fighting its wars. There was nothing new about giving land to military men in India; the practice had existed since the time of the Guptas in the fourth–fifth century AD, and was common under the Mughals and Sikhs. Political power had always rested on a ruler's military strength, and the armed establishment was kept appeased by allocating generous *jagirs* to it. Although these were usually given to chieftains, at the beginning of the eighteenth century Banda Bahadur had made cultivators themselves owners of the land on which they worked. The British, whilst ostensibly modernizing the system by giving 25 to 55 acres to soldiers, gave 500 acres and more to favoured officers, thus retaining the system's feudal colouration.

The ever-increasing representation of Punjabis in the British Indian Army dramatically altered its composition from 1875 to 1914. A third of its total strength at the beginning of this period, Punjabis were three-fifths of it by the end, more than half of whom were Sikhs. Inevitably, the British Indian Army's main recruiting centres in Bengal, Madras and Bombay had to give way to Punjab. Since land ownership also provided status, in all half a million acres were given to military veterans and serving officers and men in the nine canal colonies. (These had brought nearly ten million acres of land under cultivation in the state by the 1920s; this increased to fourteen million by 1947.) As most canal colonies went to Pakistan after the 1947 Partition, it is likely the power of the military which the British used for their ends was then used by Pakistan's military establishment for its own political ends—as is borne out by the frequency with which Pakistan's armed forces have seized political power since Independence.

Recognizing the commercial opportunities in Punjab, India's business communities—mostly Hindus and Muslims with some Sikhs—began investing in trade and small-scale industries. Between 1900 and 1944 the number of factories increased from 152 to 1,190 and the labour force from 18,191 to 1,132,480. The Punjab National Bank was founded by Indians in 1895, to be gradually followed by an insurance company and other financial institutions. In this case too, since British trading houses, banks and insurance companies, along with the imperial treasury, controlled the colonial economy, the lion's share in it went to them. But Indian entrepreneurs did lay the groundwork for a diversified economy.

In education, Lahore would in time become a centre of excellence reflecting, in essence, the British objective of creating "a class of persons, Indian in blood and colour and British in taste and opinions, in morals and in intellect." With this in mind a medical college was established in 1860, followed by seven further colleges. Punjab University was founded in 1882, giving an added fillip to the teaching of English, which was accorded a high priority from the outset, Christian missionaries being active in Punjab. The conversion of Ranjit Singh's son Dalip was the kind of breakthrough that the ruling power wrongly hoped would help blunt the fervour of a people passionately committed to their faith. The aim of the missionaries was to turn the Sikhs away from the source of their determination and strength, from their beliefs which gave them the courage to die in their defence. Missionary activities in Punjab proceeded in close parallel with other attempts to pacify the militant Sikhs "to whom our attention at first was specially directed."

An American Presbyterian mission was already established in Ludhiana, south of the Sutlej. No sooner had Sikh rule ended in 1849 than the Ludhiana mission sent C.W. Forman and John Newton to Lahore to start missionary work there. They couldn't have asked for better sponsorship than that provided by John Lawrence, who had officiated as Lahore Resident during his brother Henry's absence, and had a powerful say in Punjab affairs. He was a firm believer in Christian proselytization, and was keen to see the conquest of the Sikh Kingdom followed by large-scale conversions. Other Christian missions, led by the Church of England in 1852, soon followed. The United Presbyterian Mission in 1855, the Cambridge Mission, the Baptist Mission and the Church of Scotland were some of them. The proximity of the missions to the ruling power could have appealed to some potential converts. The conversion figures, however, are not too impressive: they stood at 4,000 in 1881, 300,000 in 1921.

An unintended spinoff of missionary activities in Punjab was the determined move by Sikhs, Hindus and Muslims to rediscover and re-emphasize the essentials of their own faiths. The Sikhs' need for self-understanding was highlighted by two almost concurrent movements. The first was led by Baba Dayal (1783–1855), who underscored the danger of moving away from the rational moorings of the Sikh faith towards worship of idols and images that were antithetical to the Gurus' teachings. Baba Dayal propounded the Sikh concept of the Formless One, or Nirankar—after which his movement was named. The Nirankaris' emphasis on austere living, on rejection of monarchical trappings and extravagant displays, and their insistence on restoring self-discipline and selflessness among Sikhs, struck a responsive chord in some.

Another reform movement by the Kukas was started by Bhai Balak Singh (1799–1862). His emphasis too was on a restoration of those religious commandments that had been relegated to the background by the pomp of monarchy. Bhai Balak Singh's devout follower and successor Baba Ram Singh, born in 1816, had served in Ranjit Singh's army. He had also fought the British at Mudki in the First Anglo-Sikh War. Deeply impressed by the purpose and rationale of the Kuka movement, Ram Singh organized it on a province-wide scale by establishing 22 districts, with wide responsibilities vested in the head of each.

Government reports expressed increasing concern at the growing appeal of the Kukas. Even more suspect was Ram Singh's aversion to British rule; his rejection of government service, English education, English law-courts, imported goods, and mill-made cloth. His emphasis on homespun cloth, as a symbolic rejection of alien economic dominance, was the earliest expression of non-cooperation which Mahatma Gandhi would adopt almost three-quarters of a century later. Understandably, the authorities kept Ram Singh under tight surveillance and severely restricted his movements.

The crisis-in-the-making, aggravated by widespread arrests, repressive restrictions and frequent jail sentences, was precipitated by the Kukas' opposition to the killing of cows. In June 1870 a band of Kukas attacked butchers' shops in Amritsar—which the Resident had earlier closed but had reopened after annexation—killing four and injuring others. Another three people were killed in Raikot near Ludhiana. In all nine Kukas were hanged for these crimes, including one man, Giani Ratan Singh, whom the outraged Kukas believed to be innocent. Several violent incidents followed, until in January 1872 around a hundred Kukas attacked the government treasury in Malerkotla, killing seven policemen and an officer.

The British response was swift and savage. The Deputy Commissioner of Ludhiana ordered 66 Kukas to be summarily executed, without benefit of trial and in a particularly reprehensible manner. On 17 January 1872, fifty of them were blown apart in his presence by cannons lined up on the Malerkotla parade ground for a crime allegedly committed two days earlier. The sixteen others were similarly executed two days later. Ram Singh was deported to Rangoon where he died in November 1885, undaunted and unchanging in his convictions and beliefs. The Deputy Commissioner was dismissed from service and the Commissioner transferred on the orders of the Viceroy, the Earl of Mayo. As a sect within the Sikhs, the Kukas have continued to stand by their convictions, with some modifications such as acceptance of the learning of English.

Despite their undeniably deep commitment to their beliefs these two movements—possibly because of their exclusivity—left the larger body of Sikhs uninvolved, although they did light a spark which found expression towards the end of the nineteenth century in a renewed assertiveness involving the entire Sikh community.

This took the form of the Singh Sabha movement. Its emergence was a cultural counter-offensive against missionary arrogance which viewed all faiths other than the Christian as either backward or bar-

baric. Western education, "representative" politics, colonial compulsions and census pressures also convinced Sikh thinkers of the need to redefine Sikh identity—especially since a census of some areas of Punjab in 1855 had classified Sikhs as a sect of Hindus. Since this was unacceptable, the Singh Sabha movement was started to revitalize Sikh thinking by not only re-emphasizing the primacy of rational thought and behaviour in keeping with Sikh scriptures, but also by preparing them for the challenges ahead. The logical interpretation of Sikhism by intellectuals of the Singh Sabha movement left no scope for the *laissez faire* drift which had allowed quaint customs, rituals and practices to cloud the clarity of Sikh beliefs. The Sabhas used the printed word to disseminate the essence and spirit of Sikh scriptures, and underscored the dangers of infiltration by elements bent on subverting their tenets.

The first Singh Sabha was founded in Amritsar in 1873, another was established in Lahore in 1879. And within twenty years of that, 117 Singh Sabhas had been established all across the towns and villages of Punjab and beyond, with what can only be described as lightning rapidity. The Sikhs' individualistic bent—as also the divergences in their approach to similar goals—inevitably led to the splintering of the Sabhas into different chapters, although each tried in its own way to intensify the momentum of reforms. Other parallel thrusts, born out of similar concerns, also contributed towards crystallizing the purposes and priorities of the faith. The Tat Khalsa, the Panch Khalsa Diwan and the Chief Khalsa Diwan provided variations in their methods and approach to the same end: to instil in Sikhs a clear sense of their distinctiveness from other faiths.

The Amritsar Singh Sabha had a looser orientation under theologians and landed gentry like Khem Singh Bedi, Thakur Singh Sandhanwalia and Kanwar Bikram Singh. They were also known as Sanatanis, and their view was that anyone following Guru Nanak's teachings was a Sikh, even if the discipline of the five Ks was not observed, and even though he or she worshipped local saints and deities. They saw nothing wrong with the idea of Sikhs as a reformist group within Hinduism. The perspective of the Lahore Singh Sabha was radically different. The two key figures in it, Gurmukh Singh and Bhai Harsa Singh, assistant professors in Lahore's Oriental College, opted for a broad-based membership of different castes and classes including professionals, businessmen and government functionaries. The Lahore Sabha opposed the worship of living gurus, and of the Ten Gurus' descendants. Aggressively reiterating Sikh separateness, it vigorously opposed Hinduism's caste structure, idols, customs and social practises. In time the Lahore Singh Sabha's assertive approach towards a distinctive Sikh self-identity won out as people increasingly gravitated to its programme of instilling pride in their institutions and beliefs.

One result of the ongoing efforts by Sabha intellectuals to restore the moral order of the faith was the re-emergence of the Tat Khalsa (Tat: the unalloyed, Khalsa: the pure; together the two words could be interpreted as "purest of the pure"), which injected a new dynamic into the drive towards rediscovery. Although the Tat Khalsa goes back to the eighteenth century—when it stood for the glorious traditions of a triumphant Khalsa—the extravagances of Ranjit Singh's court, and the debilitating intrigues of the Brahmins after his death, had weakened it. But with its ascendance once again towards the end of the nineteenth and early twentieth century, the ideologues of the Tat Khalsa took strong exception to all un-Sikh practices which were Hinduizing their faith: local gods and instant saints; deities; divination; coarse songs during weddings and other ceremonials; women fasting for their husbands' welfare; ancestral spirits; charms, amulets and roadside shrines. Equally disdainful of astrologers, horoscopes and omens, they wanted an end to all the invidious practices Sikhism had rejected and opposition to which was the *raison d'être* of their faith as it did not permit multiple religious loyalties. The faith of every Sikh had to rest on Guru, Granth and Gurdwara.

In his Punjabi novel *Sundari*, published in 1898, Bhai Vir Singh, the most significant Sikh poet and writer of the twentieth century, put the problem facing the Sikhs in perspective:

> LOOK AT YOURSELF AND SEE WHETHER OR NOT THE DECLINE OF THE SIKH NATION IS CAUSED BY YOUR VERY OWN HANDS. LEAVING YOUR GOD AND YOUR TRUE GURUS, YOU WORSHIP STONES, TREES, IDOLS, TOMBS AND SAINTS. FORGETTING SIKH RELIGION, YOU ROT IN ANOTHER RELIGION. TURNING YOUR BACK ON THE TRUE GURUS YOU TEACH SOMEONE ELSE'S RELI-

GION TO YOUR OFFSPRING TOO. YOUR CHILDREN WILL GROW
TO BE HALF-BAKED LIKE YOU—SIKH ON THE HEAD, BRAHMIN
AROUND THE NECK AND MUSLIM BELOW THE WAIST.

The new and resurgent mood reformed many religious and social institutions of the faith. In addition to bringing simplicity and a quiet dignity to marriages by replacing Brahmin rituals with Sikh Anand rites, there was an insistence on equality of women in all walks of life. Schools, colleges, research institutions, book clubs, educational societies and printing presses were established to teach the young academic disciplines and provide grown-ups with ongoing information on historical, contemporary, social, political and theological subjects. Among the institutions established was a Khalsa College in 1897 and ten Sikh schools in various parts of the province including an exclusive girls' school in Ferozepur. The aim of these was to instil Tat Kalsa values into young Sikhs.

Within a few years the number of books published in the Province of Punjab increased fivefold, and no less impressive was the increase in the number of newspapers and magazines. Amongst these were *Khalsa Akhbar, Khalsa Advocate, Khalsa Samachar, Sri Gurmat Prakasak, Khalsa Gazette, Lyall Gazette* (which later became the *Sher-i-Punjab*), *Sudharak, Gurmukhi Akhbar*, and *The Tribune* which first appeared as a twelve-page weekly in 1881. The number of printing presses and publications ended the missionaries' monopoly in this field which the American Presbyterians had established in Ludhiana in 1836. With an antiquated wooden printing press they had succeeded in turning out a vast amount of evangelical literature, setting the pace for other missions and printing presses.

In intellectual life, literature and theological research, the most sensitive and elegant leadership was provided by the Chief Khalsa Diwan which evolved in 1902 from the Singh Sabha and Khalsa Diwan movements. Emerging out of the need for a central organization which would co-ordinate the work of different institutions, it successfully affiliated over a hundred Singh Sabhas during the twenty years or so of its active existence. Those who drew up its constitution included men of distinction like the scholar Bhai Kahan Singh of Nabha, the district judge Sardar Aya Singh, Sardar Sundar Singh Majithia, the scholar Gyani Thakur Singh, Bhai Jawahar Singh—secretary of the Khalsa College Council, the barrister-at-law Sardar Gurbakhsh Singh and the engineer Sardar Dharam Singh.

Of wide orientation and learning, these men used their scholarly, academic, legal and technical skills to broaden the base of the reformist agenda and relate it to the social and political realities of the times. They were also conscious of the central role that communications were beginning to play in convincing people of the cultural and ethical qualities of their own traditions. The Chief Khalsa Diwan published a voluminous amount of literature including tracts, books, monographs and the *Khalsa Samachar*, a newspaper edited by Bhai Vir Singh. Closely involved with the Chief Khalsa Diwan throughout his lifetime, he was the main inspiration behind the Khalsa Tract Society which exercised a tremendous hold on the Sikh intelligentsia for decades.

Sadly, the Chief Khalsa Diwan, because of its liberal, intellectual leanings, came under siege from the more radical and impatient elements among the Sikhs. Its intellectual bent actually proved a bane. In less than twenty years it had to make way for the more aggressive Shiromani Gurdwara Parbandhak Committee (SGPC), which has been the spokesman for Sikh affairs ever since, acting in tandem with the Shiromani Akali Dal which was also founded in 1920 although it has since moved from religious to political activities. The term *Akali* comes from *Akal*, the Timeless One, which Guru Nanak had used to describe God: *Akal Murat*, or the Eternal Form.

The reason for the emergence of the more militant Akalis was the fate that had overtaken Sikh gurdwaras. Ever since the middle of the nineteenth century, they had slid into the hands of hereditary caretakers called *mahants*, who were often Hindus. The *mahants*, supported by the British, were anathema to the Sikhs. And so the SGPC mounted a militant—though peaceful—struggle to prise the gurdwaras loose from the usurpers. It felt the Chief Khalsa Diwan was inappropriate for this role.

Sikh feelings had been further bruised by the fact that the Golden Temple was under the control of the British Deputy Commissioner who had appointed his own man to manage it. This person had allowed idols to be placed in the temple precincts, given pandits and soothsayers a run of the place, and restricted the entry of the backward castes. Each move was repugnant to Sikh beliefs, so the stage was set for a major confrontation since some blood had already been shed over the control of gurdwaras.

As increasing numbers of Sikhs joined protest marches, demanding the return of gurdwaras to Sikh control, arrests increased daily. It was becoming clear to the British administrators that the scale of this agitation, though it was peacefully conducted, had an inbuilt potential for violence considering the recent history of this turbulent region. And so on 19 January 1922 a representative of the government handed the keys of the Golden Temple to Sardar Kharak Singh, the president of the SGPC, in the presence of a vast congregation at the Akal Takht. But the struggle was still to continue for over three years before legislative sanction ensured the successful conclusion of the Gurdwara Reform Movement. The Sikh Gurdwaras Act of 25 July 1925 made the Sikhs custodians of their places of worship, though the price paid during this struggle was heavy: over 40,000 went to jail and 400 lost their lives. The Sikhs did prove, however, that they not only had the courage to lay down their lives in battle, but they also had the courage to take on, unarmed and unflinching, the armed might of the state. M.K. Gandhi's telegram to Kharak Singh summed it up: "First decisive battle for India's freedom won, congratulations."

There had been other aggravations on the way to restoring the tarnished Sikh heritage. Some of the milestones along this troubled route had to do with the British authorities; others with the resentments of the larger Hindu community, because, oddly enough, while the Muslims—from whom the Sikhs had wrested control of territories with which to establish their empire—had no serious differences with the Sikhs, several Hindu revivalist movements did. Sadly, even Muslims and Sikhs would collide once again during the Partition of India in 1947. But that traumatic event was still some years ahead.

Two clashes out of many which the Sikhs had with the British administration remain etched in their collective memory: the *Komagata Maru* episode and the Jallianwala Bagh massacre. The former incident took place against the background of colliding aspirations of Sikhs wishing to emigrate for reasons of "mobility, enterprise, and opportunity," and the racial intolerance of British Dominions like Australia and Canada. The United States was no exception since it also subscribed to the prevailing colour prejudices.

Undaunted by these, the robust Sikhs, determined to emigrate, raised their passage money themselves. Sikh farmers were doing well; in 1904, for example, Indian wheat exports to Great Britain exceeded those of Russia and the United States, and Punjab accounted for a major part of the Indian trade. But there were racial bigots at the other end. Even though many Sikhs had gone to work in Singapore, Hong Kong and elsewhere in Asia in the late 1860s, their first foray into a white man's country, Australia, was not until the 1890s. When Australia's doors were closed by legislation in 1901 the Sikh emigrants turned to Canada, and the first few arrived in British Columbia in 1903. Their figure increased to more than 5,000 in the next four years before the Canadians too, after a short spell of unrestricted entry, openly opposed Asian immigration.

Why did the Sikhs choose Canada? "Probably the first Sikhs to see British Columbia," writes one Sikh settled in Canada, "were Punjabi soldiers from Hong Kong regiments travelling through Canada after celebrating Queen Victoria's Diamond Jubilee in London in 1897. They were impressed with the majestic landscape, the rich vegetation and the favourable climate; all quite similar to their homeland, the Punjab province in India. Word travelled fast about the opportunities in this new land and adventurous Sikhs soon started making travel plans." While it was in order to praise dashing soldiers who were helping Britain defend her colonial empire—especially if the soldiers were just passing through—it was quite another thing to let them into Canada. So liberal admission rules gave way to harsh immigration policies. One of the more devious of these was that prospective arrivals must hold through tickets from their country to Canada. This was specially aimed at Indians since there was no direct service from India to Canada, and this ordinance virtually excluded Indians from entering the country.

The Canadian authorities, however, had not taken Sikh determination into account. Baba Gurdit Singh, a very resolute man, hit on an ingenious idea for getting round this rule. He chartered an old freighter, the *Komagata Maru*, in Hong Kong, took on board 376 emigrants of whom 346 were Sikhs, and headed for Canada's West Coast. After a particularly rough passage and severe privations, the steamer dropped anchor in Vancouver harbour on 23 May 1914. The authorities, more racist even than their red-neck constituents, were unrelenting. Making a mockery of their own law, they held a fake hearing in which the Supreme Court declined to interfere in the affairs of the Immigration Department; passengers were refused permission to disembark; grapeshot was fired across the ship's decks; a deaf ear was turned to requests for medical attention for the sick aboard, and the vessel was finally forced to return to India after two months in Vancouver harbour.

Its arrival in Calcutta was greeted by a heavy police presence and a special train to take its passengers to Punjab in virtual custody. While seventeen Muslims obliged, the Sikhs refused. In a bloody encounter nineteen Sikhs and four policemen, including two European officers, were killed. Two hundred Sikhs, who were interned on reaching Punjab, were still unclear about their crime.

Although they had failed to land in Canada, the men and women who had braved the seas and bullets, to return home undaunted, struck a chord in the Punjab population and helped kindle national resentment against the high-handedness of the ruling power. The flames were further fanned by the Jallianwala Bagh massacre on 13 April 1919.

Jallianwala Bagh, an open plot of land about 225 by 180 metres in area, is located a few hundred yards from the Golden Temple in Amritsar. Though mostly a space for people to meet and pass the time of day, it witnessed a particularly large assembly on that fateful day in April, when over 20,000 persons arrived to hear their leaders speak on a rapidly escalating crisis. Resentment over two repressive bills which government intended to introduce had been building up since January, with Mahatma Gandhi deciding to launch a non-violent civil disobedience movement against them. Ignoring the mounting anger, one of the bills was passed and in March it became an Act. To aggravate matters still further, Punjab's governor, Sir Michael Francis O'Dwyer, then ordered two Amritsar leaders deported. They were arrested and taken away on 10 April. This led to a general strike with police firing on the crowd and killing around 20 protestors. An incensed crowd retaliated by attacking government properties and killing five Europeans, upon which the unnerved administration called in the army.

Brigadier-General Reginald Edward Harry Dyer, who arrived with his troops on the evening of 11 April, had "all the combined prejudices of both the British boxwallahs and the military." He also "suffered from arteriosclerosis . . . heat-stroke, sun-stroke, fever and malaria" and from the effects of "a succession of sporting accidents, most of which seem to have involved concussions with their inevitable consequences." Losing no time in establishing *de facto* army rule on reaching Amritsar, he passed an order on 12 April declaring all meetings illegal. The thirteenth of April being the day of the Baisakhi festival, a large number of people converged on the Golden Temple to celebrate the birthday of the Khalsa. From there they moved onto Jallianwala Bagh to hear some speeches. By 4:30 p.m. the space had filled and despite recent events people were in festive moods. Many had brought their children, and all were naturally unarmed. As they settled down to hear the speakers, none had an inkling of what was in the offing, least of all that the gathering, with a generous sprinkling of the old and very young, would be soon gunned down without either warning or an order to disperse. At 5:15 p.m. Dyer entered the Bagh which was completely enclosed by high buildings, and taking his position on a raised terrace next to the narrow entrance, ordered his troops to fire into the densely packed crowd.

This exchange between Dyer and the inquiry committee, popularly known as the Hunter Committee, which was set up to report on the unprovoked firing, relates the course of events:

> Q: When you got into the Bagh what did you do?
> A: I opened fire.
> Q: At once?
> A: Immediately. I had thought about the matter, and I don't imagine it took me more than 30 seconds to make up my mind as to what my duty was.
> Q: Did the crowd at once start to disperse as soon as you fired?
> A: Immediately.

Q: Did you continue firing?
A: Yes.

In their book *The Proudest Day* Anthony Read and David Fisher write: "In the crush, steel-jacketed bullets, fired at close range, tore through flesh and bone and muscle, often passing right through one body to strike the one behind. Dyer was remorseless. He directed the men to fire at those trying to escape as well as aiming where the crowd was thickest. The shooting was as calm, deliberate and cruelly aimed as target practice at the butts, with every bullet made to count." It took him fifteen minutes in all to accomplish his task, for which his men fired 1,650 rounds. The scene he left behind was of dead and wounded piled on each other; of a blood-soaked Bagh in which none dared to venture either to treat the wounded or retrieve their dead because of the 8 p.m. curfew; of a night of terror in which people slowly bled to death in the darkness. Estimates of the number killed vary from 379 to over 1,000. When the Hunter Committee asked Dyer whether his aim was "to strike terror not only into the city of Amritsar but throughout the Punjab," he replied "Yes, throughout the Punjab. I wanted to reduce their morale, the morale of the rebels."

Instead of destroying their morale, Dyer succeeded only in destroying the people's faith in the British sense of fair play. The massacre made a mockery of British justice. After the Hunter Committee's criticism and the House of Commons' condemnation of Dyer's action—with even Winston Churchill demanding his dismissal—the House of Lords voted in favour of him, and people of a conservative bent, led by the *Morning Post*, raised a purse of £26,317 4s 10d (the equivalent of around £600,000 today) for him. The British response disenchanted many like Jawaharlal Nehru, who had admired some of their qualities: "I realized then, more vividly than I have ever done before, how brutal and immoral imperialism was and how it had eaten into the souls of the British upper classes."

Freedom of speech was also a casualty. In London only *The Times* reported the tragedy in a short paragraph. In India, B.G. Horniman, the doughty editor of the *Bombay Chronicle*, was arrested and sent back to the UK for publishing news of Jallianwala Bagh. It is generally agreed that Dyer helped fuel the drive for independence which would culminate in Britain's departure from India 28 years later. An ironic light is cast on Dyer's actions by the fact that he had left Dublin's Royal College of Surgeons because he was unable to stand the sight of blood!

A spinoff of the *Komagata Maru* episode was that the Sikhs were drawn still deeper into the freedom struggle. Their commitment to it was given specific form by the San Francisco–based Ghadr Party which—incensed by the indignity of the *Komagata* incident—took up the challenge of mounting an armed rebellion against the British in India. The Ghadr Party (*ghadr* means "mutiny"), established a year earlier to generate a mood and gather resources for throwing the British out of India, was born out of various movements of protest aimed at the abolition of unfair immigration laws, racial discrimination and social injustices; its revolutionary agenda was a response to British arrogance. The party's weekly newspaper, the *Ghadr*, which started publication in November 1913, carried under its masthead the line: *Enemy of the British Government.* In addition to the United States and Canada, the paper was also distributed in Japan, Java, Sumatra, Shanghai, Hong Kong, the Philippines, Singapore, Malaya, Thailand, Burma, East Africa and India. To intensify its activities in these countries the party opened its offices in most of them.

In August 1914, soon after the *Komagata* incident and the outbreak of the First World War, the Ghadr Party declared war on the British. It also decided to send its members to work for an armed insurrection in India. The response was overwhelming. A large number of Sikhs who had emigrated to the United States, Canada and other parts of the world before emigration restrictions sold their businesses to return home for the struggle ahead. But the British, whose experience of the 1857 Mutiny still haunted them, managed to infiltrate their ranks in February 1915 and smashed the movement on the eve of the day fixed for the uprising.

British retribution was swift and the Sikhs, who constituted the bulk of the Ghadrites, paid a heavy price. Of the 291 Ghadr men tried in the Lahore Conspiracy case, 42 were sentenced to death, 114 transported for life, 93 imprisoned, and 42 acquitted. Not a single person appealed against the punishment. Of the 700 men belonging to the 5th Light Infantry in Singapore who mutinied in February, 37 were sentenced to death, as were 21 others from different military units in India. Ghadrite workers had also gone to Turkey, Iraq and Iran to persuade Indian prisoners of war and fighting troops to rise against the British. "In Iran, the party was able to raise an Indian Independence Army," Harbans Singh has written. "The Army advanced towards Baluchistan, and en route captured Kirmanshah. Then they advanced along the coast towards Karachi. Meanwhile, Turkey was defeated and the British had occupied Baghdad. The Indian Independence Army losing its base was also defeated."

The religious polarization of North India in the second half of the nineteenth century had reached a peak with the founding of the Arya Samaj movement by Swami Dayanand in 1875 in faraway Rajkot in Gujarat. Representing militant Hinduism, it was less successful in Western India than in Punjab where it established an office in June 1877. During the fifteen months the dedicated and energetic Dayanand spent criss-crossing Punjab from April 1877 to July 1878, his beliefs and convictions won him many disciples.

Born in 1824 into a wealthy Samavedi Brahmin family, he was intensively tutored in the Sanskrit language, religious texts, and the Vedas. Preferring the life of a wandering ascetic to that of a family man with all its conventional responsibilities, he left home before he could be married off, to travel, observe, absorb and crystallize his thoughts. These eventually centred on a burning desire to purify and revive traditional Hinduism by demanding an absolute commitment to the Vedas. Surprisingly, he also attacked Brahmin priests, idolatry, elaborate rituals and child marriage.

The Arya Samaj's religious militancy against the Sikhs would find virulent expression after Dayanand's death, but he himself was not averse to making the occasional impolitic statement, even though the main targets of his criticism were Christian missions and Islam, and to an extent orthodox Hinduism. His view that Sikhism was a branch of Hinduism was obviously expressed with full awareness of its impact on the Sikhs. As were his unfortunate remarks on Guru Nanak: "Nanakji had noble aims, but he had no learning. He knew the language of the villages of his country. He had no knowledge of Vedic scriptures or *Sankrata*." And so, how could anyone with no knowledge of Sanskrit, and thus of the Vedas, amount to anything?! As if to clinch his argument he concluded: "Just as idol-worshippers have set up their shop in order to get their livelihood, so have these people. Just as the priests of temples ask their devotees to see the goddess and offer presents to her, similarly Sikhs worship the book and present gifts to it."

This was mild compared to the Arya Samaj's attacks on Sikhs in later years. These became venomous after Dayanand's death in 1883 and the emergence of three radical Samajists, Pandit Guru Datta, Lala Munshi Ram (later Swami Shraddhanand) and Pandit Lekh Ram. The Brahmin Lekh Ram's anti-Muslim phobia also became more aggressive, especially towards Mirza Ghulam Ahmad, head of the Ahmadiya movement, who considered himself both the "Mahdi of Islam and the Messiah of Christianity." Ram's unrelenting attacks on the Ahmadiyas finally led to his assassination in March 1897 in Lahore.

This event aggravated a rapidly deteriorating situation in which the Samaj's programme of reconversions was already causing increasing tension between different religious communities: "The Samaj provided an ideology of militant Hinduism that had a wide appeal for Punjabi Hindus. As a minority community who, in the past, experienced Muslim and Sikh rule and who suffered from the effects of proselytization of Muslims, Sikhs and Christians, Punjabi Hindus needed a new ideology to unify and defend their community." This ideology took the form of an aggressive insistence on the infallible qualities of Hinduism, and led to an Arya agenda of reconversions which took the form of *shuddhi*, or purification, of those who had converted to Christianity or Islam. During the last decade of the nineteenth century *shuddhi* ceremonies became more frequent, and when these were extended to converts to Sikhism the Sikh-Hindu divide widened. The seeds of religious separateness were sown, and would have grave consequences.

Religious competitiveness of some, though not all, Punjabi Hindus affected the majority community's attitudes elsewhere in India. It was in Punjab, however, that religious contentions—involving estranged Muslims, Sikhs and Christians—generated the most heat. These schisms were fully exploited, first by the British, who found it easier to deal with a divided people, and then, ironically, by sections of major political parties in independent India. Whilst British designs were understandable in view of their astonishingly few numbers in the subcontinent, even at the peak of their presence, the continuing resort to communal passions in post-Independence India would betray the short-sightedness of its political groups. And during the years leading up to India's partition, increasingly assertive Muslim separatism was in direct proportion to the country's religious polarization, which was pushing it towards its eventual fragmentation.

Whatever the compulsions of the British and India's major political parties—which led to the country's partition—the Arya Samajis' role cannot be underestimated. Even a moderate Arya like Lala Lajpat Rai, despite his national perspective as one of the leaders of the independence movement, clearly expressed *Hindu* nationalism. "Within the present struggle between Indian communities, I will be Hindu first and Indian afterwards; but outside India or even in India against non-Indians I am and shall ever be an Indian first and Hindu afterwards." This position was designed to appeal to the majority community, not to India's other religious constituents.

As was to be expected, the logical extension of Arya Samaj's efforts to restore Hinduism to its Vedic origins was the setting up of a Hindu political organization—the Punjab Hindu Sabha in 1906. Not entirely coincidentally, the Muslim League was also founded in the same year to represent Muslim concerns. The Shiromani Gurdwara Parbandhak Committee and the Shiromani Akali Dal, the emergence of both of which in 1920 has already been described, were the Sikh response to this trend.

Prior to the emergence of these parties, the Indian National Congress had dominated India's political life—such as it was—for over twenty years. Established in 1885, it advocated reforms which recognized the rights of the Indian people in their own country. The idea of the Congress was conceived by a Scotsman, Allan Octavian Hume, a former member of the Indian Civil Service. The widespread discontent due to economic deprivation convinced Hume of the need for an organization of intellectuals and learned persons which could warn government of the dangers whenever it ignored or aggravated people. Such an organization, he felt, would help both the British administration and the Indian people, and it was his concern that led to the formation of the Indian National Congress.

According to R.C. Majumdar, Hume was no doubt "inspired by a genuine sympathy for the interest and welfare of India, and it by no means detracts from the merit of this noble-minded Scotsman that in setting up a political organization like the Congress, he could not possibly be, and was certainly not, inspired by the same national sentiment and patriotic yearning for freedom of India which characterized the advanced political thinkers of Bengal and other parts of India." Hume explained his own motivation thus: "A safety-valve for the escape of great and growing forces, generated by our own actions, was urgently needed, and no more efficacious safety-valve than our Congress movement could possibly be devised."

Ironically, the organization that "was brought into existence as an instrument to safeguard British rule in India" would in time spearhead a country-wide agitation for freedom from that very same rule. While two key men of the Congress, Mahadev Govind Ranade and Gopal Krishna Gokhale, both Poona Brahmins and Anglophiles, wanted to revitalize Indian society through social reforms before freeing it from foreign domination, one of the most militant voices in the movement demanded freedom before reform. Balwantrao Gangadhar Tilak, also a Poona Brahmin, disagreed with both Ranade and Gokhale and though antediluvian in many ways, was the first to say in 1908 that "Swarajya [freedom] is my birthright, and I must have it." Because of him the party's orientation towards the British rulers took a more radical turn.

Despite the presence of educated and erudite persons from different regions and of different religions, the Congress soon faced communal mistrust. At its fifth session in Bombay in 1889, the draft for a scheme of representative government was dropped because a Muslim delegate wanted an equal number of Hindus and Muslims on the Council. A year earlier, Sir Sayyid Ahmad Khan, an educationist, had gone overboard in explaining why Hindus and Muhammadans could not conceivably coexist with each other, and why it was "necessary that for the peace of India and for the progress of everything in India the English Government should remain for many years—in fact forever!" Tilak did not help matters by announcing a few years later that "Hinduism is of higher worth than other religions."

Mohandas Karamchand Gandhi, on landing in Bombay from South Africa in 1915, was welcomed at a garden party given by the Gujarati community, with Mohammad Ali Jinnah presiding over the function. Responding in Gujarati to Jinnah's welcome speech in English—because of his "partiality for Gujarati and Hindustani"—Gandhi took a dig at "the use of English in a Gujarati gathering." This could not have been lost on Jinnah and it may have set the tone for their uneasy relationship in the years ahead. In the end Gandhi was unable to work with Jinnah, who was driven to leave the Indian National Congress, of which he was also a member, in disgust. Although both men had studied law in London—Gandhi at the Inner Temple and Jinnah at Lincoln's Inn—and both had the same mother tongue, Gujarati, they were entirely different in dress, demeanour, manner and mindset.

While Jinnah enjoyed good food and drink and dressed in suits tailored in Savile Row, Gandhi had discarded Western clothes and opted for homespun cloth and modest vegetarian fare as eaten by India's poor. His preferred drink was goat's milk. Gandhi was given to fasts, passive resistance and periods of silence alternating with rambling discourses. Jinnah would have none of these: "He bowed but rarely to populist symbols, appearing only occasionally at political rallies, and shunning the display of emotion in public. Reasoned arguments and cold logic were the hallmark of Jinnah's discourse ... he was uncompromisingly committed to substance rather than symbol ... modernity rather than tradition." Nor did he believe in fasts and such.

Since Indians have demonized Jinnah a good deal, some less frequently mentioned aspects of his personality deserve stress. One of these is his courage: "the Ulema [Islamic theologians and expounders of the law] in their overwhelming majority opposed him and he made scant effort to placate them." Another is his far-sightedness. Before agreeing to join the Muslim League in 1913, he insisted that "his loyalty to the Muslim League and to the Muslim interest would in no way and at no time imply even the shadow of disloyalty to the larger national cause to which his life was dedicated." When this is contrasted with the views of those who placed their religion first and India afterward, the worth of the man stands out.

But why did Jinnah opt for a separate Muslim state? The answer is because the attitudes of many in the Congress—including Gandhi, Motilal Nehru (Jawaharlal's father), Lajpat Rai and others—compelled him to do so. He was still a member of the Congress when he joined the Muslim League in 1913, and it was during the First World War that he drafted a joint proposal (called the Lucknow Pact) on behalf of the Congress and the League for post-war constitutional reforms aimed at making the governance of India more representative, about which the British government was enthusiastic at the time. Once it had won the war, however, it reneged on its promise, arming itself instead with sweeping powers—which would drastically curtail civil liberties in India—based on Sir Sidney Rowlatt's recommendations to which Jinnah strenuously objected.

Speaking in the Central Legislative Council on 6 February 1919, he said that "the powers which are going to be assumed by the executive, which means substitution of executive for judicial, such powers are likely to be abused . . . there is no precedent or parallel that I know of in any other civilized country where you have laws of this character enacted . . . this is the most inopportune moment [for this legislation] as high hopes have been raised about momentous reforms . . ." Elated by their victory, the British overrode objections and in 1919 passed the Anarchical and Revolutionary Crimes Act. Jinnah resigned his seat on the Central Legislative Council and sailed for London to try to persuade his friends to intercede with Whitehall—to find that earlier receptivity to his views had faded.

The new Act "sought to curtail the liberty of the people in a drastic manner" by providing for "speedy trial of offences by a Special Court . . . there was no appeal from the decision of this Court, which could meet *in camera* and take into consideration evidence not admissible under the Indian Evidence Act . . . The Provincial Government was also given powers to search a place and arrest a suspected person without warrant and keep him in confinement 'in such place and under such conditions and restrictions as it may specify.'"

Meanwhile, Gandhi's anti-Rowlatt protests across the country having caught on, public anger intensified further after the Jallianwala Bagh massacre, one significant result of which was to set Gandhi and Jinnah on different courses. Encouraged by the overwhelming support for his call for non-cooperation, in August 1920 Gandhi launched a nationwide boycott of everything British: British goods, schools, colleges, laws and jobs, with the emphasis being on non-violent non-cooperation. Jallianwala Bagh had convinced Gandhi and many other Congressmen that a gradual devolution of power from the British to Indians was no longer enough. Self-rule had to be the goal and nationwide non-violent protests would be the means to achieve it. Jinnah disagreed. "India has got to keep her head cool at this most critical moment," he advised, placing his own faith in legislative and constitutional means. Gandhi was equally emphatic in support of his own approach and, as he put it, "I can imagine no form of resistance to the Government [other] than civil disobedience. I propose, God willing, to resume it . . ."

Matters came to a head the following year, first at the Bombay session of the Home Rule League (Swaraj Sabha) in October 1920, and then at the Nagpur session of the Congress in December. At the Bombay meeting, whilst Gandhi wanted the Home Rule League to opt for his protest movements and to "secure complete Swaraj [self-rule] for India according to the wishes of the Indian people," Jinnah spoke in favour of a constitutional approach for attaining self-government within the British Commonwealth. Gandhi pointedly suggested that those who disagreed with the majority's view were free to resign, which is what Jinnah—who had once chaired the Home Rule League—did.

When Gandhi asked Jinnah to reconsider and share in the "new life" which was opening up before India, Jinnah's reply was: "If by 'new life' you mean your methods and your programme, I am afraid I cannot accept them; for I am fully convinced that it must lead to disaster . . . your methods have already caused split and division in . . . the public life of the country not only amongst Hindus and Muslims but between Hindus and Hindus and Muslims and Muslims and even, between fathers and sons . . . your extreme programme has for the moment struck the imagination mostly of the inexperienced youth and the ignorant and the illiterate. All this means complete disorganization and chaos. What the consequence of this may be, I shudder to contemplate . . ."

At the Nagpur session of both the Congress and the Muslim

League in December 1920, Jinnah was repeatedly interrupted by cat-calls and crude slogans, an experience he would not easily forget. It brought home the bitter truth that national leadership for a Muslim seemed impossible in India. Knowing that bigots in the Muslim League were unlikely to behave any better, he left Nagpur without bothering to attend the League's session. The new year dawned on a disenchanted Jinnah immersed in his legal practice and reappraising his future moves on India's changing chessboard.

Above the increased political activity of the 1920s and 1930s—new alignments within and between parties, talks between imperialists and nationalists and new propositions and strategies to side-step them, round table conferences in London—hovered the spectre of religious mistrust. Of communalism, as Indians prefer to call it. Protagonists of militant Hinduism were beginning to cause concern. There was reason enough to justify a troubled view of the future.

The founding of the Hindu organization Rashtriya Swayamsevak Sangh (RSS) in 1925 was the most troubling event of all. The brain-child of five Chitpavan Brahmins,* four of whom were members of the political party the Hindu Mahasabha, the RSS's goal from its very inception was clear: if those of other, minority faiths wanted to live peacefully in India, they had to observe the rules of the Hindu *rashtra* (nation): "Let Muslims look upon Ram as their hero and communal problems will all be over . . ." The official biography of the RSS's founder, K.B. Hedgewar, placed "lower-caste assertion" with the Mus-lim threat as the "twin dangers" threatening the privileged few. According to Dr. Hedgewar: "Conflicts between various communities had started. Brahmin-Non-Brahmin conflict was nakedly on view." Not surprisingly, Brahmins dominated the RSS whose hold on the nation's political, economic, cultural and social institutions would steadily grow as a result of the efforts of many ultra-Hindu formations under the umbrella of the RSS and the Bharatiya Janata Party (BJP)—Vishva Hindu Parishad (VHP), Bharatiya Mazdoor Sangh (BMS), Bajrang Dal, Rashtrasevika Samiti, Durga's Army, and others.

Another development was the founding of another party of similar

* Dr. K.B. Hedgewar, Dr. B.S. Moonje, Dr. L.V. Paranjpe, Dr. B.B. Thalkar and Babu-rao Savarkar.

colouration, the Jan Sangh, by Shyamaprasad Mukherji, a prominent Hindu Mahasabha leader. He admired the RSS, calling it "the one silver lining in the cloudy sky of India." Alongside these and other communal bodies like the Arya Samajists were elements within the Congress openly sympathetic and supportive to militant Hindu sentiments. Many men of influence, like Purshottamdas Tandon, Madan Mohan Malviya, B.S. Moonje and others, approved of the majority community's ill-concealed assertiveness. Nor were Muslim organizations lagging behind in taking up potentially dangerous positions.

"The real winner was British imperialism," comments Sumit Sarkar. "It is not always remembered that the Hindu communalist leadership's record in bolstering up British rule is not much less notable than that of the Muslim League—from Madan Mohan Malviya, the apostle of 'Hind-Hindi-Hindu' who bitterly opposed Non-Co-operation in 1921, to Shyamaprasad Mukherji . . . who was a minister in Bengal in August 1942 at a time when the British were drowning the Quit India movement in blood." Britain was not an accidental beneficiary of the widening communal divide. It had assiduously created conditions for it: "The Montford reforms had broadened the franchise, but preserved and even extended separate electorates; there was therefore a built-in temptation for politicians working within the system to use sectional slogans and gather a following by distributing favours to their own religious, regional or caste groups."

As was to be expected, irresponsible rhetoric was soon overtaken by violence, by escalating bloodshed after each Hindu-Muslim riot. From 1921 to 1931, the frequency as well as frenzy of clashes between Hindus and Muslims kept rising each year; not just in one region of India but all across the country, from Multan in the north to Malabar in the south, from Dacca in the east to Bombay in the west, and all over Central India. Each outbreak hardened attitudes further, making unity more elusive in the face of British intransigence. Not that efforts towards some sort of compromise between the two antagonistic communities were lacking.

Jawaharlal Nehru, a promising new entrant on the scene, product of British schools, socialist leanings and wealthy, politically influential parents, gave a new impetus to efforts at bridging Hindu-Muslim communalism. "In neither case," he felt, "was it even *bona fide* communalism [i.e., the stirrings and demands of a community], but political and social reaction hiding behind the communal mask." Jinnah was no less earnest in his desire for political unity. "Believe me there is no progress for India until the Musalmans and Hindus are united, and let no logic, philosophy or squabble stand in the way of coming to a compromise and nothing will make me more happy than to see a Hindu-Muslim union."

But despite the integrity of many men and women on both sides of the divide and the earnestness of their efforts through the 1930s, the odds against the secular nationalists—those who were above narrow religious concerns—mounted, even during Nehru and Jinnah's presidentships of the Congress and the Muslim League. The experience of the first-ever elections to provincial assemblies in 1937 further distanced them. With the Congress winning 711 of the 1585 assembly seats, and a clear majority in five out of eleven provinces (UP, CP, Bihar, Orissa and Madras), against an unimpressive showing by the League, the stage was set for the alienation of the Muslims outside the "government." Some of the Congress ministries' pro-Hindu measures aggravated the Muslim mood still further and provoked Jinnah into denouncing "Congress Fascism" in the League's December 1938 session. Nor did provocative statements by Hindu leaders help. V.D. Savarkar of the Mahasabha asserted in the same month, for example: "Yes, we Hindus are a Nation by ourselves . . . Hindu nationalists should not at all be apologetic to [sic] being called Hindu communalists."

What the initial experiment of 27 months with a form of self-rule achieved, following the formation of provincial governments after the 1937 assembly elections, was to convince the Muslim League, though not all Indian Muslims, that life under Congress rule would be unacceptable; that the future of Muslims lay in a nation of their own. As Nehru ruefully conceded in October 1939, "there is no doubt that we have been unable to check the growth of communalism and anti-Congress feeling among the masses." Matters came to a head during the League's Lahore session in March 1940, and its demand for a Muslim state—Pakistan. The name "Pakistan," coined from the first letters of Punjab, Afghanistan, Kashmir and Sind, and "tan" from Baluchistan, had an ominous ring for the Sikhs since their homeland lay at the heart of the state the League now aspired to.

What the Sikhs had acquired by shedding their blood on countless battlefields would be bartered away at negotiating tables by Congress aspirants to India's leadership. The die was cast. It was in fact the Arya Samaji Lala Lajpat Rai who in the 1920s first suggested that Punjab should be divided into West and East Punjab, with the Muslims concentrated in the former and non-Muslims in the latter. Although he did not conceive of a separate nation for the Muslims, his suggestion shows how ill-conceived ideas can come home to roost. No wonder Chowdhury Rahmat Ali, who fleshed out the specifics of Pakistan, approvingly observed that "Lala's proposal was a decisive step in the right direction."

While Jinnah and the Congress's Brahminical élite drew on their immense reserves of political wile to position themselves for power, the Sikhs—not very adept at striking deals—witnessed their once vast territories divided in half by Partition, and in three different segments after Independence. The British, who had drawn on the Sikhs' fighting skills in the wars they fought around the world, betrayed them first by ignoring their interests during negotiations with the Hindus and Muslims, and then by letting the massacre of tens of thousands of Sikhs take place before the transfer of power in 1947.

Through craftily worded proposals and a shrewd mix of political skills and worthless promises the Sikhs were persuaded to accept arrangements—before and after Independence—which, when the time came, none of the signatories would honour. The most invidious agreement arrived at between the Congress, Muslim League and the British was to divide India by taking population as the basis of Partition. As 1947, the year of Partition, dawned, some very unpleasant surprises awaited Punjab. The scale and savagery of the killings on either side of the dividing line between India and Pakistan exceeded all expectations, with a bitter price paid by the Sikhs, who had neither asked for nor were expecting a separate homeland since they had always considered themselves an integral part of India. They were more dismayed than most at the very thought of Punjab's dismemberment.

That the Sikhs had options which they turned down is illustrated by an account of a meeting between their leaders and Mohammad Ali Jinnah in 1946. Jinnah suggested the meeting to the Maharaja of Patiala, its aim being to win the Sikhs over to the Muslim League's point of view. But Jinnah was reluctant to go to Patiala for the meeting. Sardar Hardit Singh Malik, the state's prime minister at the time and a distinguished member of the Indian Civil Service who was held in high regard by the Sikhs, also favoured the idea of a meeting on neutral ground and arranged it at the New Delhi home of his brother, Sardar Teja Singh Malik. The five persons who met there were Jinnah, the Maharaja of Patiala, Sardar Hardit Singh Malik, and the two Sikh political leaders Master Tara Singh and Giani Kartar Singh.

According to Malik, Jinnah was "most anxious that the Sikhs should accept Pakistan and agree to live there after it was created, and he went on to explain that if we did he would agree to everything that we would wish for to safeguard our interest as a minority." Malik, while thanking him for his generous offer, asked: "You will have a Cabinet, a Parliament, the Judiciary, the Armed Forces. What exactly will be our share in all these?" Jinnah responded by narrating a story about Zaghlul Pasha, Egypt's virtual ruler after the country became independent. When a delegation of the Copts, Egypt's influential Christian minority, went to see the pasha to seek guarantees concerning their position in the new Egypt, he asked them to think carefully about what they wanted and bring back their demands in a written document. When the Copt leader gave him the written demands at their second meeting, Zaghlul Pasha, without even reading them, wrote "I agree" on the document. Jinnah said: "This is how I will deal with you—as Zaghlul Pasha did with the Copts."

After their meeting the Sikh leaders—who were not even agreeable to the establishment of Pakistan, let alone have any dealings with it—decided to convey their reply in a manner which would also counter any false propaganda that might follow their meeting with Jinnah. That very day, as Malik recorded, "I went and saw U.N. Sen [Sir Usha Nath Sen, a veteran journalist], who wielded considerable influence in press circles in those days and was an old friend, and I said to him, 'My friend, I have never asked you to do anything for me, but today I have a request to make, a very important request.' I then told him about the meeting with Jinnah and added, 'I want you to see to it [that] *The Statesman* carries on its front page the next morning the headline in the largest letters, 'The Sikhs will under no circumstances accept Pakistan.' Sen promised to do his best and sure enough the next day *The Statesman* carried the headline that I had asked for. And that was our answer to Jinnah. We could have had Sikhistan if we wanted, as that was what Jinnah was really hinting at, because he knew full well that we could never agree to live in Pakistan. That was the price he was offering us, to agree to Pakistan."

The price the Sikhs paid, once their stand became clear to the Muslim League, is graphically described by Alan Campbell-Johnson in his book *Mission with Mountbatten*. Recording his impressions of a visit with the Mountbattens (Lord Mountbatten had just taken over as Viceroy from Lord Wavell) to Kahuta near Rawalpindi in early 1947, he wrote: "we arrived to find that the havoc in the small town was very great. Picking our way through the rubble, we could see that the devastation was as thorough as any produced by fire-bomb raids in the war. This particular communal orgy involved the destruction of Sikhs and their livelihood by Muslims . . ."

A similar story of the ruthless massacre of Sikhs in Rawalpindi in March 1947, when the Muslims murdered 2,000 in a welter of ferocity, is recounted by Leonard Mosley in *The Last Days of the British Raj*; it was repeated in the months before Independence and Partition on 15 August, while the British still ruled the subcontinent, in other parts of West Punjab, in towns as well as countryside: in Lahore, Sheikhupura, Sialkot, and Gujranwala districts. It is often said that the administration was caught unawares by the March massacres in and around Rawalpindi. This is a disingenuous argument considering that a handful of British colonialists had ruled a sprawling subcontinent largely on the basis of their excellent intelligence network. In the words of a press statement published in Lucknow on 22 March: "It cannot be an accident that those districts where serious rioting broke out are precisely those districts which are ruled by British officers. It too cannot be an accident that when people in distress go to these officers, who are paid by the province to do their duty, they are made fun of and are taunted and told to go to [the] Congress."

To the testimony of the scale of the tragedy that overtook the Sikhs in what would become West Pakistan belongs the account by V.P. Menon, the Viceroy's adviser who had a ringside seat throughout that critical period, in his book *The Transfer of Power in India:* "one must appreciate that the Sikhs had been driven out of their homes contrary to all their hopes and expectations; that they had been deprived of their lands and property, their shrines and holy places; that their losses in men and property had been comparatively greater than those of any other community affected by the communal upheaval; that nearly forty percent of the entire Sikh community had been reduced to penury and had become refugees with the necessity of having to start life afresh."

The handling of the transfer of power by the Congress, the Muslim League and Britain resulted in the massacre of hundreds of thousands of Sikhs in a few months. Among the deals that precipitated the moral and physical perversions of 1947, the most astounding was the Congress Working Committee's March decision to accept India's partition and seek the League's co-operation in "a division of the Punjab into two provinces, so that the predominantly Muslim part may be separated from the predominantly non-Muslim part." This was an obvious sellout of the Sikhs as it concerned their homeland: the only state in which they were concentrated. "Violence escalated after the Congress Resolution . . . [and] those who survived initiated the greatest mass migration in history. Their bitter memories cemented the walls of Partition," says Ajit Bhattacharjea in his excellent book *Countdown to Partition.*

By agreeing to Partition on the assumption—or so people were led to believe—that Jinnah would not accept a truncated and "moth-eaten Pakistan," duplicitous Congressmen ignored the League's determination to break with India at any cost. They refused to face the prospective human costs involved in dividing Punjab: the Sikhs stranded in Pakistan could be expected to be either killed or forced to leave their fertile lands, urban wealth, extensive properties and lucrative businesses to the not-so-well-off Muslim majority there. Which is exactly what happened. The question is: is this what the Congress mandarins wanted?

The genocidal killings of Sikhs and Hindus, starting in Kahuta and Rawalpindi and spreading rapidly across West Punjab, intensified with the Congress's ill-conceived 1947 Partition Resolution. Even Gandhi's reservations about it were brushed aside by Sardar Vallabhbhai Patel (known as India's "Iron Man," who became the first home minister of India after Independence): "It has been difficult to explain to you the Resolution about the Punjab. It was adopted after the deepest deliberation. Nothing has been done in a hurry or without full thought." These deep deliberations, whose direct outcome was mass genocide, leave many questions unanswered in Sikh minds.

The Muslim League behaved no better. Taking unprincipled advantage of the Congress Party's Partition plan, it deliberately instigated violence against unsuspecting Sikhs and Hindus, designating, for example, days of "direct action" in leading population centres, which is even more reprehensible since violence was antithetical to Jinnah's political principles and his views on minorities, his own community being a minority in undivided India. He had often reiterated that "the combination of all these various elements—religion, culture, race, language, art, music and so forth, makes the minority a separate entity in the State, and that separate entity as an entity wants safeguards. Surely, therefore, we must face this question as a political problem, we must solve it and not evade it." Presumably Jinnah's beliefs, like those of his counterpart, Gandhi, were already being ignored by his followers.

The most regrettable role in those fateful months was played by the British, largely owing to the personal agenda of Queen Victoria's great-grandson, Lord Mountbatten. Aspiring to the highest office in the navy, the ambitious Mountbatten, a darling of the British establishment, was invited to 10 Downing Street on 18 December 1946 and offered the job of India's last Viceroy, the man who would hand over power to the people of India. Drawn by the challenge of this assignment, but driven by a desire to return to his naval career at the earliest opportunity, Mountbatten was in a hurry from the very outset. On his urging the Labour government, in an official statement of 20 February 1947, agreed "to effect the transference of power into responsible Indian hands by a date not later than June 1948." Which seemed sensible. But within less than three months of arriving in New Delhi on 22 March 1947, Mountbatten advanced the date to 15 August 1947. This and other shortcuts stained his Viceroyalty despite his personal magnetism and charm.

Mountbatten's most disastrous shortcut concerned the establishing of the dividing line between East and West Punjab, the former where Muslims were in a minority and the latter which they dominated. With complete disregard for the consequences, he allowed a bare five weeks for demarcating the boundary which would also become the border between India and Pakistan. The man "entrusted with the most sensitive and potentially explosive act of social-political surgery in history," Sir Cyril Radcliffe, a British jurist and a total stranger to the subcontinent, arrived in New Delhi on 8 July as chairman of the Boundary Commission.

Within hours of reaching the capital, Sir Cyril set about the task of drawing a line which would separate millions from their friends, relatives, families, co-religionists, shrines, businesses, vocations, lands, rivers and canals, which had nurtured them for generations. As if the impossibly limited time he had allotted for the task were not bad enough, Mountbatten compounded the explosive potential of the situation by withholding Radcliffe's report until after the transfer of power, so that violent protests by those affected would not reflect on him and "the responsibility of dealing with the disturbances expected after the award would fall on the new governments of India and Pakistan. He would no longer be viceroy and the British Government would not be responsible for whatever happened."

Although Radcliffe delivered the Punjab award* on 9 August, Mountbatten sat on it. He took no steps to prevent the savaging of minorities on either side of the border, despite full awareness of the need to do so. As he admitted in a report to the British government written after Partition: "from the administrative point of view there was considerable advantage in immediate publication [of the awards] so that the new boundaries [might] take effect from 15 August, and the officials of the right Dominion could be in their places to look after the districts which had been allotted to their side, before that date." But from the political point of view, as he commented further, it had "been obvious all along that the later we postponed publication, the less would the inevitable odium react upon the British."

---

* The complete award, including the boundaries of divided Bengal, was submitted on 13 August.

Millions of Indian lives were sacrificed to avoid the "odium" of the Viceroy's decision from falling on his country. Prime Minister Attlee and the Secretary of State for India, Lord Listowel, fulsomely praised his performance. Attlee felt Mountbatten's "short tenure of the Viceroyalty has been one of the most memorable in the long list." Listowel's letter was no less effusive: "I believe your outstanding ability and fearless determination have saved India from unimaginable disaster and that your achievement will be remembered in time to come as one of the greatest feats of statesmanship in history." The reality couldn't be less so. No "statesmanship" was involved in a transfer of power attended by mass murders and migration of millions. Nor can the indescribable horror of over fourteen million uprooted Sikh, Muslim and Hindu refugees streaming towards the safe-havens of their "own" people be considered "memorable." The estimate of 600,000 who paid with their lives in Punjab because of British indifference to their fate does not take into account the countless bodies burnt, buried or dumped in rivers, nor thousands of women abducted during the frenzy that self-serving men had helped unleash on innocent men, women and children.

Not all Englishmen were insensitive to the human cost of Partition. The Governor of Punjab Province, Sir Evan Jenkins, tried hard to head off the impending disaster. He urged Mountbatten not to delay release of the Boundary Commission's report to 15 August, or even later, and repeatedly tried to get an indication of the dividing line to help him prevent violence. There was no ambiguity in his telegrams to New Delhi. "Situation here is generally explosive. Hatred and suspicion are universal and undisguised. It seems to me this is inevitable under a plan which in Punjab converts our principal cities into frontier towns and drives [the] boundary through areas homogenous in everything except religion. Explosions may be touched off at any time and I expect trouble when [the] Boundary Commission reports." His exhortations were ignored, just as the impatient Viceroy ignored all other indications of the tragedy about to overtake Punjab.

The Sikhs were not alone in paying a heavy price. Punjab's Hindus and Muslims also shared the terrible ordeal, but with a difference: the Sikhs had been offered a way out, but had rejected it. This needs reiteration, because those busy rewriting history will distort even indisputable facts. Some of them have tried somewhat laboriously to prove that separatism is endemic to Sikh politics. In search of evidence to support this conclusion—very popular in India's communally charged post-Independence atmosphere—they have reached back to the Punjab Census Report of 1891, a pamphlet by Lieutenant-Governor M. Macauliffe (1903), the Montagu-Chelmsford reforms (1919), the Cripps proposals (1942), the All Parties Sikh Conference of 1944, the Cabinet Mission's report of 1946, and much more.

No mention is made in such writings of other, more telling facts about the stand taken by the Sikhs. For instance, when in 1906 Lord Minto, then Viceroy of India, readily conceded the Muslim demand for separate electorates and reservation of Muslim seats in the legislatures, the Sikhs asked for no such accommodation. The Congress Party, on the other hand, setting aside principle in favour of political expediency in 1916, concluded a pact with the Muslim League by accepting and endorsing the concept of separate electorates. In truth, the Sikhs, in rejecting Jinnah's overtures prior to the transfer of power, made no distinction between "Sikh interests" and the interests of a soon-to-be-independent India.

The Sikhs did not see Hindus as an alien people, but a people from whom they had sprung, to whom they had married their sons and daughters, with whom they had shared their agonies and ecstasies, whose friendship had been a part of their experience of growing up, as it had been for generations before them. The stand of the Sikhs at the time of Partition resulted from their inviolable emotional involvement with their motherland, India. Misgivings would come in post-Partition years, as they saw with dismay their Hindu friends and neighbours disowning their common mother tongue, Punjabi. But that, and much more, was still to come.

The Sikhs' expectations of new beginnings in an emergent India had been bought with their blood. What they couldn't know at the time was that they were coming into a flawed inheritance, that their certitudes and hopes would be stonewalled by the same communal intolerance as that which had set the subcontinent on a suicidal course and sundered it in two.

6
Violence and Venality
1947 to the Present

On a warm, muggy day in September 1947—scarcely a month into the freedom India had longed for—Delhi exploded in blind fury. Fed by murderous hate and a desire for vengeance, violence, stoked by the plight of West Punjab's refugees, covered the entire range of human bestiality—pillage, arson, murder and rape.

Violence was not new to Delhi. The city had experienced everything in its long and chequered existence. In 1398 it was so comprehensively sacked by Tamerlane that, as one literary source has it, "for two months afterwards not a bird moved a wing in the city." On 11 March 1739 the Persian invader Nadir Shah put Delhi to the sword, and a hundred thousand persons were slaughtered in a single day. In the nineteenth century the British too proved that putting innocent people to death is the privilege of those in power. Their atrocities could be chillingly cold-blooded, as was shown by the reprisals visited on Delhi after the 1857 Mutiny, during which Captain W.S.R. Hodson took out his pistol and shot to death two sons and a grandson of Mughal Emperor Bahadur Shah—*after* they had surrendered from their place of refuge—because, as he put it, "I confess I did rejoice at the opportunity of ridding the earth of these wretches."

What Delhi witnessed in September 1947—and would again a few decades later—was, therefore, nothing new. Except in one respect. While in the past the perpetrators had been either invaders or interlopers, this time they were neighbours or friends who had lived together as fellow citizens despite distinctions of religion, region, creed and custom. Until one day one group had turned on the other in truly demonic rage. While the killers were purportedly avenging kinsmen killed in Pakistan, the victims chosen for retribution were innocent of the crimes across the border. Paradoxically, the killers and the killed on each side were victims of the communal madness their "leaders" had preached and which would haunt India long after alien rulers had been replaced by a homegrown species of purblind politicians.

The year 1947 was no *annus mirabilis* for a free India, but a year anointed by crimes, without logic or justification, by religious hate which would intensify with each decade. Needing no particular denomination to vent itself on, this hate would go beyond Hindu-Muslim hostility because there were others in India's complex religious mosaic—Sikhs, Christians and Buddhists—against whom it could be directed. Any number of permutations and combinations were possible, if the will to divide people for political gains existed, which it did in abundance, as the years after Independence would show. And which the Sikhs would experience first-hand.

Before communal madness again overtook the country, India provided convincing proof of the versatility and drive of her gifted people. There were large-scale industrialization and agricultural breakthroughs. Since famines had dogged India during the years prior to Independence, self-sufficiency in food was given high priority in the First Five-Year Plan (1951–6). Next, those in favour of rapid industrialization got the upper hand and agriculture took a backseat for over twelve years, until it was again given top priority towards the end of the 1960s. In the industrial sector, India had always been a market for British manufactures, but in the changed order after Independence the groundwork for a vast variety of industrial products was laid within the country. These ranged from steel, locomotives, heavy machinery, ships, aircraft and automobiles to the setting-up of power-generating projects, oil refineries and atomic energy plants.

The crucial role in making India self-sufficient in food was played by Punjab. The state became India's bread-basket. Sizeable government investment in developing irrigation schemes and rural infrastructure during the 1950s, combined with the robust inputs of the Sikh peasantry, produced per acre yields which put Punjab far ahead of other states. Its wheat output increased from 1 million (metric) tons in 1950–1 to 11.5 million tons in 1989–90, rice—which had scarcely been grown there previously—from 0.1 to 6.7 million tons, and cotton from 132,000 to 417,000 tons in the same period. No less impressive were increases in other sectors like animal husbandry and dairying. One economist recently put Punjab's current share of total wheat and rice production in India at 70 to 90 per cent and 60 per cent respectively.

Whilst Punjab's spectacular agricultural achievements owe a great deal to major government investments, a similar concern was lacking when it came to funding its industrialization. No large state-sector plant was located in Punjab, in marked contrast to the extent to which other states in India were allocated these. At first Punjab's exclusion was viewed as a lapse which would soon be set right, but gradually the pattern was discerned: Punjab was being denied the opportunity to industrialize. Why? New Delhi's argument that the state's proximity to Pakistan would make key industries vulnerable to attack did not allay suspicions, but increased them instead, especially since Pakistan showed no qualms about locating industries on its side of the border.

There is a view which holds that, though unwittingly, Punjab's development, in continuing to lay emphasis on agriculture, on dairying, animal husbandry and cash crops, has provided a growth model in which the balance between a large agricultural sector and small and medium industries has succeeded in ensuring ecological safeguards even as a large agro-industrial base was being created. Instead of one or two heavy industries becoming the hub of all industrial activity in the state, this argument goes, Punjab's balanced development is evenly spread within its borders.

Punjab has in fact industrialized—with small-scale enterprises accounting for a substantial portion of its overall production: about 40 per cent of output and almost 80 per cent of employment in 1989–90. Manufactures range from agro-processing industries to engineering goods, hand-tools, sewing machines, bicycles, textiles, knitwear, hosiery and sports goods. Their quality is excellent, turnover impressive, and exports sizeable. Credit for their success goes to the entrepreneurial drive and spirit of Punjab's people, including those who came as refugees. With only 2.5 per cent of India's population, Punjab accounts for more than 8 per cent of India's small-scale industries.

Although it is no one's case that the small-scale sector in Punjab has not been helped by government concessions and other incentives, the state has been denied facilities for full-scale industrialization, when Punjab's rural youth—rendered surplus by mechanization of farming—might have been provided with opportunities to develop a scientific temper and technological orientation. Even more galling to Punjabis was the fact that considerable sums of money deposited by agriculturists and others in nationalized banks in the state were being invested elsewhere in India, in preference to investing them in the state's industrial development. The Sikhs were not convinced by the argument that Punjab's per capita income of 7,674 rupees (for 1989–90) was far higher than the 4,291 rupees for the rest of India. Per capita incomes, they countered, would have been twice the present levels had the state been treated more even-handedly.

These and many other factors, mostly political but with communal undertones, would greatly add to the Sikhs' disillusionment with New Delhi, whose unconcern at their increasing alienation, despite mounting evidence of the dangers involved, would take India to the brink of disintegration. New Delhi's mishandling of the Punjab situation epitomizes the pursuit of policies contrary to the national interest—threatening the Republic's very existence soon after the end of foreign rule.

At first light of dawn on a cool and clear morning in November 1966, the people of Punjab awoke to an unpleasant reality: their state had been truncated three ways—by the carving of two new states, Haryana and Himachal Pradesh, out of it.

Partition of their homeland was nothing new. But whilst Punjab's 1947 division had taken place under the tutelage of an alien power, the second had been effected by the government of a free India. Startlingly similar considerations had triggered these momentous events.

The agenda of the colonial power was naturally different. Britain saw its self-interest served by a divided subcontinent. Two neighbouring nations, mutually hostile and embittered, are more easily managed to a former colonial power's advantage than a single, strong state whose manpower, size, vast resources and political unity would make it less amenable to outside pressures or wilful persuasion.

While Whitehall's interest in India's partition and the creation of Pakistan was understandable, the events of November 1966 in Punjab were less so. Why was this viable state slashed into three whilst Uttar Pradesh, seven times its size, was left undisturbed? Why did it take thirteen years after the formation of the first linguistic state, Andhra Pradesh, to grant Punjabi-speaking people statehood? And why was the State of Punjab whittled down to a size unworthy of its energetic people?

The response to these questions by the ruling Congress Party has invariably been that since the issue was a particularly complex one, it took thirteen years to resolve. The truth is that the delay was deliberate prevarication. But why should the government prevaricate with a people who had suffered so much at Partition, who had made Punjab India's bread-basket, and been a formidable bulwark in the nation's war-prone relations with its northern neighbour, Pakistan? Perhaps the answer lies in the Brahminical élite's ongoing determination to oversee India's destiny, as it has done in varying degrees for millennia.

Being numerically few seems greatly to have influenced the political strategies of both the Brahmins and the British. The British, for instance, were never more than 60,000 in the entire subcontinent, which even at the time of the first census in 1881 had a population of 253 million. The pre-eminent Brahmins are barely 3 per cent of India's population. Whilst India's Partition appears to have been a reflection of Britain's desire to maintain some kind of remote-controlled sovereignty over the divided subcontinent, the reorganization of its states after Independence also appears to reflect the Brahminical élite's strategy of controlling India. The exercise of power, it is obvious, requires conditions to be created which make it easier to maintain the hegemony of the few.

Notwithstanding its populist appeal, the reorganization of provinces on linguistic lines was a folly whose damaging effect on India's social fabric has yet to be fully analysed. The idea, although aired earlier, had been given specific form in 1920 when the Congress Party reorganized its provincial committees on the basis of language. Within nine years Motilal Nehru, Jawaharlal's father, committed the Congress to a linguistic reorganization of India after Independence, and spelt it out in the Nehru Report. In 1945 Dr. Pattabhi Sitaramayya, president-elect of the All India Congress Committee, reiterated his party's pledge to this goal.

There were second thoughts after the transfer of power. As practical considerations outweighed hidden agendas and populist pledges, some began to see more clearly the danger of letting linguistic chauvinism loose on a fledgling republic. There was a keener awareness, in a section of the Congress, of how language bigots could compromise national unity. Despite Jawaharlal Nehru's own apparent opposition to a type of reorganization that his father had recommended decades earlier, the ill-advised decision to divide the country linguistically was taken.

As the time for the execution of the reorganization neared, a pattern of double standards emerged. The two committees—one appointed by the government and the other by the Congress—which had been established after Independence to report on linguistic reorganization each endorsed the idea of other language states, but excluded the northern states from it, especially Punjab. According to the government commission chaired by S.K. Dar, which submitted its report on 10 December 1948, "nationalism and sub-nationalism are two emotional experiences which grow at each other's expense," and the reorganization of India on "mainly linguistic considerations is not in the larger interests of the Indian nation." But after this evaluation, the Dar Commission equivocated, calling the reorganization "a grave risk, but one that had to be taken." Despite its own concerns, why did the Commission's report recommend the formation of Andhra Pradesh, Karnataka, Kerala and Maharashtra on linguistic lines? And why did it exclude Punjab? The Commission observed that "oneness of language may be one of the factors to be taken into consideration . . . but it should not be the decisive or even the main factor." The Brahmin in Mr. Dar may have got the better of him.

Equally striking were the Congress Linguistic Provinces Committee's findings. Its members, Jawaharlal Nehru, Vallabhbhai Patel and Pattabhi Sitaramayya (two of whom were Brahmins), expressed grave reservations about the party's earlier commitment to linguistic provinces as they would create "mutual conflicts which would jeopardize the political and economic stability of the country." Then, curiously, their report of 1 April 1949 went on to state that "we are clearly of the opinion that no question of rectification of boundaries in provinces of North India should be raised at the present moment, whatever the merit of such proposals might be." If merit was not a criterion, what was? Politics, not principle.

Even before Indira Gandhi became prime minister, she was against the Centre (the Federal Government in New Delhi) conceding the demand for a Punjabi-speaking state: "to concede the Akali demand would mean abandoning a position to which it [the Congress] was firmly committed and letting down its Hindu supporters in the Punjabi Suba [i.e., a Punjabi-speaking state]." According to Hukam Singh, the speaker of parliament, himself a Congressman and a man held in high regard by everyone, "Lal Bahadur Shastri continued the policy of Jawaharlal Nehru, and was as dead against the demand of Punjabi Suba as was Nehru . . . Nehru stuck to it. Shastri continued the same, and Indira Gandhi has made no departure." So when a suba was conceded it was a mockery of what Punjab had once been.

If politics, then, was the criterion, it is easier to understand the denial of a linguistically reorganized Punjab to the Punjabis and Sikhs, and its exclusion from the Dar Commission's terms of reference. The activities of various Hindu fundamentalist organizations and groups had much to do with it, for they had gone about persuading their co-religionists in Punjab to disown Punjabi as their mother tongue, the language Punjabi Hindus had spoken for generations. Long before reorganization the ground had been gradually prepared for Punjab's Hindus and the underprivileged castes to declare Hindi their mother tongue. The timing of this campaign—on the eve of the 1951 census in Punjab—was significant since the census figures would decide who spoke which language and provide the eventual justification for carving what were in fact two Hindi-speaking states out of Punjab. The man who orchestrated these moves, Lala Jagat Narain, was not only a staunch Arya Samajist but also the general secretary of the Punjab Congress Committee. He epitomized the marriage of convenience between Congress ambitions, religious intolerance and sectarian politics.

New Delhi manipulated the media and public opinion to project a Punjabi-speaking state as a demand for a separate Sikh state. Inevitably, a purely linguistic demand, which other language groups had also made—and been granted—and which the Congress Party had declared as its goal in 1929, was in Punjab's case labelled a separatist demand. The media, ever eager to write of dark plots where none exist, willingly accepted the idea of the Sikhs as separatists and converted a linguistic demand into a confrontation between two religious communities. The Sikhs, without media of their own, were in no position to present their side of the case.

Several facts were not revealed to the public. The Sikhs in their representation to the States Reorganization Commission had pressed for a unilingual Punjab, the Hindu population of which would be 57 per cent as against 43 per cent Sikhs. Their demand in effect was not for a Sikh but for a Hindu majority state. *But it would be a Punjabi state.* The Commission rejected the proposal because it was not supported by Punjab's Hindus. For the Congress had seen to it that it would not be. Being in power in New Delhi and most states, it was in a position to do so.

It was ironic that in 1906 the Muslims, a minority, had asked the British for separate electorates in order to separate from the Hindu majority, while in independent India the Hindu majority of Punjab wanted to be separated from the Sikh minority! Such segments of Punjab's Hindu society were the real separatists.

Almost forty years after the Dar Commission's report, the Commission on Centre-State Relations (Sarkaria Commission) had this to report on the impact of linguistic reorganization of the country. "There has been a growth in sub-nationalism which has tended to strengthen divisive forces and weaken the unity and integrity of the country. Linguistic chauvinism has also added a new dimension in keeping people apart . . . unless there is a will and commitment to work for a united country, there are real dangers that regionalism, linguistic chauvinism, communalism, casteism, etc., may foul the atmosphere to the point where secessionist thoughts start pervading the body politic."

A glance at the governance of Punjab in the ten years preceding Independence will provide a useful footnote to these intrigues. Indians tend to believe that the British devised the policy of divide and rule. This is questionable. The Brahmins perfected it long before the British, who in all likelihood took their inspiration from them. Of course the British divided different religious, caste, class, regional and language groups, whenever and wherever they could. But divide and rule was never a constant, just one of many strategies by which they safeguarded their Indian empire. Their Punjab policy in the years prior to Partition proves it.

British policies of that period were based on pragmatic and hard-headed considerations. Since a coalition of different communities at that time gave stability to Punjab, which served British interests, it was encouraged. The astonishing degree of political equilibrium, in a religiously divided state, under the Unionist Party from 1937 to 1947 would not have been possible without the active encouragement of the British, or without their full support for two successive state premiers of impressive stature. Since both Sikander Hayat Khan and Khizr Hyat Tiwana's pluralistic approach to the state's three powerful communities, the Hindus, Muslims and Sikhs, helped to ensure stability in the northern reaches of Britain's Indian Empire, decisions affecting their province were left to them.

Whilst the British encouraged a stable and unified Punjab, the Indian leadership preferred a segmented one after Independence. By reducing it to a size which entitled it to only thirteen members of parliament out of 545, it considerably diminished Punjab's importance in New Delhi's corridors of power. It remains inexplicable to the Sikhs why a strong and united Punjab was viewed as a threat to the ruling party in Delhi. An increasing number attribute it to their high profile in the Indian army; their individualistic and independent temperament; their fierce pride in their religion. They also realize that Sikhism's break with its Hindu origins centuries ago continues to be viewed with disfavour by the unforgiving elements in Hindu society, and also suspect that there could be an underlying fear in the minds of the ruling mandarins that, like the traditionally militaristic Junkers of East Prussia, the Sikhs too might one day prove difficult to control and therefore have to be cut down to size by all means possible. This, in effect, was achieved by encouraging breakaway demands of two sizeable Hindu constituents of the state of Punjab, which also helped disperse large numbers of Sikhs beyond its borders.

There is still more to the story of Punjab's agony. After the principle of one language for one state had been incorporated in the States Reorganization Act of 1956—with Punjab and Bombay excluded as bilingual—Bombay was reorganized on 1 May 1960. In its place the Marathi- and Gujarati-speaking states of Maharashtra and Gujarat emerged. But it took *six more years* for a Punjabi-speaking Punjab to be formed, and that too after a bitter struggle, in which many Sikhs died, thousands were jailed, and the entire community registered the distressing fact that political clout and not principle would influence decisions in Independent India. Proof of this was provided by the time-table for redrawing state boundaries:

States formed	Date of formation
Andhra Pradesh	1 October 1953
Kerala	1 November 1956
Karnataka	1 November 1956
Maharashtra	1 May 1960
Gujarat	1 May 1960
Punjab	1 November 1966

The 1961 census figures, which determined the areas to be included in truncated Punjab, were as mischievous as those of its predecessor, the 1951 census. Thus several Hindu-majority areas where Punjabi had always been spoken—but disowned in the census—were left out. Even Chandigarh, the city designed by Le Corbusier and built as the new capital of Punjab after Partition, was made a Union Territory to be directly administered by New Delhi. In the end, what was conceded was not a genuine unilingual Punjabi-speaking state with 57 per cent Hindu population as desired by the Sikhs, but a communal Punjab they had never asked for.

Aside from the encouragement of xenophobic tendencies, lack of vision in India's linguistic redistribution is also evident from the territorial and river waters disputes which have plagued the country ever since Partition. Among the many that continue to simmer and boil over from time to time, with the ever-present danger of still deadlier confrontations, are the sharing of Cauvery river waters between Karnataka and Tamil Nadu, the Krishna river dispute between Karnataka and Andhra Pradesh, the Telegu Ganga canal project between Andhra Pradesh and Tamil Nadu, and the river waters and territorial disputes between Punjab and Haryana.

When to these avoidable conflicts are added the founding of political parties whose chief *raison d'être* is to harass and hound migrants from other states, the cost in ruined lives, to a nation divided against itself, is incalculable. Bombay's Shiv Sena party is a classic example of what crude political demagoguery has done to India's once premier city. Its increasingly inflammatory agitation even after the formation of a new linguistic state was based on the premise that Maharashtrians were being sidelined for jobs in their own state. After Shiv Sena's creation in 1966, it appealed to Maharashtrian chauvinism by attacking South Indians settled in Bombay. Not unexpectedly, this helped the Sena's political prospects, but proved disastrous for Bombay's South Indians. Worse still, encouraged by its stifling stranglehold over the once uniquely cosmopolitan and liberal city, the Sena turned on the Muslims and in a vicious killing spree in December 1992–January 1993, massacred over 1,500 in cold blood, with the connivance of a partisan police force. Religious persecution, the Sena found, provided more political mileage than xenophobia, and also bettered its prospects of emerging as an all-India party.

But even the Janus-faced approach of the Indian government to Punjab did not erode communal relations in that state. After the dismemberment of the state in 1966 the Sikhs did not turn on the Hindus, nor try to drive them out, nor resent their economic prosperity. But their indignation against New Delhi's injustice was palpable because Punjab's political clout in the polity of India had been deliberately reduced, and its demands were trifled with. Many Sikhs for the first time doubted if they had any future at all in a Union which so disregarded their interests. It had communalized Punjab's politics, created a climate of cynical indifference to principles of equity and transparency in government, and preferred political expediency to moral integrity.

Attitudes influence events, and New Delhi's attitude proved catastrophic. In the early 1970s the Akali Dal, the foremost political party of the Sikhs, which had earlier rejected religious rhetoric, changed its stand. Its new message: the Sikh Panth, or faith, was in danger. This heady refrain was far from the truth. A faith like the Sikh, whose adherents are deeply committed to it, cannot easily be endangered. But as communal-religious elements were now to the fore, the Akali Dal Party went along with them. Its members also showed a singular incapacity to identify themselves with the cause of the minorities all over India, especially the Muslims and Dalits who have suffered the most from the chauvinism of India's ruling élites. Had they assiduously built up a position of ideological integrity, as the founders of their faith and others after them did, they would not have been as isolated as they were in the 1980s.

In the 1970s, the Akalis' inability to win political power at the polls also contributed to their religious bellicosity. Their political sloganizing achieved nothing more than polarizing Hindus and Sikhs and projecting Sikhs in an unflattering light. Given the powerful ties of the Sikhs with their faith, it was altogether unbecoming to imply that the Panth was in danger. The dignity of an indestructible faith and a proud people was needlessly compromised.

The Akali defeat in the 1972 provincial assembly elections was due to a woeful lack of pragmatism and purpose in electoral politics, even within the state. Instead of winning voters' confidence through a constructive blueprint for Punjab's industrialization, power generation, communication networks and administrative revitalization—which would have been bound to appeal to the state's practical-minded electorate—the Akalis responded to Congress manipulations by playing the religious card. This was unwise, whatever the short-term appeal.

Hindu-Sikh relations had suffered many strains in the past. The Arya Samaj and Hindu Mahasabha's denigration of Sikh philosophy and scriptures, while gaining them an impressive following in urban Punjab, had adversely affected Hindu-Sikh cohesiveness. Yet these strains, not very dissimilar to those experienced by other societies, had been kept in check. The reorganization of the Indian states, however, proved more destructive since it played politics with explosive issues like religion and language.

Ironically, when the Akali policy-makers pulled themselves together, it got them nowhere. In 1977 they put forward a wise and farsighted proposal which could have benefited the entire country since it went beyond the politics of religion and language. The Anandpur Sahib Resolution was passed by the Akali Dal at its General Session attended by over a hundred thousand persons at Ludhiana on 28–29 October 1977. The first and most important of its points spelt out the main thrust of the document:

THE SHIROMANI AKALI DAL REALISES THAT INDIA IS A FED-
ERAL AND REPUBLICAN ENTITY OF DIFFERENT LANGUAGES,
RELIGIONS AND CULTURES. TO SAFEGUARD THE FUNDAMEN-
TAL RIGHTS OF THE RELIGIOUS AND LINGUISTIC MINORITIES,
TO FULFIL DEMANDS OF DEMOCRATIC TRADITIONS AND TO
PAVE THE WAY FOR ECONOMIC PROGRESS, IT HAS BECOME
IMPERATIVE THAT THE INDIAN CONSTITUTIONAL INFRA-
STRUCTURE SHOULD BE GIVEN A REAL FEDERAL SHAPE BY
REDEFINING THE CENTRAL AND STATE RELATIONS AND
RIGHTS ON THE LINES OF THE AFORESAID PRINCIPLES AND
OBJECTIVES.

The Resolution went on to point out that at the time of the Emergency in June 1975 the principle of decentralization of powers advocated by the Akali Dal Party had been openly accepted and adopted by
other political parties of all hues, including the Janata Party, CPI(M),
ADMK, etc. It endorsed "the principle of state autonomy in keeping
with the concept of federalism," and urged the government to

RECAST THE CONSTITUTIONAL STRUCTURE OF THE COUNTRY
ON REAL AND MEANINGFUL FEDERAL PRINCIPLES TO OBVIATE
THE POSSIBILITY OF ANY DANGER TO NATIONAL UNITY AND
THE INTEGRITY OF THE COUNTRY AND FURTHER TO ENABLE
THE STATES TO PLAY A USEFUL ROLE FOR THE PROGRESS AND
PROSPERITY OF THE INDIAN PEOPLE IN THEIR RESPECTIVE
AREAS BY THE MEANINGFUL EXERCISE OF THEIR POWERS.

The other points contained in the Resolution concerned river waters,
social structures, discrimination in jobs, refugee rehabilitation, abolition of duties on farm machinery, accelerated industrialization, and so
on. There was nothing unconstitutional or secessionist in any of them.

The distinguished jurist, retired Chief Justice R.S. Narula, commented in the 1980s: "The only way to save the country from disintegration is to accept and adopt the Anandpur Saheb Resolution for the
entire country—for every state unit of India."

But the Resolution was attacked as a secessionist document which
would threaten the unity of the country and lead to an independent
Sikh state! It was attacked not because it threatened the unity of the

country, but because it threatened the hegemony of the Congress Party, which, during its years in office, dismissed state governments 59 times by invoking Article 356 of the Constitution which gives powers of dismissal to the Centre. Since federalism would loosen New Delhi's control over the states, its mandarins, especially through the press, bitterly opposed it. Declared *The Hindustan Times*, the capital's leading daily: "Needless to say this would not only upset the Centre-State balance visualised in the Constitution but strengthen regional pulls to the detriment of national unity." The paper completely ignored the fact that the Resolution was along the federal axis, in favour of state autonomy, and against the Centre's hegemony.

The malevolent attacks against the Akalis and their Resolution in all general media suggested one of two things: either the government's short-sightedness was bordering on incurable blindness, or the ongoing and deliberate alienation of the Sikhs was part of a larger game plan. Certainly, an explosive situation was being created which could get completely out of hand. Which is exactly what happened.

The delay in granting Punjab statehood, its truncated size when it *was* granted, the subterfuges behind the language controversy, the attack on the Anandpur Sahib Resolution, were tragic milestones which saw the Sikhs—reluctantly and against the wishes of their majority—move away from the national mainstream. Each sleight-of-hand left the Akalis and much of Sikh opinion frustrated; each heightened religious rivalries still further.

Rajni Kothari, a respected political thinker, saw the larger import of what was happening: "By turning the Punjab issue into a Hindu-Sikh confrontation and interpreting the demand for regional autonomy as essentially one for secession based on a religious challenge, the ground was laid for communalizing not just the politics of Punjab but of the country as a whole. Punjab became a 'pivot' from which the country was spun into a new communal orbit." (Kashmir was next in line; there the duly elected Farooq Abdullah was sent packing and Congress communalized the politics of that state too.)

In June 1975 the Sikhs had once again identified themselves with a matter of grave national concern when they fielded the most sustained resistance to the Emergency declared by Prime Minister Indira Gandhi in June of that year. Under the direction of Sant Harchand Singh Longowal, over 40,000 Akali workers were jailed for their "Save Democracy" movement against this lawless act of the Congress-led Union Government. These people were the only ones in India to oppose the Emergency on such a scale. Mrs. Gandhi never forgave the Akalis their resistance and, as events were to show, she had a very long memory.

What was the Emergency about? It followed a judgement delivered on 12 June 1975 by Justice Jag Mohan Lal Sinha of the Allahabad high court, unseating Mrs. Gandhi from parliament. The judgement, delivered on a petition by one of her political opponents, accusing her of corrupt campaign practices, also debarred her from any elective office for six years. After some hesitation, Mrs. Gandhi rejected the judgement. Since this was impracticable in a country with a constitution and rule of law, she suspended both. Through a Proclamation of Emergency signed by a pliant president of India at 11:45 p.m. on 25 June 1975, India's democratic pretensions ended. Within minutes of the signing of the Proclamation, security forces were on the move across the country and over 100,000 persons including former cabinet colleagues, opposition leaders, members of parliament, journalists, academics and students were arrested. Stringent censorship came into effect, society was terrorized, political prisoners were often manacled, and midnight knocks became customary. When lawyers of the Delhi High Court Bar Association protested, over a thousand lawyers' chambers were demolished by bulldozers.

In keeping with India's ongoing Brahminical tradition, Indira Gandhi, from her number two position of power as prime minister, ensured that the president, as head of state, signed a decree which suspended India's fledgling democracy for almost two years.

The Emergency was one of Independent India's bleakest watersheds. It set the stage for a climactic showdown which witnessed the Indian army's assault on one of the most revered places of worship in the world, a prime minister's assassination, the massacre of thousands in the nation's capital, and the danger of the Republic's dismemberment.

In the snap general elections called by Mrs. Gandhi in March 1977, she was defeated, and a coalition government brought to power which restored most of the freedoms she had taken away. But a person like Indira Gandhi is not easily kept out, even less so in this case since the men who succeeded her soon found themselves in the grip of that fatal Indian malaise, factionalism. With no lessons learnt from the past or present, they were soon plotting each other's downfall. The opportunities their infighting presented were not lost on her. Drawing on her formidable manipulative skills, she engineered a revolt within the coalition which led to the ousting of the prime minister and then of his successor, to be followed by the dissolution of parliament and the announcement of general elections. Her convincing win in January 1980 once again saw her installed as prime minister.

While Indira Gandhi was making her moves to bring down the coalition government, she was also planning the opposition government's downfall in Punjab. If Punjab's ruling coalition of Akalis and the right-wing Hindu party Jan Sangh provided hope in the state's communally strained internal relations, it mattered little to the Congress. Its own goal was to unseat the state government by undermining the conciliatory Akalis, because Indira Gandhi had scores to settle with them for defying her Emergency. If the Sikhs were thus alienated still further, that was fine by her; she was willing to sacrifice their limited vote in parliament for the considerably larger Hindu vote.

Her chillingly self-serving plan called for a spellbinding Sikh who would mesmerize his co-religionists with oratorical skills, convince them of the existence of a threat to their faith, and wean them away from the moderate Akalis. Should the latter arrest him for inciting religious passions, it would antagonize the main body of the Sikhs and weaken the Akali support base, since they would appear vindictive towards a man of God. If they did not arrest him, the leaders of the Akali coalition government would antagonize their Hindu partners. And because it is difficult to manage such contradictions indefinitely, the state government would surely fall.

The person chosen for the role was Jarnail Singh Bhindranwale, a seminary preacher with a considerable knowledge of the Sikh scriptures. Seen at the outset as a devout Sikh and a man of God, he was built up—without his knowledge—with all the Brahminical subtlety and skill perfected over millennia into a charismatic leader who eclipsed the Akalis by utterances more fiery than their own; whose larger-than-life image was repeatedly projected through cannily manipulated press, radio and television. It came to appear as if he represented the aspirations of *all* Sikhs, though millions of them had no interest in him or in the Akalis. Significantly, the government did not apprehend him as long as he lived outside the Golden Temple complex. But after he had served the Congress purpose—of communalizing Punjab's politics—and had moved into its sacred precincts on 15 December 1983, the final gory scene was enacted in a carefully conceived political move which required the Indian army to unleash its firepower against the Golden Temple.

In the New Year the Akali leaders, tired of getting nowhere with the Congress for any of their demands by their usual moderate means, decided to perform a symbolic gesture of protest: to burn a page of the Indian Constitution in public. Efforts were made to dissuade them from this act, but too late. The danger was acute: the government's Machiavellian policy of blurring public perception of the distinction between the moderate Akalis and the firebrand it had so assiduously built up was now crowned with success in the fusion in the public mind between the Constitution-burning Akali leaders and the inflammatory utterances of Bhindranwale. As "Sikh extremists" became a catch phrase not only in India but around the world, the Sikhs were seen as a threat to community relations, a threat to the peace. And in taking sanctuary in the Golden Temple complex, Bhindranwale was departing from Sikh historical precedent by placing the supreme shrine of Sikhism in the line of fire.

Images of tanks rolling into the hallowed environs of the Golden Temple in June 1984 are engraved in the minds and hearts of all Sikhs. Their ostensible purpose was to flush out Bhindranwale. The use of massive power, resulting in the complete destruction of the Sikh seat of temporal power, the Akal Takht, and the loss of 5,000 civilian lives—for an entirely unconvincing purpose, simply to apprehend a "handful of men"—stunned Sikhs the world over; that it was done to improve the Congress Party's election prospects and enable Indira Gandhi to claim she had saved the nation from Sikh "secessionists" was no less astounding.

. . .

The consummation of the course of vitriol and violence was still to come. On the morning of 31 October 1984, less than five months after the assault on the Golden Temple complex, Indira Gandhi died at the hands of two Sikh bodyguards in her security detail. Before the day of her assassination ended, innocent Sikh men, women and children in Delhi, Kanpur, Bokaro and many other cities in northern India had already lost their lives. Encouraged by central government ministers and members of parliament, with mobs assembled by them, and with the connivance of the capital's police, a four-day orgy of reprisal killing and plunder in the national capital was underway. Eyewitness reports identified Congressmen and police personnel directing and often leading the killers in different areas of Delhi in which, by government's own admission, 2,733* persons were killed or burnt alive in those four days. The Sikhs dispute this official figure—which includes neither the "missing" nor unreported deaths nor bodies found in trains pulling into Delhi, nor those murdered and thrown out of moving trains.

The depravity of those days is starkly evident from case histories.

Hazara Singh and his three sons, Kulwant Singh, Jagtar Singh and Harmit Singh, with their families, lived in a two-storied house in Hari Nagar Ashram, New Delhi. They had built a business as electrical contractors and worked for clients like the Oberoi Hotel, Hyatt Regency and the Delhi Development Authority. On the morning of 1 November 1984, they found their house surrounded by a mob. Their new Ambassador car was set alight and the front part of the house looted. The family, caught unawares and unarmed, remained trapped in the rear room from 10 a.m. till 10 p.m., hoping against hope for police help. The police did finally come, and this is how the subsequent plaint in the high court civil suit filed for damages described their visit. (The defendants have denied the allegations and the case has not yet come to trial.)

LATER, DEFENDANTS NO. 11 TO 13 [THE STATION HOUSE OFFICER AND SUB-INSPECTOR AND ASSISTANT SUB-INSPECTOR

* The Citizens' Justice Committee places this figure at 3,870.

OF POLICE . . .], ALONG WITH A POSSE OF ARMED POLICEMEN,
CAME TO THE SPOT IN A POLICE VEHICLE. THEY WERE IN UNI-
FORM. AFTER GETTING DOWN FROM THEIR OFFICIAL VEHICLE,
THEY FIRST TALKED TO DEFENDANTS NO. 1 TO 10 AND SOME
OTHERS IN A FRIENDLY MANNER . . . THEN SHOOK HANDS IN A
MOST FRIENDLY WAY. MOST OF THE DEFENDANTS . . . [THEN]
JOINTLY RAISED THE SLOGAN "*KHOON KA BADLA KHOON*"
[MEANING "BLOOD FOR BLOOD"] . . .

At around 10 p.m., the defendants Nos. 1–10 mentioned in the
plaint poured kerosene oil through ventilators in the rear of the house
and set it alight. The first to come out was Hazara Singh, who with

. . . FOLDED HANDS [ASKED THE CROWD] TO SPARE THE LIVES
OF HIS HELPLESS FAMILY AS THEY WERE ABSOLUTELY INNO-
CENT. THEREUPON SOMEONE FROM AMONGST THE DEFEN-
DANTS . . . [MOST OF THEM WERE ARMED WITH DAGGERS,
SWORDS AND IRON RODS] SEVERED BOTH THE FOLDED HANDS
OF HAZARA SINGH WHICH DROPPED DOWN. THE SAID DEFEN-
DANTS ALONG WITH THE ASSOCIATES THEN ATTACKED HIM
WITH IRON RODS.

Hazara Singh's three sons were also set upon. The plaint reads on:

AFTER MAKING A HEAP OF THE HALF-DEAD ADULT MALE MEM-
BERS [OF THE FAMILY], ALL OF THEM WERE DOUSED IN
KEROSENE OIL AND SET ON FIRE. DEFENDANTS NO. 1 AND 10
DANCED AROUND AND CELEBRATED THE BONFIRE IN A VERY
GAY MOOD.

Left bereft and bewildered, the plaintiffs who are the survivors of
this massacre include widows of two of the sons with four young children in all and Hazara Singh's nineteen-year-old unmarried daughter.
Not one of the accused named in the plaint has been criminally prose-
cuted for the murder of Hazara Singh and his sons aged 27, 23 and 20,
indicative of the extent of the Indian judicial system's neglect in deliv-
ering justice in these crimes.

Mrs. Doban Kaur, of Sultanpuri, New Delhi was watching television with her family on the afternoon of 1 November 1984 when a mob of about 2,000 surrounded their house. In her affidavit before the government-appointed, one-man Misra Commission she narrates what happened:

> THEY BROKE DOWN THE DOOR AND ENTERED THE HOUSE. SOME PEOPLE HAD STICKS AND RODS AND SOME HAD PISTOLS. SOME PEOPLE PRESSED A PISTOL AGAINST MY CHEST AND THREATENED TO SHOOT ME IF I DID NOT GO OUT. I WENT AND STOOD OUTSIDE. SOMEONE WAS HOLDING ME. MY SON WAS ATTACKED WITH A STICK AND THEN HE WAS BURNT ALIVE. MY BROTHER-IN-LAW WAS ALSO KILLED AND TAKEN OUT OF THE HOUSE AND BURNT. MY FATHER AND [FOUR] BROTHERS [AGED BETWEEN 7 AND 30] WERE ALSO BADLY BEATEN AND THEN BURNT ALIVE . . . THE HALF BURNT BODIES WERE PUT INTO GUNNY SACKS . . . AND TAKEN AWAY . . .

The experience of Gurbachan Singh and his friends, residents of a housing estate at Kalyanpuri in Delhi, is a bizarre tale of a police force disarming Sikhs and facilitating their killing. But since—unlike most—they were aware of an impending attack, they fought back when a crowd of around 5,000 persons arrived on the morning of 1 November 1984. According to Gurbachan Singh's deposition before the Misra Commission:

> WE DIVIDED OURSELVES IN TWO GROUPS AND TRIED TO CONTAIN THE MOB ON BOTH ENDS OF THE STREET. THE MOB CAME A SECOND TIME AGAIN. THE POLICE, VERY MUCH A PART OF THE MOB, TOOK AWAY OUR GUNS AND LEFT. THEN THE MOB ATTACKED US . . . THE DEFENSE CONTINUED UP TO 6 OR 7 P.M. THE MOB AGAIN ATTACKED AT ABOUT 11 P.M. BUT COULD NOT REACH OUR COLONY.

The same story was repeated on 2 November when at about 6 a.m. an equally large crowd again attacked the colony and was resisted by around 40 Sikhs.

THEY CONTINUED TO ATTACK US TILL 11 A.M. BUT THEY
COULD NOT INFLICT SERIOUS DAMAGE ON US. BUT AT ABOUT
11:30 A.M. THE POLICE ARRESTED SOME OF OUR MEN . . . THE
MOB AGAIN CAME AT ABOUT 3 OR 4 P.M. OUR MEN TRIED TO
DEFEND THEMSELVES AND DID NOT ALLOW THE MOB TO ENTER
THE COLONY. AT ABOUT 5 P.M. POLICE CAME AGAIN AND
SNATCHED [THE] LICENSED GUNS OF OUR MEN AND THERE-
AFTER THE MOB ARRIVED IMMEDIATELY AGAIN. PEOPLE OF THE
COLONY DEFENDED THEMSELVES WITH STONES AND IT CON-
TINUED LIKE THIS TILL ABOUT 11 P.M. MOB ATTACKED, WE
DEFENDED WITH STONES, MOB RETREATED, CAME BACK AGAIN.
ON 3.11.1984 AT ABOUT 8 A.M. MOB CAME AGAIN, BY THIS
TIME SOME OF OUR MEN WERE INJURED AND OTHERS WERE
TIRED, STILL WE DEFENDED OURSELVES TILL 12 P.M. AT ABOUT
2 P.M. POLICE CAME AGAIN AND THEY THREATENED US AND
ASKED US TO PROCEED TO OUR RESPECTIVE HOUSES. WE WENT
TOWARDS THE GURDWARA TO SAVE OUR LIVES AND IMMEDI-
ATELY THEREAFTER THE MOB STARTED LOOTING OUR HOUSES.

Hundreds of other such sworn depositions indict ministers, members of parliament, police officials, public figures and businessmen.
Each tells a sordid story of how crowds of several thousands, abetted
and encouraged by the administration, fell upon a few men, women
and children and killed them in full view of the government of India.
Could the violence have been prevented? Easily.

Soon after Mrs. Gandhi was shot on 31 October, the General Officer Commanding, Meerut, was asked by the Defence Ministry to dispatch an army unit to Delhi immediately, to deal with any contingency
following the prime minister's death. Realizing the seriousness of the
situation, the GOC ordered a unit which had just returned from field
exercises to move to Delhi even before it could unpack. The unit—the
15th Sikh Light Infantry (LI)—consisted of 1,600 soldiers and officers.
Arriving at the capital's border on the evening of 31 October it was
stopped there for several hours—for reasons unknown—before finally
reaching its barracks in the cantonment at 11 p.m. It took up its duties
on the morning of 1 November under the command of Major J.S.
Sandhu, a Sikh officer.

Through intensive patrolling in the section of Delhi allotted to it, the 15th Sikh LI saved many lives, prevented looting and stopped the torching of businesses and houses. In the afternoon, while crossing the Safdarjung Development Area, Major Sandhu decided to investigate what from a distance looked like a house on fire. Before he and his men could enter the residential complex a man who identified himself as a senior intelligence officer tried to stop them. He said that the army had "no orders to intervene" and questioned the army's presence there. Major Sandhu brushed aside his objections and when he persisted and blocked the road with his car, the major warned him that he would order his men to open fire if he didn't remove himself at once. The man did. On seeing the military, the mob surrounding the burning house ran away, but a policeman on duty gave the information that the house was empty. Cries for help from within, however, told a different story. Fortunately, the army was able to rescue and remove the inmates to a safe place.

Within an hour or so of this, Major Sandhu was ordered to report back to Delhi Cantonment where he and his unit were confined to barracks. They stayed there throughout the duration of the killings in Delhi. Who withdrew the army on 1 November, just as violence was starting to escalate? Clearly the general commanding the Delhi Area gave the orders. But who instructed him to do so? Who was the intelligence officer whose report to the government led to the army's withdrawal? No enquiry has revealed the answers. This point was driven home by a Delhi lawyer, Harvinder Singh Phoolka—who has persevered for years in his efforts to bring the guilty to book—in a recent letter to the Chief Minister of Delhi: "The people who are responsible for withdrawing the army which was patrolling the roads of Delhi on the morning of 1 November 1984—and effectively controlling the violence—and ordering this army unit consisting of 1600 soldiers and officers to remain confined to barracks, were to a large extent responsible for the flare-up of violence which assumed such great magnitude. These persons are liable to be brought to book and punished for their misdeeds."

Had the army been kept in place, casualties would have been minimal. Was this Sikh LI unit withdrawn to facilitate the killings? And why wasn't Major Sandhu's unit replaced, a lapse which gave the mobs enough time to do their work with the tacit—and often active—support of the Delhi police? Phoolka insists that the category of people who paralysed the law and order machinery but "remained behind the scenes while taking such important decisions" must be treated as co-conspirators, "and tried for murder along with other accused."

The government of New Delhi neither stopped the killings nor brought the killers to trial. Instead, it not only confined the Sikh LI to barracks but subsequently gave a false declaration both before parliament and the Misra Commission to the effect that no army units were available to it on 1 November. Even the report of the Misra Commission (of which more later) corrects this falsehood by recording the fact that the force was available to the government from early morning of 1 November.

Even as the world's media, assembled in the capital in the aftermath of Mrs. Gandhi's assassination, watched the horror unfold, the government allowed the blood-letting to continue. John Fraser in Canada's *Globe and Mail* described how "for three horrific nights and four days, the violence was allowed to proceed . . . by which time the worst atrocities had been committed." As for setting the wrong right, Fraser wrote that "hardly had the country recovered from Mrs. Gandhi's death and the ensuing bloodshed when the Bhopal chemical disaster struck . . . While Mr. Gandhi [who succeeded his mother] is prepared for the most exhaustive inquiry possible to examine the Bhopal disaster, because the primary focus of culpability is on a US company, the Delhi atrocities . . . would inevitably point a devastating finger at his own party and at the dark side of Indian society."

Which brings us to yet another aspect of these events. Heedless of the excesses, the battering India's image was receiving abroad, and the brutality of the capital's police force, the government ordered no commission of inquiry to investigate the events. Seeing its inaction, a group of individuals got together with the intention of making up for government's indifference. This is how they explained their concern: "The mosaic of India's varied people and cultures is the very foundation of its strength, but if the bond of mutual tolerance and respect is fractured by an orgy of violence against any community, the unity and integrity of the entire structure is gravely imperiled. Such is the situation which faces our country today."

India's former foreign secretary, Rajeshwar Dayal, was the driving force behind the setting up of the five-member "Citizen's Commission" which was headed by the retired chief justice of India with the former foreign, commonwealth, home and defence secretaries of the government of India as its members. All of them non-Sikhs, their solidarity reaffirmed India's founding principle of secularism which the Congress government had treated with contempt. The concern of right-minded Hindus and Muslims, and their efforts to uncover the truth, proved that the ruling party's indecencies had not affected the country as a whole.

The government's hostility towards the Commission was expressed in various ways. It refused to allow it access to official documents, and the prime minister and home minister declined to meet it. A note to "suggest preventive corrective and retributive action; and propose ameliorative measures to restore public confidence" sent to home minister P.V. Narasimha Rao was not even acknowledged by him. The same politician, who as home minister had not stopped the carnage, would in a few years become India's prime minister.

In the preamble to its report published on 18 January 1985, the Commission noted: "The incredible and abysmal failure of the administration and the police; the instigation by dubious political elements; the equivocal role of the information media; and the inertia, apathy and indifference of the official machinery; all lead to the inferences that follow." The report's inferences and recommendations were buried by the government. As were other excellent reports like *Who Are the Guilty?* by the Peoples' Union for Civil Liberties (PUCL) and the Peoples' Union for Democratic Rights (PUDR), *Truth about Delhi Violence* by Citizens for Democracy, and *1984 Carnage in Delhi* by the PUDR. When the latter filed a writ petition in Delhi High Court seeking the Court's directions for the setting up of a judicial commission of enquiry into the events, government opposed the petition, which was eventually dismissed by a division bench of the Court on the ground that it was for the executive to take a decision in the matter.

The one-man Commission that was finally appointed—following a statesmanlike Punjab Accord (formally called the Memorandum of

Settlement) reached between Prime Minister Rajiv Gandhi and Sant Harchand Singh Longowal on 24 July 1985—fell just short of farce. To begin with the appointee, Justice Ranganath Misra, a judge of India's Supreme Court, seemed conscious of the Congress government's sensitivities. He was later appointed India's next chief justice. His moves looked carefully considered. His attitude towards human rights groups who were representing the victims was not helpful. The Citizens' Justice Committee (CJC) and the voluntary group Nagrik Ekta Manch who were allowed to participate, withdrew, complaining about the apparent arbitrariness of his procedures. The CJC, incidentally, was headed by a former chief justice of India with several retired judges, eminent lawyers and outstanding public figures on it.

Not only did the Delhi administration defend the accused before the Commission, but Congressmen—in and out of power—have even been accused of trying to obstruct justice. A Report of the Advisory Committee to the Chief Minister of Delhi has this to say of the affidavits for the accused: "Most of the affidavits in favour of the accused were cyclostyled in identical proformas on which only the particulars of the deponent were filled in by hand. Most of the deponents of these affidavits who were summoned by the Commission did not appear to support their affidavits. Some others who appeared disowned their purported affidavits."

When the CJC wanted to cross-examine the persons who had filed these affidavits, Misra turned down its request, denying it also the right to take copies of such affidavits, to examine statements of witnesses summoned at the CJC's request but examined in its absence, and to inspect records produced at the behest of the CJC. Protesting against the denial of these rights which it maintained was in contravention of some of the basic principles of law, the CJC withdrew from the proceedings.

The Government received the Misra Commission's report in August 1986, and took six months to place it before parliament in February 1987, a full 27 months after the killings. A weak and vapid report, it let key Congress figures off the hook and characteristically recommended the setting up of three more committees: the first to ascertain the death toll in the riots, the second to enquire into the conduct of the police, the third to recommend the registration of cases and monitor investigations. The third committee spawned two more committees plus an enquiry by the Central Bureau of Investigation (CBI). When one of these two, the Poti-Rosha Committee, recommended 30 cases for prosecution including one against Sajjan Kumar, Congress MP, and the CBI sent a team to arrest him on 11 September 1990, a mob held the team captive for more than four hours! According to the CBI's subsequent affidavit filed in court, "the Delhi Police far from trying to disperse the mob sought an assurance from the CBI that he [Sajjan Kumar] would not be arrested." The CBI also "disclosed that [another committee's] file relating to the case [against him] . . . was found in Sajjan Kumar's house." The MP was given "anticipatory bail while the CBI team was being held captive" by his henchmen.

Justice Misra became the Chief Justice of the Supreme Court and after retirement chairman of the National Human Rights Commission; the accused MPs, except one, were again given Congress tickets to stand for parliament; one of them, H.K.L. Bhagat, became a cabinet minister; three accused police officers were promoted and placed in high positions. As for punishment of the guilty, only five persons were given the death sentence—still to be carried out—for the murder of 2,733 persons, around 150 persons were jailed, and none of the accused MPs and prominent Congressmen has been punished. The government has not conducted any investigation into the withdrawal of the Sikh Light Infantry on 1 November 1984.

The Sikhs, determined to see those they believe to be guilty punished, continue to press for justice although fully aware of the fact that in India too, as Solzhenitsyn wrote about his country, "the lie has become not just a moral category, but a pillar of the state."

Troubled already by earlier discontents, to which was added the recent savaging of the Golden Temple complex, Punjab's Sikhs heard with disbelief and rage the horror endured by their fellow-Sikhs in Delhi. It was tyranny such as they had always encountered and resisted. Out of a steadily increasing sense of outrage, militancy against a state unwilling to see Sikhs exist as Sikhs and the desire for a Sikh homeland (Khalistan) grew in Punjab. But the portents were ignored by Delhi's politicians, by men lacking the vision and wisdom to foresee the damage this would do to the national fabric. Countless tragedies could have been avoided had wiser counsels prevailed. Though Sikh alienation started with the Arya Samajists' war of words against them in the late nineteenth and early twentieth centuries, the real aggravations took place after Independence, during the heyday of the Congress Party.

More aggravations were to follow. After the formation of Punjab State in 1966, it has been asked to share its capital Chandigarh—built to compensate Punjab for the loss of Lahore—with Haryana, though every other state has its own capital. Even Chandigarh was made a Union Territory directly administered by Delhi. The sharing of river waters also became a bone of contention, despite the fact that Punjab literally means the "land of five rivers"; and as India's granary it could ill afford the diversion of its waters elsewhere. The Sikhs perceived every act of denial as an affront to the concept of federalism, fair play and mutual trust, which drove them to seek alternatives.

For a while, following the bold initiative by Rajiv Gandhi and Harchand Singh Longowal, there was hope that violent alternatives would be avoided. The Punjab Accord provided the possibility of an end to the confrontation between the Central Government and the Akali Dal. However, in less than a month of the signing of the agreement, Longowal was assassinated and most of its provisions were sabotaged by Rajiv Gandhi's advisors who were more interested in undoing the Accord than seeing it succeed. Unable either to see through their game or to ensure implementation of the agreements reached, the prime minister allowed his initiative to be derailed, and the momentum towards reconciliation which the Accord and the Punjab elections following it had generated was lost.

This failure fed Punjab's burgeoning militancy, to which the government's response was brutal policing. Instead of serious attempts to resolve genuine grievances, official communiqués announced the numbers killed daily, mostly through faked "encounters," by trigger-happy policemen who hunted down innocent and guilty alike. Few were brought to trial and in the case of those who were, courts were seldom provided with convincing proof of their guilt. Police "interrogations" inflicted extreme forms of physical and psychic trauma on victims. Security agencies armed with extraordinary powers took away not only people's rights and freedoms—in the name of fighting militancy—but also their right to life. The democratic system of accountability was subverted by allowing security forces to exercise powers which legally they were not supposed to possess, such as torture, blinding, branding, rape and murder. While democratic systems prohibit the executive from transforming its whims into the rule of law, Indian democracy frequently encourages it, even though Article 21 of the Constitution clearly states: "No person shall be deprived of his life or personal liberty except according to procedure established by law." In Punjab, the procedures stipulated by the statute book were treated with disdain.

Inderjit Singh Jaijee, co-founder and convener of Punjab's Movement Against State Repression (MASR), in his *Politics of Genocide, Punjab 1984–1994*, has chronicled the state's contempt for human rights in a series of case histories. The text of his compilation was given to Jose Ayala Lasso, Commissioner for the United Nations Commission on Human Rights, in November 1995 at Lasso's request. Here are just three of the Punjab police's many excesses listed by him:

GURDEV SINGH KAUNKE WAS A HARD-LINER AMONG SIKH POLITICIANS AND ENJOYED A REPUTATION FOR INTEGRITY AND HONESTY AMONG THE SIKHS. FOLLOWING THE RESIGNATION OF DARSHAN SINGH AS *JATHEDAR* [HEAD] OF THE AKAL TAKHT [THE HIGHEST TEMPORAL SEAT OF SIKH AUTHORITY] IT WAS WIDELY BELIEVED THAT HE WOULD BECOME THE LATTER'S SUCCESSOR. SEEING THE DEMAND FOR HIS APPOINTMENT AMONG THE COMMUNITY WAS GAINING GROUND, THE GOVERNMENT WAS FILLED WITH APPREHENSION AS A STRONG *JATHEDAR* HOLDING HARD-LINE VIEWS WOULD STRENGTHEN THE MILITANTS' CLAIM TO LEGITIMACY AMONG THE SIKHS. HE WAS REPEATEDLY ARRESTED.

THE INTERNATIONAL HUMAN RIGHTS ORGANIZATION WAS ABLE TO PIECE TOGETHER WHAT HAPPENED TO HIM [LATER] ON THE BASIS OF EYEWITNESS ACCOUNTS (PUBLISHED IN THE *INDIAN EXPRESS* ON 17 JANUARY 1993). ON THE MORNING OF 25 DECEMBER 1992, A POLICE PARTY . . . PICKED UP THE *JATHEDAR* FROM KAONKE VILLAGE IN THE PRESENCE OF ABOUT 200 PERSONS. HE WAS THEN BRUTALLY TORTURED BY THE JAGRAON POLICE . . . AND KILLED ON THE NIGHT OF 1 JANUARY 1993. HIS BODY WAS THROWN INTO THE

SUTLEJ NEAR KANIAN VILLAGE UNDER SIDHWAN BET POLICE STA-
TION. IT WAS NEVER FOUND.

ON 29 AUGUST 1991, S.S.P. SUMEDH SINGH SAINI OF THE CHANDI-
GARH UNION TERRITORY POLICE NARROWLY ESCAPED DEATH IN A
BOMB ATTACK WITHIN JUST A FEW FURLONGS OF HIS OFFICE IN THE
CENTRE OF THE CITY. AT FIRST SUSPICION FELL WRONGLY ON A
BABBAR KHALSA MILITANT, BALWINDER SINGH, WHO BELONGED TO
JATANA VILLAGE IN ROPAR DISTRICT. (LATER IT WAS DISCOVERED
THAT THE KHALISTAN LIBERATION FORCE [ANOTHER MILITANT
ORGANIZATION] WAS RESPONSIBLE FOR THE BLAST.)

THE VERY NEXT NIGHT (30 AUGUST), THREE UNNUMBERED
JEEPS CARRYING EIGHT OR NINE MEN EACH WENT TO JATANA VIL-
LAGE AND KILLED BALWINDER'S 95-YEAR-OLD GRANDMOTHER, HIS
MATERNAL AUNT, HER TEENAGED DAUGHTER AND HIS POLIO-
AFFECTED INFANT COUSIN. THEY SET THE BODIES ON FIRE AND
DEPARTED. THE ROPAR POLICE INITIALLY ATTRIBUTED THE MUR-
DERS TO "SOME UNIDENTIFIED MILITANTS."

ON THE AFTERNOON OF 21 AUGUST 1989, A PARTY OF BATALA
POLICE (ONE WAS IN UNIFORM, FIVE OTHERS WERE IN PLAIN
CLOTHES) PICKED UP GURDEV KAUR AND GURMEET KAUR, BOTH
EMPLOYEES OF THE PRABHAT FINANCIAL CORPORATION, FROM
THEIR OFFICE OPPOSITE KHALSA COLLEGE, AMRITSAR. MANY
BYSTANDERS WITNESSED THE ARREST. THE WOMEN WERE PUSHED
INTO THE VEHICLE AND WHISKED AWAY TO BATALA, ANOTHER DIS-
TRICT ALTOGETHER. THERE THEY WERE TAKEN TO A MAKESHIFT
INTERROGATION CENTRE WHICH HAD BEEN SET UP IN THE ABAN-
DONED FACTORY PREMISES OF BEIKO INDUSTRIES. IT WAS 6 P.M.

GURDEV KAUR WATCHED S.S.P. GOBIND RAM BEAT A SIKH YOUTH
WITH AN IRON ROD THEN HE SUDDENLY TURNED AND STRUCK HER
WITH THE ROD ACROSS THE STOMACH. HE RAINED BLOWS ON HER
STOMACH UNTIL SHE BEGAN TO BLEED THROUGH THE VAGINA.
THEN GURMEET KAUR WAS BEATEN IN THE SAME WAY. GURDEV
FAINTED BUT WAS REVIVED AND BEATEN AGAIN. THE TWO WOMEN
WERE TAKEN TO THE BATALA SADAR POLICE STATION AT ABOUT
11:30 P.M. NEXT MORNING SHE [GURDEV] WAS TAKEN TO THE
BEIKO FACTORY AGAIN. HER LIMBS WERE MASSAGED BUT THEN THE
BEATINGS AND INTERROGATION WAS [SIC] RESUMED. GURDEV WAS

THE SIKHS

RELEASED AT 4 P.M. ON 22 AUGUST ON THE INTERVENTION OF HER
RELATIVE. AFTER SHE WAS RELEASED SHE EXPRESSED FEARS THAT
GURMEET HAD BEEN KILLED.

GURMEET KAUR WAS ALIVE—BARELY. SHE WAS SHIFTED FROM
BATALA TO GURDASPUR JAIL AND RELEASED. SHE WAS UNABLE TO
STAND UP AND TOLD THE PRESS THAT SHE HAD BEEN FLOGGED AND
BEATEN, HER LEGS WERE CRIPPLED BY ROLLERS, SHE HAD BEEN
MOLESTED AND THREATENED WITH DEATH.

THE TORTURE OF THESE TWO WOMEN LED TO THE TRANSFER OF
S.S.P. GOBIND RAM. (REPORTED IN *THE TIMES OF INDIA*, 27 AUGUST
AND 5 SEPTEMBER 1989, AND *PIONEER*, 27 AUGUST 1989.)

AFTER THIS INCIDENT EVEN THE GOVERNOR OF PUNJAB,
S.S. RAY, ADMITTED THAT SOME OF THE OFFICERS HAD BECOME
SADISTIC.

The excesses were not one-sided. Resistance movements the world over have crossed acceptable boundaries in fighting for their rights and ideals, and Sikh militancy was no exception. Limits were crossed, criminals infiltrated the movement, innocents were killed, and extortionists had their day. The brutality of train and bus bombings—carried out by government vigilantes as well, to discredit Sikh militants—was reprehensible and in no way less bestial than extreme police behaviour. But everyday crime was also attributed to the Sikhs—as if the state were free of all crime except for the criminal activities of "terrorists!"

The word "terrorist" was deliberately misused in the aftermath of 1984 to erase all distinctions between militant protest, the struggle for freedom, religious nationalism and self-determination. By ignoring militancy's motivations and projecting the entire Punjab struggle as terrorist-inspired, New Delhi found a *raison d'être* for state repression, but all this achieved was further agony for Punjab for over a decade and a half. It was a vicious circle in which the militants viewed the gun as their only option and the government saw greater firepower as the only response to it. Overlooked in the escalating violence and counter-violence was the fact that state repression reflected failure of statesmanship, the inability of political leaders to deal with dissent.

In her path-breaking book *Fighting for Faith and Nation—Dialogue with Sikh Militants*, the American anthropologist Cynthia Keppley-

Mahmood of the University of Maine tries to identify what prevents people from understanding terrorism. "Until it becomes fully normal for scholars to study violence by talking with and being with people who engage in it, the dark myth of evil and irrational terrorists will continue to overwhelm more pragmatic attempts to lucidly grapple with the problem of conflict. Hysterical calls to condemn terrorism from a distance, to find better ways of technologically defeating terrorists as we find ourselves less and less capable of politically defeating them, are of a piece with the failure of imagination ... There is a greater naïveté, and a greater danger, I suggest, in continuing to insist that physically exterminating terrorists is the way to eradicate terrorism. A lethal game of one-upmanship ensues which feeds the appetite for power on both sides and injures many innocent bystanders in the process. People build excellent careers in the counterterrorism forum, money is poured into the coffers of counterterrorism think tanks, yet more fresh new terrorists spring up every day."

This is what happened in Punjab in the period following the events of 1984. Between outbursts against terrorism, snap judgements, applause for police excesses, and the actions of ambitious police officers who built their careers—and feathered their nests—in the name of fighting terrorism, India came close to disintegration. Government made a mockery of the principles which democracies swear by: transparent governance, respect for human rights, commitment to constitutional proprieties, and accountability. If militancy's excesses lack justification—which they clearly do—the tyranny of institutions established to deliver justice lack it even more. Indian prime ministers, from Indira Gandhi to Inder Gujral, muddied the waters still further by launching a worldwide diatribe against terrorism through a series of joint communiqués with every conceivable head of state. Sikhs were made to appear as disturbers of the peace, the Indian state as the victim.

By acting like a petty dictatorship, the administration diminished the idea of a democratic India and showed itself incapable of living by civilized rules. To an extent sections of the Indian public were also culpable. Possibly because of their own insecurities and inability to understand the dangerous implications of a force operating outside the law, the middle class and mercantile community's adulatory endorsement of ruthless police methods contributed to their growth. The glorification of police officers who took the law into their own hands helped to embed the canker of resentments so deep that its destructive emanations will be felt for a long time among countless Sikhs.

A former militant described to Keppley-Mahmood how he joined the freedom movement: "My parents were very much hurt by the attack on the Golden Temple. My father commented that he had four sons and that even if one of them should get sacrificed for the nation he would be proud that his family had contributed something. He said clearly that nobody guilty of any crime should be spared. But he also felt that at no cost should any innocent be killed. I decided to become involved in the freedom movement, and my house became a place of shelter for the guerrilla fighters . . . Later, when I came to a leadership position . . . I never had anybody fight for me who was not a devout Sikh." Now resident in the United States, Charanjit Singh describes his experiences and baptism by fire in detail: the bloody shootouts with the police; arrests, rescues and escapes; the pain of seeing comrades slain; solidarity under fire and, finally, the irrelevance of life—whether one's own or the adversary's. In Keppley-Mahmood's view: "In its central philosophical conception of martyrdom, which not only gives meaning to the risking of one's own life but also to the taking of another's, militant Sikhism directly challenges rationalistic visions of violent political conflict."

It certainly does. If even the devout are driven to deeds in which human life means nothing, then it will always be difficult to find rationalistic explanations for their behaviour. In the aftermath of 1984 no attempts have been made in India to analyse the sense of injustice and outrage that underlay the Sikh militants' actions, nor the depth of their commitment to early but still live Sikh traditions. From the time Guru Arjan Dev and Guru Tegh Bahadur made the supreme sacrifice for their faith, the concept of martyrdom has been ingrained in the Sikh psyche. If these events transformed a peaceful movement into the most militant witnessed on the subcontinent, they also imbued Sikhs with a purposefulness they draw on during times of persecution or repression.

The attack on the Golden Temple complex and the massacre of Sikhs in Delhi were both viewed as religious repression, the avenging of which, far from being seen as a crime, became an article of faith for the militant Sikh; a choice of the individual, not of some distant authority.

"A Sikh later hanged for the murder of an Indian army general said that he imagined the rope around his neck as a lover's embrace. What sort of a world-view does a comment like that spring from?" A world-view is obviously of less importance to a militant in his fight for his faith—against a régime he considers tyrannical—than his own beliefs rooted in religious traditions. The Sikh faith, far from teaching mindless killings, emphasizes personal discipline, valour and nobility. But since it also demands the armed defence of Sikh beliefs, excesses are committed in the heat of battle, and boundaries of acceptable behaviour crossed. "The same 'saints' who uphold with valour and grace every ideal of the Sikh way of life look the other way when less saintly companions slaughter women and children on buses. These are the contradictions of being human . . ." Possibly for this reason many Sikhs justified the killing of Mrs. Gandhi even though it went against the concepts of valour and nobility enjoined on them by their Gurus.

It was again personal choice that made so many Sikhs join the various groups engaged in the struggle, especially after 1984: the Babbar Khalsa, Khalistan Commando Force, Panthic Committee, All-India Sikh Students Federation, Bhindranwale Tiger Force of Khalistan, Khalistan Liberation Force, Zaffarwal Panthic Committee, and others; each a voluntary grouping, inspired by individual beliefs. Criminals do infiltrate such movements, but most members of these groups appeared convinced of their cause.

New Delhi used disinformation to cloud the issues and to distract public attention from them. Propaganda imaginatively handled is an effective weapon in the hands of unprincipled leaderships, and Indian leaders showed consummate skill in handling it. A part of the disinformation strategy was to project Pakistan as the arch-villain; the abettor, instigator and even motivator of the Sikh struggle. The gullible bought this line. As if Sikhs had never suffered through centuries of wars, bloodshed and destruction in fighting the tyranny of invaders and Islamic rulers. As if Sikh memories—and of Pakistan's rulers too, for that matter—were so short that the past has receded altogether.

Problems with the Sikhs, it needs reiterating, were created by New Delhi, not Islamabad. Pakistan had nothing to do with the campaign to persuade the state's non-Sikhs to disown their own language, or the assault on the Golden Temple complex, or the 1984 massacre, or rewarding instigators of these killings with parliamentary tickets and ministerial berths, or stonewalling the attempts to punish them, or refusing to make Chandigarh Punjab's capital, or taking away Punjab's territories and river waters.

To assume that state violence has succeeded in weeding out discontent is a myopic view. As Keppley-Mahmood suggests: "It would be too easy to say that if there had been no Operation Blue Star [the Indian army's assault on the Golden Temple complex], no anti-Sikh massacres, no extrajudicial executions, no custodian rapes, there would be no Khalistan movement. The example of Quebec is right here to haunt us in that regard. But a great deal of the moral justification for insurgency, for many people both inside and outside the movement, wouldn't be there without this horrific crackdown. And it is clear that the repression of Sikhs makes every aspect of Khalistan activism more vehement and the potential for a kind of reactive fascism more dangerous. This is particularly the case when the *panth*, the *qaum*, the nation, is spread across several continents, and has access to education, communication and weapons on a global scale."

But it should also be remembered that not all Sikhs want Khalistan. The numbers of those who desire it could be surprisingly few. Almost all Sikhs agree, however, that the Indian state will have to adopt more mannerly policies in its dealings with them. They don't seek special dispensations, but reject discrimination due to their being a "religious minority." Equally unacceptable is the erosion of laws through repeated amendments of the Constitution, which are whittling away the rights of individuals. The Constitution, unbelievably, has already been amended more than 72 times.

This is how some of the Acts and Amendments have mocked individual freedoms:

The Armed Forces (Punjab and Chandigarh) Special Powers Act, 1983 gives "any commissioned officer, warrant officer, noncommissioned officer" the right in disturbed areas (which is how Punjab and Kashmir were designated by the government) to destroy shelters from where armed attacks are "likely" to be made, and to arrest without warrant a person on suspicion that he is "about" to commit an offence. A person's house, for instance, could be demolished because it is "likely" to be used for an armed attack against the state!

The Terrorist and Disruptive Activities (Prevention) Act (TADA), enacted in May 1985, was given even more odious powers in 1987. It poses a grave threat to everyone in India with its provisions for the arresting, indefinitely detaining and even killing of citizens by security forces. Section 21 of this Act puts paid to the internationally recognized concept of justice which holds a person innocent unless found guilty through fair and open trial. According to this Section: "the Designated Court shall presume, unless the contrary is proved, that the accused had committed such offence."

The 59th Constitutional Amendment operative from 30 March 1981 suspended the fundamental right to life and liberty. This provision was in effect virtually confined to Punjab. (It was, however, repealed from 6 January 1990 by the 63rd Constitutional Amendment.)

In all 30 Punjab-related Acts and Constitutional Amendments—specifically aimed at the Sikhs—were enacted between 1983 and 1989.

These elements of reactive fascism pose a far greater threat to India than many thoughtful Indians realize. If democratic legislation continues to be debased by repressive laws, enforced by a partisan police force, then fascism could come to India. Padam Rosha, former director of the National Police Academy, whose long and distinguished career in the police gives his views a special urgency, articulates his concerns in forthright terms: "The availability of the administration—including the police—to the party in power, for favouring its supporters, harassing its opponents, collecting money and crowds and doing whatever is dictated by the interests of the ruling junta, is now taken for granted. The police is more than willing to use this partnership for its own aggrandizement, enrichment and eventually as an insurance." Rosha rightly adds that "the seeds of fascism lie in projecting overly-ambitious and unscrupulous police officers as role models."

Religious divisions, caste prejudices and authoritarian trends, which are now tearing the country apart, show every sign of providing the necessary rationale for an open nexus between politicians and policemen. If religious nationalists, who came into political power in 1998, continue to govern at the Centre, the authoritarianism of the police—as witnessed in Punjab—could be extended to the rest of India, generating increasing tensions between a right-wing Centre and some of the more liberal states.

During the 1970s and 1980s the bias of a number of newspaper owners, editors and journalists also contributed to Sikh disenchantment. With attitudes in Northern and Central India hardening along communal lines because of manipulation by government, the situation was further aggravated by national newspapers whose reporting on the Sikhs made no distinction between a regional political party, a handful of militants, and the entire Sikh community. Even senior editors and columnists considered *all* Sikhs accountable for the actions of these three. As if the Sikhs were a compact, tightly-knit, homogeneous little group—like, say, the Amish of Pennsylvania—rather than 18 million individuals who do not easily accept the dictates of their own or other people. But these distinctions mattered little in the exciting sport of bringing the communal cauldron to a boil through sensational comment.

During those critical years *The Times of India* and *The Hindustan Times* did more to incite hostility between Hindus and Sikhs than perhaps any other English-language newspaper. According to the editor of *The Times of India*, for example, "a myth has been built, and it is currently sought to be reinforced [*sic*], about the heroic role of the Akalis in the independence struggle . . . the Akalis let us face it, were not an independent Sikh component of the larger freedom movement . . . they were the products of a British inspired movement amongst the Sikhs which emphasized their separateness from the Hindus. This emphasis was not accidental. It was part of the well established 'divide and rule policy.'"

The following facts should throw some light on the Sikhs' heroic role in the independence struggle. "Out of 2,175 Indian martyrs for freedom, 1,557, or 75 per cent, were Sikhs. Out of 2,646 Indians sent to the Andamans for life imprisonment 2,147, or 80 per cent, were

Sikhs. Out of 127 Indians who were hanged 92, or 80 per cent, were Sikhs. Out of 20,000 who joined the Indian National Army under Subhas Bose, 12,000, or 60 per cent, were Sikhs. And the Sikhs comprise only 2 per cent of India's total population!" As the non-Sikh Rajinder Puri, whose book *Recovery of India* contains these figures, observes: "Clearly the Sikhs, and for that matter Punjabis generally, do not require a certificate of patriotism from the rest of India."

Where heroism is concerned, it will be in place to mention that of the total number of Victoria Crosses awarded to Indians from 1914 onwards, "from which date VC's were able to be awarded to 'native Indians' . . . 40 were awarded to Indian soldiers of whom 21 were Sikhs (serving in various Regts), 12 were Gurkhas and the remaining 7 from assorted areas and faiths." Yet not a single Sikh general has been made army chief of staff in the half-century since India has been independent!

Other journalists of *The Times of India* followed in their editor's footsteps in writing about the Sikhs. Blaming the British for making the Sikhs believe "they were different" from the rest, one writer felt the matter was really quite simple: "grievances were manufactured, extreme slogans were put forward with which even moderate elements had to keep pace . . . In the last few years even the politics of murder was introduced. This grave situation called for necessary action which caused some unavoidable damage to the building [the Akal Takht]." By "manufactured grievances" he would seem to have meant the denigration of the Sikh faith by Hindu fundamentalists, the Centre's manipulative role in Punjab, the armed assault on the Golden Temple complex and the subsequent massacre. His brushing aside of the Akal Takht's destruction, the supreme symbol of Sikh honour, as "unavoidable damage to the building," illustrates the improprieties of commentators in those days.

Another columnist provided total justification for the armour and rockets used against a handful of militants in the shrine. "Liberals who opposed military action [against the Golden Temple complex] are in the category of Chamberlain who adopted a policy of appeasement of Hitler." A more clear-eyed commentator looked to the left of the political spectrum, pointing out that even the "leftists, particularly in the Communist Party of India, found words of praise for Operation Blue

Star which killed hundreds of innocent pilgrims in order to claim the lives of approximately fifty militants led by Bhindranwale."

The nostalgia for those heady days of police raj in Punjab has in no way lessened. As recently as January 1998, an English-language daily published in the capital editorially lamented the fact that a former chief of Punjab police, under whose tenure the force's brutal methods received the Supreme Court's strictures, had been held guilty of misdemeanour. "The latest judgement by the Punjab and Haryana High Court on the soap opera surrounding the alleged outrage of a woman officer's modesty by an outstanding nationalist and a retired police officer provides a perfect instance of the masochistic streak that pervades the Indian psyche . . . Shouldn't a grateful nation honour those who restored sanity to Punjab rather than hound them?"

In the words of the former policeman Padam Rosha, "a culture is being built up which denigrates the 'due process' of law as piddling constraints and glorifies officers who use force to teach lessons." He insists that "the use of force by the State, which is not sanctioned by law, can never carry the aura of justice," and that "this loss of legal and moral underpinning will further alienate people as the police depend on higher levels of force in dealing with them." The same policemen who are the darlings of journalists today could turn against their idolaters tomorrow once all statutory constraints placed on them are removed. Abusing the privilege of their positions by providing "moral underpinning" to brutal police methods, many editorial writers gravely weaken the rule of law and the secular character of the state through irresponsible writings.

Sikhs too are gradually weakening themselves by creating social distinctions within Sikhism which were unacceptable to Nanak and which were the very thing that set him on his own spiritual search for that essential ingredient of humanity which he intuitively felt must form the basis of a religion's appeal. Rejecting the idea of a divine being who looked at different people differently, he made this the starting point of his opposition to caste and all such divisive distinctions. What drew people to the Sikh faith was the idea of equality; of respect for people's worth and not their birth; of human beings as God's creations, not as a species to be manipulated and graded by self-appointed arbiters of the upper castes.

The devotion of its followers to this concept is evident in each unfolding chapter of Sikhism's history. All the more unfortunate that ersatz attitudes are now threatening to transform a casteless faith into a caste-ridden one. One disturbing manifestation of this is the distinction made between Jat and non-Jat Sikhs. Even within the Jat fraternity, serious distinctions are made on the basis of who comes from where: the Malwa, Majha or Doaba regions of Punjab. How the superiority of one such group over another is established is unclear; what is clear is that an emotional divide between Sikhs does exist. If these tendencies towards polarization remain unchecked, they could in time adversely affect the cohesiveness of Sikhism.

What distinguishes Jats from non-Jats? There is a school of thought which believes that the word Jat is derived from the Sanskrit term *jyest'ha*, meaning "that which is ancient." Ancient they are; some ethnologists think they are of Indo-Scythian origins and that they probably came to India around the beginning of the Christian era, occupying the northern reaches of the Indus Valley before spreading into Punjab where they had settled down by the beginning of the eleventh century. Another view is that they migrated into India along with the Aryans; yet another, that they came with a later wave. Most agree on the difficulty of differentiating between the Rajputs and Jats in the early centuries because of the close intermingling between the two.

It would be accurate, however, to say that Jats broadly represent those who work the land: the cultivators, farmers and peasants. The same robustness that enabled them to overcome the vagaries of nature and make their lands productive also made them fine soldiers— although non-Jats did just as well on the battlefield. If Jats have been persuaded to place a high premium on their own worth, so have non-Jats, in other vocations such as trade, commerce, banking and, more recently, professions like law, medicine, science, economics and university specialisms, so that a cutting edge has been added to the self-esteem of each group. The drift towards exclusivity and self-importance has affected even those whose intellectual vitality might have been expected to reject the inferior mindset of the jingoists.

Fortunately, Jats and non-Jats have no differences where their beliefs are concerned. Both accept the sanctity and supreme jurisdiction of the Guru Granth Sahib and invest immense pride in their faith; both draw equal sustenance from their heritage; both close ranks in times of adversity, and reject attempts at reinterpreting Sikhism's basic beliefs. Despite this, however, the polarization continues, creating potentially dangerous rifts.

It is difficult to say when this psychological Jat–non-Jat division began. It is often attributed to the divide and rule policy of the British, but this is an over-simplification. The growing rift is an outcome of the medieval mindset of sections within the Sikh community. This is odd since none of the ten Sikh Gurus was a Jat, nor was the warrior Banda Singh Bahadur. Maharaja Ranjit Singh certainly was, but the constellation of men around him included those of different descents, skills and vocations. It is possible that the Jats' rise to political power under him accounts for their urge to continue to control the levers of power in Punjab. It would be bad enough if the problem was confined to the Jat–non-Jat divide in the political sphere, but to make matters worse, non-Jats too have their own sub-sections like the Aroras, Ahluwalias, Ramgarhias, Khatris and others. An unfortunate spinoff of this is the increasing tendency to inbreed, to marry within their own, well, caste, which, as a recent editorial in *The Sikh Review* put it, is enough to "churn your stomach and bruise your conscience" because "there is no dearth of parents determined to divide Sikh society into a maze of compartments hooked to caste, subcaste, down to *gotra* [exogamous subdivision], etc. Their stubbornness goes to bizarre limits . . ." It certainly does. Ironically, prejudice and lack of principle are also evident in the discriminatory attitude of the community to Mazhabi Sikhs—the lower castes who converted to Sikhism because it appealed to them as a faith which rejected the prevailing caste system and treated all human beings as equal.

The Jats' monopoly of political power in Punjab, based on their large rural vote, is inexorably undermining the ethos of the faith. Their preponderance in the Akali governments—whenever they are in power—demonstrates the degree to which boundaries are being drawn. By giving preference to Jats the Akalis are making non-Jat Sikhs increasingly susceptible to those who skilfully exploit divisions.

Since Jats also control the Sikh Gurdwara Parbandhak Committee, which sits atop the formidable financial resources of Punjab's Sikh shrines, the sidelining of non-Jats on it will weaken the community still further, making it easier for their adversaries to engineer the political eclipse of the Sikhs. Corruption of the hallowed tradition of equality will exact a heavy toll.

Present religious divisions and caste distinctions which are tearing India apart are essentially no different from those that have riven this ancient land for millennia. If the pattern hasn't changed after more than half a century of Independence, the obvious question is: what keeps going wrong and why? The ideal of good governance eludes India because the Indian oligarchy feels threatened by a just order; because the caste-bound privileged few could lose control in it, which they feel they must retain even at the expense of a strong unified state which honours its moral and constitutional obligations. A similar moral dilemma faces the Sikhs, with of course some exceptions, the most obvious being that religious divisions do not pose much danger to them. Caste divisions do. If the struggle in the rest of India centres around the oligarchy's reluctance to give up power, the Jats are equally reluctant to share power in Punjab. The key difference is that whilst India's constitutional obligations have been repeatedly trampled upon by frequent amendments to the Constitution by unscrupulous leaderships, the Constitution of the Khalsa—whose directive principles are enshrined in the Guru Granth Sahib—is sacrosanct. None has the authority to change it. In this lies hope.

The injunction in the Sikh scriptures is unambiguous: "Let no man be proud because of his caste." Guru Gobind Singh, while reiterating the same message, "men are all one," constituted the Khalsa as a fellowship of inspired people. Not a hierarchical order with some more privileged than the rest but a casteless community knit by shared ideals and beliefs.

Integral to the principle of equality is the right to free speech—also ingrained in the spirit of the Sikh faith. Any diminution of this principle distorts the very concept of Sikhism, since all its traditional practices, like *panjpiyare*, *sarbat khalsa* and *gurmata*, are based on the republican ideal of encouraging people to invoke their right of free expression, a right Sikhs have enjoyed from the beginning, unfettered by the dictates of a self-centred few.

"It is the freedom to disagree that is freedom of speech," but recent moves to prevent Sikh scholars from presenting their point of view on matters of theological interest show a disturbing inclination to curb the right to disagree. The "prosecution of ideas" is an attempt to stifle debate and scholarly conjecture, reflecting an intolerance which is antithetical to Sikh tenets and traditions. Views which outrage, offend or are outside the realm of reason should certainly be censured. But as I.F. Stone suggests in his book *The Trial of Socrates:* "We must not be angry with honest men."

Harjot Singh Oberoi, Pashaura Singh and Pyar Singh are neither impious nor dishonest, nor given to creating controversies for effect. The studies produced by them have emerged from years of painstaking research and reflection, from their deep involvement with their faith. Since they did not approach their work with ill-intent or disrespect, a distinction should be made between those who seriously contribute to our knowledge of Sikh history and traditions and those who denigrate them. Yet all three were subjected to unseemly outbursts, which diminished the Sikh image of self-confidence and aplomb, making a strong faith appear fragile.

Even if some of their interpretations were unacceptable, was it necessary to pillory them so mercilessly? Is the confidence of Sikhs in the strength and durability of Sikhism so low that it can be swayed by a contrary opinion? After all, Sikhism has survived sustained and bloody onslaughts for centuries. Does it now need self-professed keepers of Sikh conscience to oversee its existence? Surely not. Pride in their faith, which resides in the hearts and minds of all Sikhs, is unlikely to be shaken by a book or two. If Dayanand and others of his ilk could not create a dent with their propaganda, what damage can the writings of three good Sikhs do? On the contrary, by conjuring up a threat where none exists, their hysterical critics have created a needless impression of insecurity over beliefs which have admirably stood the test of time.

It is odd for Sikhs—who handled some shoddy missionary writings about them in the past with equanimity and poise—to get so easily rattled over non-issues. Attempts to intimidate honest scholarship—a form of McCarthyism at best—will not do Sikh liberalism or self-assurance any good. This, in fact, is an opportune moment to highlight these qualities, especially after the disinformation successive Central governments spread about them during the 1970s and '80s, and because of retrogressive trends in India and elsewhere such as the ostracizing of Salman Rushdie.

Rushdie's persecution has contributed to the currency of the term "fundamentalism," and its unwarranted descriptive use to cover most Muslims: liberal, objective, scholarly or otherwise. One result of the unfortunate and long-drawn-out Rushdie controversy was the distasteful manner in which Mushirul Hasan, a fine and widely respected academic of Delhi's Jamia Millia Islamia University, was publicly abused—and physically assaulted—for what was viewed as his defence of Rushdie.

In the Hindi heartland of India, currents of intolerance and a tendency towards violence are making a mockery of mannerly politics at a time when many believed that the twentieth century was becoming more civilized in its closing years. Gyanendra Pandey, a noted Indian historian, feels that "the Right-wing movement for Hindutva [the movement of Hindu self-assertion] is marked by shades of McCarthyism, by its arrogant declaration of who are the 'natural' inhabitants of India and therefore the 'natural' wielders of power and by the startling ease with which it moves to a language of violence as the answer to all existing ills . . . once again, the answer to these problems is seen to lie in disciplining and control." Pandey believes that "the undisguised violence of these propositions has become a central feature of Hindu politics."

Attempts to censor freedom of expression within Sikhism lead in the direction in which proponents of Hindutva are taking Hindus, with their warnings "against *distorted* and *unIndian* interpretations of the past served up by *pseudo-secularist* historians and, more generally, *déraciné* Indian intellectuals trained in (or by) the West." Pandey pinpoints the real threat: "The greatest danger posed by the Right-wing movements is that they suppress all differences of opinion and the very possibility of debate in the name of *true* religion, *authentic* tradition, *real* nationalism." This danger—given the autocratic mindset of a few Sikhs—faces Sikhism too. And it is the responsibility of right-thinking people to curb their inclinations before they get out of hand. The "language of violence" against scholars and scribes cannot be on the Sikh agenda. They have a tradition of fighting tyrants, not those who spend years studying the origins of their faith for further insights. The findings of such men can be rejected by those who regard them as unacceptable, but those who reject them would do well to remember that debate, discussion and even controversy can often help clarify matters. Disagreement isn't per se subversive, especially since none will venerate their faith less because of a dissertation.

Spread as they are around the world, from the Americas to Africa, across Asia to Australia, and from Europe to the furthermost corners of the globe, Sikhs have proved their staying power wherever they have put down their roots. They have built magnificent places of worship everywhere, while continuing their commitment to social causes through an ongoing involvement with individuals and institutions alike, as in the first gurdwara erected in the United States in 1915 in Stockton, California, where "Charity was practised by the members and no man applying for shelter or food was ever turned away, regardless of who he was. The hobos passing by on the Southern Pacific tracks, just behind the Temple, would always be fed from a kitchen dining room, and a dormitory located on the ground floor would provide sleeping quarters."

Sikhs have not only prospered in business, industry and the professions; they are also beginning to participate in the political life of the countries of their adoption. They now sit in the parliaments and legislatures of many nations, and because they wear the outward symbols of their faith with pride, they stand out for their distinctive appearance, good humour, and just a touch of swagger.

It has been a long journey from the time the Sikhs took on formidable odds to the present. None of their assertiveness, energy or enterprising spirit has lessened. The achievements and adversities of their history have produced a compelling optimism which has helped them emerge stronger after each trial. This quality has served the Sikhs admirably over the centuries, as it will in the centuries to come.

Notes

PROLOGUE

3 On the physical side . . .: H.G. Rawlinson, India: *A Short Cultural History*. London, The Cresset Press, 1952 (1937), pp. 12–13.

"The coming of the Aryans was a backward step . . .": Romila Thapar, *A History of India*, VOL. 1. Baltimore, Penguin, 1966, p. 34.

4 a hierarchy of upper and lower classes: Louis Dumont, *Homo Hierarchicus*. University of Chicago Press, 1970, pp. 33–4.

"for a Shudra who makes money . . .": *The Laws of Manu*, trans. G. Buhler. Oxford University Press, 1886, ch. x, "Manu," p. 129.

A hymn in the Rig Veda, the oldest of the Vedas: A.L. Basham, *The Wonder that Was India*. London, Sidgwick & Jackson, 1954, p. 5.

5 "produced a high degree of ideological . . .": Rajni Kothari, *Politics in India*. Delhi, Orient Longman, 1995 (1971), p. 263.

"Indian society has been traditionally very rigid . . .": ibid.

"a kind of tolerance" which is "only another . . .": ibid, p. 264.

Vishnugupta Chanakya, or Kautilya, the astute Brahmin: Rawlinson, 1952, pp. 64–5.

6 To Kautilya is also attributed . . . *Artha Sastra* . . .: Romila Thapar, "The Date of Arthasastra," in *Asoka and the Decline of the Mauryas*. Oxford University Press, 1961, pp. 218–25.

The increasing inclination of Chandragupta's illustrious grandson Ashoka . . .: Thapar, 1966, p. 92.

Pushyamitra Shunga . . . persecuted Buddhists . . .: ibid., p. 93.

"Not by birth does one become an outcast . . .": Rawlinson, 1952, p. 52.

7 "According to Manu, the Brahmins . . .": Kunal Ghosh, "Buddha, Vivekananda, Ambedkar: Progression in Indian Thought." *Mainstream* (English-language monthly Journal), annual no., 1977, p. 64.

"whatever Manu says is medicine": ibid.

Brahmins, unlike other castes, did not pay taxes: K.A.N. Nizam, *Politics and Society during the Early Medieval Period* (2 vols). Delhi, People's Publishing House, vol. 1, 1974, pp. 192–5.

"the rule of all the Hindu princes . . .": Abbé J.A. Dubois, *Hindu Manners, Customs and Ceremonies*. Oxford University Press, 1959 (Paris, 1826), p. 290.

"Large sections of the Mughal, and even earlier Muslim . . .": Hermann Kulke and Dietmar Rothermund, *A History of India*. London, Croom Helm, 1986, pp. 136–7.

The Brahmin Rai Ranjan Patr Das was made governor of Gujarat . . .: Satish Chandra, *Mughal Religious Policies: The Rajputs and the Deccans*. Delhi, Vikas Publishing House, 1993, p. 77.

During Akbar's son Jahangir's rule, Keshav Dass Braj exercised great influence . . .: Discussion with Prof. Muzaffar Alam on 18 November 1996, Center for Historical Studies, Jawaharlal Nehru University.

Another Brahmin, Chander Bhan, was Mir Munshi . . .: ibid.

Raja Daya Bahadur and Raja Chuhela Ram Nagar . . .: Muzaffar Alam, *The Crisis of Empire in Mughal North India: Awadh and the Punjab, 1707–1748*. Delhi, Oxford University Press, 1986, pp. 45, 64–6.

8 Brahminical hold was consolidated still further in Mughal times . . .: Irfan Habib, *Agrarian System of Mughal India*. Bombay, Asia Publishing House, 1963, ch. 8, pp. 298–316.

Mughal rulers gave grants to temples . . .: Tarapad Mukherjee and Irfan Habib, "Akbar and the Temples of Mathura and its Environs," *Proceedings of the Forty-Eighth Session of Indian History Congress*. Delhi, 1987, pp. 234–50.

"even the famous *math* of Sringeri . . .": Hermann Kulke, *Kings and Cults: State Formation and Legitimation in India and South-East Asia*. Delhi, Manohar, 1993, pp. 49–50.

They received far more from regional Hindu kingdoms . . .: ibid, pp. 11–13.

"settlement of Brahmins and the establishment of royal temples . . .": Kulke and Rothermund, 1986, pp. 137–8.

In Eastern UP and Bihar, Mughals gave generous support to Brahmin landlords . . .: Anand A. Yang, *The Limited Raj: Agrarian Relations in Colonial India, Saran District, 1793–1920*. Delhi, Oxford University Press, 1989, p. 26.

"his great erudition": Stephen Henningham, *Great Estate and its Landlords in Colonial India: Darbhanga, 1860–1942*. Delhi, Oxford University Press, 1990, pp. 17–18.

"By relying on and supporting Mahesh Thakur . . .": ibid, p. 8.

9 "the Mughal forces in the conquest of Palamau . . .": ibid., p. 18.

"Places of pilgrimage have been destroyed . . .": S.R. Sharma, *Mughal Empire in India*. Agra, Lakshmi Narain Aggarwal, 1996 (reprint), p. 627.

"to the rights and honours due to a Kshatriya": Jadunath Sarkar, *Shivaji and His Times*. Calcutta, M.C. Sircar & Sons, 1961, pp. 202–3.

Brahmins from all over India let it be known . . .: André Wink, *Land, Sovereignty in India: Agrarian Society and Politics under the Eighteenth-century Maratha Swarajya*. Cambridge University Press, 1986, pp. 68–9.

During Shivaji's reign . . .: ibid.

10 Interestingly, it was a Brahmin named Sissa who invented the game of chess: Abbé Dubois, 1959, pp. 670–1.
"What can be more ridiculous than the castles . . .": ibid., p. 671.
Rajni Kothari is of the view . . .: Conversation with the author.

11 The erudite Brahmins were the obvious source of knowledge . . .: Bernard Cohn, "Notes on the History and the Study of Indian Society and Culture," *An Anthropologist Among Historians and Other Essays.* Delhi, Oxford University Press, 1987, pp. 136–71.
The reports of Jean-Baptiste Tavernier . . .: ibid., p. 140.
In the same period, Abraham Roger . . .: ibid., p. 141.
The Indian Public Service Commission . . .: André Beteille, "Caste and Political Group Formation in Tamilnad," in Rajni Kothari (ed.), *Caste in Indian Politics.* Delhi, Orient Longman, 1970, p. 269.
Of sixteen successful Indian candidates . . .: ibid.

12 Brahmins constituted 226 out of 349 Indian ICS officers . . .: *List of Indian Civil Servants in the Indian Office and Burma Office List, 1947.* London, Her Majesty's Stationery Office, 56th ed., 1947, pp. 119–384.
"In the senior echelons of the civil service . . .": Khushwant Singh, "Brahmin Power." *Sunday,* 20–7 December, 1990, p. 19.

13 The Purada-Vannan, a low-caste category in South India . . .: J.R. Kamble, *Rise and Awakening of the Depressed Classes in India.* Delhi, National Publishing House, 1979, pp. 57–8.
"In the elaborate hierarchy of caste ranking . . .": Robert L. Hardgrave, *The Nadars of Tamilnad: The Political Culture of a Community in Change.* Berkeley, University of California Press, 1969, p. 59.
"the real triumph of the caste system . . .": *Report of the Backward Classes Commission* (2 vols). Delhi, Government of India, vol. 1, 1984, p. 14.
"In modern India one born of Shudra parents . . .": *The Complete Works of Swami Vivekananda* (10 vols). Calcutta, Advaita Ashrama, vol. 4, 1962, p. 470.

14 "condescending benevolence of the upper castes . . .": ibid.
"Hinduism has an uncanny sense of what threatens it . . .": Nirad Chaudhuri, *Autobiography of an Unknown Indian.* Bombay, Jaico Publishing House, 1963, p. 232.
"While *varna* has all the appearance of a neat . . .": Rajni Kothari (ed.), *Caste in Indian Politics.* Delhi, Orient Longman, 1995 (1970), p. 11.
"all-India frame into which myriad *jatis* . . .": ibid.
"a way of thought that survived . . .": André Malraux, *Antimemoirs.* London, Hamish Hamilton, 1968, p. 207.

15 "André Malraux asked me a strange question . . .": ibid., p. 239.
"without any serious conflict": ibid.

I THE GURUS OF THE FAITH, 1469–1708

19 "He is a blessed one . . .": *Guru Granth Sahib,* trans. Gopal Singh. Delhi, Gurdas Kapur & Sons, 1962, p. 16.

21 "While weighing out rations one day . . .": Harbans Singh, *Guru Nanak and Origins of the Sikh Faith.* Bombay, Asia Publishing House, 1969, p. 90.

Notes

22 "the secret of religion lay in living . . .": Suhi, *Guru Granth Sahib*, p. 730.

23 "While [he was] at Hardwar, the Brahmins . . .": Max Arthur Macauliffe, *The Sikh Religion: Its Gurus, Sacred Writings and Authors* (6 vols). Oxford University Press, vol. 1, 1909, p. 52.

24 In Sayyadpur . . . "Your food reeks of blood . . .": Gopal Singh, *A History of the Sikh People*. Delhi, World Book Centre, 1979, p. 74.

28 "death was the privilege of the brave": Wadhans, *Guru Granth Sahib*, p. 579. "Religion lies not in empty words": Suhi, *Guru Granth Sahib*, p. 730.

29 "It was reserved for Nanak . . .": Joseph Davey Cunningham, *A History of the Sikhs: From the Origins of the Nation to the Battles of the Sutlej*. Delhi, S. Chand & Co., 1966 (1849), p. 34.

34 "the four castes of Kshatriyas, Brahmins . . .": Patwant Singh, *The Golden Temple*. Delhi, Time Books International, 1988, p. 37.
"A faith sustained only by doctrine . . .": Barbara W. Tuchman, *The March of Folly: From Troy to Vietnam*. New York, Alfred A. Knopf, 1984, p. 61.

37 "the glory of Islam consists . . .": Fauja Singh, "Development of Sikhism under the Gurus," in Teja Singh et al., *Sikhism: Guru Nanak Quincentenary Celebration Series*. Patiala, 1969, p. 12.
"had no sympathy for those who believed . . .": ibid., p. 12.

38 "to institute new proceedings against him . . .": Macauliffe, vol. 3, 1909, p. 90.
"So many simple-minded Hindus . . .": *Tuzuk-i-Jahangiri* (*Memoirs of Jahangir*), trans. Alexander Rogers, ed. Henry Beveridge. Delhi, Munshiram Manoharlal, 1968 (1926), p. 72.
"learning, valour and the discipline of war . . .": William Foster (ed.), *The Embassy of Sir Thomas Roe to India, 1615–1619: As Narrated in his Journal and Correspondence*. Delhi, Munshiram Manoharlal, 1990 (1926), p. 247.
"Jahangir stamped out the rising . . .": Rawlinson, 1952, p. 321.
He had two of his son's principal supporters . . .: ibid., pp. 321–2.
"I ordered them to produce him . . .": *Tuzuk-i-Jahangiri*, 1968, pp. 72–3.
"I bear all this torture to set an example . . .": Macauliffe, vol. 3, 1909, p. 94.
"the execution of the accursed *kafir* . . .": letter from Sheikh Ahmad Sirhindi, no. 193 in *Maktubat-i-Imam Rabbani* (3 vols). Lahore, Noor Company, 1964.
"The event marked the fulfilment . . .": Harbans Singh, *The Heritage of the Sikhs*. Delhi, Manohar, 1985 (1964), p. 50.

39 "Not to mourn or indulge in unmanly lamentations . . .": Macauliffe, vol. 3, 1909, p. 99.
"sit fully armed on his throne . . .": ibid.

40 "The Guru's imprisonment does not seem to have . . .": Indubhusan Banerjee, *Evolution of the Khalsa: The Foundation of the Sikh Panth* (2 vols). Calcutta, A. Mukherjee & Co., vol. 1, 1972 (1946), p. 14.
"the Guru had 800 horses in his stables . . .": Mohsin Fani, *Dabistan-i-Mazahab*. For sections relating to Sikhs see *Makhiz-i-Tawarikh Sikhan*, compiled by Ganda Singh, Amritsar, 1949, p. 277.
"Though successful in his first struggle . . .": W.L. M'Gregor, *The History of the Sikhs* (2 vols). Patiala, vol. 1, 1970 (1847), p. 59.

43 "I am not a king . . .": Macauliffe, vol. 4, 1909, p. 305.
"to fix his thoughts on God . . .": ibid., p. 308.

45 "His Majesty, eager to establish Islam . . .": Saqi Mustad Khan, *Maasir-i-Alamgir* (A History of the Emperor Aurangzeb-Alamgir, 1650–1707), trans. Jadunath Sarkar. Delhi, Munshiram Manoharlal, 1986 (1947), pp. 51–2.

"Iftikhar Khan . . . was using force to convert . . .": P.N.K. Bamzai, *A History of Kashmir: From the Earliest Times to the Present Day*. Delhi, Metropolitan Book Co., 1962, p. 554.

46 "fettered and detained . . .": Ganda Singh, "The Martyrdom of Guru Tegh Bahadur," in *The Panjab Past and Present* (pp. 103–14). Patiala, October 1988, p. 113.

"The Prophet of Mecca who founded your Religion . . .": Duncan Greenlees, *The Gospel of the Guru Granth Sahib*. Madras, Theosophical Publishing House, 1952, p. 87.

48 "he resolved upon awakening his followers . . .": Cunningham, 1969, p. 60.

49 "When Guru Gobind Singh inaugurated . . .": Edmund Candler, *The Mantle of the East*. London, William Blackwood & Sons, 1910, pp. 120–1.

"sharp-featured, tall and wiry man . . .": Gopal Singh, 1979, p. 263n.

52 "All military commanders . . .": *Akbarat-i-Darbari-Mualla*. London, Royal Asiatic Society, vol. 1: 1677–1695.

54 "barber-made civilizations": Puran Singh, *Guru Gobind Singh: Reflections and Offerings*. Chandigarh, The Guru Gobind Singh Foundation, 1966, p. 38.

"The orchard of the Sikh faith . . .": *Vars* of Bhai Gurdas, *Var 26, pauri 25*.

55 "the good and benefit of all . . .": Kapur Singh, *Parasharprasna or The Baisakhi of Guru Gobind Singh: An Exposition of Sikhism*. Jullundar (Punjab), Hind Publishers, 1959, p. 47.

"You are the sons of Nanak . . .": Harbans Singh, *Guru Gobind Singh*. Delhi, Sterling Publishers, 1979, pp. 46–7.

56 "an aristocracy dedicated and consciously trained . . .": Kapur Singh, 1959, p. 45.

"Guru Gobind Singh clearly seemed to believe . . .": ibid., p. 46.

57 "The Guru [has] established a new sect . . .": Harbans Singh, 1979, p. 58.

59 "Many Muslims, who considered Guru Gobind Singh . . .": Harpreet Brar, "Guru Gobind Singh's Relations with Aurangzeb" (pp. 17–33), *The Panjab Past and Present*. Patiala, April 1983, p. 19.

60 "Your name does not become you, Aurangzeb . . .": trans. from Persian by the author, Kapur Singh, 1959, p. 40, n.27.

"You are accustomed to conduct your statecraft . . .": ibid., p. 38.

"He alone is a cultured man . . .": ibid., p. 38.

"Do not wantonly spill the blood . . . I have no faith . . .": Ganda Singh, "Guru Gobind Singh: The Last Phase," *The Panjab Past and Present* (pp. 1–14). Patiala, April 1983, p. 2.

61 "The whole of the *Zafarnamah* . . .": Hira Lall Chopra, "Zafar nameh," *The Sikh Review*. Calcutta, February 1997, p. 25.

63 "When we arrive at Kahlur, the entire Khalsa . . .": Ganda Singh, April 1983, p. 7.

64 "Wherever there are five Sikhs . . .": Macauliffe, vol. 5, 1909, pp. 243–4.

Notes

2 RETRIBUTION AND CONSOLIDATION, 1708–1799

68 "pools of blood flowed . . .": Ganda Singh, *Life of Banda Singh Bahadur*. Patiala, Punjabi University, 1990 (1935), pp. 33–4.
"A will was created in the ordinary masses . . .": Teja Singh and Ganda Singh, *A Short History of the Sikhs*. Patiala, Punjabi University, vol. 1, 1989, p. 102.

69 "The example set by Banda Singh . . .": ibid.
"Of all instances of cruelty . . .": James Browne, "History of the Origin and Progress of the Sikhs," in Ganda Singh (ed.), *Early European Accounts of the Sikhs*. Calcutta, Indian Studies, 1962 (reprint), p. 28.

70 "not a man of the army of Islam . . .": Khafi Khan, *Muntakhab-ul-Lubab*, in H.M. Elliot and J. Dowson (eds.), *The History of India As Told By Its Own Historians*. Allahabad, Kitab Mahal, vol. 7, 1972 (reprint), p. 415.
"after the occupation of Sirhind . . .": "Akhbar-I-Darbar-I-Mualla: Mughal Court News Relating to the Punjab, AD 1707–1718," *Panjab Past and Present*. Patiala, October 1984, p. 19.
"to kill the worshippers of Nanak . . .": ibid. (10 December 1710), p. 6.

71 "despite the anti-Sikh and anti-Hindu measures . . .": ibid. (10 December 1710 and 28 April 1711), pp. 19–20.
"There was no nobleman daring enough . . .": ibid., pp. 5–6.
"a popular rising, such as that . . .": Ganda Singh, 1990, p. 104.

72 "*Degh O Tegh O Fateh* . . .": William Irvine, *The Later Mughals*. Delhi, Oriental Reprint, 1971 (1922), p. 110.
"the number of the dead and dying . . .": Khafi Khan, 1972, pp. 669–70.
Lohgarh was besieged by over 60,000 imperial troops: Ganda Singh, 1990, p. 115.

73 "It matters not where the dog has fled . . .": Irvine, 1971, pp. 116–17.
"calling upon them to join him . . .": Ganda Singh, 1990, pp. 126–7.
The Sikhs killed their commanders . . .: ibid., p. 135.

74 "to expel Banda from Sadhaura . . .": ibid., p. 153.

75 "that sect of mean and detestable Sikhs": ibid., p. 159.
Farrukh Siyar directed that every Sikh . . .: George Forster, *A Journey from Bengal to England* (2 vols). Patiala, Punjabi University, 1970 (1808), pp. 312–13.
"chopped heads of the Sikhs . . .": "Akhbar-I-Darbar-I-Mualla . . .": 1984, p. 141.
Banda stood his ground . . .: Ganda Singh, 1990, p. 165.
"the infidels fought so fiercely . . .": Khafi Khan, 1972, p. 456.

76 "the brave and daring deeds of the infernal Sikhs . . .": Ganda Singh, 1990, p. 168.
"stuffed with hay and mounted on spears . . .": Khafi Khan, 1972, p. 457.
"cortège of half-dead prisoners and bleeding heads": Ganda Singh, 1990, p. 176.
"were marched to Delhi . . .": Cunningham, 1966, p. 79.

77 "nearly two thousand heads [of executed Sikhs] . . .": Khafi Khan, 1972, p. 457.
"Every day a hundred brave men perished . . .": William Irvine, "Political History of the Sikhs," *The Asiatic Quarterly*, January–April 1894, pp. 420–31 and "Guru Gobind Singh and Bandah," *Journal of the Asiatic Society*, January–April 1894, pp. 112–43.

78 "1,000 swords, 278 shields, 173 bows . . .": Irvine, 1971, p. 315.

80 "Nadir Shah is said to have questioned . . .": W.L. M'Gregor, 1970, p. 115.

81 "With a force of 2,000 strong . . .": Harbans Singh, 1985, p. 130.
"It amounted to the establishment . . .": ibid., p. 130.
had the bellies of Sikhs ripped open . . .: *Haqiqat-i-Bina-o-uruj-Firqa-i-Sikhan* (Persian), MS, History Dept., Punjabi University, Patiala, trans. Indubhusan Banerjee. Calcutta, *Indian Historical Quarterly*, vol. xviii, 1942, p. 13.

82 imprisoning, starving and torturing even Sikh women and children to death: Bhagat Singh, *A History of the Sikh Misals.* Patiala, Punjabi University, 1993, p. 36.

87 "exceedingly well cultivated, populous and rich": Col. A.L.H. Polier, "An Account of the Sikhs" in Ganda Singh (ed.), 1962, p. 62.
"large revenues of the extensive and fertile territories . . .": Forster, 1970, p. 336.
"state of high cultivation": Ganda Singh (ed.), 1962, p. 17.
"in no country, perhaps . . .": John Malcolm, *Sketch of the Sikhs: Their Origin, Customs and Manners.* Chandigarh, Vinay Publications, 1981 (reprint), pp. 100–1.
Sardar Milkha Singh (Thepuria) expanded . . .: Ganesh Das, *Char Bagh-i-Punjab*, ed. and trans. J.S. Grewal and I. Banga, *Early Nineteenth Century Punjab.* Amritsar, Guru Nanak Dev University, 1975, p. 42.
"Gujranwala under Charat Singh Sukerchakia . . .": ibid., p. 105.

90 "In all contemporary records, mostly in Persian . . .": Hari Ram Gupta, *History of the Sikhs* (6 vols). Delhi, Munshiram Manoharlal, vol. 2, 1978, pp. 255–6.
"the Sikhs had now established their rule . . .": quoted in Harbans Singh, 1985, p. 143.
"the stream of immigration of needy adventurers . . .": Hari Ram Gupta, vol. 4, 1982, p. 512.

91 "that a strong army of 60,000 Sikhs . . .": ibid., p. 433.
the Sikhs, numbering about 20,000 horsemen . . .: ibid., p. 439.
"impossible . . . as the Shah was not prepared . . .": ibid., p. 440.
"defeat the Marathas": ibid., p. 442.
"if the Sikhs would not allow him . . .": ibid., p. 442.
When after his fifth invasion Timur Shah wished to place his son . . .: ibid., p. 447.
"The Sikhs, whom he had known from his childhood . . .": ibid., p. 455.

92 "presents of precious commodities . . .": ibid., p. 487.

93 "Sahib Singh, the Patiala Sardar . . .": ibid., p. 468.
"I am a Zamindar": ibid., p. 476.
"Sahib Singh received these letters . . .": ibid., p. 492.
"Guru Gobind Singh, in several battles . . .": Bhagat Singh, 1994, p. 55.

94 "In the year 1707 when Aurung-Zebe died . . .": George Forster, "Observations on the Sikhs," in Ganda Singh (ed.), 1962, p. 86.

3 EMPIRE OF THE SIKHS, 1801–1839

95 "Napoleonic in the suddenness of its rise . . .": Lepel Griffin, *Ranjit Singh.* Delhi, S. Chand & Co., 1967 (1911), p. 1.

96 "so great a reputation . . .": Syad Muhammad Latif, *History of the Punjab*. New Delhi, Eurasia Publishing House, 1964 (1889), p. 345.
"The moment he sat on horseback . . .": K.S. Duggal, *Ranjit Singh: A Secular Sikh Sovereign*. Delhi, Abhinav Publications, 1989, p. 47.

97 "Behold, grandson of Ahmed Shah . . .": Harbans Singh, 1985, p. 145.
"presents would be delivered . . .": H.R. Gupta, 1982, p. 464.
"The wisdom and energy of this extraordinary woman . . .": Latif, 1964, p. 346.

99 "My largesse, my victories . . .": K.S. Duggal, 1989, p. 62.
"God intended that I look upon all religions . . .": ibid., p. 128.

100 "based on kinship and political friendship . . .": Narendre K. Sinha, *Ranjit Singh*. Calcutta, A. Mukherjee & Co., 1960 (1933), p. 15.
"the high-spirited Sada Kaur . . .": Latif, 1964, p. 424.
"While those of the royal blood . . .": H.M.L. Lawrence, *Adventures of an Officer in the Punjab* (2 vols). Patiala, Languages Department, vol. 1, 1970 (1883), pp. 30–1.

101 "embraced Ala Singh [of Patiala] and bestowed . . .": Griffin, 1967, p. 75.
"ultimately shaped British policy towards the *cis*-Sutlej region": Bikrama Jit Hasrat, *Anglo-Sikh Relations, 1799–1849*. Hoshiarpur (Punjab), V.V. Research Institute, 1968, p. 59.
"that if protection were granted . . .": ibid., p. 61.

102 "When the British became masters of Delhi . . .": ibid., p. 60.
"Puttealeh, Jeend, Kheytul . . .:" ibid., p. 61.
"cold and servile formalists": J.W. Kaye, *Life and Correspondence of Major General Sir John Malcolm* (2 vols), London, vol. 1, 1754, p. 367.
"growing thoughtful of late": Victor Kiernan, *Metcalfe's Mission to Lahore (1808–1809)*. Lahore, Punjab Government Record Office, Monograph No. 21, 1943, p. 1.

103 "were sent away with courteous words . . .": ibid.
"not conscious that behind the bold, bad barons . . .": ibid.
"that in the Punjab one of the Sikh Chiefs . . .": ibid.
"the fear of French intrigue . . .": R.R. Sethi, *The Lahore Durbar in the Light of the Correspondence of Sir C.M. Wade*. Simla, Punjab Government Record Office Publication, Monograph No. 1, 1950, p. 4.

104 "the negotiations with Ranjit Singh . . .": Kiernan, 1943, p. 6.
"A stripling from the fifth form at Eton . . .": John W. Kaye, *Lives of Indian Officers* (3 vols). London, Strahan and Co., vol. 2, 1869, p. 88.
"an ambitious, restless and warlike character . . .": M.L. Ahluwalia, *Looking Across India's North Western Frontiers*. Delhi, Hemkunt Publishers, 1990, p. 203.

105 "In this wild encampment the bogey of Napoleon . . .": Kiernan, 1943, p. 15.
"on the run": p. 19, ibid.
"so very restless and unsteady . . .": ibid., p. 25.

106 "labours at this moment under the most cruel anxiety . . .": ibid.
"imperturbable forbearance and scrupulous non-intervention": Sethi, 1950, pp. 3–4.
"could not resist the conviction . . .": Hasrat, 1968, pp. 80–1.
"troops would advance with or without . . .": *Report: The Mission of Charles Metcalfe at Lahore*, 18 August 1810. London, Home/Misc./511, India Office Library.

107 "the British Government would not admit . . .": ibid.
"did not judge it expedient to acquaint the Rajah . . .": *Report* . . ., p. 1810.
"perpetual friendship": Sayad Abdul Qadir, "Maharaja Ranjit Singh's Relations
With the English" (pp. 154–72) in *Maharaja Ranjit Singh's First Death Centenary
Memorial*. Patiala, Languages Department, 1970 (1939), p. 159.
"more troops than are necessary . . .": ibid.
"nor commit or suffer any encroachments . . .": ibid.
108 "departure from the rules of friendship": ibid.
"weakness lay in the fact that it forever . . .": ibid.
"tantamount to a confession of defeat . . .": ibid., p. 160.
109 "The whole map will be red one day": Gurmukh Nihal Singh, "A note on the
Policy of Maharaja Ranjit Singh Towards the British" (p.173–6), in Ganda Singh
(ed.), *Maharaja Ranjit Singh*, 1970, p. 176.
"his whole conduct showed that . . .": Lawrence, 1970, pp. 32–3.
"Mr. Metcalfe certainly believed him to be so": Griffin, 1967, p. 181.
"the great sagacity and shrewdness . . .": ibid.
"in his footsteps . . .": ibid., p. 176.
112 "Was it the same as the Samantik Mani . . .": Iradj Amini, *Koh-i-noor*. Delhi, Roli
Books, 1994, p. 10.
"every appraiser has estimated its value . . .": ibid., p. 27.
116 the Emperors Aurangzeb . . .: Griffin, 1967, p. 188.
118 "Coins were struck, inscriptions were issued in his name . . .": K.K. Khullar,
Maharaja Ranjit Singh. Delhi, Hem Publishers, 1980, p. 62.
"Your excellency will reap the fruits of the alliance . . .": ibid., p. 41.
119 Dost Muhammad, who seized the opportunity of asking the English . . .: Ganda
Singh, "Maharaja Ranjit Singh" (pp. 12–45), in Ganda Singh (ed.), 1970, p. 44.
120 "the friendship of the Maharaja was valued more by Auckland . . .": ibid.
"Ranjit Singh has hitherto derived nothing but advantage . . .": G. Nihal Singh,
ibid., p. 163.
"we are now beginning to prescribe limits to his power": ibid.
121 "spurious mission": Bikrama Jit Hasrat, *Life and Times of Ranjit Singh*.
Hoshiarpur (Punjab), V. Vedic Research Institute, 1977, p. 144.
Geographical and Military Memoirs: Alexander Burnes, *A Geographical and Military
Memoir on the Indus and Its Tributary from the Sea to Lahore*. London, 1829.
122 "by the extension of British commerce . . .": Cunningham, 1966, p. 175.
"*the Government of India is bound by the* . . .": R.R. Sethi, *The Mighty and the
Shrewd Maharaja*. Delhi, S. Chand & Co., 1960, p. 136.
"Kashmir, Kabul, Sind, Ludhiana and the *cis*-Sutlej . . .": Harbans Singh (ed.),
The Encyclopedia of Sikhism (3 vols). Patiala, Punjabi University, vol. 2, 1996, p. 8.
"not to yield to the demands of the English . . .": Cunningham, 1966, p. 185.
123 "could scarcely be expected to resign . . .": ibid., p. 196.
"he should be protected from Sikh attacks . . .": Hasrat, 1977, p. 161.
"made a detailed appraisal of the Sikhs' military power . . .": Harbans Singh
(ed.), vol. 2, 1996, p. 9.
"a young British Officer prepared during Sir Henry's visit . . .": ibid.
124 "he formed an estimate of the force . . .": Cunningham, 1966, p. 193.
"the prospect of a war with the Sikhs . . .": ibid.

"died of a broken heart": ibid., p. iv.

"It has been usual to attribute the superiority of the Sikh army . . .": ibid., p. 153.

"battalions were a formidable body of troops . . .": Ganda Singh, "Maharaja Ranjit Singh as others saw him," in Gandha Singh (ed.), 1970, P. 240.

125 "in equipment, in steadiness and in precision . . .": Khullar, 1980, p. 81.

"whenever noticed, their work seems to have had the result . . .": Jean-Marie Lafont, *French Administrators of Maharaja Ranjit Singh*. Delhi, National Book Shop, 1988 (rev. ed.), p. 2.

126 for fear of the medical effect . . . .: ibid., p. 104.

"had been in the bodyguards of Prince Eugene . . .": ibid., p. 9.

"have no religious prejudices . . .": Khullar, 1980, p. 81.

127 "that Ranjit Singh's soundness of mind and body . . .": ibid., p. 201.

"in which were the strongest sauces . . .": Khushwant Singh, *Ranjit Singh, Maharaja of the Punjab*. Delhi, Orient Longman, 1985 (1962), p. 214.

"the following morning my spirits were exceedingly depressed": ibid.

128 "But so deep and sincere were the feelings of respect . . .": William G. Osborne, *The Court and Camp of Ranjeet Singh*. Delhi, Heritage Publishers, 1973 (1840), p. 219.

"the un-Sikh title of Maharaja": Kapur Singh, 1959, p. 359.

"he was sabotaging the very basis of the Sikh polity . . .": ibid.

129 "It is the self-respect, the awareness . . .": ibid., p. 366.

"was a creation of the Khalsa arms . . .": ibid., pp. 362–3.

"In pursuance of this policy of his . . .": ibid., p. 362.

130 "embarked upon a conspiracy to destroy the entire line of Ranjit Singh's descendants . . .": ibid., p. 363.

4 GRIEVOUS BETRAYALS, 1839–1849

132 "'barbarians' pressing at its borders": Umberto Eco, *Travels in Hyper Reality*. New York, Harcourt Brace Jovanovich, 1985, p. 74.

"not necessarily uncultivated . . . new customs, new views . . .": ibid.

"barbarians may burst in with violence . . .": ibid.

"had nothing to attract or attack": Hasrat, 1977, p. 215.

133 "intolerant of the English . . .": ibid., p. 217.

Sher Singh was favoured by the British: Cunningham, 1966, p. 211.

drawing the Governor-General's attention . . .: Sita Ram Kohli, *Sunset of the Sikh Empire*. Delhi, Orient Longman, 1967, p. 11.

"our dear friend": Emily Eden, *Up the Country*. London, Curzon Press, 1978 (1930), p. 22.

"foolish Kurruck Singh . . . it is just possible his dear fat head . . .": ibid.

"It was suspected by the royal physicians . . .": Hasrat, 1977, p. 216.

134 "the discretion of a statesman . . .": ibid.

"Kharak Singh's rule appeared unpromising": Hasrat, 1968, p. 187.

"the drift of Court politics . . .": ibid.

135 "I proved to them that they might be effectively removed": ibid., p. 189.

"Clerk gave encouragement to rival parties . . .": ibid.

"required for the complete subjugation of the Punjab . . .": Harbans Singh, 1985, p. 197.

"we need such men as the Raja . . .": ibid., p. 198.

136 "paved the way for the eventual enslavement . . .": Kapur Singh, 1959, p. 362.

137 The maids are said to have poisoned her . . .: Hasrat, 1977, p. 221, n.2.

138 "Sher Singh's accession was unattended by any acts of violence . . .": Hasrat, 1968, p. 201.

"while he did not write to me . . .": ibid., p. 199.

139 "I am always a little surprised at your warlike tone . . .": Bikrama Jit Hasrat, *The Punjab Papers (1836–1849)*. Hoshiarpur (Punjab), V.V. Research Institute, 1970, p. 45.

"I thought that Clerk made a false step . . .": ibid.

141 "Teja Singh, an insignificant Brahmin . . .": Kapur Singh, 1959, p. 362.

"it was soon apparent that Gulab Singh . . .": Cunningham, 1966, p. 221.

"as a most likely instrument of British policy . . .": Harbans Singh, 1985, p. 198.

142 "troublesome ambitions": Cunningham, 1966, p. 221.

"carried off the accumulated treasures of Ranjit Singh . . .": Latif, 1964, pp. 506–7.

misappropriated the revenues . . .: Harbans Singh, vol. 2, 1996, p. 121.

"We can only consider our relations with Lahore . . .": Hasrat, 1970, p. 72.

143 "In the hills Gulob Singh has succeeded in raising a religious war . . .": ibid., pp. 78–9.

"even if we had a case for devouring an ally . . .": ibid., p. 83.

"how are we to justify the seizure of a friend's territory . . .": ibid.

"we have 200,000 men pretty well up for defensive objects . . .": ibid., p. 79.

144 "the prime mover, by many considered the cause of this [the First Sikh] war": Kohli, 1967, p. 103 n.2.

"I will not fail to make him [Hardinge] acquainted . . .": ibid.

"to declare the *cis*-Sutlej possessions . . .": Cunningham, 1966, pp. 252–3.

"Broadfoot is in his element on the frontier": Hasrat, 1968, p. 253.

"British suzerainty over his *cis*-Sutlej possessions . . .": Kohli, 1967, p. 103.

"was wholly unjustifiable": ibid., p. 104.

"would have turned out to be the first shot of the great Sikh war": ibid.

145 "every act of Major Broadfoot was considered . . .": Cunningham, 1966, pp. 254–5.

"Had the shrewd committees of the [Sikh] army . . .": ibid., pp. 257–8.

"had not come to gain a victory over the British . . .": Kohli, 1967, p. 106.

"the necessity of leaving the easy prey . . .": Cunningham, 1966, p. 263.

146 "the fame of the Khalsa [could be] exalted . . .": ibid.

An assurance to the British . . .: Kohli, 1967, p. 106.

"would almost certainly have fallen . . .": Donald Featherstone, *At Them with the Bayonet: The First Sikh War*. London, Jarrolds, 1968, p. 46.

"less than two thousand infantry . . .": Cunningham, 1966, p. 265.

"the success of the English was not so complete . . .": ibid.

"the whole action was unsatisfactory and unduly costly": Featherstone, 1968, p. 66.

"wisely determined to effect a junction . . .": Cunningham, 1966, p. 265.

"the confident English had at last got the field . . .": ibid., p. 266.

147 "On that memorable night the English were hardly masters . . .": ibid., p. 267.
"was one of gloom . . .": Khushwant Singh, *The Fall of the Kingdom of Punjab.*
Delhi, Orient Longman, 1962, p. 99.
"The wearied and famished English . . .": Cunningham, 1966, p. 267.
"when the fate of India trembled in the balance": Featherstone, 1968, p. 90.
"at daybreak on the 22nd . . .": ibid., p. 101.
"India has been saved by a miracle": ibid.
"the most warlike [men] in India": ibid., p. 97.

148 "his largely untouched force . . .": ibid., p. 101.
"The Sikh leader had only to continue to fire . . .": ibid., p. 99.
"we are astonished at the numbers . . .": ibid., p. 105.
"claims that it is possible that their casualties . . .": ibid., p. 66.
"not very far removed from failure": ibid., p. 132.

149 "the Governor-General issued a proclamation . . .": ibid., p. 116.
"Even our Peninsular heroes say . . .": ibid., p. 128.
"under a tempest of shot and shell . . .": ibid., p. 129.
"they knelt to receive the dashing charge of the British Lancers . . .": Kohli,
1967, p. 112.

150 "the latter refer with staggering frankness . . .": Hasrat, 1968, p. 284.
"[Hardinge] knew that time was pressing . . .": Featherstone, 1968, pp. 134–5.

151 "The Sikhs, seeing their right had been broken into . . .": ibid., p. 143.
"Teja Singh . . . fled soon after the first assault . . .": Hasrat, 1968, p. 282.
"that the Sikh army should be attacked by the English . . .": Cunningham, 1966,
p. 279.

152 "effectually protecting the British provinces . . .": Featherstone, 1968, p. 153.
"that the Maharaja . . .": Hasrat, 1968, p. 286.
"In consideration of the services . . .": ibid., p. 382.

153 "the British Government transfers . . .": ibid., p. 384.
"Half a million, the total expenses of the war to the E.I. Co.": ibid., p. 287.
"From a financial point of view . . .": Featherstone, 1968, p. 162.

154 "Golab Singh's neutrality was most valuable . . .": Hasrat, 1968, p. 289.

155 "wild outbursts . . . overstrung": ibid., pp. 324, 332.
"exact a national reparation . . . a heavy one": ibid., p. 306.

156 "suspicious little autocrat . . . a state of perpetual excitement": ibid., pp. 318–19.
"ready disposition to believe in conspiracies . . .": ibid.

157 "we have without hesitation resolved that Punjab . . .": ibid., p. 321.
"I have drawn the sword . . .": ibid., p. 323.
"eyebrows were raised at his [Dalhousie's] determination . . .": ibid.

158 "appears to have been in some doubt . . .": Hugh Cook, *The Sikh Wars.* Delhi,
Thompson Press, 1975, pp. 141–2.
"Our acts require no explanation": Hasrat, 1970, p. 147.
"a sad affair with distressing results": Hasrat, 1968, p. 328.
"reserve salutes for real victories which this is not": ibid.
"it is no wonder that all confidence in Lord Gough . . .": ibid., p. 332.
". . . advancing British infantrymen were mowed down . . .": ibid., pp. 335–6.

159 "from within the jungle the guns opened . . .": ibid.

"a large body of Sikhs surrounded . . .": ibid., p. 337.

"we have gained a victory like that of the ancients . . .": ibid.

"subjugation without the name": ibid., p. 339.

"the preservation of our own power . . .": Hasrat, 1970, p. 189.

"Never perhaps had the British amassed . . .": Hasrat, 1968, p. 344.

160 "Fordyce's battery, which came up against the heavy Sikh guns . . .": Cook, 1975, p. 187.

"the Sikhs fought desperately and held out to the last man . . .": ibid., p. 188.

"observers who watched the surrender . . .": ibid., p. 192.

"that the British Empire was God's gift . . .": ibid., p. 203.

"that the Sikhs had risen in rebellion . . .": ibid.

161 "I do not recollect any subject has fallen . . .": Hasrat, 1968, p. 351.

"The Sikh Army fought valiantly and stubbornly . . .": Featherstone, 1968, p. x.

"I earnestly hope that your future life . . .": E. Dalhousie Login, *Lady Login's Recollections*. Patiala, Languages Dept., Punjab, 1970 (reprint), p. 95.

162 "Politically, we could desire nothing better . . .": Hasrat, 1968, p. 359.

5 FROM ANNEXATION TO PARTITION, 1849–1947

163 "had been other than they were . . .": Tuchman, 1984, p. 231.

"despite the deceitfulness of courtiers . . .": Harbans Singh, 1985, p. 211.

"No nation has ever produced a military history . . .": Barbara W. Tuchman, *Sand Against the Wind: Stilwell and the American Experience in China, 1911–45*. London, Macmillan, 1971, p. 436.

165 "The Punjab was conquered by the British . . .": R.C. Majumdar, *The Sepoy Mutiny and the Revolt of 1857*. Calcutta, Firma K.L. Mukhopadhyay, 1963 (1953), p. 408.

"who are supposed to have sacrificed their all . . .": ibid.

"It is difficult to resist . . .": ibid.

166 "transformed the endless waste and scrub . . .": Ian Talbot, *Punjab and the Raj: 1849–1947*. Delhi, Manohar, 1988, pp. 39–40.

"By the 1920s Punjab produced a tenth . . .": ibid., p. 39.

168 "a class of persons, Indian in blood . . .": H.R. Mehta, *A History of the Growth and Development of Western Education in the Punjab, 1846–1884*. Patiala, Languages Dept., Punjab, 1971, p. 24.

"To whom our attention at first was specially directed": quoted in Harbans Singh, 1985, p. 229.

175 "First decisive battle for India's freedom won . . .": Ganda Singh (ed.), *Some Confidential Papers of the Akali Movement*. Amritsar, S.G.P.C., 1965, p. 11.

"mobility, enterprise and opportunity": in Hugh Johnston, "Patterns of Sikh Migration to Canada, 1900–1960" (pp. 296–313) in Joseph T. O'Connell, Milton Israel and Williard G. Oxtoby (eds.), *Sikh History and Religion in the Twentieth Century*. Centre for South Asian Studies, University of Toronto, 1988, p. 299.

176 in 1904, for example, Indian wheat exports to Great Britain . . .: Hugh Johnston, ibid., p. 298.

"Probably the first Sikhs to see British Columbia . . .": Sarjeet Singh Jagpal, *Becoming Canadians: Pioneer Sikhs in their Own Words*. Madeira Park, BC, Canada, Harbour Publishing, 1994, p. 18.

178 "all the combined prejudices of both the British . . .": Anthony Read and David Fisher, *The Proudest Day: India's Long Road to Independence*. London, Jonathan Cape, 1997, p. 169.

"suffered from arteriosclerosis . . . heat stroke . . .": ibid.

"a succession of sporting accidents . . .": ibid., pp. 169–70.

"Q: When you got into the Bagh what did you do?": extract from Hunter Committee Report, quoted in Raja Ram, *The Jallianwala Bagh Massacre*. Chandigarh, Punjabi University, 1969, pp. 131–2.

179 "In the crush, the steel-jacketed bullets . . .": Read and Fisher, 1997, p. 8.

"to strike terror . . . throughout the Punjab": Raja Ram, 1969, p. 133.

"I realized then, more vividly . . .": Jawaharlal Nehru, *India and the World. Essays*. London, George Allen & Unwin, 1936, p. 147.

181 "In Iran, the party was able to raise an Indian Independence Army": "Ghadr Movement" (pp. 60–6), in Harbans Singh, vol. I, 1996, p. 66.

"Nanakji had noble aims . . .": Swami Dayanand Saraswati, *Satyarth Prakash* (*The Light of Truth*), trans. Ganga Prasad. Allahabad, The Kala Press, 1956, p. 522.

182 "Just as idol-worshippers have set up their shop . . .": ibid., p. 525.

"Mahdi of Islam and the Messiah of Christianity": Kenneth W. Jones, "Communalism in the Punjab: The Arya Samaj Contribution" (pp. 39–54), *Journal of Asian Studies*, vol. 27, American Association of Asian Studies, 1968, p. 46.

"The Samaj provided an ideology of militant Hinduism . . .": ibid., p. 52.

183 "Within the present struggle between Indian communities . . .": quoted in K.L. Tuteja, "The Punjab Hindu Sabha and Communal Politics, 1906–1923," in Indu Banga (ed.), *Five Punjabi Centuries: Polity, Economy, Society and Culture, c.1500–1900*. Delhi, Manohar, 1997, p. 132.

184 "inspired by a genuine sympathy for the interest and welfare of India . . .": R.C. Majumdar, *History of the Freedom Movement in India* (3 vols). Calcutta, Firma K.L. Mukhopadhyay, vol. 1, 1962, p. 389.

"A safety-valve for the escape of great and growing forces . . .": ibid., p. 392.

"was brought into existence as an instrument . . .": ibid., p. 393.

"Swarajya [freedom] is my birthright . . .": Stanley A. Wolpert, *Tilak and Gokhale: Revolution and Reform in the Making of Modern India*. Delhi, Oxford University Press, 1961, p. 191.

"necessary that for the peace of India . . .": Stanley A. Wolpert, *India*. Berkeley, University of California Press, 1991, p. 60.

"Hinduism is of higher worth than other religions": Wolpert, 1961, p. 136.

185 "partiality for Gujarati and Hindustani": quoted in D.G. Tendulkar, *Mahatma: Life of Mohandas Karamchand Gandhi* (8 vols). Bombay: V.K. Jhaveri and D.G. Tendulkar, vol. 1, 1951, p. 195.

"the use of English in a Gujarati gathering": ibid.

"He bowed but rarely to populist symbols . . .": Eqbal Ahmad, "Jinnah in a class of his own," *The Dawn* (English-language daily), Lahore, 11 June 1995.

"the Ulema [Islamic theologians and expounders of the law] in their over-whelming majority . . .": ibid., "The betrayed promise," ibid., 18 June 1995.

"his loyalty to the Muslim League . . .": Sarojini Naidu, "A Pen Portrait," in *Sarojini Naidu* (ed.), *Mohammed Ali Jinnah: An Ambassador of Unity; His Speeches & Writings, 1912–1917.* Madras, Ganesh & Co., 1918, p. 11.

186 "the powers which are going to be assumed . . .": M. Rafique Afzal (ed.), *Speeches and Statements of the Qaid-i-Azam Muhammad Ali Jinnah.* Lahore, University of Punjab, 1966, p. 85.

"sought to curtail the liberty . . .": Majumdar, vol. 3, 1963, p. 2.

"speedy trial of offences by a Special Court . . .": ibid.

187 "India has got to keep her head cool . . .": "Interview with the Press," *The Bombay Chronicle* (English-language daily), Bombay, 17 November 1919.

"I can imagine no form of resistance . . .": Gandhi to Jinnah, 28 June 1919, *The Collected Works of Mahatma Gandhi* (100 vols). Ahmedabad, Navjivan Trust, vol. 15, 1965, pp. 398–9.

"secure complete Swaraj [self-rule] for India . . .": M.R. Jayakar, *The Story of My Life* (2 vols). Bombay, Asia Publishing House, vol. 1, 1958, p. 405.

"If by 'new life' you mean your methods and your programme . . .": M.H. Saiyad, *M.A. Jinnah.* Lahore, S.M. Ashraf, 1945, pp. 264–5.

188 "Let Muslims look upon Ram as their hero . . .": Tapan Basu, Pradip Datta et al., *Khaki Shorts and Saffron Flags.* Delhi, Orient Longman, 1993, p. 12.

"lower-caste assertion . . . twin dangers . . .": Sumit Sarkar, "Indian Nationalism and the Politics of Hindutva" (pp. 270–94), in David Ludden (ed.), *Making India Hindu.* Delhi, Oxford University Press, 1996, p. 288.

"Conflicts between various communities . . .": Basu and Datta, et al., 1993, p. 14.

189 "the one silver lining in the cloudy sky . . .": ibid., p. 23.

"The real winner was British imperialism": Sumit Sarkar, *Modern India: 1885–1947.* Delhi, Macmillan, 1986 (1983), p. 237.

"The Montford reforms had broadened the franchise . . .": ibid., p. 235.

"In neither case was it even *bona fide* communalism . . .": Gyanendra Pandey, *The Construction of Communalism in Colonial North India.* Delhi, Oxford University Press, 1990, pp. 240–1.

190 "Believe me there is no progress for India . . .": Afzal, 1966, p. 295.

"Yes, we Hindus are a Nation by ourselves . . .": "The Presidential Address by V.D. Savarkar" at the Nagpur session of Hindu Mahasabha, December 1938 (pp. 317–35), in N.N. Mitra (ed.), *The Indian Annual Register, July–December, 1938.* Calcutta, The Annual Register Office, 1938, pp. 328–9.

"there is no doubt that we have been . . .": Sarkar, 1986, p. 356.

191 "Lala's proposal was a decisive step . . .": Kirpal Singh, *The Partition of the Punjab.* Patiala, Punjabi University, 1989 (1962), p. 10.

192 "most anxious that the Sikhs . . . You will have a Cabinet . . .": Sardar Hardit Singh Malik, "Khalistan: Let us keep our cool—1," *The Indian Express* (English-language daily), Delhi, 12 November 1981.

"I agree . . . This is how I will deal with you . . .": ibid.

"I went and saw U.N. Sen . . .": ibid.

193 "we arrived to find that the havoc in the small town was . . .": Alan Campbell-Johnson, *Mission with Mountbatten*. London, Robert Hale, 1952, p. 79.
"It cannot be an accident that those districts . . .": "J.P. Narain's statement to the press on Punjab disturbances," *The Pioneer* (English-language daily), Lucknow, 22 March 1947.

194 "one must appreciate that the Sikhs had been driven . . .": V.P. Menon, *The Transfer of Power in India*. Bombay, Orient Longman, 1957, pp. 432–3.
"a division of the Punjab into two provinces . . .": Resolution of the All-India Congress Working Committee, 6–8 March 1947 (pp. 117–19), in Mitra (ed.), *The Indian Annual Register, 1947, January–June*, pp. 118–19.
"Violence escalated after the Congress Resolution . . .": Ajit Bhattacharjea, *Countdown to Partition: The Final Days*. Delhi, HarperCollins, 1997, p. xxiv.

195 "It has been difficult to explain to you the Resolution . . .": Leonard Mosley, *The Last Days of the British Raj*. London, Weidenfeld & Nicolson, 1961, p. 100.
"the combination of all these various elements . . .": Jamil-ud-din Ahmad (ed.), *Some Recent Speeches and Writings of Mr. Jinnah*. Lahore, S. Muhammed Ashraf, 1942, p. 5.
"to effect the transference of power into responsible Indian hands . . .": "Indian Policy Statement of 20 February 1947" (pp. 773–5), in Nicholas Mansergh (ed.), *The Transfer of Power, 1942–47* (12 vols). London, Her Majesty's Stationery Office, vol. 9, 1980, p. 774.

196 "entrusted with the most sensitive . . .": Bhattacharjea, 1997, p. 59.
"the responsibility of dealing with . . .": ibid., p. 100.
"from the administrative point of view . . .": "Viceroy's Personal Report No. 17; 16 August 1947" (pp. 757–83), in Mansergh (ed.), vol. 12, 1983, p. 760.
"been obvious all along that the later . . .": ibid.

197 "short tenure of the Viceroyalty . . .": ibid., p. 731.
"I believe your outstanding ability . . .": ibid., p. 727.
"Situation here is generally explosive . . .": ibid., vol. 11, 1982, p. 942.

6 VIOLENCE AND VENALITY, 1947 TO THE PRESENT

199 "for two months afterwards . . .": Rawlinson, 1937, p. 240.
"I confess I did rejoice at the opportunity . . .: cited in Patwant Singh, *Of Dreams and Demons: An Indian Memoir*. London, Gerald Duckworth, 1994, p. 13.

201 One economist recently put Punjab's current share . . .: G.S. Bhalla, "Political Economy since Independence," in Indu Banga (ed.), 1997, p. 377.

204 "nationalism and sub-nationalism . . .": *Report of Linguistic Provinces Commission 1948*. Delhi, Government of India, 1948, p. 31.
"mainly linguistic considerations . . .": ibid., p. 34.
"a grave risk, but one that had to be taken . . .": ibid., p. 35.
"oneness of language may be one of the factors . . .": ibid.
"mutual conflicts which would jeopardise . . .": *Report of the Linguistic Provinces Committee*. Delhi, All-India Congress Committee, 1949, p. 15.
"we are clearly of the opinion . . .": ibid., p. 16.

205 "to concede the Akali demand would mean . . .": Indira Gandhi, *My Truth*. Delhi, Vision Books, 1982 (1981), p. 117.

"Lal Bahadur Shastri continued the policy . . .": ibid.

206 "There has been a growth in sub-nationalism . . .": *Commission on Centre-State Relations, Report: Part 1* (Sarkaria Commission). Nasik (Maharashtra), Government of India Press, 1983, pp. 15–16.

211 "The Shiromani Akali Dal realises that India . . .": R.S. Narula, "Anandpur Saheb Resolution," in Patwant Singh and Harji Malik (eds.), *Punjab: The Fatal Miscalculation*. Delhi, published by Patwant Singh, 1985, p. 64.
"the principle of state . . .": ibid., p. 66.
"recast the constitutional structure . . .": ibid., p. 67.
"The only way to save the country . . .": ibid., p. 77.

212 "Needless to say this would not only upset . . .": editorial, *The Hindustan Times* (English-language daily). Delhi, 31 October 1978.
"By turning the Punjab issue into a Hindu-Sikh confrontation . . .": Rajni Kothari, "Electoral Politics and the Rise of Communalism," in Patwant Singh (ed.), 1985, p. 84.

215 the loss of 5,000 civilian lives: J.S. Grewal, *The Sikhs of the Punjab*, The New Cambridge History of India. Cambridge University Press, 1990, p. 227; citing Chand Joshi, *Bhindranwale: Myth and Reality*, p. 161.

216 "Later, defendants No. 11 to 13 . . . folded hands . . . After making a heap . . .": plaint to the Delhi High Court. This information is courtesy of Supreme Court lawyer Harvinder Singh Phoolka, New Delhi.

218 "They broke down the door and entered the house . . .": ibid.
"We divided ourselves into two groups . . . They continued to attack . . .": ibid.

220 "The people who are responsible for withdrawing the army . . .": letter from lawyer H.S. Phoolka to the Chief Minister of Delhi, dated 13 April 1996.

221 "remained behind the scenes . . . and tried for murder . . .": ibid.
"for three horrific nights and four days . . .": John Fraser, "Sifting the Ashes of India's shame," in Patwant Singh (ed.), 1985, pp. 203–4.
"hardly had the country recovered . . .": ibid., p. 206.
"The mosaic of India's varied people . . .": *Report of the Citizen's Commission: Delhi, 31 October–4 November, 1984*. Delhi, Tata Press, 1985, p. 7.

222 "suggest preventive corrective and retributive action . . .": ibid., p. 29.
"The incredible and abysmal failure . . .": ibid., pp. 29–30.

223 "Most of the affidavits in favour of the accused . . .": *Report of Advisory Committee to the Chief Minister of Delhi*. Delhi, The Sikh Forum, 1994, p. 5.

224 "the Delhi Police far from trying to disperse the mob . . .": *1984 Carnage in Delhi: A Report on the Aftermath*. Delhi, People's Union for Democratic Rights, 1992, p. 9.
"disclosed that [another committee's] file . . .": ibid.
"anticipatory bail while the CBI team . . .": ibid.
"the lie has become not just a moral category . . .": Alexander Solzhenitsyn, *The Oak and the Calf: Sketches of Literary Life in the Soviet Union*. London, Collins and Harvill Press, 1980, p. 533.

226 "Gurdev Singh Kaunke was a hard-liner . . .": Inderjit Singh Jaijee, *Politics of Genocide: Punjab, 1984–1994*. Chandigarh, Baba Publishers, 1995, p. 88.

227 "On 29 August 1991, S.S.P. Sumedh Singh Saini . . .": ibid., p. 94.
"On the afternoon of 21 August 1989 . . .": ibid., pp. 123–4.

Notes

229 "Until it becomes fully normal for scholars . . .": Cynthia Keppley-Mahmood, *Fighting for Faith and Nation: Dialogues with Sikh Militants*. Philadelphia, University of Pennyslvania Press, 1996, pp. 272–3.

230 "My parents were very much hurt by the attack . . .": ibid., pp. 167, 170.
"In its central philosophical conception . . .": ibid., p. 185.

231 "A Sikh later hanged for the murder . . .": ibid., p. 24.
"The same 'saints' who uphold with valour . . .": ibid., p. 20.

232 "It would be too easy to say that . . .": ibid., p. 281.

233 "The availability of the administration . . .": Padam Rosha, "The Dharma of Policemen." Unpublished paper.
"the seeds of fascism lie in . . .": ibid.

234 "a myth has been built, and it is currently . . .": Girilal Jain, "What Ails the Sikh Community?" *The Times of India*. Delhi, 11 August 1986.
"Out of 2,175 Indian martyrs for freedom . . .": Rajinder Puri, *Recovery of India*. Delhi, Har-Anand Publications, 1992, p. 99.

235 "Clearly the Sikhs, and for that matter . . .": ibid., p. 100.
"from which date VC's . . .": letter dated 19 December 1996 from the Victoria and George Cross Association, London.
"they were different . . . grievances were manufactured . . .": Ram Swarup, "The Hindu-Sikh Cleavage," *The Times of India*. Delhi, 20 December 1984.
"Liberals who opposed military action . . .": Kewal Varma, "Genesis of Sikh Alienation" (pp. 8–22), *Mainstream* (English-language journal). Delhi, 1 September 1984, p. 19.
"leftists, particularly in the Communist Party of India . . .": Dipankar Gupta,

236 "The Communalising of Punjab 1980–1985," in Patwant Singh (ed.), 1985, p. 213.
"The latest judgement by the Punjab and Haryana High Court . . .": editorial, *The Pioneer* (English-language daily). Delhi, 8 January 1998.
"a culture is being built up which denigrates . . .": Padam Rosha, loc. cit.
"the use of force by the State . . .": ibid.

238 "churn your stomach . . .": editorial, *The Sikh Review* (English-language monthly). Calcutta, January 1998, p. 4.

240 "It is the freedom to disagree that is freedom of speech": I.F. Stone, *The Trial of Socrates*. New York, Anchor Books, 1989, p. 213.
"prosecution of ideas . . . We must not be angry with honest men": ibid., p. 222.

241 "the Right-wing movement for Hindutva . . .": Gyanendra Pandey, "The Civilized and the Barbarian: The 'new' politics of late twentieth century India and the world," in G. Pandey (ed.), *Hindus and Others: The Question of Identity in India Today*. Delhi, Viking, 1993, p. 2.
"the undisguised violence of these propositions . . .": ibid.
"against *distorted* and *unIndian* . . .": ibid., p. 9.
"The greatest danger posed by the Right-wing movements . . .": ibid., p. 20.

242 "Charity was practised by the members . . .": Patwant Singh, *Gurdwaras in India and around the World*. New Delhi, Himalayan Books, 1992, p. 131.

Further Reading

Akbar, Muhammad, *The Punjab Under the Mughals*. Lahore, 1948

Alam, Muzaffar, *The Crisis of Empire in Mughal North India: Awadh and the Punjab, 1707–1748*. Delhi, 1986

Alexander, Michael, and Sushila Anand, *Queen Victoria's Maharaja Duleep Singh, 1838–93*. New York, 1980

Ali, Imran, *The Punjab Under Imperialism, 1885–1947*. Delhi, 1989

Ali, Shamat, *The Sikhs and the Afghans in connection with India and Persia immediately before and after the death of Ranjit Singh from the Journal of an Expedition to Cabool through the Punjab and the Khaibar Pass*. Patiala, 1970 (1847)

Babur, Zahiruddin M., *Baburnama*, trans. A.S. Beveridge. Delhi, 1970 (reprint)

Badaoni, Abdul Qadir, *Muntakhab-ut-Tawarikh* (3 vols), trans. George S.A. Ranki. Patna, W.H. Lowe & W. Haig, 1973 (reprint)

Bal, S.S., *British Policy Towards the Punjab*. Calcutta, 1971

Banerjee, Himadri, *Agrarian Society of Punjab (1849–1901)*. Delhi, 1982

Banga, Indu, *Agrarian System of the Sikhs: Late Eighteenth and Early Nineteenth Century*. Delhi, 1978

Barrier, N. Gerald, *The Punjab Alienation of Land Bill of 1900*. Durham, 1966

————, "The Arya Samaj and Congress Politics in the Punjab, 1894–1908." *Journal of Asian Studies*, vol. xxv, pt. 1, 1966–7

————, "Punjab Government and Communal Politics, 1870–1908." *Journal of Asian Studies*, vol. 26, pt. 2, 1968

Batalavi, Ahmad Shah, *Tarikh-i-Punjab*, trans. Gurbaksh Singh. Patiala, 1971

Bell, Major Evans, *The Annexation of the Punjab and Maharaja Duleep Singh*. London, 1882

Bhai Gurdas, *Varan Bhai Gurdas Ji*, ed. Amar Singh Chakar. Amritsar, 1964 (2nd ed.)

Bingley, A.H., *Sikhs—A Handbook for Indian Army*. Patiala, 1970 (1918)

Brar, Harpreet, "Guru Gobind Singh's Relations with Aurangzeb." Patiala, *Panjab Past and Present*, 1983

Brass, Paul R., *Ethnicity and Nationalism*. Delhi, 1991

Buist, G., *Annals for the year 1848 to the end of the Sikh War in March, 1849*. Bombay, 1849

The Cambridge Economic History of India. Cambridge (2 vols), 1982–3

Census of India. Punjab volumes, 1868, 1881–1941

Cohen, Stephen P., *The Indian Army: Its Contribution to the Development of a Nation*. Berkeley, CA, 1971

Cole, W. Owen, *Sikhism and its Indian Context, 1464–1708*. Delhi, 1982

Cust, Robert N., *Linguistic and Oriental Essays*. London, 1906

Datta, V.N., *Jallianwala Bagh*. Ludhiana, 1969

Davis, Emmett, *Press and Politics in British Western Punjab, 1836–1947*. Delhi, 1983

Douie, J.M., *The Punjab, North Western Frontier Province and Kashmir*. Delhi, 1974 (reprint)

Dumont, Louis, *Religion/Politics and History in India*. Paris, 1970

Dungen, P.H.M. van den, *The Punjab Traditions*. London, 1972

Farquhar, J.N., *Modern Religious Movements in India*. London, 1947

Farroqui, M.A., *British Relations with cis-Sutlej State, 1809–23*. Lahore, 1940

Fazl, Abul, *Ain-Akbari*, trans. H. Beveridge. Lahore, 1975 (reprint)

Fox, Richard G., *Lions of the Punjab: Culture in the Making*. Berkeley, CA, 1985

Frankel, Francine R., *India's Green Revolution: Economic Gains and Political Costs*. Princeton, NJ, 1971

Garrett, H.L.O., *The Punjab a Hundred Years Ago, as described by V. Jacquemont and A. Soltykoff*. Patiala, 1971

Gopal, S., *Jawaharlal Nehru: A Biography*. London, 1975

Goswamy, B.N., and J.S. Grewal, *The Mughals and Sikh Rulers and the Vaishnavas of Pindori*. Simla, 1968

Gough, C. and A.D. Innes, *The Sikhs and the Sikh Wars*. London, 1897

Grewal, J.S., *Guru Nanak in History*. Chandigarh, 1967

———, and S.S. Bal, *Guru Gobind Singh*. Chandigarh, 1967

———, *Guru Tegh Bahadur and the Persian Chroniclers*. Amritsar, 1976

———, *From Guru Nanak to Maharaja Ranjit Singh*. Amritsar, 1982

———, and Indu Banga, *The Civil and Military Affairs of Maharaja Ranjit Singh*. Amritsar, 1987

Grewal, Reeta, "The Pattern of Urbanisation in the Punjab under Colonial Rule." *Journal of Regional History*, 1983

Grey, C., *European Adventurers of Northern India, 1785 to 1849*, ed. H.L.O. Garrett. Lahore, 1929

Griffin, Lepel H., and C.F. Massy, *Chiefs and Families of Note in the Punjab* (2 vols). Lahore, 1909

Gupta, Dipankar, "The Communalising of Punjab, 1980–1985." *Economic and Political Weekly*, Bombay, vol. 20, no. 28, July 1985

———, *The Context of Ethnicity: Sikh Identity in a Comparative Perspective*. Delhi, 1996

Gupta, Hari Ram, *Punjab on the Eve of First Sikh War*. Hoshiarpur, 1956

Habib, Irfan, "Evidence of 16th Century Agrarian Conditions in the Guru Granth Sahib." *Indian Economic and Social History Review*, 1964

Handa, R.L., *A History of the Development of Judiciary in the Punjab, 1846–84*. Lahore, 1927

Hans, Surjit, *A Reconstruction of Sikh History from Sikh Literature*. Jullundur, 1987

Hasrat, Bikrama Jit, *Life and Times of Ranjit Singh*. Hoshiarpur, 1977

Heeger, Gerald A., "Growth of Congress Movement in Punjab, 1920–40." *Journal of Asian Studies*, 1972

Henly, G.A., *Through the Sikh Wars.* Patiala, 1970

Hira, Bachan Singh, *Social Change in Upper Bari Doab, 1849–1947.* Amritsar, 1996

Hugel, Baron Charles, *Travels in Cashmere and the Punjab.* London, 1840

Husaini, Khwaja Kamghar, *Ma 'asir-i-Jahangiri,* ed. Azral Alavi. Bombay, 1978

Hutchison, J. and J.Ph. Vogel, *History of the Punjab Hill States* (2 vols). Simla, 1982 (reprint)

Irvine, William, "Guru Gobind Singh and Bandah." *Journal of the Asiatic Society,* January–April, 1894

Jalal, Ayesha, *The Sole Spokesman Jinnah: The Muslim League and the Demand for Pakistan.* Cambridge, 1985

Johar, R.S., and J.S. Khanna (eds.), *Studies in Punjab Economy.* Amritsar, 1983

Jones, K.W., "Ham Hindu Nahin: Arya-Sikh Relations, 1877–1905." *Journal of Asian Studies,* 1973

———*Arya Dharm: Hindu Consciousness in 19th Century Punjab.* Delhi, 1976

Josh, Bhagwan, *Communist Movement in Punjab.* Delhi, 1979

Jurgensmeyer, M., and N.G. Barrier (eds.), *Sikh Studies: Comparative Perspectives on Changing Traditions.* Berkeley, CA, 1979

Kalia, Barkat Ram, *A History of the Development of the Police in the Punjab, 1849–1905.* Lahore, 1929

Kerr, Ian J., "The British and the Administration of the Golden Temple in 1859." Patiala, *Panjab Past and Present,* 1976

Khan, Samanullah, *A History of Education in the Punjab.* Lahore, 1932

Khare, S., *The Untouchable as Himself.* Cambridge, 1984

Kohli, Atul (ed.), *India's Democracy: An Analysis of Changing State-Society Relations.* Princeton, NJ, 1988

Kohli, Sita Ram, *Catalogue of Khalsa Durbar Records* (2 vols). Lahore, 1919 and 1927

———, *The Multan Outbreak and Trial of Dewan Mulraj.* Lahore, 1932

———, *Maharaja Ranjit Singh.* Delhi, 1953

Kohli, Surinder Singh, *Philosophy of Guru Nanak.* Chandigarh, 1969

Kothari, Rajni (ed.), *Caste in Indian Politics.* Delhi, 1995 (1970)

Krishen, Indra, *An Historical Interpretation of the Correspondence of Sir*

George Russell Clerk, Political Agent at Ambala and Ludhiana, 1831–43. Simla, 1952

Kumar, Ravinder (ed.), *Essays on Gandhian Politics.* London, 1971

Latifi, A., *The Industrial Punjab.* Bombay, 1911

Leigh, M.S., *The Punjab and the War.* Lahore, 1922

Login, Lady, *Sir John Login and Duleep Singh.* Patiala, 1970 (reprint)

McGregor, W.L., *History of the Sikhs* (2 vols). Patiala, 1970 (1847)

McLeod, W.H., *The Evolution of the Sikh Community.* Delhi, 1975

Maharaja Ranjit Singh's First Death Centenary Memorial. Patiala, 1970 (1939)

Majumdar, R.C., *The Sepoy Mutiny and the Revolt.* Calcutta, 1963 (1953)

Malhotra, S.L., *Gandhi: An Experiment with Communal Politics—A Study of Gandhi's Role in Punjab Politics, 1922–31.* Amritsar, 1975

Malraux, André, *Antimemoirs,* trans. Terence Kilmartin. London, 1968

Manumriti, The Laws of Manu, trans. G. Buhler. Oxford, 1886

Mitra, N.N., *Indian Annual Register.* Calcutta, 1923–47

Moon, Penderel, *Divide and Quit.* London, 1961

Moorcroft, W., and G. Trebeck, *Travels in the Himalayan Provinces of Hindostan and the Punjab, in Ladakh and Kashmir, in Peshawar, Kabul and Kunduz and Bokhara, from 1819 to 1825.* London, 1837

Narang, A.S., *Storm over the Sutlej: The Akali Politics.* Delhi, 1983

Narang, Gokal Chand, *Transformation of Sikhism.* Delhi, 1956

Nayar, Baldev Raj, *Minority Politics in the Punjab.* Princeton, NJ, 1966

Nayyar, Kuldip and Khushwant Singh, *Tragedy of Punjab: Operation Blue Star and After.* Delhi, 1984

Nehru, Jawaharlal, *Autobiography.* London, 1936

Nehru, Motilal, *Report of the All Parties Conference.* Allahabad, 1928

Oberoi, Harjot S., *The Construction of Religious Boundaries: Cultures, Identity and Diversity in the Sikh Tradition.* Delhi, 1994

Page, David, *Prelude to Partition.* Delhi, 1982

Paustian, P.W., *Canal Irrigation in the Punjab.* New York, 1930

Pearse, Major Hugh, *Memories of Alexander Gardner.* Patiala, 1970 (reprint)

Petrie, D., *Confidential Report on Developments in Sikh Politics, 1900–11.* Simla, 1911

Prinsep, H.T., *Origin of the Sikh Power in the Punjab and Political Life of Maharaja Ranjit Singh.* Patiala, 1970 (1834)

Puri, Harish K., *Ghadar Movement: Ideology, Organization and Strategy.* Amritsar, 1983

Ram, Raja, *The Jallianwala Bagh Massacre.* Chandigarh, 1969

Report of the Linguistic Provinces Committee. Delhi, 1949

Sabherwal, Satish, *Mobile Men: Limits to Social Change in Urban Punjab.* Delhi, 1976

Sachdeva, Veena, *Polity and Economy of the Punjab During the Late Eighteenth Century.* Delhi, 1993

Said, Edward, *Orientalism.* New York, 1979

Sethi, Anil, *The Creation of Religious Boundaries in Colonial Punjab, 1850–1920.* Cambridge, Ph.D. thesis, 1998

Singh, Amrik (ed.), *Punjab in Indian Politics: Issues and Trends.* Delhi, 1985

Singh, Bhagat, *Sikh Polity in the Eighteenth and Nineteenth Centuries.* Delhi, 1978

Singh, Chetan, *Region and Empire: Punjab in the Seventeenth Century.* Delhi, 1991

Singh, Dalip, *Dynamics of Punjab Politics.* Delhi, 1981

Singh, Fauja, *Military System of the Sikhs.* Delhi, 1964

———, *Kuka Movement: An Important Phase in Punjab's Role in India's Struggle for Freedom.* Delhi, 1965

Singh, Ganda, *Makhiz-i-Tawarikh Sikhan.* Amritsar, 1949

———, *The Punjab in 1839–40.* Patiala, 1952

———, "The Martyrdom of Guru Tegh Bahadur." Patiala, *Panjab Past and Present,* 1988

Singh, Harbans, *Guru Gobind Singh.* Delhi, 1979

———, *Guru Tegh Bahadur.* Delhi, 1982

Singh, Hukam, *A Plea for the Punjabi-Speaking State: Memorandum by Hukam Singh.* Amritsar, n.d.

Singh, Khushwant, *A History of the Sikhs* (2 vols). Delhi, 1978

Singh, Mohinder, *The Akali Movement.* Delhi, 1978

Singh, Pritam, *Emerging Patterns in Punjab Economy.* Delhi, 1983

Singh, Pritam, and Shinder S. Thandi (eds.), *Globalization and the Region: Explorations in Punjabi Identitiy.* Coventry, 1996

Singh, Sant Fateh, *Our Stand on Punjabi Suba.* Amritsar, 1963

Singh, Wair (ed.), *Sikhism and Punjab's Heritage.* Patiala, 1990

Sri Guru Granth Sahib, trans. Gopal Singh (4 vols). Delhi, 1960–2

Sri Guru Granth Sahib, trans. Pritam Singh Chahil (4 vols). Delhi, 1992

Tabatabai, Munshi Ghulam Husain, *Siyar-ul-Mutakhirin* (2 vols). Lucknow, n.d.

Talwar, K.S., "The Anand Marriage Act." Patiala, *Panjab Past and Present*, 1968

Tandon, Prakash, *Punjabi Century*. London, 1961

Tavernier, Jean-Baptiste, *Travels in India, 1640–67*, trans. V. Ball and ed. William Crooke, Delhi, vol. 1, 1977 (reprint)

Thorburn, S.S., *Musalmans and Moneylenders in the Punjab*. London, 1885

———, *The Punjab in Peace and War*. London, 1904

Tully, Mark and Satish Jacob, *Amritsar: Mrs. Gandhi's Last Battle*. London, 1985

Vigne, G.T., *A Personal Narrative of a Visit to Ghazni, Kabul and Afghanistan and of a Residence at the Court of Dost Muhammad With Notices of Ranjit Singh*. London, 1840

Wade, Lt.-Col. C.M., *History of the Campaign on the Sutlej and the War in the Punjab*. London, 1846

Webster, John C.B., *The Christian Community and Change in Nineteenth Century North India*. Delhi, 1976

Index

Index

Index

Jahan, Shah, 40, 42, 113
Jahangir, 37–8, 40
Jaijee, Inderjit Singh, 226
Jainism, 6–7
Jallianwala Bagh massacre, 177–80, 187
Jan Sangh, 189
Jat caste, 24, 237–9
jati, 14
Jenkins, Sir Evan, 197
Jinnah, Mohammad Ali, 185–8, 190–5

Kabir, 16
Kalha, Rai, 59
Kangra, 109–11
Kartarpur, 24–9, 41
Kashmir, 113, 116–17, 153, 212
Katoch, Sansar Chand, 109–10, 119
Kaunke, Gurdev Singh, 226–7
Kaur, Chand, 137, 140, 142
Kaur, Mrs. Doban, 218
Kaur, Gurdev, 227–8
Kaur, Gurmeet, 227–8
Kaur, Mehtab, 97
Kaur, Raj, 97
Kaur, Rani Jind, 154
Kaur, Sada, 97, 100
Kautiliya (Vishnugupta Chanakya), 5–6
Khalistan, 232
Khalsa
    after Chamkaur, 61
    battles against Abdali, 82–6
    battles against Farrukh Siyar, 74–6
    Chief Khalsa Diwan, 173–4
    Dal, 79–80, 82, 87
    first five, 55–7
    formation of, 53–5
    as Guru, 64–5
    Ranjit Singh and, 129, 162
    Sher Singh and, 138–9
    Tat, 172–3
Khan, Abdus Samad, 74–5, 78, 93
Khan, Alif, 51–2
Khan, Azim, 117–19
Khan, Dilawar, 52
Khan, Dost Muhammad, 119–20, 123
Khan, Husain, 52
Khan, Iftikhar, 45

Khan, Jabbar, 117
Khan, Jahan Dad, 111–12, 114–15
Khan, Mehdi Ali, 92
Khan, Mukhlis, 40
Khan, Muzaffar, 111, 119
Khan, Nawab Muzaffar, 114–15
Khan, Nizamuddin, 98
Khan, Osman, 69
Khan, Painda, 57
Khan, Shah Nawaz, 81
Khan, Sher Muhammad, 60
Khan, Suhrab, 75
Khan, Wazir, 59–61, 63, 69–70
Khan, Wazir Fateh, 112–14
Khan, Yahiya, 93
Khan, Zain, 88
Khan, Zakariya, 74–6, 78–81, 93
Khatri caste, 24
Khusru (son of Jahangir), 38
Koh-i-noor diamond, 112–13, 161
Komagata Maru episode, 175–7, 180
Kothari, Rajni, 11, 212
Kshatriyas, origin of, 3–4

Lahore
    Afghan occupation, 82–7
    British control, 152–6
    under Ranjit Singh, 97–9
    Sikh attack on, 84
    Sikh commerce, 88
    Singh Sabha, 171–2
    Treaty of (1846), 152–4
    as urban center, 168
Lake, Lord, 102
land reform, 77–8, 87, 167
    see also agriculture
langar (communal kitchens), 27–8, 30
language, political division and, 203–8
Lawrence, Henry, 154–5, 159–61, 164
Lawrence, John, 164, 168
Littler, Sir John, 146
Lodhi, Daulat Khan, 21, 26
Lohgarh, 74
Longowal, Sant Harchand Singh, 223, 225
Lubana, Lakhi Shah, 47
Lucknow Pact, 186

A NOTE ABOUT THE AUTHOR

Patwant Singh is well known for his books and articles on India, international affairs, the environment and the arts, which have been published in India, Europe, and North America. He has broadcast frequently on television and radio in many countries, and travelled and lectured all over the world, often as the guest of governments. He lives in New Delhi.

Praise for *The Surrender*

"Wonderfully smart and sexy and witty and moving."
— *Publishers Weekly*

"A small masterpiece of erotic writing." — LEON WIESELTIER

"A fierce and funny book, intimidating and inviting in equally big doses." — DAVITT SIGERSON, author of *Unfaithful*

"Genuinely daring in its self-exposure. . . . Surely the greatest hymn to the transcendent powers of sodomy since the Marquis de Sade." — *Village Voice*

"Toni Bentley has done nearly the unimaginable: she has written about a profane act in a sacred manner, which is the hallmark of any great writer."
— BRUCE WAGNER, author of *I'll Let You Go* and *The Chrysanthemum Palace*

"Arousing, fascinating, and beautifully written, Toni Bentley's *The Surrender* is a unique testimonial to one woman's passion and intellect. Think *Story of O* with a high IQ and a sense of humor. . . . Bentley is shameless, brazen, and hot."
— JERRY STAHL, author of *Permanent Midnight* and *I, Fatty*

"The art of talking dirty has come late to women, but when we get it—and Toni Bentley has—the pages burst into flames."
— NANCY FRIDAY, author of *Women on Top* and *My Secret Garden*

"An extraordinary book, *The Surrender* is written by a real woman with an ax, and an ass, to grind. It's touching, even heroic, possessing, like its author, more than one exciting passage." —BARRY HUMPHRIES

"What Bentley has achieved in these pages is something rare and unexpected. Hers is an erotic journey neither prurient nor grandiose, resulting in a work of high literary ambition rendered unforgettable by its unflinching candor."
—DAVID M. FRIEDMAN, author of *A Mind of Its Own: A Cultural History of the Penis*

"Toni Bentley has gone into territory other writers are afraid of, and that has been considered male territory at that, and done so bravely and sexily."
—PHILIP WEISS, author of *American Taboo: Murder in the Peace Corps*

Also by Toni Bentley

Winter Season: A Dancer's Journal

Holding On to the Air: An Autobiography
(by Suzanne Farrell with Toni Bentley)

Costumes by Karinska

Sisters of Salome

The
SURRENDER
An Erotic Memoir

Toni Bentley

ReganBooks
An Imprint of HarperCollins Publishers

A hardcover edition of this book was published in 2004 by ReganBooks, an imprint of HarperCollins Publishers.

HarperCollins books may be purchased for educational, business, or sales promotional use. For information please write: Special Markets Department, HarperCollins Publishers Inc., 10 East 53rd Street, New York, NY 10022.

FIRST PAPERBACK EDITION PUBLISHED 2005

Designed by Kris Tobiassen
Cover painting by John Kacere

The Library of Congress has cataloged the hardcover edition as follows:
Bentley, Toni.
    The surrender : an erotic memoir / Toni Bentley. — 1st ed.
      p. cm.
    ISBN 0-06-073246-6
    1. Bentley, Toni. 2. Women — United States — Sexual behavior — Case studies. 3. Women — United States — Biography. 4. Ballet dancers — United States — Biography. 5. Anal sex. I. Title.
HQ29.B45 2004
306.77 — dc22
  [B]   2004050807

ISBN-10: 0-06-073247-4 (pbk.)
ISBN-13: 978-0-06-073247-9 (pbk.)

05 06 07 08 09 RRD 10 9 8 7 6 5 4 3 2 1

Virginia Woolf believed that no woman had succeeded in writing the truth of the experience of her own body—that women and language both would have to change considerably before anything like that could happen.

—CLAUDIA ROTH PIERPONT

I once loved a man so much that I no longer existed—all Him, no Me. Now I love myself just enough that no man exists—all Me, no Them. They all used to be God, and I used to be a figment of my own imagination; now men are figments of my imagination. Same game, different positions. I don't know how to play any other way. Someone must be on top, someone on bottom. Side by side is a bore. I tried it once for a few wildly disorienting minutes. Equality negates progress, prevents action. But a top and a bottom, well, they can get to the moon and back before equals can negotiate who pays, who gets laid, and who gets the blame.

My transformation, however, was not from bottom to top, but from bottom to bottom: from my wretched emotional submission to my blessed sexual submission. This is the story of my switch—and of paying its price. Very expensive. Priceless.

The SURRENDER

THE HOLY FUCK

> This pleasure is such that nothing can interfere with it, and the object that serves it cannot, in savoring it, fail to be transported to the third heaven. No other is as good, no other can satisfy as fully both of the individuals who indulge in it, and those who have experienced it can revert to other things only with difficulty.
>
> **—DONATIEN DE SADE**

His was first. In my ass.

I don't know the exact length, but it's definitely too big—just right. Of medium width, neither too slender nor too thick. Beautiful. My ass, tiny, a teenage boy's, tight, and tightly wound. Twenty-five years of winding as a ballet dancer. Since age four, the age when I first declared war on my daddy. Turning out the legs from the hips just winds up that pelvic floor like a corkscrew. I worked my gut all my life standing at that ballet barre. Now it is being unworked.

His cock, my ass, unwinding. Divine.

As he enters me I let go, millimeter by millimeter, of the tensing, pulling, tightening, gripping. I am addicted to extreme physical endurance, the marathon of uncoiling intensity. I release my muscles, my tendons, my flesh, my anger, my ego, my rules, my censors, my parents, my cells, my life. At the same time I pull and suck and draw him inward. Opening out and sucking in, one thing.

Bliss, I learned from being sodomized, is an experience of eternity in a moment of real time. Sodomy is the ultimate sexual act of trust. I mean you could really get hurt—if you resist. But pushing past that fear, by passing through it, literally, ah the joy that lies on the other side of convention. The peace that is past the pain. Going past the pain is key. Once absorbed, it is neutralized and allows for transformation. Pleasure alone is mere temporary indulgence, a subtle distraction, an anesthetization while on the path to something higher, deeper, lower. Eternity lies far, far beyond pleasure. And beyond pain. The edge of my ass is the sexual event horizon, the boundary to that beyond from which there is no escape. Not for me, anyway.

I am an atheist, by inheritance. I came to know God experientially, from being fucked in the ass—over and over and over again. I am a slow learner—and a gluttonous hedonist. I am serious. Very serious. And I was even more surprised than you are now by this curiously rude awakening to a mystic state. There it was: God's big surprise, His subtle humor and potent presence, manifested in my ass—well, it sure is one way to get a skeptic's attention.

Anal sex is about cooperation. Cooperation in an endeavor of aristocratic politics, involving rigid hierarchies, feudal positions, and monarchist attitudes. One is in charge, the other obedient. Entirely in charge, entirely obedient. There is no democratic, affirmative-action safety net swinging below ass-fuckers. But they'd best be of firm action, very firm. You can't half-ass butt-fuck. It would be a travesty. There are no understudies, no backups, for anal Cirque du Soleil. It's a high-wire act—all the way up.

The truth always shows itself with the ass. A cock in an ass operates like the arrow on a lie-detector test. The ass doesn't know how to lie, it can't lie: it hurts, physically, if you lie. The pussy, on the other hand, can lie at the mere entry of a dick in the room—does so all the time. Pussies are designed to fool men with their beckoning waters, ready opening, and angry owners.

I've learned so much, maybe the thing of most importance, from getting fucked in the ass—how to surrender. All I learned from the other hole was how to feel used and abandoned.

My pussy proposes the question; my ass answers. Ass-fucking is the event in which Rainer Maria Rilke's hallowed dictum to "live the question" is, in fact, finally embodied. Anal penetration resolves the dilemma of duality that is introduced and magnified by vaginal penetration. Ass-fucking transcends all opposites, all conflicts—positive and negative, good and bad, high and low, shallow and deep, pleasure and pain, love and death—and unifies them, renders all one. This, for me, is therefore The Act. Butt-fucking offers spiritual resolution. Who knew?

If I were asked to choose for the rest of my life only one place of penetration, I would choose my ass. My pussy has been too wounded by false expectations and uninvited entries, by movements too selfish, too shallow, too fast, or too unconscious. My ass, knowing only him, knows only bliss. The penetration is deeper, more profound; it rides the edge of sanity. The direct path through my bowels to God has become clear, has been cleared.

Norman Mailer sees the sexual routes in reverse: "So that was how I finally made love to her, a minute for one, a minute for the other, a raid on the Devil and a trip back to the Lord." But Mailer is a man, a perpetrator, a penetrator, not a recipient, not a submissive. He hasn't been, I assume, in my compromising position.

My yearning is so large, so gaping, so cavernous, so deep, so long, so wide, so old and so young, so very young, that only a big cock buried deep in my ass has ever filled it. He is that cock. The cock who saved me. He is my answer to every man who came before him. My revenge.

I see his cock as a therapeutic instrument. Surely only God could have thought of such a cure for my bottomless wound—the wound of the woman whose daddy didn't love her enough. Perhaps the wound is not psychological in source at all, but truly the space inside that yearns for God. Perhaps it is merely the yearning of a woman who thinks she cannot have Him. A woman whose daddy told her long ago that there is no God.

But I want God.

Getting fucked in the ass gives me hope. Despair hasn't got a chance when his cock is in my ass, making room for God. He opened up my ass and with that first thrust he broke my denial of God, broke my shame, and exposed it to the light. The yearning is no longer hidden; now it has a name.

This is the backstory of a love story. A backstory that is the whole story. A second hole story, to be entirely accurate. Love from inside my backside. Colette declared that you couldn't write about love while in its heady hold, as if only love lost resonates. No hindsight for me in this great love but rather behind-sight—cited from the eye of my behind. This is a book where the front matter is brief and the end matter is all. After all, my end does matter. When you've been ass-fucked as much as I have, things get both very philosophical and very silly very quickly. My brain has been rocked along with my guts.

Having a cock in her ass really gives a woman focus. Receptivity becomes activity, not passivity. There's just a whole lot to do. His cock pierces my yang—my desire to know, control, understand, and analyze—and forces my yin—my openness, my vulnerability—to the surface. I cannot do this alone, voluntarily. I must be forced.

He fucks me into my femininity. As a liberated woman, it is the only way I can go there and retain my dignity. Turned over, ass in the air, I have little choice but to succumb and lose my head. This is how I can have an experience my intellect would never allow, a betrayal to Olive Schreiner, Margaret Sanger, and Betty Friedan, and an affront, from the rear, to many modern "feminists." Oh, but once there, there is no going back—not to control, not to being on top, not to men more feminine than me. This is simply how my liberation manifested itself. Emancipation through the back door would never be, for any rational woman, a choice. It can only happen as a gift. A surprise. A big surprise.

This story is about my coming to experience—and sometimes understand—terms that allude to spiritual endeavor. I have learned more of their meaning and power through being sodomized than through any other teaching.

Anal sex is, for me, a literary event. The words first started flowing while he was actually buried deep in my ass. His pen to my paper. His marker to my blotter. His rocket to my moon. Funny where one derives inspiration. Or how one gets the message.

I knew after my initiation that I must write it all down. To keep track, bear witness to myself, to him, to the harmonic energy we generated. Enough to burn holes through the parameters of my existing world. Enough for the word God to take on meaning. Enough for gratitude to flow like water.

I didn't want, afterward, just a memory. Memory would inevitably mar the truth with the vanity of nostalgia and the self-pity of lost desire. I wanted documentation, like a police log, which noted at the time—or moments later, an hour at most—the details of the crime, the crime of breaking and entering my ass, my heart. This record would say: this did happen, this did indeed come to pass in my own life, under my own watch.

Besides, if I didn't write it all down, no one would ever believe it—least of all me. I didn't believe it two hours after he left my bed. So I wrote it all down to make it last longer. To make it real. Words seemed the only way to mark the spot, to preserve my transitory experience of eternity. This is a testamentary document. Do not miss the message, distracted by the profanity of the act.

I am, you see, a woman who has been in search of surrender my whole life—to find something, someone, to whom I could subsume my ego, my will, my miserable mortality. I tried various religions and various men. I even tried a religious man. And then he found me, the agnostic who demanded my submission.

"Bend over," he'd say, gently, firmly. I can hear it now—echoing in the bowels of my being.

Ass-fucking is the great anti-romantic gesture—unless of course, like me, your idea of romance begins on your knees with your face in a pillow. Poetry, flowers, and promises till-death-do-us-part have no place in the backland. Ass-entry involves the hard edge of truth, not the soft folds of sentimentality inherent in romantic love. But butt-fucking is more intimate than pussy-fucking. You risk showing your shit, as metaphor and reality. You let a man into your bowels—your deepest space, the space that all of your life you are taught to ignore, hide, keep quiet about—and consciousness is born. Who needs diamonds, pearls, and furs? Those who've never been where I have been. The promised land, the Kingdom.

If you can let a man ass-fuck you—and only the truly sensitive lover should have that privilege—you will learn to trust not only him but yourself, totally out of control. And beyond control lies God.

Humiliation is my greatest devil, but when the eye of my terror is entered, I experience my fear as unfounded. It is through this physical surrender, this forbidden pathway, that I have found my self, my voice, my spirit, my courage—and the cackle of the crone. This is no feminist treatise about equality. This is the truth about the beauty of submission. The power in submission. To me, you see, I have happened upon the great cosmic joke, God's supreme irony.

Enter the exit. Paradise waits.

BEFORE

THE SEARCH

Finding Paradise began decades ago with my search for God. I've been looking for Him since I was five, when my family moved to the Bible Belt. Everyone there seemed to know God personally except me. I asked my father. He was right about everything. "No, there is no God," he explained. "That is for people who need it. We don't."

But I did. Everyone at school was God-fearing and churchgoing. Could they all be wrong, and their parents, too? I was certified at birth an atheist. The deed was done. I figured that I could break the big news to all my classmates that God didn't exist, or I could investigate God on my own, just in case they were right about Him.

Now I think that one can come to believe in two ways. Either you are indoctrinated by your family and that belief stays with you for life, despite rebellion or evidence to the contrary; or you have an actual experience of God that is powerful enough to contradict your original indoctrination. So I assumed a difficult identity: that of the atheist who longs to believe—but can't. Preordained doubt always left me yearning for a God who couldn't exist. The Conflict was born, the Search began.

The previous year, at age four, I had begun ballet classes. This simple, once-a-week affair developed over the course of the next two decades into a ten-year professional career in one of the world's best dance companies. My mother's original intention, however, was simply to give me a physical workout to encourage my nonexistent appetite, and to keep me out of team sports that used balls: as a child, I had an outright terror of balls of any size heading in my direction. Ballet had no balls, and thus my fears were allayed. I concentrated instead on cute outfits, red ballet slippers, and highly controlled movements.

It was in the world of ballet that my investigation of God found its greatest laboratory. Quite simply, all the best dancers believed in God—each and every one. I conducted several private surveys over the years, and continued my God-watch right through my professional career, where the evidence was the strongest. In ballet school, around 60 to 70 percent of the young ladies believed in God; among those who had crossed the hurdle and become one of the chosen few for the company, the percentage rose to about 95 percent. I deduced that the key to these dancers' superiority lay in their ability to believe. They retained faith when things went badly. When I had a bad class, I was bad, which then led to more bad classes. When they had a bad class, they believed it was a "lesson," "God's will," a blip on the screen, and proceeded to have a good class next time and therefore improve in a steady and predictable manner. Being an atheist, I had no one to blame; self-doubt blossomed in proportion to my bad classes.

After ten years of this kind of training, even a good class looked bad to me; I had perfected not only my pliés but my ability to criticize myself. I sure wished I could put those bad classes on God like the other girls—what a relief it would have been. But they were living under an "illusion," while I held up the banner of truth, and so I soldiered on, a martyr to my atheism. God, I was jealous. Not of their dancing—of their faith.

My anxiety about this haunting intangible found a productive outlet when, at age eleven, I taught myself to crochet from a book. My mother knitted and had taught me the two-needle knit-one-purl-one routine, but there was always the possibility of a lost stitch, discovered too late to correct. The risk of this appalled me. With crocheting, however, there were not only far more possibilities for patterns but there was also no way to lose a stitch.

I began with scarves and berets and graduated to ponchos, turtleneck sweaters, bags of every size, lacy blouses with ruffles, ties for men, bedspreads, and intricate doilies made with very fine sparkling thread. All those stitches, all that yarn and mercerized cotton, all those pastel colors, in and out, up and around, winding and unwinding, knot after knot. I was fast, I was good, I was compulsive, and I was relentless with my hook and thread—everyone in my family wore some strange woolly item I had made for them. I always had several projects going simultaneously, so my hands never rested.

Stitchery, I see now, was a perfect repository for my ambitious anal tendencies: each article grew in a controlled and foreseeable manner, and was not subject to the irrational chaos of my existential anxieties. I crocheted my way right through adolescence while sewing ribbons on my toe shoes and attempting to emulate the ethereal faith of my peers.

I believe now that dancing is about two things: good behavior and faith made visible. For me the first was easy, the second impossible—hence more desirable. Being a dancer was my earliest, and perhaps most earnest, attempt to have faith. But it was like trying to be a nun without believing in God. I had effort in abundance, but I could not will faith.

Denying myself food all day long while dancing all day long seemed a good place to begin trying, however. At least I was exercising some self-control, making sure that my body would be as svelte as those belonging to the believing girls. I could do that part without God. Just don't eat until the evening. It felt good. Powerful. With food—or, rather, without food—I could compete with the believers. Why, I could even be thinner than a few of them. I learned early how to transcend pain, deny pain: the bloody toes and strained tendons, the horrid loneliness of being an atheist. Very useful. If I could deny enough, I reasoned, perhaps I could even deny my denial of God.

I became a professional dancer at age seventeen and began performing in public eight times a week. It was then that I started crossing myself before going onstage. I had seen the best dancer in all the world do this, and I thought perhaps this was her secret. So I tried it, in the wings, alone, unseen, before an entrance. It was like performing one more step in the ballet. I wanted it to mean something. And it did. Though it did not bring God into my consciousness, it did demonstrate my belief that ritual was the way to invoke Him, in the unlikely event that He should ever be willing to take me on.

On tour in Paris one summer, I started collecting rosaries from the antique stores on the Boulevard St. Germain—old ones, with chips in the mother-of-pearl. I figured that if they were old and European they would already be suffused by the faith of previous believers and thus, despite my miserable Darwinism, some of their faith might rub off on me. I wore one as a necklace for a while, though I was told it was sacrilege. No matter, I needed that rosary around my neck, massaging its history into my heathen skin.

The rosaries led me to the saints. By age eighteen, I was reading voraciously about them all—Francis, Thomas, Jerome, the two Teresas—but I then honed in on the women who starved, who bled, who beat themselves with birch branches, who licked the oozing wounds of lepers, who woke up screaming in the middle of the night, pierced by God's love. This was really interesting stuff. I briefly entertained the idea of switching professions from ballet dancing—already rather nunlike in its dedications—to being a saint. Certainly nothing seemed more worthwhile, and sainthood appeared to demand the disciplines with which I already had substantial experience: self-control and self-denial. Just how much pain and suffering could I endure, could I choose, could I cause for myself? Testing my strength in this way sounded immensely attractive.

But after considerable consideration, I reconsidered: becoming a saint would entail even more pain than I could imagine. And what if one suffered all that pain and still didn't see God, still didn't have that mystical union? The risk was very high indeed. Besides, I didn't want to suffer just to suffer. Dancing had taught me about pain for gain, pain for beauty. Pain for pain was self-indulgent, whereas my youthful masochism was both ambitious and realistic. Saint Teresa of Avila would have no competition from me.

Instead, I would stick to dancing and continue plunging my toes into the beautiful, tight, shiny sheaths called pointe shoes. And there was the miracle, made manifest daily on my very own feet. Despite blistered and bloody evidence to the contrary, my feet didn't hurt at all while ensconced in the shoes, while dancing. They only hurt when the shoes came off, when my foot was released from its satin prison. This curious experience, the ironic marriage of physical discomfort and euphoria, taught me the power of transcendence. My pink pointe shoes became my fetishistic ally, my crown of thorns, my bed of nails. I adored my toe shoes.

Alongside my saint obsession, I developed a passion for reading. This passion, I came to believe, detracted from my ultimate success as a dancer by luring me from the circumscribed, nonverbal world of movement to the limitless plains of thought. The Book Phase included: Simone Weil (beyond my scope to emulate); Nietzsche (Thus Spake he to me); Henry Miller (the romance of poverty in

Paris!); D. H. Lawrence (John Thomas and Lady Jane); Anaïs Nin (sexual liberation between the sheets and on the page—in Paris); Freud (incest is best—or at least inevitable); Thomas Mann (the poetic profundity of X-rays); Henry James (I *am* Isabel Archer, living in the wrong era, in the wrong wardrobe); Virginia Woolf (diary after diary right into the river); Erich Fromm; Eric Hoffer; Ernest Becker (*The Denial of Death,* every page underlined in red); and Søren Kierkegaard (seven tomes in a row, with voluminous notes on either legal pads or index cards . . . I loved Kierkegaard).

These books and their revelations constituted my secret life until I was nearly twenty. Then I lost my virginity. And although my deepest interests have perhaps never changed, they immediately became irrevocably diverted to deriving answers—dancing had presented all the questions—from experience, not only books.

But while all this reading and searching for external connection went on in the early morning and late at night, my deepest allegiance and dependence belonged elsewhere during the day: on the walls of the dance studio, where I could not escape my savage self.

MY MIRROR, MY MASTER

Ballet dancing is learned in front of a mirror. Hours and hours and hours and hours in front of a mirror. As a little girl, as a serious student, and then as a professional adult in both classes and rehearsals, I learned that every arch of the foot, every glance of the eye, every angle of the arm, every turn of the leg, every smile, every grimace, every strain is simultaneously performed and witnessed by one's self, that nebulous entity called consciousness. One becomes both subject and object.

I have calculated that in twenty-five years of dancing I spent approximately eighteen hundred hours performing in front of a live audience—and eighteen thousand hours practicing in front of the huge floor-to-ceiling mirrors that are a principal feature of every dance studio. This relentless and intense daily exposure has an acute effect on one's so-called self-image. Contrary to popular supposition, it is not narcissism or vanity that is fostered by so much time spent scrutinizing oneself. Quite the opposite. We watch ourselves with eyes trained to be critical, competitive, and comparative. Yes, every now and then, the view is pleasing, beautiful, something worth looking at. But far more often it is the image of an imperfection—of body, of line, of face, of outfit, of movement. Frequently, this single flaw actually seems to obliterate all one's efforts, even one's entire existence.

The mirror shows the impossibility of perfection. And thus a curious intimacy was born: I was constantly shaping, changing, improving, and restyling myself, while the mirror—cold and constant—sat in judgment, like God. The mirror was now jailer and savior, the source of self-contempt and yet the only source of affirmation. I was humbled before the mighty looking glass with its illusion of three dimensions in two. I submitted completely. While God felt distant, the authority of the mirror over me felt absolute.

I eventually realized that, like Dorian Gray, I had relinquished my entire perception of myself to my reflection. The troublesome result of this submission to what I saw—me, but flipped—was that once onstage, where the orchestra pit and black hole of an audience replaced my own image in the mirror, I could not even feel my body move. I existed solely in the mirror; onstage I was my own shadow, a vapor. Only the next morning, back at the barre, could I find myself in the mirror and once again confirm my existence.

At the age of twenty-three, while still dancing, I attempted to marry God. It was all very sudden. His father was a minister and he was a believer, and so my searching, frustrated atheist self tried to get religion the only way she could: by marrying into the family. My husband was the first man who reflected back to me an image of myself preferable to the one in the mirror. Thus I quickly transferred my dependence to his point of view. Now I existed, but differently. He adored what he saw and told me all about it; it was a lovely thing. Once again, I had good reason to suspect that I had an existence.

As time went on, however, he became far less reliable to show me to myself on a daily basis. He was an acquisitive man of many artistic passions, and others eventually took my place. My reflection became blurred; too many fingerprints upon the once-clear looking glass. Smeared, reduced to a smudge in his mind, I found myself dancing numbly in the black hole one more time. God had turned off the spotlight.

Where am I? I cannot see. I cannot feel. I must not be.

SEX HISTORY

I had my first orgasm, alone, at age sixteen, after going to a French porn movie called *Exhibition* at an Upper East Side art house in New York City with an equally curious girlfriend. Despite the legitimate location, this was my first moviegoing experience where my feet stuck to the floor in front of my seat; this was rather disturbing to my virgin soul.

While watching the woman in this movie masturbate, however, I realized that I had simply not persisted long enough with my own explorations to get to the big bang. I went straight home after the movie and imitated my new mentor, with instant results. Thus began my long and secret career as an aspiring porn star.

I continued practicing for my debut, but saw no reason to employ a man for the job. A year later, a geeky young boy put his tongue down my throat at a party while pressing something very hard up against my belly. This confirmed my suspicions. Men were gross.

Sometime later, a handsome womanizer who knew I was a virgin persisted in pursuing me, and managed to change all these negative feelings. He was famous, strong, charismatic, and sexy as hell. Don Juan. After much resistance, which amused him, I allowed him in. Excitement, pressure, a pool of blood, and awakening.

I had never seen an erect penis before. Totally shocking. But once he started in on me, I got over it. He dominated me—physically, completely—and it was the most thrilling thing that had ever happened to me. I don't believe, however, that I ever had an orgasm with him: I was too excited. And totally in love with him. He suggested a world beyond my own.

I fell in love for two years although the affair lasted less than three months. Looking back, I now realize that his first sexual comment to me was, "You have a great ass." Must have been my fate, even then. But I didn't know it for many years. I look good, from the back.

After I lost my virginity, my pussy became a place of great interest to me. I had not realized until then that that hidden hole below my waist was the entrance to my heart. Others came to the now-opened gate, and I proceeded to have what everyone else seemed to be having: consecutive monogamous relationships of varying lengths. It never occurred to me that you didn't have to become monogamous the moment a guy put his tongue in your mouth. That's just the way it was—sealed with saliva—and I didn't have enough experience to think that I might have a choice in the matter. The second and third boyfriends—both "nice" and "appropriate" young men—introduced me to orgasms through oral sex and I became hooked on that, on their tongues, but not so much on them. The intercourse that followed just seemed like their part of the deal. And there were a few more boyfriends after them. Same thing.

The only time I had sex that was not defined by monogamy was with a stagehand I met in a bar. Long blond hair, gruff language, tattoos. I was having a drink with friends one night when he turned to me and whispered, "I want you to sit on my face."

"Excuse me?" I said. I had no idea what he was talking about. He thought I must be joking, but I wasn't. So he explained. I had another vodka, left the bar with him, and sat on his face. I'd never done that before. He had big hands that handled me like meat, prime. It was my second taste of being with a man who was "wrong" for me, a man with whom I knew there would be no "relationship." Fucking him, I felt the fantastic power of a completely other being crashing into mine. I could not lose myself with a peer, only with a man who was impossible.

But then I fell deeply, suddenly, and totally in love with the man who became my husband—it was like being hit with a cement block on the head, *crash,* and there I was at the altar—and bad boys were banished. It never even occurred to me to have an affair while I was married. I loved him too much, it was unthinkable.

He was my fate, my husband. But I had thought that meant my ending, my final destination, when, in fact, he was my beginning, my wretched beginning. God, that hurt. The profound disillusionment of having the great love of my life founder on the rocky road of reality was a blow too great for my own consciousness to bear, much less comprehend.

After ten years I left my husband. He couldn't see me any longer; and he never even knew I had an asshole. I had retired from dancing some years earlier because of a hip injury that had first surfaced six months into my marriage. Funny, that: life's wicked signposts. A friend says hips represent where you hold trust in your body. Hokum? Maybe. Either way, both my right hip joint and my trust were shot.

I became intolerable both to myself and my husband. A wailing banshee, a celibate nymphomaniac with a suitcase of resentments and matching lingerie. I listed fifty-two of the former and left with the latter. Freedom. Fear.

THE MASSEUR

This bed thy centre is, these walls thy sphere.

—JOHN DONNE

My first affair began a week after the end of my marriage. Amazing
what two phone calls can precipitate: one ended a ten-year relationship, and the other booked a one-hour massage that began the rest
of my life.

The adorable masseur. I had already had two massages from
him for my wounded hip, and I'd held my breath to conceal my desire: I was still married. But by the next massage I wasn't, and I took
my first bold step. I could tell that he was too professional to make
an overture, so I decided it was up to me. I planned beforehand that
if (ha!) I was aroused again, I would say something by the end of the
session—but what? I didn't want to embarrass myself; the risk
was high.

At the end of that third massage, dripping with a decade of

sublimated desire, I asked him in a general kind of way, "Do your clients ever get aroused?"

"Yeah," he ventured, and got up from a chair on the other side of the room to come back to the table where I was lying. "But I just let it be." He was young and handsome, with big blue eyes and soft full lips, but this was not the source of my attraction. It was those magic hands. He placed one below my throat and I lost all decency and self-control. He did not retreat but slid his hand under the sheet. In the next few hours, I learned about how his mouth and tongue held the same magic current as his hands, and I thought I would die from the pleasure he gave me. It was a dream of pleasure, of love—yes, love, physical love. And no fucking, just sucking.

When he left I was dazed: never had I been so receptive. My clit had come out of hibernation, no longer hiding, no longer scared, but reaching out, reaching for direct contact with heaven. For the first time, I was in submission to my own orgasms, trying only to survive the contractions, to stay conscious despite annihilating pleasure. I knew right then that my decision to leave my marriage and break those vows taken before God was worth it. Worth it all for those two hours. I was sure, of course, that it would not happen again. Why would I be so blessed when I also felt so guilty? Guilt, pleasure, and the impossible man: the ingredients of sexual ecstasy were becoming apparent.

I waited the requisite week, counting the days, and called for another massage, expecting nothing, wanting everything. I jumped when the doorbell rang: bathed, perfumed, and obsessed. Again it happened. Again, and again, and again.

One day he suggested a couple of rules—he'd been thinking, like me, about how to make this thing happen when it shouldn't happen. He didn't play with clients: I was the first, so keep it quiet, very quiet. Of course. The other rule: no intercourse. No problem. "We're just going to play," he explained, and I came to understand just what playing really was. Fucking wasn't so interesting to me, anyway. At best it was a return offering for receiving a good licking. Now licking was the sole activity. And he never, ever, in all the time I knew him, took off his shoes. His shoes became our mutual marker that we were still within our limits of decency. Sort of.

He presented me with the first sex I'd ever had that I thought about in words, that I wanted to describe and preserve in words. And so the scribbling began. Every time he came, and left, I went straight to my notebook and wrote it all down. I was experiencing an impossible pleasure, and having it on paper would prove that the impossible existed.

I knew something profound had happened to me: I had shifted from being my small, hurt, wounded, and unhappy self to being a conduit of a pleasure that was far greater than myself, a pleasure that I did not own, but that I could feel. And I could not experience this in silence. I had to tell some unknown, undefined audience. Perhaps that audience was really me, my unbelieving atheist self being told by my transformed sexual self about hope.

He kisses my belly, inside my thighs, my pubic hair. Eventually with a very soft, very gentle tongue, contact is made with my pussy, my clit. My eyes open. I see his lovely eyes, looking at me, mouth buried in my cunt. My knees drop open 180 degrees, my feet press on the sides of his chest, my pussy is pushed into his mouth, contact, contact, contact. He is there a long time. I have many small, very intense orgasms. He moves his tongue and mouth quickly side to side, then stops on the tip, on my center, a tiny pinpoint where my whole being of emotion, power, and love are centered. Legs and belly convulse, contract, vibrate. Through these releases I know it's not over, not finished. Possessed, I explode. My torso rises off the table over and over, his tongue works furiously, my legs are all over, my arms flailing. I am crying, whimpering, never before so conscious of tears of joy, that someone had been so kind to me.

Every time I called, the pleasure was given and received. His tongue held close and soft and fast on my clitoris became the center of the world. And fingers everywhere—fingers on my clit, fingers in my pussy, fingers up my ass—how many tendrils can one man have? I stopped tipping him. But I did buy a series of ten massages at a reduced rate. He insisted, for his own moral welfare (and perhaps mine), that he always give me a massage—although on more than one occasion the massage came after we did.

I was surprised at how much I liked sucking his cock. It was because he had shown me love first, and filled with gratitude, I headed down. I gave this guy the first good blow job I had ever given, one that came from my guts and brought tears into my eyes. It was the first time I was that grateful to a man.

We never saw each other outside of the room in my apartment. We stayed in the bedroom, only going to the kitchen for liquids and the bathroom for rinses. The bedroom was the world. No dinners, no dates, only phone calls to make an appointment. Because my damaged hip had ended my dance career, the massages were paid for by insurance. Insurance for the resurrection of my deeply injured sexual desire.

I was obsessed with my masseur. I tried to fill the time between sessions, wondering, Did I live to see him, or did I see him so I could live? I learned with him that I am most alive, most observant, and most intelligent when sexually engaged. And I experienced for the first time the intense beauty of having a time and place for a lover where sexual pleasure is the mutual purpose, the only conscious intent. After all, you never know where a dinner date is going to end up. So often the conversation runs amok and preempts the possibility of sex afterwards. I like to know when I'm going to have sex—it's too important to leave to chance.

Boundaries around the erotic . . . my theory grew wings. A room, a bed, two bodies, music, no intrusions. This was the life I wanted to explore and did—once a week for over a year. "The frame is a border hermetically sealing-off the object, so that all you are experiencing, all that matters, is within that border," wrote Joseph Campbell. "It is a sacred field, and you become pure subject for a pure object." Ugliness, I realized, only enters my love life when real life does. Cars, calls, bills, mortgages, food, family, schedules, money—these are the subjects of controversy and control, and they destroy the erotic bond.

Did he love me? Did he fantasize about me? Did he dream of marrying me? Did he wonder if I had other men and hate it? Did I infiltrate all his waking moments? Did he wonder what our kids might look like? If mental obsession is the evidence of love, I don't think he was in love with me.

But he loved me in the time we were together. Did he focus all his attention on me? Was he gentle and nasty and charming and completely devoted to multiplying my pleasures? Oh yes, he loved me all right. And this kind of love became the kind I wanted. I began distrusting mental men, talking men, and love's verbal declarations. One cannot love by words alone. I had tried that. Giving and receiving words of love, however witty or Shakespearean, is a ruse propounded by poets with inept dicks. One loves by act. Language can clarify and explain and amuse, but it cannot change your being. Experience can.

Sure, I was in love with him. Until I wasn't. I don't believe love is only real when it endures for many years and is marked by the ring of marriage. My wedding ring had only confined me, robbing me, eventually, of freedom and love alike. Love, for me, exists only in a moment of choice in a moment of time: there is no other manifestation except for the one available right now. Repeating those moments is the key.

But the masseur was not real, I decided. He was only my transient sexual angel who kept reappearing with his heavenly message in my bedroom at preappointed hours. Perhaps, I thought, deep in my unexamined soul, I really am a conventional girl who simply got thrown out of orbit, and a boyfriend is what I need. Perhaps the masses knew something I didn't about men and women and love and sex. So I also tried dating. Six weeks per male, quick to sex, oral, but every time they fucked me I felt fucked over and fired them, one by one. They'd get in, get off, roll over, and I'd feel used and underpaid.

So I kept calling the masseur—whom I paid. It was a better deal.

Disappointment is a great teacher—if one survives the lacerations to one's romantic ideal. After my marriage ended I was willing, open, and angry, and nothing that others did or "society" suggested in terms of conducting relationships necessarily held any merit for me. Everything I knew hadn't worked, so I was free to try anything. Most of all, I had valuable firsthand experience that "relationships" that exist in "real life" sooner or later lose their erotic excitement. Not a particularly original notion, but one I now owned. At the same time, being a dreamer, I was adamant that there had to be another way. All was now backwards to me: fuck love and love sucking.

I was discovering that while the theatrical stage left me numb and afraid and invisible, the sexual stage brought out a spontaneous theatricality and confidence that I knew was my truest self—or at least the one that amused me most. So, like a sexual scientist, I set out to test my theories, to adjust them as needed, and to formulate new ones as they evolved. I had already lost everything, so I had nothing to lose. Thus I vacillated between experiments in the nightmare of attachment with nice-nice sex and the thrill of naughty sex without attachment—take your Tantra and shove it up your yoni.

There were only two rules that governed my behavior. One was relentlessly safe sex—I became the Queen of Condoms. The second was the importance of quality control. If the sex isn't awesome, or at least fascinating, get out, stop, shift gears, and change direction with minimum discussion. There were, as a result, plenty of discarded bodies floating in the moat around my castle, but the drawbridge was always down, inviting new specimens into my laboratory. They came in droves.

NEW YEAR'S EVE

A year later. A petite, Pre-Raphaelite redheaded dancer kept flirting with me at the gym where I exercised. She could tell I was a dancer, too: lean, hard-bodied, physically intense. I had never been with a woman, though I had thought about it plenty. The reality seemed far, far away. It wasn't quite as far as I had thought. She had been trying, she told me, to get this Young Man, who also worked out at the gym occasionally, to have sex with her, but had yet to succeed. She was recently out of a seven-year live-in disappointment. Heroin, lies, other women. Her mental masochism, like mine, needed a rest.

One day, I was at the gym in a corner stretching on a mat when I saw the Young Man nearby, resting between exercises. I had hardly ever noticed him before. He was self-effacing, quiet, and ventured carefully. Sitting, stretching over my toes, I asked him for a push on my back. It was not a sexual overture; I wanted a push. I got one.

His hands touched the middle of my back, moved up and down, pressing my tightness, and I released—even moaned a little. We said nothing. Just his firm fingers pushing deeply, consciously, up and down my back. Time stood still until he took his hands away and I lifted my head, flushed and clear-eyed, as if I'd just come.

We looked at each other, said nothing, stood, went through a fire-exit door into an empty hallway, and slowly pressed into each other, my back to the wall. No words: just eyes and an electric current with European voltage. So much power in one man's hands. It must, physically, be some kind of vibrational force, a quixotic dance of a million molecules. His touch was very strong, very unafraid, and yet so tender. And humble. My belly started contracting involuntarily, and he started trembling through his strength. Yielding, we slid down the wall, stunned. I had never before felt such immediate impact from a man's touch, much less from a stranger. I didn't even know his last name.

It was New Year's Eve that day. The redhead suggested to us both that we spend the midnight hour at her house. Still feeling the effects of his electric field, I agreed. I had no other plans. Neither did he. Would it be him? Her? Both? I didn't know, but I was so willing to find out. And thus fate had her three ways with us.

We convened at the redhead's house at 10:30. Now, this woman knew ambiance like she was born in a harem: red velvet curtains not only on every window but dividing every room; gold fixtures galore; no electric lighting, just candles and incense burning like in a Catholic church; sexy music emanating from unseen speakers; potted palms; naked images of herself in various theatrical guises on the walls; and mirrors, mirrors everywhere—a narcissist's nirvana. I was learning from this woman already, learning about myself, learning what I liked.

After a glass of champagne in crystal flutes at midnight, we ended up on her Persian carpet on some lush pillows watching Fred Astaire in *Top Hat*. The Young Man had never seen it before. He didn't see it that night, either. He and I were the first to touch, relinking from earlier that day. As we grasped hand to hand, she watched like a Cheshire cat, and slowly linked herself, too, to me, hands to legs.

Before long, they had conspired to remove my clothes, mesmerizing my body with touch. Four hands, two faces, male and female, urgent, loving, sexual, groping, they swept me up in waves of love. Gently, they fought over my pussy; he got there first, but she edged him out. The pleasure was illegal. What's wrong with girls with girls? Absolutely nothing. But I wanted to come in his mouth, and in my only move, I pulled his face into me. As I gave him all I had and then some, Fred was still twirling in his top hat on the muted black-and-white screen.

Then the redhead and I stripped him. He allowed it, willing and erect. She and I gathered like good girlfriends around his cock, which was hard, big, and beautiful. Four hands, two mouths. Every few minutes the Young Man raised his head to look down at the scene of angels praying together over his vertical altar. His eyes rolled back in his head, and with a smile and a groan he fell back into his pleasure. But he never came. She commented on his endurance. He said he'd always been that way. She seemed to know a whole lot about cocks and pussies, and I just sucked it all in. He was one of the blessed, she said, a man who can really take a woman on a ride. I found out later for myself just what kind of ride this could be.

Soon after, the redhead announced that she was tired and was going to bed. She showed us a futon that rolled out over the Persian carpet, kissed us both on the forehead, placed two condoms and a bottle of water beside the futon, and disappeared to her own bedroom. She was our fairy godmother, she had felt it between us, she had seen it, and she sanctioned it, even engineered it—despite the fact that she had wanted him. I'd never had a woman do that for me before. I loved the redhead and her house of Freudian mirrors.

And then the blessings really began. Thus far, there had been no fucking that night. Now love poured out of this guy's body like oil. When he entered me, I knew. I just knew. He fucked in love, not frenzy; in tenderness, not anger; in ease, not desperation. What his cock could do for me seemed to be the question he was answering. It did plenty for both of us. Finally, a fuck I liked. A new year, a new world.

I saw him once more, alone, before he went to Europe for two weeks, but I simply didn't have the courage to love him, so I got myself one of those temporary boyfriends—monogamy, weekends away, dinner parties, friends, plans. When the Young Man returned, he called, and I told him I had a boyfriend, I couldn't see him. He was too good to be real, I told myself, so I chose instead a small, jealous man who didn't even like to eat pussy. Why? Self-hatred, lack of faith, and a fear of what is beautiful: divorce can make you nuts. But after the boyfriend snooped in my diary one morning six weeks later and confronted me with questionable evidence—I had kissed the Young Man at the gym and had written it down—I fired him on the spot, my outrage being greater than his. I never saw him again.

So I continued to date some men (dinner) while fucking others (no dinner). I was learning a lot—well, two things anyway. I preferred sex on an empty stomach, and to eat alone with a good book.

MEN

Despite all this emerging knowledge, convention dies hard and I still kept trying out boyfriends—whom I always bitterly resented afterwards for allowing me to entrap myself. But between these misguided debacles there were several amusing forays. The impossibly handsome actor who modeled Jansen bathing suits but whose riveting blue eyes seemed to look into mine only to see their own reflection. It was the first time I witnessed a man's narcissism that was undoubtedly greater than mine—how unbecoming, I thought. His cock was huge and, I suppose, impressive, but it smelled antiseptic and I kept away. The big neighbor who looked like Nicolas Cage was a bit of a jerk, but he fucked so slow that I cried at the beauty, at the sadness. Then there was the other neighbor, the biker. I'd never had a Harley man; never done it before on a Harley, over a Harley. Lost an earring I loved. The cute newspaper boy: the cliché was too good to resist. And he did deliver.

I tried returning to a former boyfriend. Great friend, not a lover. Then there was the guy who held me fast with one arm, his tongue buried in my mouth, his cock vertical against me while madly waving with his free hand for a cab to take me away. This has become my favorite image of male ambivalence.

There was the magician who could produce my jack of hearts out of sealed cement only seconds after I handed it to him but who, remarkably for a trickster, couldn't eat pussy to save his life. Talents vary. One Paul Newman–like prospect found me at Starbucks and caught me with his eyes. He could ejaculate, stay hard, and come again, often three times in row. Remarkable. I wondered if they were three full orgasms, or if he had simply learned to parse out one big one to impress the girls. He even attempted boyfriend status, but his patronizing butt-patting made me crazy. One evening, when he arrived for a date and asked to hang his clean shirt for the next morning in my closet, I knew I was done with him. What presumption. Sex does not mean breakfast.

Happily, the beautiful boys—tall, svelte, toned, thoughtful, loving, full of poetry and music—never considered sleeping over, but they did not yet know how to fuck, either. I was intrigued by two feet guys. Sucking, kissing, rubbing my feet in stilettos, they garnered erections like steel. But was it me or my shoes? I do have some great shoes. They both had big cocks—about the height of my heels, strangely enough—dispelling any misconception I might have had that their fetish was compensatory.

A charming young Frenchman produced the thickest cock I'd ever seen up close. He knelt above me, shoving this enormous protrusion toward my mouth, saying "Suck it, suck it," with a strong French accent. It was the size of a corncob. I was terrified. Condoms didn't fit, they kept rolling back to the tip like a bad joke that was very funny. Finally, I rolled one on three inches with much cock to spare and we had a three-inch, fat fuck.

After seriously considering the evidence of my current sexual escapades, I concluded that I did not like intercourse. The Young Man had been a strange exception. Either they were not so big, and I felt little, and the whole event felt feeble: the Princess and the Pea. Or they were so big it hurt and my anger would increase with every thrust until I became the victim of a monstrous rage.

Besides, I almost never had an orgasm from fucking except for the one guy who would direct me to climb on top and "make" myself come. He would just lie there, rigid in body and cock, and I would follow his directive and rub my clit on his pubic bone. But, I thought, this was not coming from intercourse, this was masturbating with a live dildo. I ended up resenting his orders until my only defense, ironically, was *not* to come.

Every man who fucked me risked my contempt—and most earned it. The smart ones stayed away or insisted on friendship, while the arrogant ones plunged in to their enormous satisfaction— and eternal regret. There were also, of course, the romantics, who thought they wanted a woman like me—but they didn't, not really, not once they'd seen my version of romance.

Was I gay and wasting my time with men? I adore beautiful, feminine, bright women: if I was so anti-penetration and so clitorally oriented, maybe they were the way to go. But conquering men—or, rather my resentment of them—has always seemed a far more interesting challenge. I reckon every woman wants a cock between her legs, ultimately. The question is: Does she want one of her own, or can she tolerate one belonging to a man?

SCANTY PANTIES

It is perhaps no surprise, given my theatrical background, that props, costumes, and ceremony became increasingly essential components of my newly expanded private life. My bed became the stage for that intense human drama called sexual interplay. I knew from public performance that artifice, ambiance, and ritual could propel the participant into a state of truth and beauty far more effectively than thoughts or good intentions. In my bedroom, where I exchanged my tutus for corsets, my tiaras and toe shoes for blindfolds and stilettos, the poetic logic was obvious. And crotchless panties fit perfectly (they always do) into the tragicomedy that was now my sex life. This vastly underrated, overlooked undergarment is so rarely celebrated, or even mentioned, that I must digress for just a moment to rectify this enormous oversight.

While the thong has been elevated to a sexual status far beyond its actual utility, the crotchless panty is really where it's at, or at least where my clit is at. I actually—optimistically and sadly—bought my first pair while still married. Black, transparent little nylon bikinis without any crotch between the leg elastics. The moment I saw them—draped over a red silk hanger at a sex store I visited while in Copenhagen on vacation—I got a warm rush. Ah, another Danish souvenir to bring home along with my crotchless Little Mermaid statue. But this lonely item simply ended up gathering dust in the back of my underwear drawer—until found, washed, and resurrected in my new single life, years later. The first time I put them on for a lover was a brave day indeed. But they received a most encouraging reaction. I needed another pair. But where to shop?

Crotchless panties are usually found in sex-toy stores and occasionally, in small supply, at Frederick's of Hollywood, where the variety is also quite limited. Despite their titillating sell, Victoria's Secret stops just short of offering their slutty little panties with crotch slits. But where, after all, is "Victoria's Secret"? It sure isn't at their return address in Ohio. I guess this is where those masters at monitoring the boundary between decency and vulgarity draw the line to maintain their legitimacy. But the sex stores have a different reputation to maintain, and they are well stocked. Costing on average just slightly more than your basic cotton thong but far less than La Perla's little nothings, these crotchless wonders will definitely get you more bang for your buck.

Crotchless panties are actually little works of art, and the art is clearly in the details—or carefully placed lack of detail. They are, in short, pussy-framing devices—hence their great potential for lovers, even going so far as to guide those who are directionally challenged right into the center of the playing field. Contrary to popular assumption, they come in many different styles—each with its own *je ne sais quoi*. I currently own five styles, with a few duplicates of my favorites.

There is the very normal-looking bikini style—mine are deep purple—that upon closer inspection (which is the aim, after all) sport a very nasty little three-inch, black-lace-lined slit in the middle of the crotch that basically forms a glory hole for a searching tongue—or cock. In their apparent innocence, these are in some ways the naughtiest of the assortment—but then again perhaps not . . . There are the transparent black ones that carry the slit concept to infinity: the slit, red-ribbon-rimmed, simply runs from the waistband in front all the way down and around to the waistband in back. These are actually very practical panties, allowing for clit, cunt, and ass access, although with one's legs held together, they appear quite decent.

Then there is my little-girl pair: white with tiny pink roses. These are stylistically quite complex. While they retain the usual waist of a panty, the entire crotch has been excised, leaving only two delectable little elastics traveling between one's legs with zippo in between except one's very own jewelry box. Carefully coiffed pubic hair in front acquires a really lovely triangular frame in this style, and I'm especially charmed by the petite pink bows decorating the crucial junctures where skin and panty meet. Taken as a whole, this truly "crotchless" design is perhaps the most elegant of the bunch, but I'm also fond of a rather amusing pair that has clearly been based on the design of a ballerina's tutu. Sporting a split thong between the legs and a witty little tutulike black gauze ruffle around the waistband, they are quite adorable.

But the very best of all, my favorite, is the Butterfly. I have these in both black and powder pink. These are the most expensive and it is clear why—they have the least fabric of all. These petite, delicate works of art best embody the great irony of this particular garment: they are classy crotchless panties.

G-string style, the upper pubic area is designed and woven in the shape of a spread-eagled butterfly complete with wings sprinkled with beads and shimmering sequins. I just adore glitter, pomp, and circumstance around my pussy—I'd wear red velvet curtains with gold-tasseled tiebacks between my legs if I could. But the real pièce de nonrésistance in these particular panties lies in the two slender elastic straps that connect the lower wings of the butterfly to the center of the thin elastic waistband in the back. Properly placed, alongside the outer pussy lips, they pull up ever so slightly, visually accentuating from the front the beginning of one's slit.

But one day those two little straps slipped—ooh la la!—and demonstrated yet again that accident is the mother of invention. With those elastics placed securely inside, on either side of one's clit and hood, the butterfly soars. Oh my, oh my, oh my—that feels good. And it looks absolutely beyond porn queen, like the summit of high art—like a Modigliani by Mondrian.

To be so framed, positioned, and exposed and then have a lover find his target—well, I could come right now just thinking about it. It seems to me to be, at the very least, respectful to utilize these various crotchless darlings to aid and abet those men whose only object is my clit and whose only reward is my clit.

HOUND SEX

In those first years after my marriage, I discovered that the great antidote to bad fucking—or no fucking—is fantasy, and that fantasy's greatest aide is the Pussy Hound: the man who lives to dive. Every woman should have at least one; it can mend years, even centuries, of patriarchal ramming. Thank heaven, then, that women's liberation has fostered what appears to be an entire generation of this particular man: the male masochist who can now masquerade, legitimately, as the feminist man, the male lesbian. They can be spotted on street corners everywhere. I say grab one, girls, and give him a job!

The masseur had taught me how to make my orgasm, not his, the main event, how to allow oral sex to compete successfully, even override, intercourse. After all, for women, cunnilingus is a much more dependable pleasure. This is a hard lesson for a nice girl to learn, what with so many dicks always demanding attention. Hounds help. And so do crotchless panties. In fact, it is with a headstrong Hound that crotchless panties find their true place.

First as a good girl, then as a married woman who didn't dare imagine having sex with anyone but her husband, I'd had a fairly impoverished fantasy life. But once the masseur came along and became a real-life fantasy, that potent world was cracked open and my desires came tumbling out.

All those unlived scenes told me a lot about myself. There was the rich woman who pays for cunnilingus—and I did pay, cash. There was the trashy girl in six-inch heels and crotchless wonders— "Lick my shoes! Lick them clean!" And then there was the virgin in Victorian white cotton whose rich father pays the "healer" to give her her first orgasm: it is the only way to save her life, for she is, of course, mortally ill. She resists mightily, feigning sleep and frigidity, and comes like a rolling avalanche—brought back from the brink of death by the anonymous roving tongue.

The whore fantasies were prolific and my fee enormous. I found it fascinating that the man who materialized in these heated encounters was more often than not almost physically repugnant to me—a beast-man. Being a sucker for beauty in general, I gave this unexpected scenario a great deal of thought. I concluded that every woman must have a man—real or imaginary—to whom she is a whore, for whom she is a whore. I have always wanted, alas, to be some man's bimbo. I don't mean just acting like a slut or being desired for sex alone, although these are both excellent goals. I mean that the sex is for profit—be it financial or otherwise—more than for physical desire. If a woman is driven by a physical craving, she is vulnerable; with a beast-man, obviously, she retains her power. But that is not the most interesting part.

I also discovered that imaginary sex with a man for gain is incredibly sexy. One's inner whore gets a real workout, so to speak. Selling one's sexuality, by choice, frees a woman's desires from the incriminations, restrictions, and suppressions of good-girlness that proliferate when one is "in love." And thus the paradoxical surprise: love is released as gratitude in great gushes of incredible uncensored sexual energy. With my fantasy beast-men I achieved orgasms that were, finally, entirely guiltless; they were, after all, my job. You see, I have an impeccable work ethic, whereas in matters of the heart I have no idea of my rights, much less their application. When sex becomes my work, I'm home free—cash in hand.

I found that if I allowed these various fantasies to rove uncensored, they would uncover parts of myself that were otherwise entirely hidden. I became particularly interested in the fraction of time that preceded the moment of orgasmic inevitability. What thought, what dynamic, what image would cause that final, magical, loss of control? That was the pivotal moment that seemed to join consciousness to the divine—and more often than not, I found this lofty pathway to be inspired by completely slutty activities (see above—and below). This meeting of the galaxies in the gutter fascinates me still.

I learned, for example, that I often reach the point of inevitability through the inspiration of a dire "last-resort" thought or image that renders me, my pussy, my clit, the most exposed, the most seen, the most helpless. Loss of responsibility—it's-not-my-fault—does it every time.

My OB-GYN fantasy works extremely well: I am the guinea pig, for a fee of five hundred dollars—I really need the money; it's only for the money—for the final semester of classes for the advanced medical students. I am behind a big white sheet, just doing it for the dough, awake, and above it all—this is work. On the other side of the sheet my feet are in stirrups, my thighs are wide, and my pussy is spread for show-and-tell. The doctor teaching the class first uses a pointing rod to direct the ten students to the sites of the female sexual anatomy. Then, naughty doctor, he starts to use his fingers to better explain the details. And all those students, male and female, are gazing intently at my shaved, pink little pussy while I read the *New York Times* Arts & Leisure section on the other side of the sheet, blasé and anonymous, feeling nothing . . . I think.

The final class is devoted to the clit and female sexual excitement, with the doctor suggesting that for thorough knowledge each student get up real close for a single, well-earned lick before their lunch break. By now I am somewhat distracted and wondering why the *Times* doesn't have a horoscope section, and then the good doctor finishes me off, showing all those young men and women just how expert a physician he really is. Now I know my horoscope: it's a "good day," full of "unusual opportunity" with a "tempting offer" for "a lucrative position promising unexpected personal reward."

About anonymity and sex. I find it very shortsighted to dismiss the concept of "anonymous" sex—real or imagined—as "impersonal," and shamefully indicative of one's unresolved "intimacy issues." This is a terrible misunderstanding based on the post-

Freudian world where "individuality" and "self-expression
been raised to unworthy heights of worthiness that leave one
dled with the heavy burden of "being oneself" at all times. Who can
be "themselves" during sex? Not me.

In anonymity lies freedom from oppression—from the personality of one's partner, and from one's own demanding ego. Blindfolds
are your friends, concealing your shame and the identity of your all-
too-human lover. Anonymous sex is not about avoidance. For me, it
is about a kind of harmless grandiosity: when I am anonymous, I exist as something far greater than my particulars. I become an arche-
type, a myth, a Joseph Campbell goddess spreading my legs for the
benefit of all mankind for all time. This imagined generosity brings
me the most profound orgasms.

One heroic diver would come over, eat me out, slowly, slowly,
daring me not to come. Sometimes I'd last over an hour. How wonderful to be in the position of trying to hold back, of not praying to
come. There was one thing he did want, to lick my ass. Okay, I said,
go ahead. But he didn't just lick my ass, he fucked my ass with his
tongue, very impressive indeed, never had a tongue deeper to date.
He never took his clothes off, and he had the good taste to never kiss
me on the mouth.

There is risk, however, with the Pussy Hounds. The final fading
of my respect has sometimes happened when a man is so eager to
suck my pussy that I know he indulges his need to please rather than
an actual love of pussy. It's distracting. Intention is all—I can feel it
with my clit. It is more important to me that a man love pussy in

general than mine in particular. After all, if he likes them as a whole, then mine is a slam dunk. But if a man likes only mine and not all the others, well, I just don't trust him. With this type of man I have learned to guide my orgasm with fantasy, and, like him, play the using game. While he licks furiously, indulging his codependence, I file through my Rolodex of every man I've ever known, all in the audience, erections puncturing the air, watching this one lap at the altar they all still covet. Works every time.

It is my altruism, not my narcissism, that fosters this fantasy. After all, a man can acquire such wisdom at the source of a woman's orgasm: how to slow down, speed up, be consistent, be nonlinear, be persistent, be unpredictable, be patient, be outrageous, be generous, be witty. There is, in fact, nothing of value, philosophically and practically, that he can't learn if he can turn the delta of Venus into the site of Vesuvius.

Most men will lick and suck and drink a pussy—and I'm not complaining. But it is the rare man who does so with his whole consciousness poised on his tongue. It is this awareness that will move a woman; when her consciousness—on her clit—encounters his, orgasm marks their meeting. Ultimately, it is here—or rather, down there—that a man will learn how to be a winner or a loser, with women as in life.

TRINITY

If old-fashioned fucking-for-two remained a minefield for me, fucking-for-three continued to be a delight. The Pre-Raphaelite redhead plotted reunions, and we three got together every month or so with unplanned regularity for over a year. I returned to my New Year's Eve lovers again and again, hungry for love and freedom—a previously impossible duet in my experience. Says Jesus in the Gnostic Gospel of Thomas:

> *When you make the two one, and when you make the inside like the outside and the outside like the inside, and the above like the below, and when you make the male and the female one and the same . . . then you will enter the kingdom.*

One day, I ventured down on the Pre-Raphaelite. First time. Terrified. Curious. I wanted to see her pleasure in order to know my own. She was a genuine redhead. Eating pussy when you are a heterosexual woman is overwhelming. To confront a pussy that close for the first time—you can't ever get that close, at that angle, to your own—is like looking narcissism in the face with a resounding Yes! Profound. Wet.

It can sometimes be so hard to be oneself in one's own sex life. With another woman, a woman's identity receives a brutal jolt: she is me, I am her, her pleasure is mine, mine is hers. The source, the center, the origin of the human race becomes your only view. I bonded with my own sex and learned to love myself. I also developed a new compassion for the male divers. A pussy is a wild and watery landscape of hills and valleys and ravines and mighty holes that suck one in like quicksand. Once in, you cannot escape. Diving is an act of bravery.

The redhead, however, demonstrated less hesitancy, and ate me like a woman who knows how. Naughty, considerate, and relentless. Her fingers felt like tongues, her mouth like a baby's, sucking. I resist men's fingers. Too rough, too big, too fast. My shield goes up, my clit hides. My orgasms with her were long, open, and free.

The next New Year's we three reconvened and she had a surprise for us: her beautiful young Belgian friend who was mourning the loss of her rock-star lover. One-two-three-four, three of one and one of the other. She and me and him . . . and her. I did a striptease to Led Zeppelin, swinging around the luscious green velvet curtains at the door of her boudoir—a kind of *Gone With the Wind*–Vivien-Leigh-Gone-Wild moment.

The Belgian girl was shy, but she didn't shy away. The redhead

and the Young Man looked at each other slyly, and before I knew it
they had lined me and the beautiful Belgian up on the bed side by
side; he devoured my pussy while the redhead ate hers. I looked to
my left, catching eyes and hands with the Belgian. I felt so safe. Later
he and I lay faceup underneath the soft white ass of the kneeling Belgian, our lips close to hers, as we took turns licking her. "Eat her," I
say, and watch him dive and suck and drink pussy, another pussy. It
made me wild with joy. Later we rolled out another futon and slept,
all four, side by side. In the morning I climbed on his hard cock
while the other two watched, the Belgian reaching out and holding
his hand while we fucked for her, for us. Loving and hot . . . like hell
on fire. That was New Year's Day. This was my unmarried life.

The Young Man and I fucked alone as well. But when the redhead
told me she had seduced him without me, I didn't like it—no, not
one bit. It was legal and democratic—the three of us had no rules—
but it felt horrid to be left out of the party. And horrid, in my new-
found sexual bravado, to experience something so shameful as
jealousy. I had never felt this particular pain before, having only
been with faithful men. The three of us met at his place and tried to
talk about what was hurting me.

I was playing with fire all right, but it burned so brightly that I
could not, and would not, acknowledge the warning that had just
come my way. Between all the forbidden ecstasy I was having, I
was still weeping on a regular basis over my marriage, and still

interpreting all grief as emotional weakness. It seemed such an awful bore to be jealous, so bourgeois. Surely I could overcome this
feeling with practice, with the right bohemian attitude.

They countered my fear—fear of loss of him, of her, of our
magic triangle—by telling me how much they both loved me. I told
them that I loved them, too . . . and that I wanted to see them fuck. I
put the condom on him and, leaning over his back, guided his cock
between her legs and into her. We both looked down on her, the
delicate little redhead, as he fucked her, and I saw myself: pale, vulnerable, and pierced. But I was also him, fucking her with a big
beautiful cock, riding his back as he pulsed in her, me.

Later I lay on my back and she climbed on top of me, small,
white, fragile. Breast to breast, mouth to mouth, we lined up our
pussies, redhead and brunette, hers mine, mine hers. Over her, he
entered me, six legs atop one another. I looked up at their two faces
beaming down on me as he fucked me. I held them both and knew
that this was one of the great moments of my life—of being overwhelmed, ensconced in love. He is me is she is he and we are
rolling, fucking, oozing, laughing, being.

This layered, fucking sex sandwich became the image for my final theory of us three. He and I deeply connected, with her as our
midwife, our buffer, our catalyst, our crazy glue. As Colette observed, "Certain women need women in order to preserve their taste
for men." She lightened us, separated us, and spread around the
shattering intensity between us. She diminished the terrible anxiety
of love.

Several months later, he announced he was leaving town for a job—for months and months, maybe forever. We hastily arranged a rendezvous. After he arrived, she called to suggest we begin without her, she would be late. She knocked just as we finished fucking. We greeted her naked, but she was in red velvet and green silk with freshly cut white baby roses strewn in her hair, like Ophelia.

They told me to just lie there, and relax, as they connected over their prey. He had fingers on my clit, up my pussy, and inside my ass, while she leaned over me, soft, with red, silky hair everywhere, whispering "I love you, I love you, I love you, I love you . . ." The waves started coming and still he continued, still she whispered, caressing my face, "I love you, I love you, I love you . . ." The waves continued, on and on, with orgasms so sweet building to ones less sweet but more intense.

And then it happened. A wave began in my feet and legs, traveled up my belly, my chest, my throat, and my soul burst out the crown of my head. It was the deepest experience of pleasure-love I had ever known—or witnessed. She later explained the technical name was a "Kamikazi-Mega-Hiawatha." That sounded precisely right.

Then he left town. Gone. Gone.

She and I met one sunny afternoon holding each other in her bed, with wandering fingers—but I missed him. Sweet sisters without a cock between us.

MAN OF GOD

The loss felt devastating. Would such joy never be more than momentary? Probably not. My inability to tolerate this knowledge led me into yet another flirtation with God. This time I met him at Home Depot.

I was in a back aisle with a tape measure and a saw trying to cut a seven-foot wood pole in half to use as a curtain rod. The pole kept rolling off the cutting bench, and things were not going well. Finally, as I made the first slice into the wood, my sequined handbag slipped off my shoulder, and the saw went flying out of my hand. He caught it and asked if I would like some help. "Oh yes!" I said, relieved. Well, maybe this was only the carpenter son, but I wasn't going to fuss about generational details at this crucial moment in the lumber aisle. I just knew that he'd saved me.

He was tall, handsome, fair-haired, and soft-spoken. He carried the freshly cut pole to the checkout for me and put it in the trunk of my car. He asked if he could buy me something to eat and we crossed the street to a burger joint. For a four-hour lunch.

How can a single, liberated woman have the indescribable pleasure of illicit sex? No, not with a married man: that's never appealed to me. With a celibate man. Mr. Home Depot was a born-again Christian. *And* a former "sex addict." He said he'd often fucked seven or eight different women in a week! Oh my God! Could this be the perfect man? God and Pervert and Hound all neatly packaged in a six-foot-two Texan. And he was handy, too.

He told me the story of his conversion. Early one October morning on the beach in the Bahamas, after a night of drugs and debauchery, God—unsolicited—had spoken to him, saying: "The time is now." Being a seeker myself, I was jealous. Why hadn't God ever talked to me? I asked if God had spoken out loud—would I have heard Him, too, if I'd been there? But I couldn't get a clear answer on those details. From that day forward, in any case, he had been sober and celibate. This man hadn't had sex for fifteen years. My imagination reeled at the thought of all those lonely erections. Nice, too, that he wasn't newly born-again, but long-term born-again. He knew every book of the Bible, backward, and taught Bible school every week.

The Forbidden married to the Unattainable was my magical aphrodisiac: I realized at that first long lunch that Born Again and I would never, ever have sex, and thus my heart began to open and my pussy to yearn. Once again, the impossible had coalesced before me. He had the biggest hands and feet I'd ever seen. Listening to his story, I began feeling a Christian conversion rapidly coming my way.

He said that it was difficult to find a nice Christian wife—the only way he could legitimately have sex again. I didn't understand; he looked so incredibly eligible. Then he admitted with a shy grin that he liked his women a little slutty—*trashy* was the word he used. Admittedly, I couldn't be a genuine Christian, but I had been practicing slutty and trashy for a few years already. This man's contradictions were as epic as my own.

I asked him just how far could he go sexually before God got mad: "Where is the line?" An hour later, I still hadn't gotten an answer, just a discernible sigh as his tongue hit my clit on the roof of a nearby car park. He had suggested looking at the view. God was now speaking to me, too, and the time *was* now and the view superb. And thus, I, too, died and was born again.

I have never seen a man before or since look at a pussy the way this guy did. I felt penetrated by his gaze alone. He projected an innocent, open-eyed hunger layered with filthy lust and divine desire. It is forever fixed in my mind's eye and, easily recalled, can make me come in a jiffy.

The risk of being caught in public did wonders for Born Again. One afternoon I sucked his cock in a Denny's parking lot, just as the lunch crowd of blue-haired ladies was heading for their Pontiacs. He had a great way of staying calm, cool, and on the lookout above while fucking my mouth furiously below. Jekyll and Hyde, sacred and profane, horny man of God.

Another time he stuck his hard cock through my vertical mail slot, humping my front door, as I sucked him on the other side while neighbors passed behind him in my courtyard. Perhaps this was a man I could actually date. But shortly afterward he told me that both Darwin and the Dalai Lama were, in general, wrong about most things, and my brief hope for a man who combined the erotic and the spiritual disappeared. When he told me that he didn't believe in evolution (so I came from a monkey but he didn't?), I suggested we stop talking entirely and find a nice mail slot through which to communicate.

This guy name-dropped God like they were buddies, and his heresies became my self-righteous obsession. Though invited to enter their bliss for a three-way, I simply couldn't override my own intelligence and do it. Witnessing his religious arrogance in all its shameless glory, however, inspired my own libido to new heights, and every erection became a tangible victory over his troubled piety. Dressed in my red stilettos, fishnet stockings, and a thong, I invited him one night to come into my backyard. Camouflaged in my bushes, he spied through the bedroom window into the candlelight as I pranced, stripped, and touched myself. All was quiet but I could see his hypocrisy harden as his hand moved furiously back and forth on his cock. Was God watching now as my pussy took precedence over Him? I couldn't have God myself, so I settled for treating Him like the competition. In fact, each time Born Again touched me in public, I felt a kind of religious potency emanating from my pussy.

I was angry at Born Again for not being who he thought he was. And who I hoped he was. I wanted him to be for real, a real Man of God. Once again, I found myself not fucked by God but fucked over by His apostle. This man's flaws shone all the brighter in the light of my massive expectations and subsequent frustration. I had, you see, loved him. A little. He couldn't win with me, and eventually the games wore out and I ended our X-rated morality play. The Holy Fuck never took place. Perhaps this was how he kept things straight with his buddy.

THE LAST BOYFRIEND

Contrary to appearances, perhaps, I was by now finally beginning to acquire some semblance of romantic discipline. After the disappointment of the truck-driving, gun-toting, sex-addicted Republican Christian, it was time for the Volvo-leasing, pot-smoking, monogamous, left-wing atheist. And a liberal lesson in disappointment.

I refused to mourn for the impossible Young Man and the crazy Christian. So I attempted the possible—a boyfriend with an out-of-control dick—and found this, too, impossible, but in a different way.

There are two types of out-of-control dicks: the first one insatiable, the second merely undisciplined and poorly behaved. I prefer the former, but often found myself with the latter.

In some strange, inexplicable throwback to my premarriage years, I had agreed to be monogamous with this guy after one mad make-out session on my couch on the first date. He asked and I delivered. Perhaps I was having a conventional moment of my own after the transcendent Trinity and the byzantine Christian affair. Naughtiness in the moment was definitely the most fun, the most erotic, but it had a price—the anxiety of impermanence.

Immediately, however, I was reminded of something even worse: the anxiety of permanence. I had hitched myself to a single flawed human being. What was I thinking? Weekly therapy, where I howled bloody murder, kept me "working" on the "relationship" for more than the usual six weeks. For over a year I tried to be his girl-friend, kicking and screaming every step of the way. I even considered Prozac in this last attempt to be "normal" and "conventional." Aren't drugs, after all, how everyone else tolerates monogamy?

I hated being the object of a desperate, controlling passion but felt that it was somehow the morally dutiful stance when the man "loved" me. I was finally cured when I found myself in a fetal position on the floor of my bedroom while the Boyfriend put me on hold for a business call. I had humiliated myself beyond recognition.

What is wrong with me? The wretched question always beckoning my shame, the shame of the little girl who was deemed "overly sensitive." But with the Boyfriend I made progress. I stayed long enough to allow the pain to slice right through my mental masochism and discovered the relief on the other side: my sadism.

I considered the radical possibility that there might be nothing "wrong" with me. Except perhaps choosing guys who adored me, seduced me, and then couldn't control their dicks, and therefore had to control me. I'd protest, get upset, and the discussion would be successfully diverted from their penis to my hysteria. Oh, the myriad insecurities, baffling behaviors, addictions, and possessive outbursts that inhabit the man in search of control. There is only one kind of control that really matters.

My nice-girl martyrdom over, I turned to its heady antidote, the liberation of tyranny. I would no longer accommodate penis problems—whether they were insecurities about length or width, or issues of control lost and not found. If a damaged dick and his owner threatened to raise their heads in my direction, I would simply move out of their reach, and be on my way.

I told the Boyfriend that either we were finished or he could retain me as his mistress—meaning my own mistress. I even wrote down the rules—a parody of a best-selling treatise by a couple of housewives on how to lead a man to the altar. My rules led to slavery instead.

THE REAL RULES

1. See each other a maximum of once a week, except in special circumstances and when it's a mutual decision to do so. A week is defined as Monday through Sunday—hence there can be a Saturday encounter and then a Tuesday encounter but then not until the following Monday, when a new week begins.

2. One encounter is defined as any time spent together with no specific limits on hours, etc.—a late-night horny rendezvous and a weekend away both count equally as one encounter.

3. "Don't ask, don't tell" policy on nonmonogamy issue. But when together, completely together—no procurements, flirtations, etc.

4. Outside issues to be carefully avoided: work, friends, and family.

5. Phone calls are for only two purposes: to plan an encounter, or, if desired, a thank-you follow-up call, postencounter. No long, in-depth discussions of any nature on the phone—not about others, not about our relationship, not about current sports events.

6. Both parties are equally free to initiate the next encounter and the one who calls preferably has an "offer," a "plan." Examples: Be ready at 6 P.M. Friday with an overnight bag, sunglasses, and a jacket; or meet me at Café Lulu at 9 P.M., I'll have no panties on; or movie, dinner, and sex; or a 10 P.M. call—I'm coming over to suck your cock; or pick me up and I'll surprise you; or let's talk and not have sex. . . . Anything and everything can be an encounter, and imagination is all.

7. While together, refinements, additions, and subtractions to rules can be discussed and negotiated, although avoid getting stuck in having the encounters be entirely about the encounters.

8. All these rules, limitations, and boundaries are designed to enable and protect the possibility of fully, deeply, freely exploring the erotic realm and whatever else goes along with it.

9. Can give gifts to each other, but absolutely no obligation in this area.

10. Any amendments to these rules must be very clearly discussed and agreed upon together.

I faxed them over. These rules were a serious, insane attempt to legislate separation, to eliminate all areas of contention, to edit our sex life into our only life. Well, it was worth a try. In truth, #3 was the only rule I really cared about. It legislated hope.

Mistressing worked for a few months. One by one he tested every rule like a naughty boy. He bought me dresses and handbags, and in his arrogance thought he would win me from the competition. But it was too late. Show me an arrogant man, and I'll show you my machete—ah, the legitimized anger of feminism! I had freed myself at last from men whose shit was so deep that I thought it was my own. What I've learned from each relationship is how much emotional pain I'm willing to take. This was the last conventional connection I've had with a man.

This relationship had an unexpected silver lining, however. It goes like this. When I met him, the Boyfriend was deep in therapy with the first shrink of his life. He adored her, praised her, and wanted me to meet her—wanted her approval. I was evidence of how far he had come. Meanwhile I had a shrink, too, who

helped me deal with my divorce, but I didn't adore her. I agreed
to meet his.

Within a couple of weeks of seeing him, I was already in a state
of complete agitation, and so we went to see her together. And I
adored her, also. Oh dear.

"Can't I see her, too? You know, separately?" He thought it a fine
idea—same mom, common ground, and similar information. She
was less enthusiastic, but she finally agreed. Great—I finally had
the shrink of my dreams, and she could now help me deal with the
very annoying man who came with the deal.

Here was a different kind of triangle—not sexual, per se—but
more insidious. All my conversations with the Boyfriend were about
our different, and occasionally mutual, therapy. In bed with Mom
we certainly were—trouble was, I came to love Mom more than I
loved him, while he remained convinced that he was her most cher-
ished client. Just like when a man has bought three lap dances from
a stripper, has a raging hard-on, and declares in all seriousness, "I
think she really likes me!"

When I initiated mistressing, our dear therapist announced that
one of us had to go—or both. If we were potentially not monogamous and she knew it, the therapy would be poisoned. The
Boyfriend announced that he'd had enough therapy and was ready
to hit the road alone, comforted by the notion that when a man
chooses his lover over his therapist it is a sign of his newly found independence and maturity. This was fortunate because I announced
that I would definitely not give up the shrink no matter what. I

chose my therapist over my lover, which was a sign of my own growing maturity: I had finally decided to choose a woman over a man.

After four or five months of mistressing, I ended it completely
and during the last phone call with the Boyfriend the elegant irony
became apparent: he had now lost not only his lover but his shrink
as well.

I see it like this: you just never really can know what a particular
connection is about—until later. The Last Boyfriend was about me
finding a woman who would not only witness and analyze my misery but whose very presence in my life echoed my never-before-pos-
sible ability to endorse myself above, and beyond, any man. And
when A-Man entered my world, she endorsed me from behind as
well—while I learned to embrace my masochism sexually and leave
it out of my life.

DURING

A-MAN

You just don't know when he's going to show up. The one who is going to change everything forever, the one who's going to rock your world. He might even be someone you already know.

The Young Man had been gone for two years. In the meantime, I had acquired the Boyfriend, while the redhead Pre-Raphaelite had acquired a tall, skinny, rocker musician who wore more makeup than she did: they painted each other's nails and were mad in monogamous love. So when the Young Man called, I knew it would have to be a two-way; the safety of a three-way sandwich was no longer an option.

I was petrified. My male dilemma was personified in these two men before me: the Boyfriend was dependable in life but not in sex, while the Young Man was dependable in sex but not in life. Can't a woman win? My experiments so far said no. The Boyfriend was too safe, too arrogant, too possessive. But the Young Man was too dangerous, too sexy, too young, too not here. But I had Rule #3 at my disposal, so at least he was legal, technically.

In fact, the decision to see the Young Man the very afternoon he called was surprisingly easy. Earlier that day, the Boyfriend had juiced up my anger to the point of murderous rage by pontificating about "our" relationship—he was in "our" relationship alone, as far as I was concerned. And so it was arranged. It was three, the Young Man would be over at four. Love in the afternoon, like Gary Cooper and Audrey Hepburn. Well, not quite. I didn't have a cello.

With one hour to prepare, I had no time to think. Just as well, because there was no sense in it. But the ones who made sense drove me crazy. I had already caught several men desiring matrimony—and married the best of them—and had found misery to spare. Catching a man and hauling him to the altar was not what I wanted. I had a creepy suspicion that all those "proposals" were more about insecurities and jealousies than about love, more about tying me down emotionally when I needed tying down physically. I didn't want a lifetime commitment; I wanted a sexual commitment. For a few hours, anyway.

Trembling, I got on my knees, not knowing what else to do, and prayed to my unknown God to allow me to surrender to this man, in this moment, for this afternoon only. No more. I could not imagine more. I can only fuck one fuck at a time. Could I have the courage to not be afraid of the beauty of the Young Man just this once? To go all the way in with him, not knowing if there was a way out? I got up off my knees and turned on the bath.

I bathed, shaved my legs, powdered my whole body with honey dust, set up the music, closed the curtains, fed the cat, lit the incense and candles, and then—very excited, very apprehensive—I put myself into a black thong, a black bra, and a long black velvet gown.

The doorbell rang, late. I opened the door and he stepped inside and then stepped inside of me. He folded me into his big arms, no words, and pressed me close. I was his from that moment forth. I allowed it, and then it took on a life of its own. For the next three hours, I melted into this man in a way I never had with any man before.

As his cock entered me to the full, the pressure made me flinch. He looked down at me and said gently, "I won't hurt you." Actually, it did hurt—he had a big cock—but somehow I understood intuitively that it wasn't *about* hurting me, it was about something else. As with dancing, I knew that I had to work with my discomfort, embrace it, to get to the next level.

And then he fucked me in the ass. Is this what he learned while out of town? It was the first time for me. Ever. My God, he was good. I mean bad. What nerve he had. So graceful. It was very slow, very careful, very connected and painful. It was here, in there, that I first tasted the experience of moving through pain and fear to that plateau on the other side where I met this man in a foreign land called Bliss. Bliss is not a pain-free zone; it is a postpain zone. Big difference.

His cock inside me on that virgin voyage was an emotional and anatomical miracle: the impossible had come to pass in my ass. Now God had my total attention. If I had walked on water I couldn't have been more amazed. This was my first act of sacrifice that was not mired in the vicious circle of self-reflective narcissism, the first that delivered me to an entirely new place, instead of a new angle on the old one. I have been changed ever since. Forever changed. And it began physically with his cock in my ass—the act that proposed the mystery—and psychically with my decision to allow it, the best one I ever made. I simply wanted to let this particular man into me, literally. I wanted who he was deep inside who I was.

Of course, it also took his balls, the balls to want and try and dare to fuck me in my tiny, tight ass. I'll respect him forever for that. Finally, a man who was not afraid. The Young Man, 3-Way Man, was transfigured before my eyes. A-Man was born.

Something else happened that first afternoon. I stopped mourning my marriage. The mourning ceased, I believe, because someone else had entered my consciousness deeply enough to override the grief, transforming the previous loss into a blessing, making space for a new entry. No one had tried my back door before. That was where my power resided and where it shifted. As hostess at my front door, I was, as you now know, the critical Queen, the impossible Princess, the angry child. But with A-Man in my ass, I became sweet again. So sweet.

Within days, I told the Boyfriend that we were done. All done. I couldn't be sweet with him, only mad. He may have resided in "reality," but those three hours with A-Man clarified everything for me: "reality" was not my home.

WHY THERE?

Once gravity reasserted its hold on me, I immediately started examining my experience. It felt like my new job. I'd been given a gift and now I had to attempt some understanding. Why? Why me? Why him? Why *there?*

I had given my vaginal virginity to the first man who paid me any consistent sexual attention. I would have married him as only a virgin would: with adoration and ignorance. Eight penises later, I married one. Ten years later, when I departed that union, I was horny as hell, like never before—a bunny on a hot tin roof—but intercourse was not what I wanted. I needed love, admiration, and pussy worship. This insatiable desire ruled my life. But then A-Man came along and shook my overanalyzed ego off its self-important pedestal.

I was an anal virgin. He showed me, physically, where my rage resided. Anger thrives in your ass. A Dickensian alley, the ass. Despite its tiny, ignored entry, once opened, it contains literally yard upon yard of coiled past traumas, the internal gripping of the emotionally unbearable. A-Man penetrated the site of my anger and cauterized my wound.

I was now being given a second chance—not on the well-trodden vaginal trail, but in a place entirely new to my consciousness—and it quickly became the site of my consciousness. Truly virgin, once again. With the discovery of this new world, I experienced all the wonder and beauty that a deflowering might be but rarely is.

And so it began, in naive complicity, once a week, twice a week, three times a week. Mostly late afternoons. He was an expert and I was willing. I began to count. It just seemed like the right thing to do.

#41

Ablaze afterward, he stood up, still hard, and slugged some water from a blue bottle.

"What is it about?" I asked from the bed, flushed and dazed.

He stopped drinking, looked over at me, paused, and said, "Vibrations."

He says we're learning something about time. The passage of time, the experience of time, the truth of time, the eternity of time. The best time.

ENTERING THE EXIT

Once initiated, I couldn't help thinking about anal everything. Including the mechanics. The digestive system is a one-way pipe where peristaltic contractions urge food from mouth to anus. Assfucking entails the bold—and contrary—attempt to travel the route in reverse.

Fucking a pussy is entering a cave with only one pinprick exit—the hole in the cervix that enters the womb. (And, of course, it is an "exit" to parenthood.) Under normal circumstances, the pussy is a pretty closed, if expandable, place. The vagina is a receptacle. The anal canal, on the other hand, is directly, though complexly, connected to the mouth, the point of entry, the place that feeds the life. Thirty feet or so of digestive track from rectum to colon to small intestine to stomach to esophagus to throat to mouth is the route entered by the anal fucker.

A-Man and I exist in the land beyond the intercourse that breeds babies. That is good, too, don't get me wrong. We do that, too, warm-up. But we live in the land beyond, behind. The place where depth is infinite and the love seems infinite, ever growing. Deep penetration, deep love. The physical depth somehow leads into that other depth as if my soul slept in my bowels and is now awakened.

The directions are clear: if you want to procreate enter the front door, but if you really want to become a part of a woman's internal workings, to penetrate her being most deeply, the back door is your portal. Anxiety, that ever-present agony, exists because of the inescapable knowledge that all must end. Enter an ass and you enter a passage that does not end. It is the exit to infinity. The back door to liberty.

Besides, pussies have just been through too much. Give them a rest. They are old news—tired, betrayed, overused, reused, abused—and have been overly publicized, politicized, and redeemed. They are no longer naughty, no longer the place for defiance, rebellion, or rebirth. Pussies are now too politically correct. The ass is where it's at: the playground for anarchists, iconoclasts, artists, explorers, little boys, horny men, and women desperate to relinquish, even temporarily, the power that has been so hard won and cruelly awarded by the feminist movement. Ass-fucking realigns the balance for a woman with too much power—and a man with too little. (I think this explains the prevalence of butt-fucking in heterosexual porn: masses of men, refugees from feminism, watching, hard and ever-hopeful.)

In his forays inside me, A-Man hits new walls, new angles, new ends, and that self-preserving voice of "too much" echoes through my brain as I feel a kind of pressure, a resistance. But I have never said "too much." Never. I breathe through, adjust the angle, and stay where he pushes until I open and receive him in farther. I expand into him and the pain subsides, transforms, into a profound sensation of freedom—freedom from pain, freedom to be crazy, freedom to harmonize with the universe. This is all physical. And it is the birth of love. His cock is my laser healer. Every point it probes inside me pierces my armor, the armor of self-protection, and the two fears—love and death—momentarily lose their grip and I experience a moment of immortality.

#75

Vertical fucking. Upside down, legs over my head, knees by my ears, ass up, he perches over me like an acrobat and points his cock down into me. He thrusts downward to Earth's center, and I am grounded. I point upward, outward to the sky, to the Milky Way, to heaven's gate, and I see clearly between my legs his cock pumping like a piston. Angle is everything.

We achieve a kind of gravity-free coordination, complete transcendence of the "fight"—the fight that is life—total trust allowing his deep, hard, long, and fast plunges entirely without self-protective gripping. Undulating . . . and great inner peace as I am rocked like a mermaid in the ocean.

THE DOUBLE-SPHINCTER THEORY

More mechanics: the inner anal sphincter is not within conscious control. It is regulated by the brain in the gut, the enteric nervous system, and is reflexive, opening on demand. The external sphincter, the internal's sister sphincter, is, however, connected to the conscious brain, regulated by conscious control—witness the ability to grip and hold when necessary, when angry, when scared, when stressed. Unconscious internal sphincter, conscious external sphincter, only centimeters apart. Where else is one's unconscious and conscious mind so intimately connected, so readily regulated, so easily probed? It is a psychological playground of the most intriguing potential. Put an ass on the couch and much is revealed.

But the external sphincter did not begin with consciousness. For the first year or so of life it was unconscious, reacting in conjunction with the internal and letting go on demand—hence diapers. The brain and spinal cord at birth are not yet developed enough for conscious control.

And then comes toilet training. When the brain is sophisticated enough and the parents encourage (or scream) enough, the little eighteen-month-old becomes conscious of that external anal sphincter and learns to grip it, control it, and not to let the shit fly at every urge. Shame is born. All this is to say that when I get fucked in the ass, I have learned to play with, and even reverse, that long-ago, probably traumatic coming to consciousness about gripping my ass, holding on to it, showing it to no one. After all, Freud hypothesized that one's shit is the first gift one offers one's parents—one's first creative production.

Only now—ninety-seven ass fucks later—is the enormity of the power that lies in this area dawning on me. It is emotional and physical therapy on the deepest level: revisiting and literally learning to trust enough to open the forbidden exit and enter the forbidden zone. As a baby, the first big resounding NO from the world as we know it is the NO perpetrated upon a loose and unconscious external anal sphincter. Getting ass-fucked is the most extreme form of rebellion against one's parents in which one could possibly indulge—returning not to adolescent transgressions, but rather to the original injury.

I experience a regression to a very young age when he's in my ass. I goo and gaa and giggle and feel the joy that must have existed before anxiety took over. As if all I ever wanted was to be loved while not gripping my ass, but allowing it to be as it is. And what is released along with my anal sphincter? A love that is enormous, a love waiting decades to be released, a love that flows freely, a love that is infinite at the moment of its conception.

Okay, I understand. You're thinking: Infinite love is good, but what if I bleed en route? To be on the safe side I have never not used a condom, but I have also never, ever bled. This can be a question of the skill of one's lover but it also may be that some assholes, like mine, are just more able, more resilient, than others—a genetic blessing. If you bleed, don't do it. I wouldn't. Period.

I also know that when some of you hear anal sex you see nothing but shit—shit, shit everywhere. Shit on the bed, shit on his cock, shit on your ass. I am here to tell you it just isn't like that. Hardly a trace, ever. All you have to do is include in your regular bathing a nice little finger-in-the-ass bath prior to an anal visitation. What woman doesn't wash her pussy before sex? Same thing, just rinse out your ass, too. Shit is not my thing, either—don't want to see it, smell it, or clean it up. Ass-fucking is not about shit. It's about not being afraid of your shit, going past your shit—to find the shit that matters.

#98

He fucked me in the ass at 11:20 last night so long, so hard, so smooth, so hilariously, so slowly, so fast, so very, very deep. After forty-five minutes of this he says, "Now I'm gonna fuck your pussy." And he fucked my pussy 360 degrees around. Then he says, "I'm gonna get me some sacred spot." And he does, anointing my sacred place—the grave of my past—with his blasphemous baptismal juice.

"I think it's your greatest gift," he says after.

"What is?"

"Submission."

PROFILE OF AN ASS-FUCKER

Ass-fucking a woman is clearly about authority. The man's authority; the woman's complete acceptance of it. A man must have this confidence, in himself and his cock, to fuck a woman in the ass. If he does not have this control, his cock will direct the action; he will move too quickly, hurt the once-willing woman, and rarely, rightly, will he be given a second chance.

Why A-Man has this authority I do not know. Psychology might find childhood reasons, but I believe, ultimately, that it's something God-given, a deep knowledge of personal responsibility. This kind of self-possession and lack of desperation can get a man a long way with a woman . . . or at least partway up her ass. In the end, it's who you are that will get you somewhere. Or nowhere.

He told me once that he likes being where he shouldn't be, crossing the velvet rope, hand in the candy jar, late to work, cock in my ass, an ass too small for his cock. A-Man made it so deeply into my ass because he dared. No one else really tried. Anyone who dares to be that intimate, that crazy, well, he might just get somewhere he never got before.

I am in the throes of coming at the moment of first touch, my body, pussy, ass so open they peel outwardly to suck him in. I was never that open before. If I were that open to someone else, would I feel the same joy of openness? No. They would annoy me long before I was that open. It's all that yakking that ruins it; it reveals too much. A-Man is the least annoying man I've ever known. And the only one who never yields to my will.

At the same time, contrary to easy supposition, I do not believe that it is the arrogant, macho man who is the great ass-fucker: he is the asshole. That guy probably doesn't even like women, he's too busy competing with other men. In my limited experience, the great ass-fucker is the patient, gentle man, the one who knows how to listen to a woman, how to be with a woman, and has the equipment that can slow her down. He is the one who can imaginatively experience her submission—her release of control—with her, and thus know precisely how to get her to that place: he absorbs all that she gives up. He is a kind man, A-Man.

OBITUARY

After such a stunning start, I prepared, as any bright woman would, for the end. Great love always brings thoughts of death and separation. This was a war—between decency and desire, between convention and pleasure, between me, myself, and I—and that great aphrodisiac fueled my craving. With the assumption, or expectation, of longevity gone, the moat of self-protection and the apathy of safety disappear and passion floods the world. Well, it flooded mine, anyway. Now is all there was, all I had—and I knew it.

The aphoristic obituary was especially comforting. My testimony would serve if he died, if I died, or—worst of all—if he flaked on me.

He had the biggest, hardest, and most gentle cock I ever knew.

He was the one who fucked me in the ass, missionary-style, before he fucked my pussy.

He was the one who looked beautiful to me when we fucked, the others all looked like men with contorted faces—best not to look.

He didn't grunt, or groan, or squeak during sex. He beamed and glowed, eyes wide open, shaking his head, saying, "Wow! Wow!" and then he'd fuck me some more.

He was the thirty-third man, and the only one I really liked to fuck. The others were just men and I allowed it. Resentfully.

Most men fuck in and out, in and out, in and out, on and on. But he fucked like he was actually going somewhere. And he was.

He was the only one who took time to be friends with my cat. The others regarded my little fur ball as a hindrance, an obstacle, even a threat. They just didn't get it: love me, love my pussy.

He was my blood.

He was the one who never got real.

He was the one I never conquered.

He was one I had the most fun with.

He had the only cock I worshiped.

He was the one with whom I couldn't tell whose pleasure gave me more pleasure. With the others my pleasure was the only pleasure.

He was the guy who could fuck for three hours . . . and still not come.

He was the one who showed me real physical joy. The others just made me come. With him I came to . . . the Kingdom.

He was sweet-sweet-sweet.

He was the one who oozed love. Through his fingertips, his movement, his skin, and his cock.

He gave me nothing outside of bed. In bed he gave me everything that I, as a woman, could ever desire.

He fucked like a rolling ocean.

I didn't have those powerful but so brief and geographically specific outward climaxes with him, it was the building of an inward tidal wave that flooded my body, my brain, and then spilled into my soul.

He never, unlike the others, asked me to be "his"—but I was.

He was the one who treated me like his—in bed. All the others treated me like theirs out of bed, but in bed I could smell their fear.

With him sex was about transcendence, with the others power.

He swooped in and out of my pussy, my ass, my life. Others smothered, wishing, foolishly, to colonize what they coveted.

Fucking him was like breathing in wide open space.

If I never loved again I would die having known a big, big love.

There was always that moment when he fucked me when all my thoughts ceased and turned to God: I was entering His territory.

He didn't please me. He possessed me.

He, you see, was the one I really loved.

Having now imagined its demise, I mustered the courage to proceed with the affair.

#101

He stands by the bed naked, hard, and beautiful and says, "Show me your pussy." He watches as I take off my thong, lie back on the bed, and bend my knees up and apart. Looking at my pussy, he says, "Spread it apart." With a hand on each side I open my little pink pussy lips to him. He kneels before me and sucks on my clit, sings on my clit like a troubadour breaking all the rules. I flowed into his tongue and he murmured, "You like it when I eat your pussy, don't you?"

"I would die for it," I admitted.

I cannot imagine feeling greater love in all my life, nor do I expect to ever feel greater love, except for him. Nor would I ever ask or want greater love than I feel for him.

With any others, after him, I will need to rest.

THE UNWRITTEN RULES

We are not domestic. We stay in the desire, in the bedroom—and out of the kitchen, the laundry, the office, and any other room that would threaten to bring in reality. We have, on a few occasions, when famished after sex, cooked dinner—well, actually he cooked it, but then we ate it in the bathtub with candles, floating a large metal bowl filled with tender rare meat between us. Both of us in the deep end, of course. We've never been to a movie and don't plan on going to one, ever. Why would we? We are the movie: the porn that can never be—visually astounding, spontaneously inventive, genitally graphic, and viscerally soul-searing. It isn't predictable with A-Man. The sex, the ass-fucking, that is the only constant. We never don't fuck.

We are not monogamous. Never have been and never will be. Neither of us has ever asked for it and neither of us has ever offered it. Offering it is the only way it could happen—neither of us would intrude on the other's free choice. Free choice is at the core of what is hot between us. The subject has been discussed only to establish what is mutually understood. "Don't ask, don't tell" is the basic policy. He says, "I don't need to know." He pays attention to what is, not what isn't.

Having never done this before, I thought about it plenty. If one has sex with someone other than the Beloved, what happens? Does one risk diminishing one's affection for the Beloved? Does it contaminate the love? Or does it merely confirm the love in every way, the contrast illuminating the beauty of the Beloved yet again, in yet another way, from yet another angle. And this gift to each other—the freedom to allow for other experiences—only enhances the love. Love without chains is love.

The experience of being truly free, without recrimination, without judgment, to choose at any time, on any day, this one or that one, only reinforces love of the Beloved, reinforces the choice of the Beloved as the Beloved. Not being monogamous, and exercising that option, secures the great love—always being tested, it is confirmed, strengthened, reshaped, redefined.

If a man can possess a woman sexually—really possess—he won't need to control her ideas, her opinions, her clothes, her friends, even her other lovers. In my experience of many lovers, only he has truly possessed me and so set me free. He fucks my ass for hours with a dick an inch too big for the job: *that* is possession. After a round like that he doesn't need to infiltrate my life, my psyche, my time, or my wardrobe, because he has infiltrated the core of my being—the rest is just peripheral decoration. Domination—total and complete domination of my being—that is where I find freedom.

I assumed from the beginning of our affair that he was probably fucking this other woman here or there or somewhere. And he knew that I knew. This was not the Pre-Raphaelite redhead but a pretty, quiet brunette who also exercised at the gym. I was even turned on by the power I assumed he had over her. I knew about her, but she didn't know about me, and this worked just fine. I even had my own fantasies about her. About seducing her myself, about him telling her to eat my pussy while he watched. I ran into her on occasion at the gym and we were always friendly; she seemed like a nice woman, self-effacing.

He and I had even discussed the idea of a three-way with her—we always reminisced fondly about the magic of our times with the red-head and wondered if it could be reproduced with someone else. But he said he was not sure that I would like her body. Proportion is important to me in matters of beauty, and though she was slim, she had no tits and a wide ass. Good enough for him, obviously, but per-haps not for me. A curious assessment, but probably correct.

As time went on, however, this woman became increasingly ab-stract. A-Man was fucking me so often and so well that she was eas-ily dismissed, often forgotten. That he is free to fuck whomever he likes and yet repeatedly calls me, comes to me, fucks me, seems a greater proof of love and desire on a daily basis than a commitment of monogamy would be—especially if it was made only to prevent insecurities from rising to the surface.

Is his love as deep as mine? I don't care if it is as superficial as mine is deep as long as he, and his rock-hard desire, show up at my back door several times a week. Sodomy ignites a gratitude of great scope. I suspect that until he shattered the control panel of my being—my mental acuity and my physical power—I had never really loved before.

How do you know it's love, real love?

When you meet the one with whom you are not afraid to die. The one who takes away that constant gnawing fear of death and gives one air to breathe.

Not afraid to die, this is the feeling he generates when he fucks my ass. Pussy penetration does not delve this far into my psyche; does not break the barrier; does not stop the fear.

Did the love or the sodomy come first? Love grows from lust. This I know. Besides, I don't trust love. I've heard it declared too often. But I trust lust completely.

#121

After, I say, "Maybe it's not even sex. Something else. Beyond sex."
Did I have a regular battle-to-the-end clitoral orgasm? No. Had I
even thought about it? No. Only a fool would hold on to what she
knows while being shown some land of release beyond orgasm. The
land of harmony, of deep harmony with another human being.
Family. He is my family.

K-Y

"What's your afternoon like?" It begins.

He has an appointment at six, will be over at three. It is now two. One hour. The courtesan takes over. I turn on the bath, all hot, and let it fill.

I check the condom stash and refill it, always having plenty, at least five, more is better, a feeling of bounty, of possibility, like popcorn. I check the K-Y tubes, pushing the insides to the opening end and then rinsing them off under the tap, sticky from last time. The heat rises as I wash those tubes. I use my pink nail brush to wash just under the ridge on the cap where his thumb pushes it open. Dirt always collects there; it's how I know that tube was used. I adore washing those tubes smooth.

In the beginning, I bought the tiny little travel tubes, good for one or two sessions, small, discreet, deniable. Once I knew, initially, the ecstasy of the act, I also knew it could only be a very rare occurrence, sort of like a birthday special. I reasoned that it would not be healthy for my little asshole to be so invaded too frequently. I reasoned that bliss was not free, not plannable, and definitely not something that might come my way very often. Such reasoning led me to buy those little travel tubes. But those tiny tubes kept running out and denial became an effort. Ass-fucking was part of the regular repertoire. The next time he opened the drawer, he pulled out a giant, phallic-sized white-and-blue tube, looked at it, and fell off the bed howling with laughter. It was a risky move for me. Presumptuous. Practical.

After several months of using one large tube after another, I put two large tubes in the drawer at the same time. That is how he developed the ritual of dispersing the tubes while I sucked his cock. The beautiful man with a fierce erection tossing large white-and-blue plastic tubes around the room (wherever we land he can fuck my ass, right there, right then, no reaching): it is an image of promise as close to a guarantee as I've ever known with a man. The gold band on my left ring finger guaranteed far less. Soon there are as many as five tubes in the drawer at one time, each in a different stage of emptiness, the emptier the better.

I still haven't figured out how many ass-fucks per four-ounce tube. Probably about eleven. At $4.19 a tube, that is about 38 cents a fuck . . . add that to the price of a condom (thirty-six for $14.99) at 42 cents, and the best thing in the world costs less than a buck. Then I found the tubes discounted at Costco, two for $4.00, and bought six. That brings the whole affair down to 60 cents per cum shot. (Ass-fuckers: use dark glasses for K-Y shopping and don't turn around in the checkout line: they're all staring at your butt in disbelief.)

I'm going to buy stock in K-Y. The Lexus of lubricants. Grateful for the smooth ride.

I heard a television talk-show shrink quizzing a cross-dressing man to test if he was gay or straight. Playing quick word association, she says "football," he says "beer"; she says . . . he says . . . she says "KY," he says "Kentucky." She announces triumphantly that he is heterosexual. And, I would add, clearly not a heterosexual sodomite.

Of the liquid lubricants, Astroglide is king. But be forewarned: if you pour Astroglide onto K-Y during a single vigorous ass-fucking, then expect a large amount of froth. Froth everywhere.

What do the K and Y stand for? According to Johnson & Johnson, which has been manufacturing the jelly since 1910—their service reps were very friendly on the phone—they don't stand for anything, just arbitrary letters assigned by the original research scientists. But they have come to mean plenty.

TRACELESS

Now that I have fallen into both sin and love, my scribbled daily tes-
timonies serve to keep my anxiety of loss just barely at bay. With
him I live on the ledge of the abyss. The terror that this experience
might end competes with the even worse terror that it might be lost
forever.

Because he and I are not fused, except during sexual contact, I
must constantly confront the spaces between us. He never overstays
his welcome, and thus cultivates an air of scarcity, an erotic component of powerful and paradoxical consequences. On the one hand,
the element of instability is clearly an essential factor, perhaps the
central factor, in generating the total thrill of each and every encounter. The lost heat that monogamous couples constantly mourn
is always there for us. And yet this unpredictability also leaves me
with ample time and space for the insecurities of love to blossom.
Thus I doubt, I question, I worry and heap indignities upon myself
for which there is neither evidence nor refutation. The lingering
voice of convention is always attempting to diminish and deride my
own transcendent experience. And yet I have never tried to control

him in order to avoid this anxiety; I have always known that he is not an extension of me but a clearly separate human being.

Besides, I am well aware by now that if a man exhibits too many signs of attachment I lose interest and the sex becomes laden with obligation. Desire is sexy, a show of free will; attachment is the enemy of free will. A-Man, with his scarcity, has become the first man to keep me poised at that delectable point where I both thrive and suffer: always-in-desire, never-having-enough.

It is easier to want something than to have it—and so often when you do get the thing you've wanted so long, you're busy with numerous substitutes. With him somehow the wanting and the having combine, simultaneously. He is my very real yet eternally impossible fantasy: a man I can respect.

Living entirely in the moment, he leaves no traces. He is here when he is here. He is gone when he is gone. Others linger when they are gone, like a bad smell, even when they were never really here in the first place. He is the most present, and as a result, the most emphatically, painfully absent.

He recoils from nostalgia, detects sentimentality across a room, and the only hard evidence of our encounters is his relentlessly hard cock. Hardly something a girl can hang on to after the act. He keeps his private life private. I've not met his friends and do not know what he does during time not spent with me. He rejects gossip, refuses photographs, and eschews the love note. He is not a romantic, he is a practitioner of the here and now. He acts like a man unafraid of death—or else joyously defiant. I, however, am mortified by my mortality, and so I scribble on and on, searching for evidence, creating evidence, of our affair.

He says he doesn't need devotion. He says he doesn't even really need to be listened to. If he isn't heard the first time, he'll say it again. What he does want, he says, is the adventure, the ride together, the opportunity to enter a time warp with someone.

A-Man is a man with many tools. He can hang a mirror with toggle bolts, clean a skylight, grill a rack of lamb, pose naked in the garden like a Rodin sculpture, and fuck my ass. He's a doer, not a thinker, and he openly admits that he wants a woman to be smarter than he is. I have never before met a guy brave enough to want that. It is the confidence of a man who owns his cock and knows exactly what to do with it and where to put it. Thinkers, in my experience, can't fuck; they're too busy with the meaning and the metaphors, too busy avoiding their tool, afraid of entering a hole without a clearly marked exit. He is an underthinker—and overfucker. A-Man leaves the meaning of the metaphors to me.

He has given me almost no material gifts. Except one. A twelve-pack stack of yellow legal pads. I am writing on one now. Smart guy.

Why him? Four things:

1) *He loves me.*
2) *He knows how to fuck me.*
3) *He doesn't take me seriously.*
4) *He is not afraid of me.*

No one else had all four. Most only had the first, and even that was usually merely a sentiment, not a course of action. If you love me you shall fuck me without fear. I don't want to be a whore to a man's insecurities. I want to be a whore to my own.

STATISTICS

Enough—for now—of my story. What about yours? I am not alone, you know, in my sometimes unlawful obsession. Despite the landmark 2003 Supreme Court decision *Lawrence v. Texas* that renders all antisodomy laws unconstitutional and unenforceable, the statutes are still on the books in twenty-two states and Puerto Rico (and I suspect that Disneyland has an ordinance somewhere in the fine print). Every state in the Union had an antisodomy law until 1962, when Illinois became the first state to repeal the law. A steady spread of repeals in twenty-seven more states and the District of Columbia followed—good to know that all that ass-fucking in the nation's capital has finally been legalized.

Of the states where antisodomy laws can still be found in the legal literature, Kansas, Missouri, Oklahoma, and Texas are unique in that "the unspeakable vice of the Greeks" remains illegal only for homosexuals, whereas Alabama, Florida, Idaho, Louisiana, Michigan, Mississippi, North Carolina, South Carolina, Utah, and Virginia forbid it no matter what your sex—or species.

Definitions vary: in Rhode Island, for example, where the law

was repealed in 1998, sodomy was a felony, an "abominable and detestable crime against nature" meriting seven to twenty years in
jail—unless, of course, you were married. Then it was totally okay.
To think that you had to get married to get legally "abominable and
detestable." I really respect that sort of legal logic.

South Carolina is the only state that still defines sodomy as
"buggery," an affectionate nod, I assume, to the state's original
position as a British colony. This state also claims the impressive distinction of the most prosecutions: between 1954 and 1974, there
were no less than 146 buggery cases, resulting in 125 convictions.

A 1977 attempt in Oklahoma to repeal its antisodomy law was
unsuccessful due to a vote-delaying "chorus of giggles," according
to the official records. In Arkansas, where sodomy was defined as a
misdemeanor only for homosexuals, the bill was explicitly "aimed at
weirdos and queers who live in a fairyland world and are trying to
wreck family life." Good thing this law was declared unconstitutional in 2002, if only to deflect attention from the Arkansas legisla-
ture's propensity for queer and weirdo prose.

Minnesota gets high marks for animal rights: there was once a
curious addendum to their law, since repealed, stating that sex "between humans and birds" is strictly prohibited—sounds like some
sick fuck got his chicks confused. As a woman who prefers most animals to most people, I will say without reservation that I think this
particular statute should be reinstated to prosecute those particular
Homo sapiens who threaten the avian community.

The penalties that accompanied these laws varied widely: in

Utah, you could get off with a penalty of a thousand dollars, rendering the state one of the cheaper places in the Union in which to perform illegal sodomy. Back in 1857, a twenty-one-year-old Mormon man was ordered shot to death for "bestiality" with his horse, but, in a brutal reversal, the Mormon was spared while the horse was shot. Very sensible.

Speaking of Utah, I can't help wondering how Mormons feel about anal sex—with humans, that is—what with all those extra wives and orifices around the house. Does one prohibited penchant for multiple options lead to another?

One had to be very careful, however, in adjacent Idaho, where the same act could get you life in the slammer with all the other newly converted sodomites. This huge variable of penalty in such close geographic proximity suggests that the hundred-and-fifty-mile border between Utah and Idaho might be packed with cheap motels—Buggery Row—filled with Idahoans enjoying some bargain borderline behavior.

Despite its new legal status, sodomy remains the last taboo, sexually and socially. Oprah Winfrey talks about everything—rape, child molestation, incest, adultery, murder, drugs, homosexuality, bisexuality, even threesomes—but never, ever, about sodomy except in the guise of abuse and criminal behavior. Always a scandal, never an advertisement. "Odd how nineteeth-century literature is sealed off at both ends by an anal scandal," the theater critic Kenneth Tynan observed. "Wilde up Bosie's bum, Byron up Annabella's."

All this evidence leads me to believe that entering the exit will never become mainstream. Even the spell-checker on my computer that recognizes more than 135,000 words does not recognize *sodomize*. But that's okay. I know how to spell it.

PUBLIC INTEREST

There is, however, a growing underground movement of heterosexual backdoor behavior, according to the largest and most authoritative national survey of sexual behavior ever published in the United States. "Our data shows that anal sex was much more prevalent than might have been expected," begins the dry admission from the unsuspecting researchers. Overall, 25 percent of men and women try it in their lifetimes, and 10 percent have done so in the last year. Only 2 percent, however, on their "most recent" encounter—I just love statistics.

Nevertheless, between the ages of thirty and fifty, the likelihood of male heterosexual sodomy rises to a respectable one third of all men. One out of three. Think about it next time you're at a party and looking around the room. A curious footnote points out that all these percentages are only based on men's and women's two primary sex partners. Meaning: if someone is having anal sex with their #3 lover, then it is not reflected in these figures. Does it not count as statistically valid behavior if you're anal only with #3? Why are they not included? I suspect foul play. Who paid for this survey anyway? Or, perhaps, the trackers were onto a hidden truth: whoever is fucking your ass is never gonna be #3 or even #2. Ass-fuckers are always #1.

When they start breaking down the anal prospectors into socio-economic categories, things get even more interesting. The higher the level of education, the more anal sex. What are they teaching in college these days?

Unsurprisingly perhaps, both male and female atheists are the most likely backdoor enthusiasts, but the Catholics run a very close second. For the former it is pleasure, perversion, and possibly their only chance for the religious experience of submission; for the latter, no doubt, it's merely birth control.

While white women are the most common sodomitic recipients (Sue Johanson, Canada's Dr. Ruth, says 43 percent of all women have tried anal sex), their male counterparts appear not to be their most likely perpetrator. Hispanic men are the white woman's most likely ride for a trip to the other side. To think that anal sex actually encourages integration!

Perhaps even more politically correct is the less mainstream, but nevertheless significant, "bend-over boyfriend" movement. This movement certainly deserves . . . ah . . . well, these guys must deserve something for facing not only the terror of homosexuality but a girlfriend wielding a dildo bigger than their own dicks. And what a movement it is! The chance to be a girl, the chance to find out just how much submission it takes to have a hard, seven-inch cock up your bum. Come on, guys, bend over . . . take it like a man.

And there it is: the curious double standard common to so many straight men: terrified of getting it, but all too eager to give it. What is that about? How can they expect a woman to take a cock up her ass when they squeal if anything larger than a pinky finger is waved in their direction? Not that I'd want any man of mine to be bending over too eagerly. Definitely not. Protest is the only dignified position for a straight man to assume when he's consented to be ass-fucked. Protest every inch of the way, I say.

There is plenty of protest in Eve Ensler's popular play *The Vagina Monologues*. But why is it that in all those interviews, all those questions, all those monologues, there is not a single mention of a woman's asshole? So close and yet so far; the space that could change the world. All that "liberated" Pussy Talk, and yet so avoidant about what lies behind their sacred place: the hole of no return. Oh, well. It would be treason, I suppose, to advocate surrender at the rear for those who are just finally claiming victory at the front. Victory from behind, however, seems so much more, how can I put it . . . honorable. I can't but wonder if my play, *The Anal Dialogues*, could find a venue even off-off-off-Broadway? Perhaps in some dark performance space down some little-traveled back alley?

Clearly, yelling about butt-fucking from the rooftops—or on the national radio waves—is not advised. In April 2004, it was proposed that Clear Channel Communications, the nation's largest radio broadcaster, be fined no less than $495,000 by the Federal Communications Commission for a single twenty-minute segment of the *Howard Stern Show* in which Stern discussed, at some length, what he refers to as "anal." (It probably didn't help matters that the conversation was frequently punctuated by fart noises.) Thank God that having anal sex is so much cheaper than talking about it.

Despite this new trend of sodomitic censorship, ass-fucking has made several auspicious appearances recently on screens both big and small. The subject came up regularly in the popular TV series *Sex and the City*, whose heroines discussed not only men's growing interest in "the ass" but also their own willingness to accommodate those interests, the appropriateness of doing so on a first date, and the basic lube how-tos. Perhaps even more surprising was its mention in the Hollywood hit *Bridget Jones's Diary*. At one point, when Bridget is lying in bed after having sex with her caddish lover, Daniel Cleaver, she reminds him that what they just did is illegal in several countries. To which he replies, without missing a beat, that that's one of the reasons he's so pleased to be living in England today.

Is Daniel Cleaver the latest incarnation of the bad-boy lover, the zipless fuck for the twenty-first century? After all, the zipless ass-fuck simply takes zipless to a new hole level. So does missionary-position ass-fucking. The term itself conjures up such perfect contradiction: the most patriarchal position, the most biblically sanctioned, and yet, well, what a difference an inch can make. The experience on the other hand—best achieved with a nice firm pillow under the ass—makes me feel downright missionary. After all, here I am spreading the word, sharing the epiphany like a born-again believer, a convert, an anal zealot.

#145 and #146

We just completed both 145 and 146 consecutively in the course of an hour and a half. He never went down. I grabbed the base of his cock shortly after he had pulled out and shot vertically up my arched back, arcing over my face. His jizz landed squarely on a black velvet pillow with a satisfying splat. That look was still in his eye, that crazy fucking look, and I asked, "May I lick your cock?"

"Yes," he said gently, generously. And we did the whole thing all over again. Double bliss, double cum, exponential fun.

GETTING READY

If you want the whole thing, the Gods will give it to you.
But you must be ready for it.

—JOSEPH CAMPBELL

I dry the freshly washed K-Y tubes on my bath towel and put them back in the bedside drawer. I turn off the bathwater and strip into the wet heat. Knees drawn up, I fill my pussy with water and shoot it out like an underwater fountain. I watch the ripples in the water, sometimes lifting my hips so I can watch the fountain above water. After soaking, soaping, and shaving, I pull the plug, crouch on two feet, and with a slightly soaped middle finger reach gently into my ass and give it a good warm water bath. You could eat out of my ass, and on my ass; it's that clean.

Out of the tub I dry, cream, and powder my entire body—calves, thighs, ass, stomach, arms, neck, breasts—brush my teeth and hair, perfume my wrists and neck, and stain my lips red with a liquid rose potion.

I prepare the bedroom, clearing all books, papers, magazines, and remotes off the bed and piling the pillows at one end. From the closet I retrieve Pink Square, a rectangular pillow I bought because I liked its fleur-de-lis pattern. It doesn't match the colors of the other pillows, but it fits perfectly under my hips, raising them to cock height. It is one of A-Man's favorite amenities and once, when I forgot to put it on the bed, there was a moment when I saw him scanning the bedroom, perturbed: "Where's Pink Square?"

I go in my closet and plan an outfit. Sometimes a black bra and thong, or, occasionally, crotchless panties when I want to be a slut. Applied slutdom doesn't do much for A-Man, though, he just smiles indulgently when he sees those dainty crotchless wonders. But they don't turn him off, either.

A long silk or velvet gown, elegant but easily raised, is the most frequent choice. If I'm feeling like more exposure, I'll choose high, tight shorts and a skimpy top. Lady or slut, I wear high-heeled mules and keep them on throughout—or, at least, I try to. The sound of those shoes hitting the floor, pounded off me, one by one, is his sign that things are going well, that now we're rocking, that now she's lost control of her facade, her fears, even her shoes. It's usually when he's deep in my ass that I can't cling any longer to those heels.

I lay out my outfit on the bed and fill a couple of water bottles and place them around the room and open him a cold beer. I draw the curtains and light candles—at least ten of them. Frankincense adds to the smoke, the chapel is prepared for his confession—and my baptism. I turn off the phone machine and turn on the music. I gravitate to New Age spiritual and chanting monks—to which he comments with a grin, "Oh, we're having a holy fuck today?"—or Leonard Cohen or Tom Waits groaning as only they can: with inimitable angst. But Ella singing Gershwin is best. Ella is sexy but not slight, happy but not saccharine, serious yet funny—and completely subversive. Ella lilts, she taught me how. She is all about floozies, trollops, Delilah, and "boy-and-girl enjoyment." But in the end it's the rhythms. They are blow-job rhythms. Ella inspired me to suck cock like she sings—smooth, easy, deep, surprising, naughty, indulgent, clear.

Then the final cue. The phone rings and he whispers into my ear, "It's Time." This gives me ten minutes for the final ritual. Pussy shaving. I do this last, out of habit. In the beginning I was so distrustful that he would really show up, so unwilling to believe that I could have this pleasure yet again, that until I got that final call I was too fearful to shave. I wouldn't want to coif my mound for nothing. A freshly prepped pussy without a party to attend is a sad site indeed. It would be more disappointment than I could bare. So I shave last.

I am naked now, but in high heels. Can't shave my pussy without the heels on, never have, ever. They elongate my legs, turning my body into an easel displaying the canvas, my crotch, for the upcoming design. It makes me think of Jackson Pollock for some reason—though I am more precise than he in my execution.

Taking two new pink Daisy razors out of the drawer, I remove the plastic protective tip from the first one. I line up the tools: mirror, baby powder, aloe gel.

At this defining moment, ready to commit, but before the first cut, I always read the William Blake poem I keep on the bathroom windowsill in a tiny green-and-gold frame. It is called "Eternity."

He who binds to himself a joy
Does the wingèd life destroy;
But he who kisses the joy as it flies
Lives in eternity's sun rise.

This four-line poem is the reason I have had the courage day after day, month after month, to lay aside my fear of loss and proceed with A-Man in the present, the only place we exist together. In these lines I find the courage to shave my pussy, risking my dignity with every passage of the razor. Each swipe of the blades reveals my vulnerability far more than my sex. I bet Bill Blake never thought his profound little ditty would find such practical use for so profane an act on such sacred ground. Never mind, he is my seer.

Now, pussy trimming is an interesting subject. I am a complete believer. Trim down that wild bush, girls, let him get a view, let him get access. Waxing doesn't really work. It's good for a week, but then there's three weeks of bumps and stubble till you can wax again. I cannot tolerate bumps and stubble for three weeks. So I shave, every single time. I do it dry, using lots of baby powder and two new two-blade disposable razors each time. Against the grain, but gently. It never cuts and never takes off a layer of skin like wet shaving.

Then there's shape. I began with the simple side trims, the tutu trim, from my ballet-dancing days—a nice isosceles triangle. But then I went to a few strip clubs and got jealous of those very exposed, hairless pussies. Now I shave everything in between, smooth, smooth lips, and leave a nice little triangle on top—though carefully, carefully I trim on either side of the top of my slit, just to highlight and expose the magic crevice—very sexy, very porn. On the bed, legs over the head, mirror in hand, I shave the few hairs around my ass—smooth as a baby. I have, with this view, really come to see what he sees, what he loves, where he goes. My rosebud—not Citizen Kane's.

I dress. There are three firm knocks on the door. I'm ready.

New Year's Arithmetic

Eighty-four anal fucks this year—that averages 7 per month, that's 1.75 a week, one every 4.3 days. But he was out of town 21 weeks, in town 31 weeks, which averages 2.7 ass-fucks a week, which makes one every 2.6 days. I like the math; I do it to believe. Me and the Marquis de Sade: he counted, too.

HIS COCK

I always found cocks rather ugly—better not to look too closely. Wrinkled, asymmetrical, disparate shades of color. Dangling and silly when down, curved, veiny, and just plain weird when up. Was this foreign protuberance supposed to get me wet? Visually, it dried me up. Visually, it was humorous. And scary. And they all want you to lick it, suck it, and rub it. Ugh. The only thing I liked about it was the metaphor, a monument of vertical desire. And that unruly hair all over the place. It's insulting. When I deigned to go down on a man, hairs always caught on my tongue—and it can take ages to find that one curly culprit. In short, a cock was not a thing of beauty to me.

Now, women, they are beautiful. Breasts, hips, curves, asses, faces, eyes, lips, smell, pussy—everything about a beautiful woman is, well, beautiful. Would my eyes ever see a cock as an object of beauty? I tolerated them at worst and felt a mild, passing affection at best. And since they rarely did much for me during intercourse, I really had no proper place for them.

Then he came along and it all changed—in those first three

hours. The epiphany of the cock. I love his cock. Every millimeter, every centimeter, every movement at every moment. His was the first that spoke to me, that took me personally, that never failed me. A-Man remains calm in the face of his own erection—the ultimate test of male dignity.

In my experience, most men, when hard, don't act as if their penis is their own, but as if they have suddenly become subject to some kind of erectile radar device that forces them to relinquish all responsibility for its erratic behavior. A-Man, however, presents a complete paradox. Filled with the same juices, the same desires, the same hardness, he never loses his head. He uses his desire to create an event, to push boundaries, to do something not done before. He is the only man I've seen who can walk around a room with a killer erection and still look like a man with a mission—focused, alert, self-contained, and mischievous. He has the most noble erection I've ever met.

Sometimes we discuss just where exactly is his cock going in my body. Somewhere into the center, behind my belly button. We have even measured with the tape measure. Hard to tell the exact angle. What is sure is that he stirs my guts from right to left, forward, upward, sideways, and back. It really gets your attention, having a large cock in your ass, concentrates the mind. Each time, rebirth. Nearly a hundred and fifty so far. That is a lot of starting your whole life over. You might think, after all that ass-fucking, why am I still counting? I'm anal! There you have it. Back to the terrible twos.

The best way to feel, to know, a man's cock is through one's ass, where the walls cling to every inch all the way to the head. A pussy has less feeling, fewer nerves, less strength, less muscular power—and, often, less interest.

A pussy, genetically, wants impregnation, the juice; an asshole wants the ride of its life. Both holes, I would postulate, reconcile the problem of mortality as caverns for creation: vaginas for babies, asses for art.

Speaking of Michelangelo, there is the question of trimming the bush, the male bush. A-Man trims. In the beginning he didn't, and then one day I suggested that a trimmed rim around the base of his cock would look superb, like a samurai warrior. "Depilation is the act of a fastidious lover," states the *Kamasutra*. He thought about it for a minute and then promptly went into the bathroom and sat on the edge of the bathtub. As I held the flashlight, he trimmed. And trimmed, and trimmed. He went far beyond the original idea and just cut down the whole bush—sides, top, balls, underballs, everything. Now there's no going back to the bush. I have much better hand and mouth contact, no little curly hairs in my mouth, and his cock and balls look beautiful. Why doesn't every man trim? Vanity. The hair camouflages their shame. No hair, no shame.

THE LONG AND SHORT OF IT

All this talk about size. From where to where do you measure? From the front side? Belly side? Belly-button side to tip? Or from the base in front of the balls? Or, for that matter, from the more neutral two sides? And then do you measure the penis in a freestanding erection, or can you grasp the base and press down and in toward the body and use that extra inch or so in the measurement? And what are you measuring with? A ruler that doesn't bend? A tape measure that slips? The palm of a hand? A "good eye" combined with a good guess?

And who is doing the measuring? A doctor? A lover? The man on himself? (Can't trust that data.) What with all the possible—and probable—discrepancies, I would say that the calculation of penis size is a most inexact science, a study subject to such extreme variations that when men go on and on and on about size, I don't think they are even comparing penis to penis. In her book *Woman: An Intimate Geography*, Natalie Angier says the average erect human phallus is 5.7 inches (I wonder if she acquired this very precise number from first—or second—hand research? The term *hand job* suddenly takes on new meaning.) Less than half a foot. Yards shorter than a whale's dick, but almost twice the size of a four-hundred-pound gorilla's. God's humor.

Size matters. The perception of size, that is. By the man. In the end, size is more about attitude than inches—but attitude can come with inches. The size of a man's attitude about his penis is more important, and effective, than an extra inch on a small-minded man. On the other hand—or in the same hand, or even both hands—a bigger dick can take a woman farther, farther into herself, deeper into herself. But some women may not wish to go there, be taken there.

How a guy thrusts with his hips is a huge, often overlooked, fucking factor. A small dick with a strong thrust can achieve greater dominance than a big dick that hardly moves, that cannot do the dance. Personally, I cannot love a cock that cannot dominate me. Otherwise I retain too much power. And become totally tyrannical.

And then there's width to consider, something far less frequently referred to by men, which serves to prove yet again that men care more about other men than about their women. A thicker dick can generate an even deeper feeling of domination than a long one—in a pussy, where the most feeling is at the threshold. In an ass, length counts more. Harder to get a long one in, but more profound once there; it feels like it's knocking on your brain as it invades your soul. In short, when it comes to dick size, width for the pussy, length for the ass is the ideal formula . . . which of course underscores the importance of variety. While, obviously, a big cock is not the whole answer—it could of course be attached to an asshole—it can be your hole's answer, which is one place to start.

Women are taught that size doesn't matter, that it's the motion in the ocean. But this is a theory propagated by those bright guys with insecurities who need big theories. The guys who love their dicks are too busy fucking to care. They put their dicks where the others put their theories. Like a good girl, I believed the theory—until I found out I'd been had, not so much by little dicks but by men who thought they had little dicks.

I have learned to be careful with a man who doesn't love his penis. Suspicious of the myriad ways, physical and psychological, that he will compensate. Money, literature, flowers, poetry, promises, proposals, and proficient pussy diving are a few of the camouflages I've been subjected to. But it is always, in the end, a case of the emperor's new clothes, and the insecurity leaks out.

Now, there will always be plenty of women who are happy, happier, with the camouflages. So those men needn't worry—just make sure you get a chick who prefers a real pearl necklace to the washable kind, and a house with a mortgage to your dick in her ass.

I'll admit to penis envy, but only for a big one—if I had one of those, I'd fuck every pretty pussy I could find, nailing each to the cross of her servitude with my big cock. I'd consider it my job, my duty, my destiny. But in the end—in my end, anyway—it is not inches that matter. I have no sense of actual length in my ass, no ruler on my anal walls. I sense size by presence, by pressure, by depth. A-Man is a depth junkie. Of his emotional and spiritual depths I cannot speak with any authority, but I do know that he searches out the depths of my bowels like a demonic Victorian explorer, a gentleman possessed. Like Sir Richard Burton entering Mecca, he is the first Westerner to have infiltrated the tangled jungle of my bowels, my uncharted territory, the heart of my darkness. And he does so with a weapon of singular penetration.

#156

He hangs a large gilt mirror in my bedroom and then I suck his cock in front of it, profile, testing the reflection—it proves worthy. He then sits on the bed and says, "Now just slide back up onto my cock . . ." We're facing the same way. Obedient, I move too fast, too eager, and my ass is pierced with that anal virgin pain. "Okay, okay," he soothes, "I'll do everything . . ."

He turns me over, places me on Pink Square, and rests his cock at the entrance to my ass. Not moving, he reaches around, finds my clit, and pulses her until my ass releases. He then pumps my ass to kingdom come.

THE LESSON

One day we had a conversation. Having discovered how to surrender, I was committed to continue doing so. This entailed remaining passive, ready to submit, willing to let him manhandle me, to let him enter my ass. On this particular afternoon, he said that he loved fucking me—and my ass—that everything was terrific, and if it stayed as it was, he would still love it. But, he continued, if I learned how to suck his cock really well, that would be a real bonus. After swallowing my pride, I said, "Okay, teach me." And he did. So well. And then I started adding things of my own.

Sucking a dick is an art form. He gave me some basics. Wet, wet, wet, the wetter the better. Circling the base above the balls with a strong grip is good. So is circling the cock and balls with a one-handed grip. Mouth: no teeth, ever. Smooth, wet, tongue in, or better, tongue long and licking. Then we got to variations of movement, speed, tension, and rhythm. Change course, he suggested—surprise is good. Don't just do one movement over and over. Do one movement over and over and then switch. For example: base circled by the thumb-middle-finger cock ring, soft lips around his cock, down his cock, build up a consistent rhythm, watch his face, see him get closer, then pull out and lick down the back side of his cock, over the balls, and then suction them into your mouth one ball at a time, wet, wet, and with a mouthful of balls roll them around on your tongue like almonds, then lick back up the spine and deep-throat the whole throbbing thing. And variations on this.

Deep is good. Gagging is good. If you won't gag for your man, how can you really love him? Juices more slippery than saliva come up through the throat and coat his cock. It is the throat orgasm.

My blow jobs also made yet another marked improvement in the visual arena, after I sucked his cock in front of several different mirrors. Experimenting with various angles, I learned showmanship, delineation of movement, clarity of intent.

Learning to suck his cock was about concentration. This is the act now, and the only one; it is not a warm-up, it is the main event in that moment. I took these few pointers and practiced, and practiced, and practiced. It's all practice, like ballet, nothing but practice. The more I practiced, the more I discovered, the more I adored his cock, the more I adored myself, the more I adored him, the more I loved sucking his cock, the happier he got. Now he gets so happy that his eyes travel from mine and roll up into his head and his breathing changes and his cheeks flush and I fill with joy like an empty tank at a gas station.

It was while preparing to suck his cock one sunny afternoon that another pillow besides Pink Square found its place. I had been given a tiny, decorative heart-shaped pillow one year for Valentine's Day. It measured only nine inches across, was firmly stuffed, and boasted pink, black, and gold satin stripes on its cover with pink tassels around the circumference. The first time A-Man saw this rather silly little example of female frivolity, he grabbed it in his palm like a football, asked with amused bewilderment, "What's this?," and promptly tossed it off the bed.

He had never seen anything so completely useless being called a pillow; a pillow was for support and comfort, and this particular item promised neither. Until that inspired afternoon when the ostracized little pillow suddenly came into its own. As A-Man sat up at the end of the bed, I grabbed the heart pillow out of his way and, angling the pointed tip toward his ass, placed his balls on it. And there they sat, supported, cock on top, like a royal offering surrounded by shimmering gold threads and dangling pink tassels. We both looked down at the scene in silence. After a brief pause, he announced triumphantly, "It's the Ball Pillow!" We both laughed so hard that his imminent cocksucking was delayed for quite some time. And after that day, he always asked, along with Pink Square, for the Ball Pillow.

He never, ever comes in my mouth. I can suck his cock for forty minutes and he'll hold his power throughout, allowing me to give more, allowing me to love him. Receiving as he does really is a gift to me. I didn't know what a great art cocksucking could be, or what a practitioner I could be, until I found a man who could withstand so much pleasure for such extended lengths of time. So difficult with those guys who come at the mere sight of your mouth on the tip of their cock. It leaves me disabled, impotent.

After I suck his cock more fabulously than ever before, that much deeper, that much slower, that much faster, with a bunch of ball sucking, then, after his eyes roll up into his head several times over and he looks seriously disoriented, he takes my head firmly in his hands, refocuses, looks me straight in the eye and says, "Good girl."

To think I've been through all this, come this far, just to find out that all I ever really wanted was to be a good girl, Daddy's good girl. Finally.

THE UNFORTUNATE
AND BORING PLIGHT OF
SO MANY WOMEN

I am the victim of the unfortunate and boring plight of so many women—Daddy didn't love me enough way back when. And my life with men has become the long trail of my mostly subconscious and sometimes desperate attempts to fill that gap, to feel that love, to heal that hurt, to address that loss. Daddy loves me now, accepts me now, respects me now—and I love him. But this is irrelevant. That hole was dug early and is now part of me. My father can no longer fill it.

Besides, who would I be if he were not my father? Not me. Not me writing this. No, sir. So, in the end, I'm grateful. After all, I wouldn't want to be my unwounded self; she might not like ass-fucking and then where would she be? Certainly not in my privileged position, propped on Pink Square, ass in the air several afternoons a week. She'd probably be doing four loads of laundry for her husband and three children at about that same time and wondering about how to fill that emptiness she feels.

I've only ever met one woman who said that she not only had always adored her father, but that he adored her, always had, and she proudly stated that he was the most beloved man in her life. All the men wanted this woman. She had no hurt, no anger, and no edge. Eventually she married an insanely wealthy entrepreneur. But the rest of us are hurt, angry, and very edgy. Time bombs. Defusing the bomb is a challenge to the feminist man, and arrogance makes him think he can succeed. He can't. It's my hurt, my pain, and who are you to take it from me? I don't need rescuing, I don't need pity, I don't need opinions, I need fucking—and maybe a nice little spanking for indulging my anger.

I have always embraced David Copperfield's challenge to be the heroine of my own life. I just always thought it would involve great public deeds or heart-wrenching sacrifices, but no, it's not like that at all. When I suck his cock and he fucks me in the ass, I am that heroine. It is the deep and sure knowledge that finally, finally, I have really loved a man with no agenda except to love. After my daddy, that is miracle indeed.

He has unwound my wound.

My ass began life as the tiny pale recipient of Daddy's angry hand. It was the place of shame, the site of humiliation, the area to hide from The Hand. It received the proof of my shameful badness, my seemingly unavoidable wrongness. I was Bad and I was Punished. And now that same ass—older but wiser—is the coveted arena of a lover's pleasure where I am naughty and rewarded. And so my ass remains the strongest point of contact with the most important men in my life. It holds my deepest and oldest emotional nerve endings.

Is there a direct connection between getting spanked on the bottom, as I was as a child, and my inclination to being anally penetrated? Possibly. If every father who spanked his little girl thought he might be creating a hungry little sodomite, well, that might be a deterrent.

Being sodomized now, by choice, reconciles this injury with a scenario of the dominant male and the obedient little girl. Instead of rejection and criticism, I am told, "Good girl, good girl." The nastier I am and the better I suck his cock, the better I am, until I'm the goodest little girl in the world. I am finally loved. The relief it brings me is profound.

I, with my total submission, in fact wield a great healing power: the more I submit the more excited he gets, until I enter the deepest phase of surrender and he comes. He only comes when I've given it up. It takes a lot of surrender, discipline, and love to let a man fuck your ass hard enough, long enough, deep enough, and fast enough to shoot. His orgasm is my victory over my lesser self, over the pain of my anger. It fills the hole; I'm finally whole.

#162

Owwww! My dad just left after a lovely friendly visit of a week, and three hours later I was doubled over in literal gut-wrenching pain lasting a solid twenty-four hours. Like I'd been punched in the stomach, like I'd rewound in one hour 161 unwinding ass fucks. So the only logical thing to do was go for #162. Jesus, that hurt. New levels of tolerance, new levels of release, new levels of discipline. As he entered I thought, not so painful, I'm already healed by being naked with my ass on display. I was wrong. By the time he got in five inches and then some, he was pushing into the fist in my gut and rolfing me from the inside. It hurt like hell but I didn't say a word. I just maintained the pain level just past bearable and adored the challenge all the while thinking, Girl, you really are Daddy's little masochist.

DEVOTION

A-Man does not require my devotion, he says, but he has it anyway. Sometimes I give up so much power to him, give up even more than I have, and this leaves me vulnerable just beyond my own capacity to endure. The best antidote for this is not biting the bullet and suffering like some deeply ethical woman—I have, at least, matured beyond that. No, the antidote is another guy. It's called "The Two-Guy Solution." Every woman should subscribe when necessary. Many already do without admitting to it. As one friend put it, "If you're having trouble with one man, just call another man." For me, A-Man with the occasional Hound form the ideal combination. Someone needs to give to me as I give to him—power, that is.

While it is my greatest desire to surrender to him, with anyone else I am dominant. I never fuck anyone else, and no one else goes in my ass with their cock.

On one occasion, shortly after #169, I felt the need and called an old Hound friend. He announced, to my surprise, that he really wanted to fuck me—which was out of the question. But he let it be known that for a price he would eat my pussy: amazing how demanding Hounds can get when left alone too long. The money would give him detachment—he would be a tongue for hire. I loved the idea of turning a man into a whore—though it did feel a little too politically correct. But before even negotiating a price, he proposed that he would give me a freebie under the condition that I be entirely dominant, dictating every turn, every move, fulfilling my every desire. Okay, okay, I said—but just this once. I can, on occasion, be compliant with a Hound; I could be a dominatrix for a night. It would, however, have been easier to pay him. We were now both "topping from the bottom"—and I wasn't sure who was actually in charge anymore.

He came over and I was ready for him, reclining on my bed in my boudoir in black lingerie. First I asked for admiration while he sat in a chair. Why was I the hottest chick at the party? He explained. In his life? He explained further. I found this game to be quite fun. In the whole world? He explained still further, but this time I was not convinced. Next game. We examined my ass in the mirror from all angles, and he pointed out every curve and line to explain why it was the best ass—best in the boudoir, anyway. Then we looked at how my shaved pussy lips peeked through my thighs below my ass when I bent over. This was really fun—right out there with it all, shamelessly.

So far he hadn't been allowed to touch me. Lying on my bed, I then asked for a back massage, then a breast and stomach massage, then a butt massage, then a hip and thigh massage. Then I told him to go back to the chair, sit down, take out his cock, and stroke himself while I displayed my pussy to him like a stripper girl on the runway, spread lips, swollen red clit, long lean legs, killer shoes. He got pretty fucking hard.

Then I asked that he lick my pussy for a while, taking long strokes from my ass to my pussy to my clit and back again, the whole wet package. That was great. Really just great. Next I asked him to concentrate on rimming my asshole with slowly increasing pressure until his tongue started forcing its way inside: "Like you want it." "Like?" He did want it. Then he served me four or five inches of a red chili pepper vibrator up my ass. I hadn't asked for that part, so to speak, but it was hot so I didn't object.

Then followed some straight-on clit licking, for as long as it took while I tried to hold out. During this time I indulged all my fantasies, flipping randomly through my Rolodex. Of A-Man watching this other guy lick me and being amused at my outrageous indulgence, approving, and saying to him: "You keep doing that till she's had enough, then I'll fuck her ass." Then I fantasized that A-Man was licking my clit relentlessly—but that was way too exciting, so I had to stop. Then I imagined all the men I've been with, and dumped, in a lineup, outside my bedroom window, watching. I displayed my pleasure and my juice like a whore. On and on with the fantasies until the final one, the finishing one: Reality.

This man, for reasons I don't really understand—could it be love?—is willing to be slave to my orgasm, licking until I have had enough (and enough for me, of course, is a lot). This overwhelming experience of abundance pushed me, unexpectedly, into a state of gratitude that manifested in a full body, curved, deep, silent orgasm that took twenty minutes to return from. The Hound, dear, darling Hound, left me quietly, so I could bask in the enormity of the blessedness of my life and the peace of power returned: his submission to me balancing mine to A-Man. Now I'm ready to be fucked in the ass again. I'll do whatever it takes to be ready for A-Man. This is a measure of my devotion—and, I suppose, of the Hound's, too.

RAZING THE BARRE

Training as a classical ballet dancer, as I did, is surely the most intense physical training possible for a young body—day in, day out, hour after hour of meticulous sculpting, shaping, and coercing the body, the belly, and the limbs into shapes, angles, and lines that reach far, far beyond one's natural physical state. Always going for more of everything, more length, more turns, more turnout, more strength, more-more-more. It takes both body and mind into a place of existence that is beyond normal experience. I learned from the age of four to experience my life through my body, inside my body, always on the brink of perpetual endurance.

All this, I believe, prepared me for getting fucked in the ass. It answers the call of my physical masochism. It re-creates the physical extremism of dancing, the discipline, the striving for perfection. It is my being in extremis. Now that I am retired from dancing all of life has a dull edge—except this. A-Man calls it "the Hard Edge of Truth."

Dancing is about being in service to the choreographer, to the steps, to the music. Allowing this man into my ass reproduces this dynamic of service, of yielding to something greater than myself. Learning to go past—way past—one's physical comfort level, and to love that moment of going past, is intrinsic to a dancer's training. It is only in passing this place that one finds that Edge where Risk is real and Rapture resides.

If you have a ballerina's tight ass like mine, the pain and pleasure of the internal pressure of sodomy are inseparable. Ballet school perfects the desire to be perfect, and you can end up a delightful and disciplined little slave. I understand that receiving a cock in your ass goes right in tandem with the psychology of perfectionism that afflicts high achievers like myself. To begin with, we need it: being perfect results in a very tight ass. Secondly, the challenge to remain perfect while being anally penetrated is one of the greatest challenges one could entertain. To succeed surely proves one's inner and outer perfection of being, shape, health, and resilient attitude. Recipient sodomy is a perfectionist's dream, a masochist's nirvana.

But—as with most things anal—the opposite is also true. Getting ass-fucked while wearing one's metaphorical tutu is perhaps the ballerina's most propitious—and scandalous—debut. But it is also her crucifixion, her ultimate sacrifice to transcend the human to find the divine. Never on the stage, however, did I feel as safe as I do when I obey A-Man completely and he covers my face with his big, strong hand and rocks my ass onto his cock. An incredible sense of relief—I have completely let go not only of all control but all responsibility and have given it to him. The sense of safety is so high with him because any time spent with him is the only waking time when my anxiety is gone, when I am not afraid.

#175

Well, I did just give him a truly insane blow job—cock, balls, ass-hole—the full run over and over, ending every now and then with full cock-throat immersion. Every blow job for me is an act of insanity because I feel every one could be the last, and so every one contains all I have. Fuck on the edge. Suck on the edge. All ways.

OLD ORGASMS

Is anal sex sex? I keep on wondering about this. My connection to him is primarily penetrative and, specifically, anal. Is this sex? Or merely an act of spiritual submission, divine submission?

My orgasm arc with him is an act of giving, opening, giving. With others it is withholding, a battleground of control. In the past, I have achieved orgasm through the paradoxical experience of maintaining control of my pleasure all the while that my orgasm, with a life force of its own, desires its own fruition. The battle—and it is a battle—always ends with an orgasm more potent for its release than for any emotional pleasure. There are quite a few men out there who want nothing more than to please. For them I come in angry triumph: the greater my contempt for their wishing-to-please, the greater my resistance; the greater my resistance, the greater my orgasm. This is the pleasure, literally—and clitorally—of the war between the sexes. Afterwards, so sensitized, I shun all touch and, like Garbo, want to be alone. To take notes, eat dinner, and read *The New Yorker*. Is this any way to come? Well, it is one way.

With him I have learned another. The way of no resistance. Of infinite contractions and many arrivals. And it was not a struggle to give up the struggle. It just happened with him, as if my body knew—I sure didn't—that he was the one, the one man I could trust, the one man I could give to without his misinterpreting the gift, taking advantage of it, making it mean what it didn't mean. Perhaps it was his beauty. DNA to DNA. He does have, objectively speaking, the most beautiful physique of them all. Maybe my clit knew he was my sexual mate long before I did. Just as it knew that resistance was necessary to all those men whose DNA was not a match for mine. With them I come from hostility, with him from love.

#181

Last night—181.

I tell him, after, "A hundred and eighty-one." And I point out that that is just ass-fucks, that does not count pussy warm-ups.

"What does that tell you?" I say.

"That tells me three-hundred and sixty-two," he said, "that's what that tells me. Three sixty-two tells me it's a good year."

SOUVENIRS

As we approached two hundred, I found that my desire for continual repetition, for impossible guarantees, was intensifying. Managing my relentless need to be in that place with him became a full-time job. There was the disastrous day when the cleaning lady grabbed his well-worn shirt off my bed with the sheets and I came home and saw, to my horror, that she had washed, dried, and neatly folded my aromatic lifeline. I had slept every night with the shirt that smelled like him. Now it smelled like Bounce.

All these endless words thrown toward this act, this Holy Fuck, all in the attempt to believe it, believe in something so deep and powerful, to hold on to it, to not let it expire into the black hole of my private terror. My demons are like an infection in the soul and they desire to devour and destroy the truth—and even the beauty—of my very own experience. They are the Devils. My Devils. Damn the Devils.

It's all about evidence. My quest for evidence. Evidence of attachment because attachment predicts repetition. Once one has been taken to the land of primal joy, revisiting that land becomes one's sole desire. Words, a call, a look, a sigh, the third erection of the afternoon, all are evidence. A condom shot through with cum; two condoms, one shot through with cum, the other empty because he pulled out and shot up my back and into the soft hair at the nape of my neck. His worn shirt, his scent—my madeleine. Or it can be a fuck count. That is why I count, to know it really happened, to know it might happen again. Like a detective, I amass the evidence of love, love that was, love that is, and therefore try to convince my internal jury that love will be. All too often, however, I don't believe the evidence. Until the next time. Another number, another reprieve. Another shot, another high.

I am an anal addict, but only with him. I want it consistently, frequently, repetitively, ritually, and if I don't get it I become sad, tearful, lonely, beleaguered, unhappy, grouchy, faithless, and miserable. I want to mainline him. Only his penetration of my ass excavates my fear and restores my faith, the faith he created.

When an experience of love arrives that demotes all others to impostors, it brings, inside the joy, a haunting fear. How could this delight have been showered upon me, a mortal woman with the usual sins, unhealed wounds, desperate anger, and fierce desire?

"Why me?" says my voice of disbelief.

"Why not me?" says a small, faint voice not my own, echoing up from my gut.

Then I found the best evidence of all—the one that actually worked, that relieved the withdrawal symptoms and gave me solace. He had a game, the postcoital fling-the-condom-into-the-wastebasket-by-the-bed game. Not surprisingly, his aim was amazingly accurate. After he left, I would resituate the condom so that it dangled over the top edge of the basket, the pocket of cum weighing it down, the rim secured by the still sticky K-Y. And I would leave this trophy there where I could easily see it, until the next time he called and said, "It's Time." Time to shave my pussy, time to turn off the phone, time to make way for new DNA, time for time to end. With this ritual I contrived to never be without his molecular makeup near me at all times.

Whenever I looked at that condom, and I looked a lot, I felt the rush of his beauty. I've always been a sucker for symbolism; this dangling rubber provided me with the opaque evidence of what was, and will be again. I clung to his DNA until given the next deposit—as if my subconscious took refuge in the theoretical knowledge that there was a possibility at all times of re-creating his essence. Those condoms comforted me, reminding me of the fourth dimension, the dimension beyond bills, anxiety, self-loathing, and desire, the dimension where bliss reigns, and I am its babbling slave.

#200

Always before, I doubt.

Always after, I don't.

Two hundred entries into my bowels, two hundred times I doubt and then believe.

What's it going to take? Two hundred and one.

FOREPLAY

Knock . . . knock . . . knock. When I open the front door, he is always slow to enter. He is in no rush; A-Man knows where he's going. And where he's coming, too. He steps inside, I lock the door, and we are sealed inside together. I feel the warmth rising already. Then the hug, the holding. The full-body holding that starts the coming, his and mine. Strong, enveloping, possessive. I start moaning and I feel his cock pushing at me. He grabs my hips and presses them into, onto, his cock. It's hard to break the hug, but we must get to the bedroom; it's imperative. If we don't make it there, tchotchkes always get smashed. The bedroom is our padded cell, where insanity can be unleashed without excessive material damage.

Sometimes he just turns me around, facing forward, his cock pressed up against my ass, and keeping the contact, leads me to the bedroom as we synchronize our walk so as not to break position. But before the first step, I find my speaking voice, and ask if he wants any food, if he's hungry. He always declines, but I always ask. We are very polite with each other.

Once we're in the bedroom, the hug is often revisited. Those first hugs establish Loveland, but now it's time to leave that invisible place and travel to Lustland, where things are visible and tangible and so unreal. Now he's totally hard, his pants aren't fitting right at all. He backs away from me and slowly, carefully, deliberately takes off all his clothes, keeping his eyes on me the whole time. I just watch and wait. He'll let me know what he wants. He always does.

Sometimes he'll speak softly and say, "Get on the bed—on your knees—now pull up your dress." Then he eats me out, from behind. Other times, he will just take my body and position me where he wants me—crouching on a pillow before him as he feeds me his cock, or flat on my back on the bed while he pinches my nipples through my dress or . . . But whatever happens now, it's all in slow motion. After a lot of cocksucking, and I mean a lot, he moves me around and grabs a condom and then I know we are about to enter the next stage.

Pussy sex is foreplay. Sometimes he skips my pussy altogether and goes straight to my ass, really nasty, only ass—the exit stage. But usually he does pussy first. As he enters me I feel him push up against my cervix, push into my cervix, and it always startles me. I enter the Zone of Release. Sometimes he'll get so far up there and then start pulsing, with expert little thrusts, pushing my walls outward, upward, further into my being. Every pulse wants more and gets more. This is the beginning of moreness, a state of body longing that craves without cease. The waves of pleasure roll in slowly, then more quickly, but they never stop. Pinnacle after pinnacle, most might deem it the best ever, even transcendent. But he and I are greedy and know where to go for more. There is this amazing moment where love is saturating the room and yet loss is not present. We're just beginning. Just warming up.

After he has had enough pussy (always his choice), he pulls out and situates me — sometimes on Pink Square, sometimes on all fours, sometimes sideways, hip curved upward like a Henry Moore. However he sees it, he gets it. Already well fucked, I am now at my most obedient. My will is now about 40 percent depleted, but I am still holding on to my consciousness, to my awareness, and to my high heels. I have much more to give. Much more. I have the power to give, give power. Other lovers never even got 10 percent of what I have to give. They didn't have the power to ask for it. He does . . . and then he asks for more than that.

REAR ENTRY

He places me on my left side, two pillows snug under my hip, raising my ass in a fetching little upward sideways arch. I rest my left
cheek on the bed, turn my head, and look up to him—it's always up
with him, never down. He grabs one of the tubes of K-Y scattered
about the bed. I adore the sound as the top clicks open. Looking at
me, he squeezes a gob onto two of his fingers. Looking to my ass, he
spreads my cheeks so deliberately I cannot believe my luck. He rubs
the gel gently, firmly onto my asshole, into my asshole, rimming the
entryway, smoothing the passage. There is the most wondrous look
on his face as he does this, alternately gazing in my eyes and gazing
to my ass. He slips a finger inside, then two, watching my face,
keeping the gaze as I feel his fingers turning inside me, connecting
us internally and externally, full circle. Sliding his fingers out, he
squeezes more K-Y onto his fingers and rubs it smoothly along the
length of his cock, hard as a rock.

It's Time.

Holding his cock, he guides it toward the crack in my ass, like a
canoe aiming down a narrow ravine. I feel the smooth tip, both

hard and velvety on my skin. The center of my asshole, like a magnet, gravitates toward the pressure. We meet. His key to my door, his positive to my negative, his plug to my socket.

And the light goes on.

Center to center, he nudges, I breathe, he pushes, I release, he pulses, I open, he pushes, he pushes, I open, he plunges in, our eyes lock, and he sends me home.

Sometimes he'll then pull back, and thrust short at the entry for a while, other times he'll slide inward, downward, slowly, slowly until he is buried in my ass with no cock to spare, only balls outside. He'll stay there for a moment, not moving. Then he'll pulse farther. Sometimes he will move me into a different position—on my hands and knees; or standing up while bending over, hands plastered to the wall; or on my back, feet to the ceiling; or, a favorite, legs over my head and ass to the ceiling. Whichever position I'm in, he remains above me, always looking down upon me, watching me, loving me. And he'll usually make these shifts without pulling his dick from my ass. Totally fantastic. But whatever the angle I can feel his cock growing inside me, stronger, harder, deeper, pressing into my anxieties, my pettiness, my pride, my vanity. Like a vacuum to dust, he sucks out my lesser selves, removes my sins. One by one they are suctioned away and underneath he finds my goodness, my innocence, my four-year-old before she was hit by The Hand and got mad. This is what he was looking for. This is what he finds. This is what he gives me.

Fucked off my feet, my shoes fall to the floor with a thud, one by one. He smiles and says affectionately, "Now we're having fun." Now I'm traveling on the fast train to paradise. Unschooled as I am in the process, tears often fall out of my eyes. Like a true gentleman, he will shield my eyes with his broad hand, giving me privacy, while he fucks me harder and harder, faster and faster, squeezing out the tears.

When I finally release everything, not one centimeter of my being holding on to anything at all, when my ego is annihilated, then the laughing begins. It can begin while I'm still crying, the energies are the same, though the tears are more familiar. But somewhere, somehow, along the way, my unconscious bursts open and I laugh and laugh and laugh. The harder I laugh the harder he fucks my ass until the whole thing makes no sense at all. Now we are really having fun. He looks at me laughing, and then, content that I'm on the road with him, he fucks me some more, ever vigilant, ever present. My laugh sometimes deepens and I laugh like I never laughed before. I recognized it immediately the first time it happened—the cackle of the crone. It is the sound of a woman who is caught inside the mystery of the universe, in the irony of the angst, in the place that ego abhors. Bliss.

At first the pleasure was unbearable and I'd try to pull away, try to know what was happening. But he doesn't let me, fucking me so relentlessly that any attempt to backtrack to control is useless. It is here that his domination is complete. I am his slave and he forces harmony upon me, against my ferocious fear. With repetition I have come to accept it, and now I don't only visit but have learned how to stay there. Meanwhile he is looking at me, all tears, giggles, and gut-laughs, and says, "You are CRAZY, girl." He looks a little dazed himself, but unlike me, he maintains total control, total awareness.

I look up as he kneels above me, deep inside me, and I see the most beautiful thing I ever saw. Like Michelangelo's *David*, his chest is broad, his skin is smooth, his hands are huge, his face beatific. I see the beauty of this man, the beauty of man.

I never saw this before.

#220

I fell madly, quickly, and completely, forever, the first time he fucked my ass. Now it's #220 and my love has only deepened—220 times deeper. I adore him, for good and better (it's never worse), and it is a kind of rapturous indulgence to so unconditionally adore the entire skin surface of another human being's body. Before I liked men in parts—their lips or eyes, their hands or chest, only occasionally the cock itself. With him I love all those and every nook, cranny, and space in between—and his cock, balls, and asshole most of all.

In worship lies freedom. The freedom of withholding nothing, which propels one into the elliptical realm of love.

ANAL ORGASM

As I learned how to stay in the bliss, I found something else. I have become pure vehicle for his cock, no resistance. I can relinquish all power. I feel such a gravitational pull to this man, who can, and will, disempower me, so willing to give everything away, to bestow it upon him. I never knew how much power I had until I gave it all to him through my ass. My ass is a pipeline for power.

I am, I have come to realize, his runway, his launchpad. And after numerous runs to the edge of inevitability, the final one begins. I can tell it's the one because it coincides, always, with my ability to commit to complete submission, to remain completely open without reserve, without limit. Once he feels this, he aims for the gold. If I show any sign on my face, or inside my ass, of reneging on my submission, he slows down and works me until my ass believes that there is only one choice, only one way. No choice but surrender is surrender. I am his entirely, body, soul, and asshole. I relish my freedom.

Molded onto his cock, I feel its urgency. The road to orgasm is a straight line into my ass, into the center of my being, into the center of the world. I don't know who starts the coming. I do, however, know that he is the only man whose orgasm interests me more than my own—no small feat. On one level, I feel like his cock sets off my contractions and my contractions then set off his . . . but then his set off mine . . . Contractions in my ass, involuntary contractions: anal orgasm.

I ride his orgasm like a jockey on a wild stallion, never losing contact but never in control. He explodes. My ass has sucked us together into an airless vacuum and we are one thing. Fused in a timeless space, I experience my destiny directly as being that moment and no other.

We are very happy after. We usually don't speak, just eyes in eyes. I used to like discussing the event once I regained my voice. What is it? What is it really about? Why does it happen? What, in fact, is happening? On and on. We don't discuss it now, because I know I shall never really understand. Now I am just grateful. Now I just want a three-hour ass-fuck where I give him all my power, he takes it, and takes me to visit God. That's all I need. Over and over and over. I want to die with him in my ass.

#246

Last night I am home from a three-week trip. He is over, and we are silent. He fucks my mouth and my pussy both, long and hard. Then, in my newly virgin ass, slow, deep, one plunge to the hilt. When all in, with my ass suctioning about his cylinder, he finally speaks. "Welcome home."

"Welcome home," I echo, sucking him in.

Later, tired, jet-lagged, overwhelmed, I start to cry—though nothing is particularly wrong. He looks at me weeping and tells me how wonderful my life is and then places my clenched little hand over his crotch, saying, "And I've got this big cock here for you— you can hold it if you like." I break from my self-pity and grab in his shorts, finding his cock in the folds, the gearshift that drives my life. I look up to his face in the shadows and see his eyes are glistening. Then a drop runs slowly down his cheek . . . and another. Astonished, I ask why he is crying. "I don't know," he murmurs. Almost 250 ass-fucks got us here, into the essence of unspoken sweetness.

THE BOX

A beautiful, tall, round, hand-painted Chinese lacquered box.
Black and gold. Shiny. A pussycat with long white whiskers on
the lid.

The collection.

The collection of the collection.

The condoms. Used. Filled. Hundreds.

Latex, sealed with K-Y.

Evidence. My mortality. His immortality.

DNA. The X and the Y. The Code. Forever.

My homage.

My altar.

My treasure.

His life.

PARADISE

I have learned a few things, by now, about Paradise.

Paradise is not that thing in the nebulous, far-off future, in another place, or another world, or another galaxy. It is not a state of mind, or a place in the mind. Nor is it the exquisite sexual pleasure of pulsing blood and moaning desire. Paradise is not achieved only after great suffering. There may well be great suffering before or after Paradise, but it is not the requirement for entry. Wounded ego and rampant narcissism demand suffering. Paradise is just there, here, if you really want it.

I am sitting on the threshold. Perhaps this is the final paradox of God's paradoxical machinations: my ass is my very own back door to heaven. The Pearly Gates are closer than you think. Sacred and profane united in one hole.

Paradise is free. A gift. A state of grace. A dance of time and space. It resides inside the ego and outside the ego, a place of pure harmony, another body riding your ass like it was the last fuck on earth.

Paradise is an experience that in real time may last only seconds.

But in those immeasurable fragments, time stops, and only when time stops does death die and Paradise is entered. It is revealed in the spaces of time when the self is penetrated so deeply that it is pried wide open and love rushes in like an ocean through a porthole.

And Paradise, once known, becomes the goal of every waking moment, its loss inherent in every waking moment. This is the burden of Paradise found.

#262

*He's back! He was gone but now he's back. A phone call and he's
over. Declarations. Tears. Hilarity. Clarity. In front of the blazing
fire, insane kissing, sucking, and fucking. Insane. Completely insane.*

*I am clear. Clearly blinded. I am his mother, sister, daughter,
and friend. He is my father, brother, son, and friend.*

After, we watch the flames and he says, "See what we've done?"

"What?"

"We've created love out of sex . . . And we've only just begun."

"Yeah," I say, "Maybe I'll fuck you in the ass next."

*He grins, pauses, and tells me to stand in front of him, turn
around . . . and he bends me over . . .*

No dice with A-Man.

REAR-ENDED

Where do you go once in Paradise? What happens when Adam and Eve enter Eden? And eat the apple? I will tell you. Perfection cannot be maintained. With time, cracks appear in the walls of the Garden—and reality, insipid reality, slithers in with its insidious poison. The snake of knowledge.

At some point well past the two-year mark, my relentless attempts to trust that A-Man was real and really in my life paid off. I had finally convinced myself that there was some form of unpredictable continuity to our connection. Before, I had only one focus: the need to believe in our existence. But once I finally accepted "reality," the rest of the world soon followed. I tried to plug the leaks, ignore the signs, deny the chaos—but the world proved to be even stronger than my passion for A-Man.

He was constantly leaving town for work; sometimes for weeks, sometimes for months. I found his absences increasingly difficult to manage. One time, I hired a pretty woman in a pink-sequined minidress to come to my house and pray for me, while I cried, for a hundred and fifty dollars. That's how bad it was.

Then he called. Prayer answered. All's well, he says, except one thing. His cock won't reach across four states into my ass. Things are funny and good again, for a few hours. And I don't tell him just how difficult things are for me. Never told him. Ever. Why would I? Reality was oozing in anyway, but why open the door wide?

Another time I consulted with a friend, afraid that after his three-month absence he wouldn't return to me as before. My friend laughed: "Two-hundred and sixty-something ass-fucks and you need more evidence?" The only one that counts, I explain, is the next one. And I am dead serious. I then explored a sex and love addiction twelve-step program, went to a few meetings, and read the textbook. From its point of view—which I tried adopting for a week or so—he is my drug, I am an addict, and abstinence is the beginning of re-covery. This information was horrifying—my situation was an ill-ness! And comforting—I could follow their plan to heal from this illness, in the company of similarly sick people, and get all the sup-port I wanted.

But I was assailed by doubts. When is it love and when is it ad-diction? Did I, once again, want to pathologize myself, especially af-ter my hard-won sexual liberation? Did I wish to regard the great opening of my heart and ass as a problem to be solved rather than a gift to be honored? Did I wish to view this flawed, flesh-and-blood man as nothing but a projection of my own illusions, obsessions, conflicts, and screaming sexual desires? This felt like a limited per-spective. Besides, the first thing a sex addict must do is to stop hav-ing sex. I'd suffered celibacy in my ten-year marriage; was I now going to choose it voluntarily? The textbook had a whole chapter on just what hell to expect from withdrawal—I found little solace in it. It would be hell indeed to withdraw from loving whom I loved. Perhaps this was not the pain of an addict in the grip of disease but simply the pain of a woman in love confronted with the loss of her beloved. (When I told A-Man, much later, after #270, that I was "addicted" to him, he looked highly amused and responded without missing a beat, "You damn well better be.")

There were other disincentives to "recovery." The meetings were mostly attended by men with a lot of compulsive-masturbation and Internet-porn obsessions. I imagined their computer monitors stained with crusty semen drips and their sexual fantasies running wild as they shared their distraught and ambivalent hopes of abstinence. It felt dangerous to be an attractive woman in their presence. Then, at the end of one meeting, a reforming addict held my hand with just a little too much sympathy and I never went back. My problem was love; his was lechery.

I then turned to Buddhist meditation to deconstruct my suffering—to accept it as a karmic consequence of my past lives and present life, to tolerate it without blaming anyone, even to welcome it as part of life's natural cycle. I tried to look at my own contribution to my unhappiness. I would meditate on the suffering of others, and attempt to lay the groundwork for less suffering of my own the next time he left town. I would try to remember that the pain of my loss and attachment is an illusory phenomenon.

I thought about how simple life might be if one removed sexuality from the equation. Between the search, the conquest, the fucking itself, the residual emotions, and the desire for repetition, my sex life was almost a full-time job: without it, I could save a great deal of time and energy. A very great deal. For what? Compassion for all rather than obsession with one?

But after months and months of all this "spiritual" work, I still wanted A-Man in my ass—as frequently and as predictably as possible. I was, it appeared, incurable.

There I was—searching, searching, searching for the solution to my pain to no avail. Then she found me.

HER

One day, walking into the locker room at the gym, I saw the quiet brunette, the one I assumed A-Man fucked on occasion. I said my usual warm hello, but instead of her usual warm smile back, I was greeted with an icy stare and sulky silence.

The next time I saw A-Man, I recounted the exchange. Did he know why she might have snarled at me? Well, yes, he did know. Apparently she had recently confronted him, demanding to be told if he was fucking anyone besides her. (Surely, I thought smugly to myself, she already knew the answer to that particular question.) He said that he asked her if she was certain she wanted an answer, and she insisted that she did. So he said yes. But she didn't stop there. She wanted to know who. So he told her about me. Apparently this was a total surprise to her. She had known we were friends, but I guess she didn't know the whole of it. Or the half of it. Or the back half of it. Well, he told me, she couldn't stop crying. He clearly didn't feel good about this, but he also knew that he'd only told her what she'd insisted on hearing.

Was she sorry, I wondered, that she'd asked? It seemed like such an obvious error on her part. She was not, apparently, only snarling at me, but very angry at him as well. I was slower to realize that I, too, had asked about something better left alone; if I had never queried him about my encounter with the mousy brunette, A-Man would never have mentioned their blowup. It was us women asking for information that we didn't really want that precipitated the events that followed. On that day, however, I just listened, feeling somewhat aloof. If anything, I enjoyed that slight thrill of drama in our midst as we proceeded into the glory of ass-fuck #272.

But the next day, and the one after that, I realized that I had been given unsolicited confirmation that he *was* fucking her on occasion and I really hadn't wanted to know that. This made her real to me in a way that she never had been before. Were we competing for A-Man? She clearly thought so, and was putting up some sort of fight, or at least a protest. I had always assumed that there was no fight, no competition, because I was simply in the far superior position to her or anyone else that A-Man might have been fucking. It was technically impossible that he could have been having anything greater or even equivalent with anyone else—there simply wasn't time in a day, or cum in his balls . . . Or was there?

And thus my mind started working. What was their connection? How was their sex? Was he with her the way he was with me? Did he mold her onto his cock the way he did me? Did he fuck her ass, too? What had he done to make her so attached? And what about her kept his interest? Was she to him what a Hound was for me—a balancing act? Now that his little harem was in my face, I couldn't pretend it wasn't there. The jealousy began and I couldn't stop it. But I was determined to try.

This, I reminded myself, was the price of not being monogamous. Perhaps it was time to review the price of monogamy.

If I asked A-Man to be monogamous, then I would always know I had taken his freedom, and I loved him basking in his freedom. I did not want to control him. I remembered him saying once, "You go out with a chick, you sleep with her once, and she hands you an armful of 'do nots,' and you're looking at her great tits and her hot pussy and you're looking at the 'do nots' in your arms and you hand them back. 'Hey, I think these are yours.'" I had admired that— that's why he was A-Man and not Any Man. He was not going to compromise himself for pussy, like so many men do. And I didn't want to compromise a man with my pussy, I wanted a man to be true to himself . . . while desperately wanting my pussy.

But this was only idle speculation, for I knew that A-Man would not be monogamous, even if I asked. He had told me long ago that he had tried being a boyfriend several times and always failed miserably. Better not to even try. I agreed. Failure is the great anti-aphrodisiac.

Besides, if I wanted him to be only with me then I would have to return the favor and be only with him. And I knew that I couldn't do that. I loved him too much. I was too vulnerable to give myself entirely to him. Without a commitment that might be broken, at least any pangs I might be feeling about the mousy brunette were not compounded by the self-righteous pain and anger of betrayal.

So, I told myself, Do you know what you have to be if you're not monogamous? Not jealous? No, jealousy is inevitable. Worth it. You've got to be worth it. He's got to be worth it. The fucking has got to be worth it. Worth the occasional, gut-ripping insanity of jealousy.

WAR

As the days passed, however, I started feeling this overwhelming need to assert my authority over the mousy brunette. When I next saw A-Man I slyly suggested that we all get in bed together to assuage everyone's pain with love and sperm. He smiled at me, loving that I was the kind of woman who would solve a problem with an orgy. Well, better than bayonets. He then said that he had actually suggested this to her during that first confrontation but that she had only cried harder in response, confessing that she would be too jealous. Damn. I knew if we could get her in bed, I could win. Suddenly winning became imperative. Winning what, exactly, I wasn't sure, but the stakes seemed very high indeed. It was not about having him exclusively, it never had been; it was about knowing I was the most beloved.

It subsequently became completely imperative for me to distinguish myself from her in my own mind. A-Man had told me that she'd had affairs with married men in the past; I decided that she must have a history of playing second fiddle to other women. Whereas I, on the other hand, am always lead masochist, head girl, first-best, or I don't play. Period. I also became inordinately, insanely fixated on the size of her ass. It was, after all, twice mine, if not more . . . maybe two and half times mine . . . If A-Man so loved my tight ass, how could he love that wide one, too?

Then, a few weeks later, we all had the misfortune to overlap at the gym. Having finished my own exercise routine, I was leaving through the check-in area and there they both were, sitting on the couch: she was scowling, and he looked as if he'd rather be anywhere else. What had happened to the sex god who strode about my bedroom with the killer erection? This man pulled his legs under him on the couch and stared at his knees, barely breathing.

I breezed through on my way out the door, saying a bright hello to both. What else could I do? And while I didn't expect her to respond, I was, I realize, testing him. And he failed me. Silence. No acknowledgment of me in front of her. Outside, devastated, I burst into tears. I needed something from him and I wasn't getting it. And I wasn't going to get it. Assurance. But of course—and this was the catch-22 that lay at the core of our whole affair—had he given me the assurance I so desperately needed, of my place in his hierarchy and his heart, the fire between us would most likely have been extinguished. It was always just the right balance of that element of not being sure that kept me so in love, so full of desire, so very excited about him. He had never bent to my will, and that wasn't going to change now. He had always shown me his love; but he wouldn't confirm it on demand.

∽

It was clear to me that A-Man was going to do nothing to resolve this problem. So I had to do something. I got this idea in my head to discuss with the mousy brunette, in a girlie kind of way, the problem, our problem: him. This woman's agony was now threatening the safety of my world with A-Man, and perhaps if we talked, she and I could work something out. Besides, it wasn't just her pain anymore; it was also mine. The story was becoming about her and me, with A-Man watching from the sidelines. Was this some unresolved Electra thing? Maybe, but I had no time to think about mythology right now. This was war. And, with her, I had no intention of surrendering.

Contriving to run into her at the gym, I approached her boldly in my carefully planned outfit and asked if we had "something to talk about." Although she was not sure that we did, she said she was willing to talk. I asked her what had happened. She said that she had been so unhappy with him, with having so little of him, that she'd asked him about the other women in his life. The Truth Will Set You Free Strategy: she'd suspected that his answer would hurt her, but she'd hoped that it would give her the courage to stop seeing him.

Well, clearly it hadn't, because almost immediately she was trying the same strategy again with me, asking me all these intensely personal questions. How often did he and I fuck? Did he sleep over? Did we eat dinner together? And I found myself doing the most awful thing. I found myself answering her, praying that this time her strategy would succeed, even though I knew it wouldn't.

And so we all limped along: no monogamy, no threesome, more fucking, no resolution.

#276

He directed me onto all fours. He stood behind me and gently but insistently tapped my pubic bone skyward. I raised my ass to meet him. He tapped the insides of both thighs. I separated my legs. I laid my head down on the bed, ass high, back arched. He parted my pussy, found my little clit, and began looking and sucking and flicking. I imagined that other chick, the one with the wide ass, sitting in a chair, naked, legs spread, as he knelt before her pussy. Not an ugly pussy, but a bigger pussy than mine, a different, mousy pussy, and as she sat slumped, spread and slutty, he sucks on her clit, her obvious, swollen, big red clit. She is uninvolved, shameless. I am watching this secretly from behind a door. He knows I'm watching and spreads her pussy more and more so I can see her clit. She doesn't know I'm watching. As her clit stands out, like a small erect cock, proud, flagrant, and hungry, I come. Conquest of the other woman is my orgasm, my pleasure. The other woman is my whore—the whore in me. Then he fucks my pussy and then my ass. My clit runneth over.

THE BANANA

The memory of humiliation is the bleeding scar of reliv-
ing it. . . . Humiliation, I believe, is not just another experience in our life, like, say, an embarrassment. It is a
formative experience. It forms the way we view ourselves as humiliated persons.

—AVISHAI MARGALIT

Funny—well, not really—how I began to lose the ability to receive
pleasure directly from A-Man but had to siphon it through another
woman, his other woman. So sexy in bed, so catastrophic out of
bed. And thus I erected yet another Freudian triangle as I fantasized
pulling her into bed with us so I could control what I couldn't control. What I could never control: my dignity in the face of someone I
adore. Losing it was the first thing I ever learned to fear; the cause of
all my fear. My Waterloo in love.

I am four years old. I am a very thin and little girl. So thin and little that my mother actually takes me to the doctor to make sure I'm healthy. After examining me, he allays my mother's fears with one statement that quickly becomes family lore. "She is just 'tin' child!" he declares, in his thick German accent. He suggests I be given more exercise to stimulate my tiny appetite. So I am sent to my first ballet class.

After school one day, a short while later, I ask my mother for a banana. (I now don't remember particularly liking bananas—I liked fish sticks and macaroni with ketchup—but on this particular day I wanted a banana.) The request is refused on two counts. One: we don't eat between meals in this house. Two: you won't eat your dinner if you eat a banana now. But I am headstrong in my desire and beg so hard that I am finally handed a large, bright yellow banana. It is longer than my face. Victory.

I go to the landing at the top of our staircase and look out the little picture window with my banana in hand. I peel down the top an inch or two and take a couple of bites. And stop. That's all I want.

My father, having witnessed the battle with my mother in the kitchen, comes up the stairs and tells me I had better finish that banana since I had asked for it. I know my father means what he says. Ten minutes later, he passes me and the banana again on the landing. The few inches of peel are now drooping around the few inches I have eaten, but the rest remains unpeeled, untouched. Again I am warned that I had better eat that damn banana, waste is not allowed in this household: you ask for it, you eat it. Daddy is very serious.

But being such headstrong little girl, I just will not eat the rest of that banana. Now comes the lesson.

As my mother looks on apprehensively—angry eruptions are frequent in our house—my father comes up to the landing, grabs the banana, pulls off the peel, and squashes it all over my face, rubbing the excess into my hair. As I stand there, frozen, I hear my mother cry out from the bottom of the stairs, "Don't, don't, I'll have to wash her hair!"

I don't remember anything after that moment, not how I felt, or what happened next—my mother probably washed my hair. But the quest for my lost dignity has become a lifelong obsession, a relentless search for the face beneath the banana. It's a face I've never seen. I was, in effect, erased from my own existence. It was the birth of my shame. And my rage.

This unfinished crusade has somehow led me here, to an obsession with an act of voluntary, disciplinary action that restores me to a sanity lost so long ago I can't remember it. I still love to control my food intake. And I have grown into a "tin" woman. A woman who has learned to embrace her terror of humiliation by choosing and desiring what to many is the ultimate act of humiliation: anal penetration. The weapon has become an instrument of pleasure in my adult world, and I am hell-bent on taking those last few inches of cock down my throat and up my ass. To this day, however, I don't finish a single banana without pulverizing it first in the blender.

Sometimes I wonder if the appeal of being ass-fucked, contrary to appearances, is that you can indulge in the naughty sensation of shitting on a man. When you open your ass enough to be fucked without pain, the sensation achieved, and then enjoyed, is that your bowels are open and you could be shitting on the cock that has been so bold as to enter. As such, perhaps being sodomized could be viewed as my answer to the banana, the ultimate act of revenge.

Out of the world of my bedroom, however, I fear that I will always be a little girl with banana dripping off her face, unable to forget that at any moment I am under the threat of humiliation from someone I love. The more I love, the greater the threat. When I am deprived by A-Man's absence or the possibility of his loss, the threat of real humiliation, unchosen humiliation, lurks nearby like a predator awaiting its prey. The waiting is agony and the perceptions of humiliation multiply like a virus. They become so powerful that I experience them as real and endure the same annihilation of identity my father accomplished wielding a half-peeled piece of fruit.

#291

As we approach year three, we approach three hundred ass-fucks. I love symmetry.

After eight days without his cock in my ass, I'm ready to be certified. Insane from deprivation. We arrange a Power Hour and a Half. Unusually, I want to talk and I tell him of my pending insanity.

I suggest to him that I am fully aware that he is not my answer (though my ass is convinced that he is). He concurs enthusiastically.

"I am definitely not the answer," he says. "I'm the question."

I immediately envisioned his cock entering my little asshole, his question firmly planted in the center of my being. I had it backwards, of course. My ass is the answer—for both of us.

He strips, sits on the end of the bed, knees apart, and puts a pillow on the floor between his feet. I get on my knees, and as sucking begins, my heart is relieved. He takes my head between his hands, I put my own hands on either side of his hips, resting on the bed, and he slowly, smoothly guides my head, mouth rounded, open and wet, down the length of his cock. Very slowly, all the way until the tip of his cock meets the back of my throat. I give him to-tal control, and become head and mouth for cock alone. It is so slow and his cock is so hard, the edge of cement. Beauty flowed back into my being and all my insanity flowed out like bilgewater.

Then he fucked my ass, only my ass, and as his cock began en-try he whispered, "If you ever forget, remember this, this is the point of connection, always."

SAVING FACE

I was, however, now making other connections.

When I confronted the mousy brunette that day, I asked her if she loved A-Man. I hadn't planned on asking, but I guess I wanted to know. Well, no, I already knew. But I wanted, just as she had, confirmation. My sadism (to her) and my masochism (to myself) were—perhaps more than at any other point in my life—each struggling for dominance. Her big brown eyes filled with tears and she murmured, "I try not to." And in that moment, all my desperate attempts to separate myself from her dissolved.

Unlike her, I was too proud to admit to jealousy or let her see my grief, but they were both there, like hers. No longer different from me, she *was* me, and I suddenly recognized what I had been searching for all my life—the face beneath the banana, the face of a little girl crushed and humiliated by love. My tears were rolling down her cheeks. And it was horrid. For weeks afterwards, I was haunted by that reflection of myself that I had never seen before.

But then the most astonishing realization gradually entered my consciousness. The brunette was, just as I had been, incapacitated, unable to act on her own behalf; she was not capable—not yet, anyway—of leaving her own pain behind her. But I was no longer incapable. I could make the decision for both of us, I could take action, because now I had the strength to leave the triangle, as I never could before. It was a kind of miracle.

What a strange gift this woman gave me, the ability to accomplish what all my spiritual searching, ultimately, could not—the ability to break the chain of pain, right here, right now. Not only for me, but for my fragile four-year-old self. She did, after all, live with me still. It was time to dry her face and take her home.

AFTER

ACCOUNTING

4/3/3/3/3/3/3/1/2/0/0/0/0/0/2/0/0/0/0/3
/2/1/2/1/2/1/1/0/0/0/1/1/2/3/1/2/2/3/1/
1/0/0/0/0/0

The above is an accounting of anal penetrations per week for year three. All the zeros represent one of us being out of town. Except the last five.

Number 298 was our last. The walls I had so carefully constructed around our love had split wide open. The world was in, and we were over. I sent A-Man away. It was Time.

Yes, it was that sudden. That unexpected. Totally unplanned. Time to end the pain, time to end the beauty: they had become inseparable, a sadomasochistic adagio.

So the search for the end of my end ended as abruptly as it had begun three years before. A symmetry of sorts. A single, swift, clean cut. No negotiations, no begging, no manipulations, no blame. After #298—it was again a Friday afternoon—it was over with A-Man while it was still hot as a volcano and beautiful as art. Try that for courage. Though for me, it wasn't courage at all, it was necessity. I never would have had the courage to send him away.

Curious how another woman was always the catalyst for him and me: the Pre-Raphaelite had joined us and, now, the mousy brunette separated us. I must have much unfinished business with women, with my mother. But this is the Daddy story, not the Mommy story—or so I thought.

I started counting the zeros week after week after week, as if they would add up to something other than zero. Zeros marking the empty space in me where the nearly unbearable pain of loss grew and grew. I festered.

And I died.

The core of me that he had touched died.

I felt that I would grieve for him all my life. And I do. I had been grieving for him since the first time he came in my ass; why stop now just because he was no longer there?

If heaven is a taste of eternity in a moment of real time, then hell is an eternity of loss in a moment of real time.

Completely bereft. We didn't even make it to three hundred.

RECLAMATION

After many months without A-Man, the love bubble in which I had lived for so long began to deflate. I couldn't keep living like this. I used to be such a happy little sodomite; now I was a miserable little sodomite with only memories to taunt me.

There were some things to tidy up. I put the few clothes of his I had inside several plastic bags and hid them away. I resisted smelling them one last time, and in doing so, I knew I would have the strength to do what was necessary to move on. The few notes and photos I had I hid in a drawer, along with the small plastic bag of his pubic hair, the hair from that first trim. Nothing was thrown away, all was carefully preserved. You throw things away when love has turned to hate. That wasn't what had happened to me.

And then there was the Box. Sitting on my dresser, overflowing with the evidence of all I was trying to overcome, get beyond. I realized that I needed a bigger box—and one with a lock. There it was, waiting for me in the antique store: square, with a hinged lid, a red satin lining, and a tiny padlock with a key. In gold leaf. Perfect. I made the transfer, took one last, long, searing look, closed the lid, and locked it. I put the tiny key away. The casket was sealed—with tears, K-Y, and a wink to its future finder.

This shrine of sacred relics was my monument—to the divinity of my masochism, to the great joy that once so frequently passed my way, to a state of consciousness I can no longer access, to a chemical connection that reached far beyond any logic or rationale, to the sacred insanity that so blessedly pervaded my being. Now, where to put it? Nearby . . . but out of reach. Like a smoker's last pack, close by . . . but out of sight. Available . . . but forbidden.

Climbing out of love with him, I felt like a pelican trying to extract itself from an oil spill: lurching, falling, getting up, trying again. But even if the bird breaks free, its feathers remain saturated, forever marked. I realized that until the pain of loving him no longer interested me, I wouldn't be able to move on. Why was the pain so very interesting? It felt as though the key to my soul was buried inside it. The unmatched enormity of the ache begged for attention.

Taking solace in other compulsions, I made lots of lists. Lists of pros and cons. Lists of what I lost in losing him and what I would have lost if I'd kept him. Lists of what I have gained, what I have accomplished, whom I've dated. They meant nothing in the end, those lists, but they gave me something to do while I cried. I realized that I had to change in order to not want him. Who I had become wanted only him. I had to become someone else, yet again.

This is how my former self died, how I killed her. But she did not go quietly into the night. No, she raged herself into extinction with one last blast of scorching pain. Pain to stop the pain. But perhaps masochism never heals, just changes form. Different objects, different manifestations. I feared I could not be happy without my pain. But I had to direct it outside myself now; inside I was soaked to the bone.

After a while I started fucking men again—one by one. No longer obedient, I started telling them how to do it—"like this," "like that"—and they obliged. Having been slave to the King, I was all Queen with them, spreading the word to my jesters, even as I closed my eyes and pretended they were him. Every now and then it worked. And when it worked, it was worst of all: the tears streamed down my cheeks while they thought I was in ecstasy. Is not every affair after the Great One just another state of mourning, prolonged and disguised as some form of continuity or bravery when there is neither?

But I didn't let anyone else—and a few tried—into my sacred backyard. Now a tunnel of despair, it had become hallowed ground, a battlefield, now quiet, but filled with ghosts. If those walls could talk . . . I figured no one else would ever get in there. How could they possibly earn the right? Who could ever be worthy? Who, in their right mind, would even dare?

BACKDOOR BUDDHA

The loss continued, intolerable and relentless, and the other men only made it worse. I needed help. Badly. Peace of mind was a distant intellectual concept; I was crying every day. I had finally suffered enough. Enough to finally say "enough." My dignity was shattered. In an effort to wrest myself out of my self-pity, I signed up for a two-week retreat with seventeen hundred Buddhists five thousand miles away in an obscure part of England. To leave where he was. It was like tearing off my own flesh to escape the hold he had on me. Free, I had no skin. Like a burn victim.

The Buddhists I met were truly lovely people, welcoming me into their world without judgment despite the fact that I was probably only there for a quick fix in my moment of desperation. But even the wisdom of a quick fix, if it's Buddhist, can linger long after one's ego has regained its footing. And so while they all meditated on peace for all, I meditated on peace for me, feeling like the child among them.

Everyone I met at the retreat, all strangers, asked me with genuine interest how I was. And so I told them. One after the other smiled broadly at my tale of lost love. "Ah! But you are so fortunate!" said one man, beaming. "So very fortunate!" He almost looked envious. The explanation: any experience of great pain is releasing negative karma, and this release is nothing more than a cleansing, a clearing of the way to nirvana.

Well, while nirvana without A-Man in my ass seemed a most unlikely prospect, I had now become the one thing I wasn't before: willing. Willing to entertain the possibility of sanity without him, just as I had been willing three years earlier to entertain the possibility of giving myself to him for just one afternoon—and look where that had led me. One by one, over and over, again and again, my new Buddhist friends rejoiced at my great sadness . . . until the tears finally stopped. They just ran right out.

There was a young Englishman, also attending the retreat, who was staying at my B&B in the nearby town. Every morning at breakfast, he would smile at me as we ate poached eggs on toast at opposite ends of the communal table. Eventually we talked. He had been a devout Buddhist for eight years already, although he was only twenty-four years old. He even lived at a Buddhist center in northern England, where he was finishing his university education. Tall, with clear white skin, full red lips, and long curly black hair, he was handsome as hell; he reminded me of John the Baptist, whom Salome so loved. He was also kinder than kind, paler than pale, and sweeter than honey. And, I assumed, monklike—given his Buddhist devotion. After all, the one thing I thought would never happen at a Buddhist retreat was hedonistic sex. But, oh no, those naughty, wonderful Buddhists, sex is A-okay with them—so long as no one is getting hurt, and all karmas are properly aligned. Clearly more experienced in this than me, he began our alignment.

When I told him that I was leaving the next day, he suggested meeting up, after the evening meditation. I can't remember exactly how the proposition was phrased—it wasn't dinner or a movie or even a date—but he ended up in my cozy room with the Laura Ashley curtains, two narrow single beds, tea bags, and an electric water heater. Outside, needless to say, it was raining.

This beautiful Byronic Buddhist not only fucked me royally on the last evening of the retreat, but also performed a particular kind of surgery I had only vaguely considered being of any possible use. He became the second man to fuck my ass in my whole life— gently, wildly, eagerly, Buddhistically. It was amazing. The sex, yes, he was so able, so young, so ready . . . and then ready again. But more amazing was that it happened at all, that I allowed it when others had tried to no avail. But when he asked, I looked into his saintly sexy eyes and saw that he could be the one. The one kind enough.

It was like being vaccinated against the very illness I had so long been afflicted with. A-Man was the FirstMan, was the BestMan, but he was no longer the OnlyMan. The spell was broken. Buddha had found his way into my backyard. To think that God, that sly devil, had sent me a Buddhist John the Baptist to show me the way out of hell. Or at least to break the seal that bonded me to another but never to myself.

How does one let go of the best thing one has ever known in the hope of something better? With a crazy, illogical leap of faith. I left early the next morning, feeling blessed for the first time in a long time.

Time to shop.

HEELED

Upon returning home, I decided that I would not find a replacement or a continuation in a single man; I must find something entirely other. This plan got legs when I bought some new shoes. The right pair of shoes, at the right time, can really change a woman's attitude. And these weren't just any old shoes. These were the shoes in which I would find a new identity. Just as toe shoes had shaped the contours of my young life, these shoes would guide my life when submission to a man was no longer possible. These weren't nice, elegant, sleek Manolo Blahnik pumps. These were nasty, heavy, spiky heels—useful shoes, practical shoes. No more easy-to-lose mules for me; these were serious strap-ons with buckles galore. I like a shoe with a good metaphor to support me. Toe shoes, hooker shoes, it's all just bondage in the end.

I got a lot of shoe for fifty bucks. I called them my "Don't-Fuck-With-Me" shoes. They also, ironically, looked a lot like "Fuck-Me" shoes. Ah, the double-entendre shoes, the key to Freud's question "What do women want?"—"Fuck me!" but "Don't fuck with me!"

Black, heeled platforms. The front pedestal raised the ball of my foot off the ground two and half inches, and the heel, that gloriously slim yet strong heel, raised me up a solid seven inches. Finally, for the first time since being on pointe, I felt myself to be taller than the truth. But most important, my feet were far above the ground: it is the place where I am at my best in both mind and body. And, if necessary, these shoes could deliver a very healthy kick.

My new shoes became both shield and armor in the battle for a new way to live. I ended up buying pairs in all the other colors: silver, sky blue, and serious pink. Once strapped on, these shoes changed my entire demeanor. I became my own Amazon—Aphrodite, Artemis, and Athena rolled into one. A-Woman was born.

Equal in height to most men, I was now taller than many. I walked slowly, deliberately, proudly, stupendously on my shimmering, high-heeled weapons. Hope sprang alive as I peered about from my new perch. No longer looking up, I was looking down. No longer Slave, I was Mistress: the only refuge for a submissive with no Master. I started wearing my shoes around the house. With sweatpants, with underwear, without underwear, dusting a shelf, doing the dishes. One time I even shaved my pussy in the heels in order to do the dishes. Therapy. And I continued to rinse out my ass every time I bathed—a gesture of hope in a vacant lot.

Then, one day, as Leonard Cohen was singing "Dance Me to the End of Love" through the speakers, I started swaying to the music—"moving like they do in Babylon"—and I knew that I would be dancing again before too long in my "Don't-Fuck-With-Me" shoes. I was healed.

I had made the leap across the open chasm. It wasn't as wide as I'd thought. All those abbreviated M-words were never bridge enough to the other side. I never really liked being a "Miss." Too prissy. It was slightly better in French—"Mlle."—but still felt wanting—too petite for my budding enormity. Then came the opportunity for "Mrs." which felt horrendous, like my mother, and its dry, neutered alternative, "Ms." The problem with them all is that what followed was always a man's name—a father's or a husband's. Now I only recognize titles befitting a woman who belongs to herself.

Having traveled the long and twisted road from Masochist to Mistress . . . What next? Madam? Muse? And with whom? Perhaps with a man who is difficult to love. A-Man provided no challenge in this regard. Loving him was so easy, too easy; not loving him was hell. So perhaps the opposite: loving that is difficult, leaving that is easy. Would I not then learn some tolerance?

A-Man is now long gone. But was he ever really here? Did he ever really inhabit my ass and me? Was he indeed the demon-lover who avenged my anger, the ever-ready erection to which I so willingly and joyously martyred myself? Or was he the God of my own creation, the God I always wanted but couldn't have, couldn't find? Perhaps I finally found a place for Him, and A-Man entered my expectant space.

I believe the equation goes like this: sex can only be truly deep, truly life changing, truly transcendent if you are being fucked by

God; if you love your man like he was God. But—and here's the rub that no lube can assuage—if your man is God and shifts your world, then you are, by definition, in the very center of your female masochism, open, willing, vulnerable. A-Man was my God, but he was my Last God. I fear no man can be God again for me. Lucky for all of us, perhaps: less far to fall. But I mourn this with all my being; it is the loss, finally, of my insistent innocence. It has been a long process, the extrication of him and the excavation of my soul. He no longer lives in my ass. I live there now. What a place.

I have been to the precipice. I looked over, and fell off the ledge. But now I am back, back from the great valley of my masochism, back to bear witness—for myself but also for you—to my survival, to my return from a world where depth was all that mattered. If you don't fuck with death chasing you, you are mistaken. So long as love, crazy, crazy love, can be survived, there is no excuse. No excuse at all.

Go. Come.

Slowly, resentfully, I have moved out of slavery, though I cannot forget its freedom. But I am no longer blinded by obsession. I can now recognize what is commonly termed reality, wretched reality. I even live in it on occasion, when feeling perverse. I have endured the loss. Choice is mine. But I know what to do—and where to go—should I need a fix of beauty, of submission, of relief, of bliss. And, besides, I still have the Box. It does not only contain his DNA. It contains my very own madness—safely captured under its gilded lid.

But I don't need to open it. I have the key.

Acknowledgments

I would like to extend my deep appreciation to Alix Freedman for true friendship and to John Tottenham for being the first to say, yes, you must. I am eternally grateful to David Hirshey whose inexhaustible good humor and unwavering enthusiasm kept me laughing and gave me faith when mine faltered. And to Alice Truax, thank you for everything: guidance, intelligence, impeccable taste, and relentless pursuit.

I am very grateful to my persistent and brave agents Glen Hartley and Lynn Chu, and to Catharine Sprinkel for the handling of so many things. And to Michael Wolf, a lawyer with real integrity, many thanks.

At ReganBooks I want to thank—and applaud—Judith Regan, for her courage, Cassie Jones, who made it all happen on time, and Kurt Andrews, Paul Crichton, Michelle Ishay, Adrienne Makowski, and Kris Tobiassen.

And my great gratitude to all my beloved and delightful advisers and friends who offered wonderful suggestions as well as numerous pictorial responses to my work: Elizabeth Alley, Christopher d'Amboise, Jeff d'Avanzo, Erin Baiano, Beverly Berg, Jim Bessman, John B. Birchell Hughes, Laura Blum, Mary Bresovitch, Steve Brown, Leonard Cohen, Bonnie Dunn and Le Scandal, Alfredo Franco, Janet Goff, Bruce Grayson, Gregory Jarrett, Paul Kolnik, Elizabeth Kramer, Marc Kristal, Maureen Lasher, Gillian Marloth, Michele Mattei, David Mellon, Carolyn Mishne, Adam Peck, Quentin Phillips, Ray Sawhill, Michael Schrage, Michael Sigman, Michael Solomon, David Stenn, Neal Tabachnick, Bill Tonelli, Vicky Wilson, Leslie Zemeckis, Robin Ziemer, and, of course, A-Man, always.